The Literature of Exclusion

The Literature of Exclusion

Dada, Data, and the Threshold of Electronic Literature

Andrew C. Wenaus

LEXINGTON BOOKS
Lanham • Boulder • New York • London

Published by Lexington Books
An imprint of The Rowman & Littlefield Publishing Group, Inc.
4501 Forbes Boulevard, Suite 200, Lanham, Maryland 20706
www.rowman.com

6 Tinworth Street, London SE11 5AL, United Kingdom

Copyright © 2021 The Rowman & Littlefield Publishing Group, Inc.

Interviews with Allison Parrish, B. R. Yeager, and Mike Bonsall used with permission.

Excerpts from *Falling Out of Cars* by Jeff Noon used with permission.

All rights reserved. No part of this book may be reproduced in any form or by any electronic or mechanical means, including information storage and retrieval systems, without written permission from the publisher, except by a reviewer who may quote passages in a review.

British Library Cataloguing in Publication Information Available

Library of Congress Cataloging-in-Publication Data Available

ISBN 978-1-7936-1463-6 (cloth)
ISBN 978-1-7936-1465-0 (pbk)
ISBN 978-1-7936-1464-3 (electronic)

For Christina, with Love

Contents

Acknowledgments		ix
Introduction: The Literature of Exclusion		1
1	Metaphor and Metanoia: Linguistic Transfer, Cognitive Transformation, and Exclusion	31
2	The Radical Poetics of Impersonality: The Posthuman, the Inhuman, and Dada	59
3	The Divine Neutrality of the Apparatus: The Self-Reflexive Conceptual Horror of B. R. Yeager	81
4	"Something Is Taking Its Course": Zero-Player Games, Proceduralism, and Samuel Beckett's *Endgame*	109
5	Blossoming Ghost: Memetic Engineering, Hauntology, and Metamorphiction in Jeff Noon's *Falling Out of Cars*	141
6	Swarm Annihilation and Supermodern Transcendence: Chaotics, Granular Synthesis, and the Glitch Poetics of Kenji Siratori	181
7	The Electronic Literature of Exclusion and Autopoiesis: Obsession and Fictionalism	223
8	The Electronic Literature of Exclusion and Allopoiesis: Asemic Word Processing, Technical Images, and Allison Parrish's *Ahe Thd Yearidy Ti Isa*	251
Conclusion: Extro-Science Fiction, Hyper-Contingent Literatures of Exclusion, and Unthinkable Thought		277

Bibliography	291
Index	303
About the Author	313

Acknowledgments

This book has been in the works for quite some time. Originally planned as a short monograph with Zero Books in mind, it gradually took on a broader scope. I had been examining works of avant-garde science fiction narratives since 2007 as a graduate student at the University of Regina under the supervision of Dr. Nicholas Ruddick. I continued this work as a PhD candidate at the University of Western Ontario from 2009 to 2013 with Dr. Jonathan Boulter as my mentor and supervisor. During my studies, a pattern continually emerged: that the avant-garde and automated technologies are both inextricably linked to each other and modernism. Slowly, an idea rich enough for a book began to emerge. None of this would have been possible without my mentors' guidance, so I would first like to thank Nick and Jonathan for their patience, astuteness, kindness, and support.

I would also like to thank Dr. Allan Pero and everyone at the Centre for the Study of Theory and Criticism. The graduate seminar, "From Dada to Dank Memes," that I taught at the Centre in 2018 was one of the most fruitful and enjoyable intellectual semesters of my teaching career. So, I would like to thank the students from the seminar: Michael Bodkin, Austin Chisholm, Alex Harasymiw, Alex Hudecki, Dylan Hughes, Maxwell Hyett, Won Jeon, Jennifer Komorowski, Taylor McGoey, Vikram Panchmatia, Eric Shepperd, Jeremy Smith, and Andrew Woods. Discussions with this brilliant group had a major impact on this book's content, and I cannot thank them enough.

I also extend my gratitude to Dr. Kathleen Fraser, Brock Eayrs, Shelley Clark, and the Writing Studies faculty at the University of Western Ontario for all their help, support, and advice over the past five years. Additionally, I extend my thanks to those I have come to know, befriend, and learn from at the University of Western Ontario and Fanshawe College: Drs. Peter Schwenger, Steven Bruhm, Michael Groden, Stephen Adams, Thy Phu,

Manina Jones, Bryce Traister, Mark Stephenson, Edward Matthews, Richard Moll, Gabrielle Ceraldi, Tom Cull, Mark Feltham, Rasmus Simonsen, Michael Sloan, Nicholas McGinnis, Zeinab Mcheimech, Phil Glennie, Tim DeJong, Paul Frehner, and Christopher Keep.

A huge thanks also to Colin Herrick and his endless energy, creativity, and kindness for creating an original analog collage for the cover of this book.

Thanks to Lexington Books for publishing this book and to Dr. Graham Harman for reassuring me that Lexington Books was a great place for this title. I am also particularly thankful to Holly Buchanan at Lexington for her help with preparing this manuscript for publication.

Much love, respect, and thanks to Chuck Blazevic and Alice Hansen for their sincere friendship, music, and endlessly enjoyable conversations.

A massive thanks to my dear friend Andrew Weiss for the great conversations, long walks, and invaluable help polishing this book.

Thanks to Allison Parrish, Mike Bonsall, B. R. Yeager, Kenji Siratori, and Jeff Noon for generously sharing their insight and giving their time to discuss their work with me. I loved these correspondences and thank the authors a thousand times.

Endless gratitude to my parents, Daryl and Susan Wenaus, and in-laws, George and Linda Willatt, for all their support, encouragement, and love. Thanks to my sisters Sarah, Ila, Emma, and Stephanie for the great conversations, intelligence, jokes, music, and love. Special thanks to my brother William and my brother-from-another-mother Sandy Junek for the limitless thoughtfulness, broken bones, and love over the years.

Finally, I owe everything to Christina Willatt. Thank you, Christina, for reading my work, providing critical commentary, making music, and offering years of love and support. More than anyone else, you inspire everything I do.

Short sections of the book appeared in different versions in the following articles: "'Zero, zero, and zero': Beckett's Endgame, Automation, and Zero-Player Games" in *Chiasma*; "Twilight of Information Illiteracy: Kenji Siratori's Asemic Cyberpunk" in *Foundation*; "'Spells Out The Word of Itself, and Then Dispelling Itself': The Chaotics of Memory and The Ghost of the Novel in Jeff Noon's *Falling out of Cars*" in *Journal of the Fantastic in the Arts*; and "Coping with Zero to a Million Decimals: Mike Bonsall's J.G. Ballard Twitter Bots and Procedural Psychopathology" in *Deep Ends: The J.G. Ballard Anthology 2019*. Some passages from my dissertation *Metaphor and Metanoia* (2013) appear scattered throughout the book as well. For full references, please see the bibliography.

Introduction
The Literature of Exclusion

We are rapidly accelerating into the future, and, as novelist J. G. Ballard remarks, there are dangerous bends ahead. So, we need to make a choice: should we slow down or should we speed up? The past century indicates that the tendency is to accelerate, in general, and to accelerate the rift between human agency and autonomous technologies, in particular. Yet, this inclination is not necessarily new. As early as the thirteenth century, Catalan polymath and mystic Ramon Llull proposed a combinatorial system that aimed to evangelize Christianity using a careful set of definitions and rules that would guide a sequential argument through finite permutations. For Llull, this logical, algorithmic process would guide thought toward a prescribed truth: Christian doctrine. Over three centuries later, this dream was revived by German polymath Gottfried Wilhelm Leibniz. Seeking a combinatorial and algorithmic mode of reasoning, Leibniz, like Llull, advanced the proposition that the world is fully computable through finite analytical, algorithmic, and permutational possibilities. For Llull, the project was primarily epistemological and theological; for Leibniz, the dream of the combinatorial arts was to discover all things and create new ideas through elegant permutation. By the twentieth century, the dream of procedural reasoning, permuting, and calculating the truth became a reality in computer programming and autonomous, processual calculation. Today, these processes are ubiquitous and central to the functioning of supermodern society at all levels, from global systematics to the unconscious, but the implications of this new semiosis, however, remain ambivalent.

In 1959, Japanese novelist Kōbō Abe, for example, reminds us that "programming is essentially the operation of reducing the qualitative to the quantitative."[1] Such reductionism ultimately superimposes an ideology of combinatorialism on the chaotics of world: while permutational systems are finite, the poetic impulse to articulate mind-independent reality is boundless. As a result, combinatorialism, calculation, and permutation delimit potentialities, offer prescribed guides to results, and abstract signification from the concreteness of everyday life. Both Llull's and Leibniz's systems are beautiful, elegant, and admirable; they are also, however, artificial selectors that steer epistemological potentialities by deforming the disorder and chaos of actuality into computable subcomponents. Combinatorialism is beautiful and elegant, yet it excludes potencies and potentialities. It may create new ideas, but only so much as such ideas are prescribed in the permutational possibilities of its initial conditions. In short, it is a closed system that eschews poiesis. Here I mean poiesis in the broad sense of creating a new idea or thought that transcends prescribed combinatorialism and offers wholly novel concepts. By delimiting the unpredictable emergence of novel potencies and unruly potentialities, both useful and useless, combinatorialism prescribes limits to poietic alternatives and, ultimately, reduces the human to the quantifiable.

In this book, I examine what effects the shift from a culture of language to a culture of combinatorialism, algorithms, and digital code has on lived experience and self-narration. I also consider the relationship between this shift and the role narration plays in agential cultural engagement. The study rests on the structural similarity between linguistic metaphor and the mind as defined by cognitive linguistics. Working from the conceit that the human mind is linguistic and that language is an artifact of the human mind, I extrapolate upon the "psycho-ecology" of narrative involvement: a knot of reflexive level-crossing between text and mind as the constituent of lived experience and agency. Far from being a remote, abstract process, psycho-ecology refers to the ways that unique textual engagement transforms how we see and understand the world. In this sense, the more one nonhabitually engages with unusual modes of language, the more one may exercise agency in the way they restructure their thought and lived experience in an era of algorithmic, neuro-totalitarian steering, an era characterized by what I am here calling "dataism."

Since data is without desire, value, or meaning, its closest literary analog may be Dada and its vehement rejection of sense, authorial agency, and purposeful programs. At first glance, data and Dada seem like an unlikely combination; however, the two meet in the twenty-first century with experimental literature that confronts the moment when literary narration comes up against processual algorithmic combinatorialism. Here, I turn to works of literature that scrutinize this incommensurability between the human and autonomous information technologies. Each literary work that I analyze in this book is either written about algorithmic culture's effects on the human nervous system, composed using computers and algorithms, or both. Some texts appear in print, while others are composed entirely with computers and are accessible only with a computer. In each case, these texts simultaneously protest against and praise the threshold that separates human autonomy from self-optimizing, autonomous technologies, and hold that the instance of exiting into the logic of combinatorial, algorithmic culture is an entry into an inhuman future where humans are excluded from their own autonomous, poietic self-narration. At this junction, I ask what it means when a dramatic shift away from language (as the governing medium of culture and value) is rapidly being replaced by digital code and autonomous self-optimizing processes.

This threshold, though optimized, is not smooth. The mind does not operate according to the rigid, processual selectivity of code. Artificial intelligence (AI) and self-optimizing algorithms operate in ways that are radically unlike the way we think, create, and, as a result, self-narrate. If language is both constituted and constitutive of the human mind, the implications of a shift toward a culture organized through calculation, combinatorialism, number, programming, and digital code will have major effects on individual agency, epistemology, and innovation. Byung-Chul Han explains: "No insight into the self can result from data and numbers alone, no matter how exhaustive they are. Numbers do not recount anything about the self. Counting is not recounting. A sense of self derives from giving an account. It is not counting, but recounting that leads to self-discovery or self-knowledge."[2] For Han, data cannot operate as an analog to language; its narratives are not our narratives, its combinations and quantifications do not yield creation, nor do they acknowledge subjective, singular qualia. Language shapes and narrates agency; it is an ongoing, constructive, chaotic, open process. Code, however, is procedural and processual; it is rule-governed, self-optimizing, and rigid. Language innovates and opens the *self*, while code updates and completes *itself*. Through language, we tell our own imperfect stories; those stories then narrate the self, which equips the subject to tell new stories, which then narrate the self, and so on. The more unruly errors, ambiguities, and inexplicable minutiae these stories contain, the more resulting richness. Unlike human storytelling, code calculates, combines, completes, and concludes a prescribed task. While code is frequently goal oriented, it proceeds without intention; instead, it functions efficiently. This shift from language-driven narrative to code-driven narrative ultimately has implications that are psychic, social, political, and aesthetic; in each case, however, algorithmic culture expels and negates the messy and fuzzy desires that fuel experimental self-narration.

Today, this expulsion manifests itself as the nonconsensual exclusion of individual agency in nearly every aspect of daily life. Through the ubiquity of information technologies and the cultural logic of algorithms, this exclusion largely takes place in the form of everyday banalities rather than, say, technological transcendence. Such an ambient and electronically mediated society may be best explained by Vilém Flusser's concept of the apparatus. The apparatus makes it difficult, if not impossible, to distinguish knowledge from inhuman processes that are ontologically indeterminate, procedural, and self-optimizing. "The inherent contradiction in the apparatus arises because it functions just as the universe does, namely, automatically," writes Flusser,

> its programs are games in which possibilities occur randomly, programmed accidents. The difference between the apparatus and the universe is that the apparatus continues with its programmed tasks . . . and the universe runs past the programed task toward heat death. For this is, in fact, the definition of *automation*: a self-governing computation of accidental events, excluding human intervention and stopping at a situation that human beings have determined to be informative. The difference between the apparatus and the universe is, accordingly, that the apparatus is subject to human control. But it cannot stay this way forever: in the longer term, the autonomy of the apparatus must be liberated from human beings. This is why the negative entropy of the apparatus changes to entropy.[3]

Nearly four decades after Flusser wrote this, the cybernetic homeostasis is off-balance, and the apparatus is breaking free of human control. This poses a conundrum. Our sense of agency and self-knowledge is largely an a priori function of language; however, language is being subsumed by an algorithmic procedure that functions from *without* yet continues to *shape* us. As a result, storytelling that is experimental in both content and compositional methodology is appropriate for supermodern self-narration.

The literature that confronts the instance of excluding the human from our own narrativizing is what I call the literature of exclusion. While Ezra Pound writes that "Great Literature is simply language charged with meaning to the utmost possible degree,"[4] the literature of exclusion, on the other hand, is literature that both desperately grasps for meaning *and* confronts the thresholds of human meaning-making by moving deeper *into* the inhuman logic of algorithmic culture. Examining the process that transforms the unpredictable, poietic, and empathetic operations of human self-narration into the proceduralities of calculation, programming, and code, the literature of exclusion is neither utopian nor dystopian. Instead, it is a heterotopian literature concerned with the ultimate *other* place of supermodernity: the inhuman *outside* of automated, mind-independent information processes. The literature of exclusion is explicitly modernist in tone, compositional methodology, and difficulty; it is always an experimental, avant-garde literature and is never traditional or conventional in its approach to the technological threshold that separates human from inhuman narration. As a supermodernist literature rather than a postmodernist one, it acknowledges that a culture of algorithmic determinism is not open, multivocal, multiplicitous, or playful, but a structurally closed, indifferent, steadfastly alien, delimiting *sýstēma* (a whole comprised of finite, permutational parts). Such accelerated agential exclusion asks whether we are, and will remain, equipped for our own cultural and political steering or whether we are being programmed to become functions of prescribed functionalities. But how did we get here? How did structural signifying systems slip from the care of human use in the sensual sense to pure, autonomous abstraction? To examine this threshold, my methodology is itself combinatorial and paratactic. By bringing together diverse, unusual combinations like an analytical Dadaist collage, I hope to both examine and demonstrate the struggles we encounter at the threshold where human-written narratives give way to narratives that write themselves. So, to begin, we turn to an unusual junction: semiotic abstraction in finance and poetry.

WHERE WORD BREAKS OFF: LANGUAGE, FINANCE, AND AUTOMATED SIGNIFICATION

In the 1914 poem, "Das Wort," Stefan George writes, "Where word breaks off no thing may be." Four years later, a Romanian poet in Zurich literalizes this severing. Dada, Tristian Tzara wrote in his 1918 manifesto, *signifies nothing* and means "no thing." It was the proclamation that the word must break off. This statement proved to parallel the emerging semio-capitalism of the time: an instance where the impersonality of calculation seemed increasingly poetic while poetry was becoming impersonal and calculated. Modernity moves inward; it knots with itself, feeds back into itself, and intensifies itself through recursive self-reflexivity. It acknowledges that self-governing, structural systems operate in ways that can be abstracted from material reality and that we are as much a creation of such systems as we are their creators. The management of revenues, in other words, could be as immaterial as any other signifying system. Outside language, however, no thing may be. Mind-independent reality cannot be known wholly, and language itself becomes a closed system of feedback loops. So, the same process becomes acceptable with number, calculation, and finance. As the indifferent, alterior word became more poetic and strange, the poetic became increasingly impartial, neutral, and non-agential. Such systems self-reflexively operate autonomously and abstractly, and need not recourse to the human. This poses the problem of anthropic exclusion from daily practice. In short, such alterior systems operate autonomously and efficiently but do not *need us* and are, as Flusser argues, liberated from human beings. These systems signify no thing and operate where no thing may be. Indeed, we no longer need to sculpt the apparatus, yet it persists in sculpting us.

As poetry and literature retreat from the intimately personal, economics and finance become the innocuous narratives that sculpt everyday life. The self-generating autopoiesis of the word, writes Franco "Bifo" Berardi, "takes place on two levels," and it is these two levels that initiate the replacement of language by code. First, the word is subjected to "monetarization and subjection to the financial cycle," that is, the word is reduced to and constituted by its functionality consistent with the logic of finance and the management of semiosis. Signs, Bifo continues, "fall under the domination of finance when the financial function (the accumulation of value through semiotic circulation) cancels the instinctual side of enunciation so that what is enunciated may be compatible with digital-financial formats. The production of meaning and value takes the form of parthenogenesis: signs produce signs without any longer passing through the flesh."[5] Rather than the poietic function of language, the word is thus transmuted into the logic of monetary value, and "monetary value produces more monetary value without being first realized through the material production of goods."[6] Ultimately, Bifo argues that money and finance function free of material constraint. Money and finance, however, do not *mean*.

The logic of finance deals with managing the exchange of components in closed systems. In short, it is combinatorial. As a result, Bifo identifies indexicalization as central to the word's subjugation to combinatorial intensities. Indexicalization is when signs point to other signs, all of which are delimited by a closed system. Think of the way an internet search engine works: "two algorithms," Bifo writes, will "define the reduction of linguistic meaning to economic value via a Google search: the first finds the various occurrences of a word, the second links words with monetary value."[7] Meaning does not arise in such a system; instead, indexicalization reductionistically reconfigures the same set of signs within determined parameters. This process, Bifo continues, is what neoliberal capitalism and semio-capitalism utilize to capture language-as-function while halting the poetic by delimiting semiotic exchange to a *sýstēma*.

While this all sounds remarkably unpoetic, Bifo reminds us of the aesthetic modernism privileges: abstract, scientific, and technological insight into the arts. "Poetry predicted and prefigured the separation of language from the affective sphere," he writes. "Ever since Rimbaud called for a *dérèglement de tous les sens*," Bifo continues, "poets have experimented with the forgetting of the referent and with the autonomous evocation of the signifier."[8] This is the poetry of pure imagination: where words engage with other words rather than with the world outside. "Language has infinite potency," Bifo writes, "but the exercise of language happens in finite conditions of history and existence. Thanks to the establishment of a limit, the world comes to exist as a world of language. Grammar, logic, and ethics are all based on the imposition of a limit."⁹ The recognition of this limit, and the joy of playing games *within* it, he writes, begins with the Symbolist poets: here "words became polysemous evocations for other words, and thus became epiphanic."¹⁰ Ultimately, Bifo's identification that the word's severing from the world in symbolist poetry at the end of the nineteenth century parallels the financialization of the economy and reminds us that the limits of language can be pushed while the limits of finance are more rigidly well defined. By "internalizing linguistic potencies,"¹¹ finance permits the monetary signifier to function free of its referent: the calculation, circulation, and denotation of physical goods, products, and labor. Money creates money through money "without the generative intervention of physical matter and muscular work."¹² And this well-defined financial parthenogenesis ultimately restricts "social and linguistic potency, dissolving the products of human activity, especially of collective semiotic activity."¹³

Poetry itself, not calculation, is the enunciator of language. Poetry attests to the "reemergence of the deictic function (from *deixis*, self-indication) of enunciation."¹⁴ It is the spatiotemporal presence of the embodied human making manifest meaning. But, it is now subsumed by this self-referential, calculative procedurality of delimiting financial, managerial logic. In this sense, signification—both financial and linguistic—is no longer the domain of the anthropic but, instead, is handed over to a self-referential, autonomous recombinatory function. While the symbolist poets do indeed sever the link between the word and the world, the *author* remains the craftsperson, and the mental site where poetry unfolds is largely the author sharing with others their own private articulation. However, in the realm of number, calculation, and managerial combinatorialism, *the closed-system optimizes itself*, and its articulations are not shared but innocuously imposed. This semiotic analog sets the stage for the era of the apparatus and its liberation from human steering.

Symbolist poetry, of course, did not actively conspire with the self-referential semiotics of financial capitalism. However, the zeitgeist fostered "dereferentialization" and the emergence of the word abstracted from the world. As a result, the qualitative is indeed reduced to the quantitative: language serves the apparatus, currency serves the apparatus, regulatory exchange serves the apparatus, and the economy serves the apparatus. Symbolism severs the word from the world. Later, the significantly more extreme Italian Futurists called for the word to be set free. But Dada goes altogether further: "A line of poetry is a chance to get rid of all the filth that clings to this accursed language, as if put there by stockbrokers' hands, hands worn smooth by coins," writes Hugo Ball in 1916. "I want the word where it ends and begins," he continues, "the word has become a thing by itself . . . the word, the word, the word outside your domain."¹⁵ Aiming for the semiotization of no thing, the Dadaists sought the word autonomously proceeding without intention and operating as the subject of its own hyperreal theatre. Indeed, nearly a century before Jean Baudrillard provocatively heralded that the Gulf War did not take place, the Dadaist Johannes Baader, in 1920, proclaimed that "the World War is a newspaper war. In reality, it never existed."[16] Autonomous semiotics is no longer *for us*; instead, it set the stage, not just for hyperreality, but for dataism.

DIGITAL MODERNISM

If the twenty-first century optimizes itself, reorganizes itself, affirms, and, crucially, *narrates* itself through combinatorial media technologies that reduce the qualitative to the quantitative and exclude the human, this should come as little surprise since modernity has always been as much about developing—and being developed by—media technologies. In the late twentieth century, with the widespread availability of home computers and increased processing power, the appearance of exciting, avant-garde, demanding, and fresh approaches to narrative—both *about* and *using* computer technology—begin to emerge. Indeed, many of these narratives also draw attention to this new medium and, as a result, explicitly examine the prospective implications of the apparatus' self-liberation. The texts I consider in this book are those that are less interactive and playful, and instead texts that express ecstatic anxieties. These texts acknowledge the innocuous ease by which media technologies and the apparatus operate with, beside, and beyond personal engagement. Consequently, the literature of exclusion is distinctly modernist.

Jessica Pressman remarks that there is a notable modernist quality to *digital* texts (electronic literature generated with computers and read using computers). She calls this "digital Modernism": electronic literature that invites close reading, seeks "inspiration and validation in a literary past," reinvigorates "modernist aesthetic practices," and assesses "the state of electronic literature, and of literature in general in our digital age."[17] Like the modernists, these authors aim to "raze and rebuild."[18] While "electronic literature has been celebrated as a postmodern literary form that grows out of technologies, subjectivities, and poetics from the middle of the twentieth century,"[19] Pressman focuses on "an alternative genealogy" of digital narrative by emphasizing works of electronic literature that, rather than stress interactivity and playfulness, "employ a strategy of renovation that purchase cultural capital from the literary canon in order to validate their newness and demand critical attention in the form of close reading."[20] Pressman also notes that the works of electronic literature to which she is drawn are "text based, aesthetically difficult, and ambivalent in their relationship to mass media and popular culture" and "support immanent critiques of a society that privileges images, navigation, and interactivity over complex narrative and close reading."²¹ Rather than a celebration of novelty, however, such works are confrontations with the aesthetic and consumptive values of the early twenty-first century.

This ambivalence at once tightens the self-reflexive feedback loops inherent in time, place, and aesthetic value while simultaneously losing the grip of textual involvement, interactivity, inclusion, and participation. Consider Pressman's definition of modernism: "I understand modernism to be a strategy of innovation that employs the media of its time to reform and refashion older literary practices in ways that produce new art. In other words, . . . modernism is centrally about media."²² Ultimately, "making it new," she insists, is about renovating the past *through* media. In this sense, her work is situated in a lineage of Stephen Kern,²³ Edna Duffy,²⁴ Friedrich Kittler,²⁵ Lev Manovich,²⁶ and Marshall McLuhan. "Digital modernism," Pressman suggests, "allows us to reconsider how and why media is (and always has been) a central aspect of experimental literature and the strategy of making it new."²⁷ In identifying modernism—and digital modernism—as *about* and *through* media, Pressman argues against considering electronic literature postmodern and grounds this reasoning on two concrete observations.

First, the "great divide" between high art and mass culture described by Andreas Huyssen no longer seems to hold. And secondly, that the era of incredulity toward metanarratives, identifications of differends, and debates around aesthetic pastiche and parody, in the work of Jean-François Lyotard, Fredric Jameson, and Linda Hutcheon in the 1980s, describe a historical moment that is now past. The intensification of neoliberalism, techno-capitalism, personal computers, mobile devices, e-commerce, and semio-capitalism is emblematic of what Pressman, citing Henry Jenkins, calls "convergence culture." However, while such changes in media technology elicit changes in electronic literature's participatory nature, "digital modernism," Pressman asserts, "rebels against this cultural situation and the affective mode exemplary of it—interactivity—by returning to an older aesthetic of difficulty and the avant-garde stance it invokes."²⁸ In the course of this rebellion, it is the rigorous confrontation with exclusion, *not participation*, which works of digital modernism provoke. Ultimately, modernism was (and still is) as much about media as it is about the impersonal abstraction of the author and reader from self-narration.

While postmodernism consumes and repositions all critique leveled against it, as Jameson argues, digital modernism reconditions the skepticism toward such conclusions by reinvigorating a dynamic and aesthetic spatio-temporal movement *back, forward*, and *through* to *renew*. The conscious and unconscious reenvisioning of the high modernist ethos in the early twenty-first century offers, on the one hand, provocative potencies for aesthetics while, on the other hand, a reason for hesitation and careful consideration regarding the political consequences of such potentialities. While "digital modernism is aligned with strategies of the avant-garde" as it "challenges expectations about what art is and does,"[29] it also challenges the degree to which ubiquitous digitality and exclusion may affect the future of participatory democracies. "In our culture of technophilia, most people are users of ever-more complex media products containing ever-more sophisticated interfaces that hide the interworking of the technologies and the ideologies behind their design," Pressman writes. She continues remarking that "most users lack the skill to think critically about these objects and about how these objects formally operate. How do we understand the interface of the Google home page? How does it formally produce meaning?"[30] Indeed, the era of digital modernism is also the era of surveillance capitalism, social media misinformation, and information illiteracy. Just as liberal democracies require an informed and literate *dēmos*, the twenty-first century demands not only that the general public be able to answer not only *what* Google does but also *how* such proceduralities—used by Google and beyond—shape the narratives that we *adapt to* and *adopt as* our own.

Digital modernism and the literature of exclusion thus invite close reading as confrontation. This careful, slow mode of interpretation may serve to inform the ways that we examine types of avant-garde art online and in print, and also can operate as a rehearsal for how we may transpose such heuristic practices to our participation in the ever-accelerating flow of information in daily life. While high modernism looks both into the past and future in ways that were at once conservative and iconoclastic, digital modernism does so *again* as a kind of ongoing, recursive feedback loop. Modernism calls at once for more intensive engagement with the past, present, and future via, paradoxically, a new impersonal identity. It aims to establish a new kind of human being that is equipped to adapt to and engage with its own exclusion and nonparticipation from the technological forces shaping and self-generating cultural and political narrative.

DIGITAL SUPERMODERNISM: DATAISM, PSYCHOPOLITICS, AND NEURO-TOTALITARIANISM

While a central despair and delight of the modernist period was the human merger with machine, a similarly ambivalent response to our merger with information, code, and calculation is taking place in the late twentieth and early twenty-first centuries. "The disproportion," Bifo writes, "between the arrival rate of new information and the limited time available for conscious processing generates hypercomplexity,"[31] and the hypercomplexity of supermodernism anesthetizes the human. While the individual in the early twentieth century agonizes over the alienation from daily life and the fear of being turned into a cog in a machine, the individual in twenty-first-century supermodernity merges, not with large industrial machinery, but with information, calculation, and dopamine-driven feedback loops. While the machinery of modernity is inhumane in its disciplinary brutishness, the processual and procedural calculation of supermodernity is inhuman in its smooth, insidious invisibility and ease. Both exclude, but to differing degrees of abstracting intensities. To recognize this requires, paradoxically, that we at once accelerate our aesthetic while also slow down our interpretative and heuristic practices.

Despite its capabilities to connect us, information technologies—as dataism—also isolate, infiltrate, and occupy the mind's very prereflexive processes. A century ago, mass industrialization and emergent media technologies heralded what appeared to be, according to Han, the apex of the "first Enlightenment": a ubiquitous everything operating as rational clockwork machinery at the expense of human imagination, desire, and autonomy. "The imperative of the second Enlightenment," however, "declares: everything must become data and information," Han continues. "The soul of the second Enlightenment," he writes, "is data totalitarianism, or data fetishism. Although it announces that it is taking leave of all ideology, dataism itself is an ideology. It is leading to digital totalitarianism":[32] psychopolitics, "neuro-totalitarianism,"[33] and a "totalitarian apparatus."[34] Such digital totalitarianism, for Han, is ultimately one that does not punish the body, but, instead, harnesses the psyche. This process manifests itself in ways different from the barbaric logical conclusion of the first Enlightenment. With the second Enlightenment's obsession with information, data, and calculation, Han remarks that it "is summoning forth a new kind of violence,"[35] and this new kind of violence is one that parasitizes autonomy through processual procedduralities. Ultimately, "disciplinary technology . . . reaches beyond the physical realm, into the mental sphere."[36] He remarks that Bentham's panopticon affected moral sense, but did not invisibly infect the psyche.[37] The digital, combinatorial processes of supermodernity and neoliberalism, on the other hand, *do* level-cross *into* and *with* the mind and psyche. In this sense, neoliberalism co-opts a "more efficient technology of power"[38] by inoffensively making individuals subordinate themselves to the apparatus by becoming dependent on its proceduralities. Indeed, our very conscious and autonomous *involvement* in our own agency is retreating from its wordly source. In a way, the apparatus yields deeply intimate, nonconsensual hallucinations *from without*.

As a result, digital modernism and the literature of exclusion also confront the dawn of digital psychopolitics by marking a definite shift from disciplinary technologies and surveillance to the "active steering" of the nervous system.³⁹ For Han, the major crisis of our time is that neuro-plasticity and "free will itself [are] at stake."⁴⁰ And, perhaps for the first time in history, this is not rhetorical hyperbole: "Big Data is a highly efficient psychopolitical instrument that makes it possible to achieve comprehensive knowledge of the dynamics of social communication. This knowledge is knowledge for the sake of domination and control . . . it facilitates intervention in the psyche and enables influence to take place on a pre-reflexive level."⁴¹ The horizon is dominated by information technologies predicated on goal-oriented, deterministic algorithms. These processes execute, reorganize, and self-optimize until a predetermined goal is achieved. Yet, for humans to act as free agents, "the future must be open," Han remarks. The eerily accurate ways that Big Data can predict human behavior marks the inception of technologies that can invisibly direct and shape human behavior; with digital psychopolitics and neuro-totalitarianism, "persons are being positivized into things, which can be quantified, measured and steered" by Big Data,⁴² Han remarks, and this announces the end of autonomy and agency.

However, what makes this process even less intuitive is that Big Data, like the apparatus, is itself without autonomous agency. It is a hypercomplex procedure that proceeds without agential intention. "Big Data lacks comprehension—it lacks the Concept," Han adds, "the absolute knowledge intimated by Big Data coincides with absolute ignorance."⁴³ That is, the programmed procedures that steer supermodernity are without value judgment, without empathy, and without meaning: "*No one* rules the empire," writes Han. "It is the capitalist system itself, which encompasses *everyone*. Today, exploitation is possible without any domination at all."⁴⁴ Ultimately, the algorithmic procedures that make the apparatus possible assemble into an automaton without physical components, interlocking parts, or identifiable contours. That which rules is at once ubiquitous and fundamentally *without*, namely, the apparatus steers us blindly *from within* yet *exists outside*. As a result, to examine the apparatus' effects on the personal, one must approach it obliquely. To narrate the self in the face of dataism, one must be willing to narrate the *effects* that the apparatus has on agency; to do so requires the enigmatic adoption of modernist impersonality. And no modernist movement sought a more paradoxically impersonal, spontaneous, automated approach to resistance than the Dadaists.

THE VOICE OF THE UNKNOWN: DADA AND THE SUPERIDIOT

N. Katherine Hayles writes that a "nothingness would confront us if we could take an impossible journey and zoom into a computer's interior while it is running code. We would find that there is no there there, through a layered architecture correlating ones and zeros with human language. From the nothingness of alternating voltages emerges the complexities of digital culture."[45] Because digital psychopolitics, neuro-totalitarianism, and the black box of everyday interfaces operate from, paradoxically, neural intimacy *and* alien immaterial proceduralities, the role we play in shaping meaning and cultural narratives proves an urgent concern. It is this digital *outside*, occupied by the apparatus where *no thing* makes manifest its objectives, into which we must gaze if intervention with nothingness is indeed possible. It is this no thing, nothingness, and "no there there" of the digital that is the subject matter of the literature of exclusion, thus distinguishing it as a subset of digital modernism. Rather than the electronic manifestations of high modernism in the lineage of Pound, Eliot, Woolf, and Joyce, we turn to the peculiar legacy on the digital by the most iconoclastic, extreme, nihilistic, and revolutionary form of modernism: Dada.

For Han, the relation between the semantic unraveling of Dada and the asemantic functioning of data is not ambiguous: "Dataism, it turns out, is amounting to digital Dadaism,"[46] he writes. Like dataism,

> Dadaism also takes leave of meaningful contexts of every kind. It empties language itself of sense: "The acts of life have no beginning or end. Everything happens in a completely idiotic way. That is why everything is alike. Simplicity is called Dada." Dataism is nihilism. It gives up on any and all meaning. Data and numbers are not narrative; they are additive. Meaning, on the other hand, is based on narration. Data simply fills up the senseless void.[47]

However, in filling up the senseless void, data self-animates and motivates its self-optimized parasitism of the psyche. By narrating the recursive psycho-ecological feedback loops between the mind and the apparatus, the literature of exclusion ultimately aims to confront the nihilistic, valueless, indifferent, processual encroachment of the *no there there* here. However frequently popular media attributes anthropomorphized, superhuman qualities to AI and the apparatus, the fact remains that the apparatus is ultimately without mind, intentionality, and meaning. Indeed, the apparatus cannot *think*. "The capacity of society as a whole, as a collective brain,"[48] writes Flusser, is still more intelligent than the apparatus. While it is inhumanly fast at making everything happen through pre-set combinatorialism, apparatuses are "exceptionally fast idiots that forget nothing, but they are idiots nevertheless."[49] The apparatus is idiotic, and idiocy is Dada: both exemplify the *outside* in the sense of "the idiot" as that which only concerns its own singular, autonomous functionalities.

Just as the emergence of financialism in the twentieth century finds itself tangled with the French and Russian symbolism of the later nineteenth century, the coming into being of a mindless automaton *in place of* cultural negotiation is knotted with the Dadaists. Financialism and symbolism free the signifier from the referent; however, it is with Dada that semiotics break free of human agency and intentionality altogether.[50] When applying this semiotic discontinuity to dataism and autonomous technologies, the breaking off is sometimes called the technological singularity. The technological singularity refers to the instance when exponential technological acceleration moves beyond the human capacity to comprehend or control technological development. As a result, the theory purports, society, culture, and everyday life will be altered in irreversible ways. Indeed, while the singularity is often discussed in terms of superintelligence, here we consider it in terms of the apparatus' teleology: indifferent, efficient, inhuman superidiocy. As self-optimizing, autonomous superidiot, the apparatus is the absolute outsider. This is technological Dada and emblematic of supermodernity.

Dada aims to seek a new kind of human being while it also annihilates the site of knowledge. In a sense, this antiepistemological teleology results in the following enigma: how might one know the disappearance of knowledge if the site of knowledge itself is transformed in irreversible and unidentifiable ways? When the technological singularity arrives, human involvement in its processes and development will have already waned to the point of exclusion. As a result, the narratives of transcendence so frequently coupled with discussions surrounding the singularity are upturned. Rather than transcendence, humans will *experience the banality of the singularity*: the breaking off absolutely of the apparatus into functions so abstract and inhuman as to become imperceptible. Calculation will function, but it will signify no thing. Once shaped by humans and the shaper of humans, the apparatus will eventually optimize its own procedures; it will develop new languages (rather, processes) unintelligible and without use for or even recognition by humans. This instant will mark the apparatus' full realization, and its exponential data, like Dada, will signify nothing and will no longer be *for us*.

While it is now common to encounter comparisons between the mood post-2016 to that of early twentieth-century Europe, it is nevertheless evident, in the early twenty-first century, that something is "in the air," as André Breton wrote in 1927, "as everything is said to be in the air."[51] And indeed, this progressive melting into air has been unfolding for well over a century. During the early twentieth century, the turbulence in Europe saw the avant-garde shift from art for art's sake to art as lived experience and revolutionary gesture. Dada was at the center of all this and disrupted the human faith in rational, agential involvement. The movement was motivated by disgust toward the bourgeoisie and its support of the Great War.[52] The Dadaists in Zurich, Berlin, and New York wanted to disrupt and destroy every way of thinking that could lead to such a hyper-technologized slaughter. So, they waged war on the epistemic practices and institutions that they blamed for the conflict: language, rationality, and logic. Yet, Dada's legacy is both positive and destructive. It aims at multiplicity over reductionism and freedom from everything while it simultaneously presses for the breaking free of the semiotic parameters of language. Dada is the deliberate *human* dismantling of humanism.

The psychical and physical trauma and upheaval of 1914–1918 splintered confidence in the project of democracy, humanism, and Enlightenment. While Dada shared much in common with Italian Futurism in its bombastic approach to manifestos, destruction, and avant-garde typography, the movement did not have a program and, in fact, was against programs of all varieties. In his Dada Manifesto 1918, Tristan Tzara writes that Dada was "born for a need for independence, of a distrust toward unity. Those who are with us preserve their freedom. We recognise no theory."[53] Such absolute independence forbids any form of censorship and, as a result, its destructiveness is balanced by the proliferation of new aesthetic and anti-aesthetic practices. Contradictions reigned: "Dada's propaganda for a total repudiation of art was itself a factor in the advance of art,"[54] writes Hans Richter, "the absence of any ulterior motive enabled us to listen to the voice of the 'Unknown'—and to draw knowledge from the realm of the unknown. Thus we arrived at the central experience of Dada."[55] Indeed, it is listening to the voice of the unknown, hearing the non-articulation of the outside, that is inseparable from the core experience of Dada and its continuing influence on modernity through supermodernity.

Dada was meant, however, to at once be nihilistic ("DADA MEANS NOTHING"[56] writes Tzara) and a strange kind of affirmation: "Freedom: DADA DADA DADA, a roaring of tense colours, an interlacing of opposites and of all contradictions, grotesques, inconsistencies. LIFE."[57] Yet these pursuits, both political and individual, abstract and concrete, nihilistic and affirmative, took place against a backdrop of chaos and catastrophe, a colossal blind force that proceeded on its own inhuman terms: "The sort of human or inhuman being who used reason as a juggernaut, crushing acres of corpses—as well as ourselves—beneath its wheels."[58] In the midst of tragedy, it makes sense to embrace the absence of sense, to express ambivalence and paradox, and to declare a "raging *anti, anti, anti,* linked with an equally passionate *pro, pro, pro!*"[59] In a way, we can consider Dada as a collective melancholia, mad laughter, revulsion, and rage: an experience of profound grief[60] deepened by disgust in the past, revolt against the present, and endlessly assembled from an increasingly technologized, calculative, inhuman future where the exclusion of the human was always thought inevitable.

Dada, as a result, both emerges from and accelerates a newly optimized and mediated cybernetic merger of human and apparatus. Such reflexivity is vital to understanding modernity because it closes in on itself, affirms itself, and negates itself via self-iterating, self-regulating, and ever-mutating feedback loops. Hayles, in *How We Became Posthuman* (1999), defines reflexivity as "the movement whereby that which has been used to generate a system is made, through a changed perspective, to become part of the system it generates."[61] This dual turning inward activates the symptoms of modernity while also being symptomatic of it: a feedback loop that rapidly produces new ways of accelerating technological, scientific, cultural, political, and artistic change that curves in on itself, reiterates itself, and affirms itself, while at the same time dismantling and undermining itself. "The unsettling conundrum at the heart of Dada negation," writes Jed Rasula, "is that saying no is still saying something. The negative adds to a positive sum."[62]

Like financialism, Dada's abstraction finds its roots in symbolist poetry. Stéphane Mallarmé, in a letter to Eugène Lefébure, dated May 17, 1867, writes that his "work was created only by *elimination*, and each newly acquired truth was born only at the expense of an impression which flamed up and then burned itself out, so that its particular darkness could be isolated" so he "could venture ever more deeply into the sensation of Darkness Absolute. Destruction was my Beatrice."[63] The spirit of Mallarmé's practice of creation via elimination is emblematic of this process: appearance then disappearance, creation then destruction, illumination then darkness. Mallarmé was one of the first to clearly express the journey more deeply into a nonorientable reflexivity that would come to dominate the twentieth century and define the early twenty-first century. Essential to this loop is the *nil* or darkness absolute; indeed, Mallarmé closed his eyes and "saw that [the eliminated, the absence, a nothingness] existed."[64] In the 1860s, Mallarmé may have willed a journey into the void; his poetry freed the signifier from the signified; word was loosened but not severed. By the early twentieth century and certainly in the early twenty-first century, the reflexive vortex that eliminates as it creates is a reality principle. While destruction was Mallarmé's Beatrice, optimized, functional nothingness is the apparatus' Beatrice.

Because psycho-ecological reflexivity marks technology as an extension of the human body and mind—and the human body and mind as extensions of technology—this cybernetic assemblage is suspended above and apart from a collective, ongoing loss so traumatic that it fuels and self-generates an abstract tool that severs itself from the tool-user. Human and apparatus are tangled in a self-reflexive, self-referential, self-optimizing loop without orientation. The severing of this loop, as a result, thus mostly goes unnoticed. When William Butler Yeats famously wrote in 1919 that "the center cannot hold,"[65] the observation was remarkably apt, as the absent center proceeds toward its full realization *as* apparatus: a nothingness that accelerates both the collective grief of a century while operating like a tranquilizer to anesthetize endless anguish and a centerless, self-reflexive loop, accelerating its momentum to the point of casting off the human altogether.

Indeed, with modernity, "the center is missing," writes Mark Fisher, "but we cannot stop searching for it or positing it."[66] While Hayles also suggests this center is missing—with supermodernity, the center has shifted to zero-dimensional digitality—Fisher adds that even if we were to identify the inhuman procedurality of the apparatus, we would find that "what is there is not capable of exercising responsibility."[67] The apparatus, rather than an optimizing collective consolation, propagates and perfects itself as an indifferent, idiotic force that will continue to operate in increasingly innocuous and invisible ways throughout the twentieth century, into the twenty-first century, and well after it has abandoned us to pure information. Indeed, the technological apparatus that optimizes the mechanization of catastrophe ultimately instantiates absolute loss in such a way that it inhumanly slouches toward redemption by optimizing the absence at the heart of catastrophe. The result is damning for human agency. Before we are fully anesthetized, before the human-apparatus merger splits, a collective human psychopathological force will be mobilized to confront disaster by denying it and embracing it. Indeed, to reiterate Tzara, the acts of life have no beginning or end. Everything happens in a completely idiotic way, and with increasingly innocuous ease.

POWER IS ALL ABOUT MAKING THINGS EASY: NEURO-TOTALITARIANISM AND POIESIS

Iconoclastic shifts in literary practice coincide with broader epistemic changes. The literature of exclusion explores anxieties, grief, and ecstasies that are deeply intimate; yet, the effects of atomizing the individual also have profound effects on the way individuals may act as autonomous political agents. The early twentieth century saw the rise of authoritarianism, nationalism, and xenophobia in a way uncannily similar to what we have seen in the early twentieth century. Behind this political theatre, the apparatus proceeds without intention. We may fear the police officer's bullets, but we generally do not fear our smartphone or GPS. When we sit down at a computer terminal, use our ever-at-hand mobile device, or tap at our tablets, we are met with a comfort akin to the smoker lighting the day's first of many cigarettes. Despite its complexity, the reductive and calculative functioning of the apparatus, its ontological unknowability, and endless ease at crafting the social sphere while benefiting the few can be summarized as follows: the new "power is all about making things easy."[68]

Our reliance on the apparatus isolates even as we aim for electronically mediated connectivity. "Contemporary society," writes Han, "is not shaped by multitude so much as solitude ... privatization now reaches into the depths of the soul itself."[69] Social solidarity, political freedom, and collective empathy are rapidly, efficiently, and stealthily replaced by the "techno-linguistic automatisms"[70] of the apparatus, while collective social choice is transcoded into "psychic automatisms embedded in social discourse"[71] by the apparatus. Because the apparatus embeds itself in the unconscious, it thrives on the infinite libidinal and irrational flows of emotive, addicted, and reactionary psychic automatisms. It optimizes itself by seizing "on emotion in order to influence actions on this pre-reflexive level."[72] We do not resist the apparatus because we have not acknowledged its purely efficient idiotic, functional rationality and ability to steer "the person as a whole"[73] on a psychopolitical level. Authoritarians may seize opportunities from these psychic shifts, but even they are not in control of them. Indeed, the authoritarian far-right does not understand the apparatus, but it does know how to exploit its effects. And while authoritarians are always eventually overpowered by the oppressed, the apparatus, nevertheless, processes and possesses power silently, invisibly, and inhumanly.

For this reason, the literature of exclusion is obliquely political: its psychic trials are typically inward, isolated, automated, and immobile. It does not concern itself with riots, protest, disruptions, brute oppression, or celebratory liberation. Instead, it examines the apparatus' occupation of the nervous system and its resultant self-brutality. Expressing psychic automatisms that discipline and reeducate the self, it is a literature of "inner space" occupied by the inhuman automatisms of dataism and, as a result, at once inevitably embraces the apparatus while struggling to resist it. While the Dadaists took to the art galleries, cabarets, theatres, and the streets, dataism concerns the bidirectional, self-reflexive inner riot for and against the self. This is the central paradox that the literature of exclusion aims to understand: complicity, indifference, and resistance are all heterarchically valuable data to the apparatus' expansion.

It is in this psychic theatre, where rationality and irrationality function like an idiotic, intentionless, self-regulating ouroboros. "Rationality is defined by objectivity, generality and steadiness,"[74] writes Han. The apparatus functions as an idiotic, optimized, efficient rationality; it consumes then constitutes its opposite—human irrationality—by adapting, adopting, and offering volatilities that will fuel further the accumulation of future data by provoking pre-reflexive reactionism, thus automating human emotionality. The apparatus dismantles all forms of duration, continuity, and sustained empathy by "pushing the emotionalization of the productive process forward."[75] Remarking that human rationality is "slower than emotionality," Han notes that the apparatus' rationality is faster than emotionality, in fact faster than any pre-reflexive affect. For humans, "the pressure of acceleration now is leading to a dictatorship of emotion."[76] The apparatus is absolute speed, the great organizer and reorganizer, a hypercomplex indifferent assemblage of processes blindly accumulating, delimiting, and consolidating every discernible feature of referentiality itself *as* data. It is this intractable problem that the literature of exclusion attempts to both occupy and unravel.

The literature of exclusion, however, is not a defeatist, hopeless, or miserabilist mode; instead, it offers poiesis as a mode of human intervention into the apparatus. As a member of the Dadaist lineage, the literature of exclusion is animated by the contradictory enigmas arising from the subsuming of autonomy to data-optimized automatisms. That the homeostasis between human and apparatus is currently unstable proves an opportunity for evanescent acts of intervention. "Autonomy" requires, Bifo remarks, "the ability to escape environments where the positive feedback is switched on."[77] Because this positive feedback loop operates innocuously and seduces with its ease, the task of the literature of exclusion is to make its processual proceduralities visible and to offer, via conspicuousness, alternatives. It may not offer immediate solutions, but the literature of exclusion is nevertheless a laboratory of experimental tactics. Indeed, while Bifo suggests that "only the poetic revitalization of language will open the way to the emergence of a new form of social autonomy,"[78] Han and Flusser would suggest that poiesis will simply transcode into further metadata, thus accelerating the optimization of the apparatus. Perhaps our only *choice*, paradoxically, is accident, excess, and avant-gardism that is at once profoundly human and deeply impersonal, deliberate but without intention, *for* and *against*: Dada. Such acts of paradoxical self-narration can become concept generating, poietic *human* input that may, if anything, steer *inhuman* output rather than inhuman output determining the steering of human behaviors.

THE APPARATUS TURNED HUMAN: AI AND SELF-NARRATION

The processual counting of the apparatus is essential for its self-optimization, while human recounting is essential to self-knowledge. Complicating this process is the emergence of modern AI since AI is the apparatus made human and the human made apparatus. While AI is not technically new—it may be traced back to the abacus[79]—its recent manifestations in the twentieth century as intelligent computer programs mark the bridge between the apparatus and the human. Of course, AI is neither fully human nor fully apparatus. The apparatus constitutes AI, while AI functions as autonomous goal-oriented problem solvers in the world. While AI simulates aspects of thought via computer processes—sometimes anthropomorphic, though more often according to very different modes of cognition—the apparatus does not think. Because it does not think, it cannot narrate beyond the parameters of combinatorialism. AI, that is, "has no access to what is *wholly Other*."[80]

While there is lively debate about what constitutes AI, John McCarthy, who coined the term in 1955, offers a concise definition: AI is "the science and engineering of making intelligent machines, especially intelligent computer programs. It is related to the similar task of using computers to understand human intelligence, but AI does not have to confine itself to methods that are biologically observable."[81] What precisely "intelligence" denotes is another point of debate. McCarthy suggests that the reason for this uncertainty is that though AI need not confine itself to biologically observable methods (think, e.g., of the programming and code operating in the "no there there" of a smartphone predicting the subsequent word in a text message), the qualitative interpretations of its processes are done by humans. As a result, AI is always understood in relation to *us*, while AI, if it can be said to understand, understands in relation to its own processual programming. Intelligence means very different things to humans; because intelligence itself is language and understood through language, it is remarkably ambiguous, tenuous, and drifting. AI, on the other hand, need not *denote* intelligence; instead, it is a computational, programmed process that *demonstrates* intelligence to humans. That is, it shows an "ability to achieve goals in the world,"[82] while procedurally operating regardless of biological observation. AI *is* a science; the apparatus, however, is the autonomous, cumulative, and alterior effects of this science. The apparatus, unlike AI, is an objective made manifest as an abstract object.

Most computer intelligence cannot currently create beyond the self-reflexive loops it has been handed in its program's initial conditions. The implications here are significant in addressing what McCarthy identifies as the task of using computers to understand human intelligence. Han remarks that "intelligence means *choosing-between* (*inter-legere*). It is not entirely free in so far as it is caught in a *between*, which depends on the system in operation. Intelligence has no access to the *outside*, because it makes a choice between options in a system."[83] In this sense, intelligence does not operate freely; instead, it is selective and combinatorial. It may be an aspect of the apparatus, but it—like linguistic human intelligence—cannot offer special insight into the apparatus because it cannot access the outside. Ultimately, a system provides particular offerings a priori from which intelligence can then choose by following, not a system of logic, but "the logic of a system."[84] Han asserts that intelligence is "system-immanent" whereby "a given system defines a given intelligence."[85] Such AI may attempt to solve the "problem" of poetic, varied, fluid, and singular human variability by reducing the qualitative to the quantitative. By optimizing and standardizing, for example, consensus around brand loyalty, political opinion, group identity, or collective attitudes—that is, by organizing and delimiting the dissemination of multiplicity and alternatives—such AI select from already-given datasets in order to achieve a teleological end. In the task of using computers to understand human intelligence, the following problem arises: that of prescribed delimiting, rather than discovering, the parameters of human thought.

The apparatus, however, constitutes these closed systems, but cannot be delimited to them. Instead, it is a superidiotic process *without* intelligence: an ultimate outsider—literally, a fool or idiot. It is dataism as Dada, and electronic Dadaism as data. Self-optimizing by incorporating all information, the apparatus escapes closed systems by constituting them from without, deserting intelligence, and glistening "with intelligence that has been overcome."[86] The apparatus-as-superidiot as the ultimate outsider makes subordinate not only the human but also AI.

This poses a problem for those who wish to harness the apparatus for political and ideological ends. AI measures, solves, quantifies, and selects more rapidly and efficiently than humans, and it is through AI—whether visible or invisible—that we *experience* a cybernetic relationship. Indeed, a specialized few program and profit from AI's ability to measure and quantify every aspect of our daily lives in the form of metadata gathered from internet use, smart objects, GPS, purchases, and phone calls, that is, every aspect of a connected life. Our participation, even embrace, of the user-friendly, addictive interfaces ultimately provide AI with information from which it can select and optimize to, then, reinforce and encourage selective behavior from users. Its power is all about making things easy. And yet, while Zhongguancun and Silicon Valley innovate astounding AI technologies, neither have access to the apparatus itself. As the superidiot, the apparatus abstracts the constitutive totality of intelligent technologies from without: where intelligence breaks off, no thing may be except the autonomous objective made object.

The sum of all data cannot answer the most basic problems of self-knowledge and self-narration. This is because the "Quantified Self"[87] is reductive, essentialist, and appeals to the without. However, to *consider* the apparatus, we should inhabit the threshold of the quantified self and acknowledge it as an experimental "Dadaist technology"[88] so that we may wholly empty the self of meaning and aim to produce (post)human narratives *alongside* inhuman combinatorialism and processualism and, via analogy, expand the possibilities of self-narration. While Han laments the recent disappearance of the *human* fool or idiot as a consequence of AI procedures that amplify the human compulsion to conform, Dada in the twenty-first century may be a force of idiotism appropriate to narrating the human by both confronting and using technology as a means of intimating the apparatus. While "the attendant violence of consensus is suppressing idiotisms,"[89] Dada offers dissensus and the singular. Dada is contradiction: order, disorder, various, individual, self, other, art, and anti-art. It is non-denotative, asemic, and unpredictable. With—and as—a Dadaist technology, we may *rehearse the outside* and recognize the thresholds of self-narration. Tzara writes that

> This world is not specified or defined in the work, it belongs in its innumerable variations to the spectator. For its creator it is without cause and without theory. *Order = disorder; ego = non-ego; affirmation = negation*: the supreme radiations of an absolute art. Absolute in the purity of a cosmic ordered chaos, eternal in the globule of a second without duration, without breath, without control.[90]

It is *from* such paradoxes that the human may renew the social and acknowledge our merger *with* and co-option *into* the self-reflexive, level-crossing loops of the apparatus. As a Dadaist technology, the human may resist its co-option as a dataist technology through mad techno-poiesis. In narrating our omission from automated technological processes, the literature of exclusion actively accepts new modes of impersonality as an invitation into as much as a confrontation with the apparatus.

Seeking the poietic potencies of the human, the literature of exclusion provokes the instance where word breaks off and where calculation operates indifferently, efficiently, and autonomously. It is a literature—both poietic and thanatotic—that seeks the voice of the unknown by engaging the superidiocy of the apparatus and by enacting the idiot who "communicates with the In-communicable."[91] If the apparatus combines, calculates, and counts tirelessly in silence, then the human must dismantle, disrupt, and recount in parallel. Indeed, such narratives seek order in disorder, the self in the non-self, affirm through negation, articulate the inarticulate, and recount the horizon of the future.

THE CHAPTERS

The overall purpose of this study is to explore works that stand at the threshold where literature confronts the "no thing" upon which digital and algorithmic culture rests. Each chapter in this book examines a different example of the literature of exclusion through close reading. My goal is to consider how the literature of exclusion, as a contemporary Dadaist avant-garde, is both complicit with and resistant to the apparatus, and to consider how new forms of fiction may offer novel alternatives for the future of self-narration. Chapter 1 examines the structural similarity between language and thought via cognitive linguistics and functionalism. This chapter establishes certain assumptions about the psycho-ecological relation between mind and language, and how such relations are transferable to considerations about the relation between mind and code. Chapter 2 considers an updating of the modernist poetics of impersonality as a means of both acknowledging and resisting psycho-ecology and the struggle between the posthuman and the inhuman.

In chapter 3, I discuss B. R. Yeager's cyber-Gothic novel *Amygdalatropolis* (2016) and its examination of the human merger with the "divine neutrality" of the apparatus. Rather than a kind of cyberpunk techno-transcendence, Yeager posits this transcendence as a *descent* into a valueless, neutral, processual void: the apparatus is neither posthuman nor superhuman, but an inhuman procedurality. In short, this chapter considers the asemantics of the apparatus and its assault on narrative. Ultimately, Yeager's work articulates the banality, not the sublimity, of the technological singularity.

In chapter 4, I consider Samuel Beckett's *Endgame* (1957) as a zero-player game: a simulation or game that plays itself without a player. Theodor Adorno comments that, in the work of Beckett, "poetic procedure surrenders . . . without intention," and we may consider this procedure as akin to the processual proceduralities of autonomous technologies. Taking Beckett's phrase, "something is taking its course," as its central conceit, this chapter is a meditation on the status of the extra-diegetic—the reader—as a literalization of agential exclusion.

In chapter 5, I look at Jeff Noon's experimental novel *Falling Out of Cars* (2002), hauntology, and Noon's permutational remix writing technique that he calls "metamorphiction." With Noon's metamorphiction, the past haunts the present via textual sampling, the present haunts the past via mourning, and the lost potentialities of the future haunt the present. This formal experiment is mirrored in the content of the novel: a woman mourning her daughter's death. The overwhelming sense of grief and loss in *Falling Out of Cars* is expressed by a diseased England succumbing to "the noise"—a mysterious illness that dismantles semiotics and establishes a hyper-contingent world. The noise operates as a dual metaphor in the novel: firstly, the loss of a child signifying endless grief and a promised future unfairly stolen and, secondly, a broader loss of language and narrative in the face of the apparatus. Ultimately, *Falling Out of Cars* is a profound meditation on the contemporary state of the novel in the digital era.

In chapter 6, I examine the work of Japanese multimedia artist Kenji Siratori. Siratori's work poses a contentious question: at what point does digital literary experimentalism transcend literacy? Furthermore, how might a hyper, digital Dadaist "glitch poetics" *employ* illiteracy to confront the apparatus. Siratori's antinovel *Blood Electric* (2002), for example, evokes "the coming to consciousness of an artificial intelligence" via "a devastating loop of language" that is connotatively dense yet does not communicate meaningfully. Beyond the surface of the chaotic noise in Siratori's project is a gesture that is as lucid as it is timely: the radical opening up of language through glitch poetics *resists* the processually steered swarm behavior emerging from algorithmic culture. Much like Noon's experimental novel, Siratori's work suggests that as literary experimentation is pushed to extremes, new languages of code and programming suggest the dawn of new arts; our *exclusion* from the apparatus may also be an opportunity to reclaim from the digital swarm a renewed social spirit of the human.

While both Noon and Siratori employ digital techniques to differing degrees in the composition of their works, chapters 7 and 8 turn to works generated entirely with computers and which are accessible only through computer interfaces. I consider these projects examples of the "electronic literature of exclusion," since each is a work of electronic literature that expresses the same concerns as the literature of exclusion more broadly defined. Chapter 7 examines the work of Mike Bonsall and his J. G. Ballard Twitter bots as well as Benjamin (a Long Short-Term Memory Artificial Intelligence) and its science fiction screenplay *Sunspring* (2016). Bonsall's spreadsheet Twitter bots—and their regimented, tireless regularity as an intensified realization of Ballardian obsession—offer insight into ways that procedural Markov Chains may operate as a kind of metaphor for the processual compulsions of the apparatus. In Benjamin's *Sunspring*, alternatively, we have a short film entirely written by an AI. The surreal, nonsensical script (and its filmed component featuring human actors) elicits a unique kind of laughter from the audience: but, is this laughter an expression of joy, anxiety, fear, ridicule, anticipation, or a combination thereof? At the heart of Benjamin's script, however, is not simply the words but the fact that these words are organized by number and combinatorialism. The implications here are significant: perhaps part of our uneasy response to Benjamin's script rests on whether mathematics is, like language, an ingenious tautological human invention (called "fictionalism," anti-realism, or nominalism), or whether mathematics does indeed refer to the *outside* (mathematical realism or mathematical Platonism), and what the implications of either of these can mean for narrative in a combinatory future.

While the works of both Bonsall and Benjamin are autopoietic systems (combinatorial systems that generate and sustain themselves self-reflexively and indexically *from* themselves), chapter 8 examines Allison Parrish's *Ahe Thd Yearidy Ti Isa* (2019) and the way that the work resists autopoiesis. Rather than autopoietic, *Ahe Thd Yearidy Ti Isa* is allopoietic in that the system produces something radically different from the system's own processes. By drawing attention to asemic word processing—glyphs on the screen that *look* and *feel* like a language but are instead indecipherable and generated by machine learning—Parrish's asemic novel denaturalizes word processing and reminds us of what Flusser calls the technical image: a technologically generated image that, rather than operating through representation, functions through combination, recombination, and code.

To conclude, I reflect on how "literature thinks" in ways that philosophy, science, mathematics, and AI cannot. Here, I reconsider the *outside* by turning to "speculative realism" and the work of Quentin Meillassoux. While not a unified school of philosophy, what speculative realists have in common is a rejection of psycho-ecology (or what Meillassoux calls correlationism) and an embrace of the possibilities that speculating about mind-independent reality may yield. For Meillassoux, the one thing we can know about a mind-independent reality is that it is hyper-chaotic and contingent: for all we know, everything *could* change without any causal precondition. This radically changed reality would, however, posit an outside that is incongruous with the apparatus. While the apparatus is a superidiotic procedure that selects based on an immense, finite corpus predicated on *probability*, hyper-chaotic contingency *is absolute possibility*. Ultimately Meillassoux calls for an "extro-science fiction" to express a mode of world-building where the only absolute is this absolute possibility itself. From this would arise a form of contingent science fiction narrative that rests outside the laws of science and mathematics. I suggest that extro-science fiction at its best will be a kind of literature of exclusion: a hyper-contingent literature that can think the unthinkable thought and narrate possibilities as a way of staying abreast to the apparatus' accelerating quantification of every aspect of daily life.

NOTES

1. Kōbō Abe, *Inter Ice Age 4*, trans. E. Dale Saunders, drawings by Machi Abé (New York: Alfred A. Knopf, 1970), 97.

2. Byung-Chul Han, *Psychopolitics: Neoliberalism and New Technologies of Power*, trans. Erik Butler (London: Verso, 2017), 68–69.

3. Vilém Flusser, *Into the Universe of Technical Images*, trans. Nancy Ann Roth (Minneapolis: University of Minnesota Press, 2011), 18.

4. Ezra Pound, *ABC of Reading* (New York: New Directions, 1934), 28.

5. Franco "Bifo" Berardi, *The Uprising: On Poetry and Finance* (South Pasadena: Semiotext(e), 2012), 17.

6. Ibid., 18.

7. Ibid., 18.

8. Ibid., 18.

9. Franco "Bifo" Berardi, *Breathing: Chaos and Poetry* (South Pasadena: Semiotext(e), 2018), 31.

10. Berardi, *The Uprising*, 18–19.

11. Ibid., 19.

12. Ibid.

13. Ibid.
14. Ibid., 21.
15. Hugo Ball, "Dada Manifesto (1916)," *100 Artists' Manifestos: From the Futurists to the Stuckists*, ed. Alex Danchev (Penguin Random House, 2011), 128–129.
16. Johannes Baader, "Germany's Greatness and Decline," in *The Dada Almanac*, ed. Richard Hülsenbeck, trans. and ed. Malcolm Green (London: Atlas Press, 1993), 101.
17. Jessica Pressman, *Digital Modernism: Making It New in New Media* (New York, NY: Oxford University Press, 2014), 2.
18. Ibid.
19. Ibid., 2.
20. Ibid.
21. Ibid.
22. Ibid., 3–4.
23. Stephen Kern, *The Culture of Time and Space 1880–1918* (Harvard University Press, 1983).
24. Enda Duffy, *The Speed Handbook: Velocity, Pleasure, Modernism* (Duke University Press, 2009).
25. Friedrich A. Kittler, *Discourse Networks 1800/1900*, trans. Michael Metteer, with Chris Cullens (Stanford University Press, 1990).
26. See Pressman, *Digital Modernism*, 28–55.
27. Ibid., 5.
28. Ibid., 9.
29. Ibid., 10.
30. Ibid., 21.
31. Berardi, *The Uprising*, 10.
32. Han, *Psychopolitics*, 58.
33. See Franco "Bifo" Berardi's *Neuro-Totalitarianism in Technomaya Goog-Colonization of the Experience and Neuro-Plastic Alternative* (Los Angeles: Semiotext(e), 2014.
34. Flusser, *Into the Universe of Technical Images*, 76.
35. Han, *Psychopolitics*, 58.
36. Ibid., 33.
37. Ibid., 33.
38. Ibid., 26.
39. Ibid., 22–23.
40. Ibid., 22–23.
41. Ibid., 22–23.
42. Ibid., 22–23.
43. Ibid., 76.
44. Byung-Chul Han, *In the Swarm: Digital Prospects*, trans. Erik Butler (Cambridge, MIT Press, 2017), 13.
45. N. Katherine Hayles, *Electronic Literature: New Horizons for the Literary* (Indiana: University of Notre Dame Press, 2008), 185.

46. Han, *Psychopolitics*, 67–68.
47. Ibid., 67–68.
48. Flusser, *Into the Universe of Technical Images*, 76.
49. Ibid., 76.
50. Consider the various definitions of data. While the word Dada appeared for the first time *in print* on June 15, 1916, the origin of the word is, appropriately, uncertain. The Dadaists themselves, however, are deceptively helpful. There are various tales recalling how Dada was named. Richter's catalog is central to this tangled narrative: Raoul Hausmann, in his *Courrier Dada* (1960) believes that he discovered Dada in 1915. Alternatively, Claude Rivière suggests (in *Arts* winter 1962) that Francis Picabia is the founder of the movement. Alfred Barr, director of the Museum of Modern Art in New York, suggested that Dada appeared rather simultaneously (and somewhat independently) in both Zurich and New York. Richter claims that this is, in both Dada fashion and in actuality, equally correct and incorrect. As early as 1915, Dada-like works appear in Russia and, even earlier, the Italian Futurists, particularly the work of F. T. Marinetti, were proto-Dada before the first decade of the twentieth century was over. Hugo Ball suggests that in Romanian *dada* is the double affirmative "yes, yes"; in French, it signifies a hobby horse; in German, Richter suggests it signifies idiotic naivety and fixation on procreation; to the Kru people in West Africa, dada refers to the tail of a sacred cow; and in Italian dada can refer to dice. Hans Arp is comically more certain on the matter, claiming that Tzara invented the word on February 6, 1916, at 6:00 p.m. at the Café de la Terrasse in Zurich. The poet and physician Richard Hülsenbeck claims that he and Ball discovered the word accidentally while flipping through a French-German dictionary while looking to create a stage-name for the cabaret singer Madame Le Roy. Richter also lists proto-Dadaists: Mark Twain, Jean-Pierre Brisset, Alfred Jarry, Christian Morgenstern, Apollinaire, and Herostatus. Ultimately, these various, contradicting definitions enact, rather than denote, Dada. Such contradictions also demonstrate how Dada is at once historically bound and also a memetic tendency that transcends history.
51. André Breton, "'Max Ernst' by André Breton (1927)," in *Beyond Painting: And Other Writings by the Artist and His Friends*, by Max Ernst (Solar Books, 2009), 130.
52. In many ways, Dada can be seen as a protest movement as much as an art/anti-art movement.
53. Tristan Tzara, "Dada Manifesto 1918," *The Dada Reader: A Critical Anthology*, ed. Dawn Ades (Chicago: University of Chicago Press, 2006), 37.
54. Hans Richter, *Dada: Art and Anti-Art*, trans. David Britt (London: Thames & Hudson, 1997), 50.
55. Ibid., 50.
56. Tzara, "Dada Manifesto 1918," 36.
57. Ibid., 42.
58. Richter, *Dada: Art and Anti-Art*, 65.
59. Ibid., 35.
60. In a way, the First World War never really found closure, and the twentieth century proved to be endless militarized conflict and tragedy. The loss experienced

through the First World War is incomprehensible. Over nine million soldiers died, and seven million civilians died as a result of conflict, starvation, and genocides. Throughout the twentieth century, it is estimated that 108 million people were killed by war. The impossibility to fully conceive of this catastrophe established a void out of which collective grief could not escape. Quantifying catastrophe, however, is ineffective; when devastation is of such a scale, it resists concretization and remains forever abstracted from consolation. As a result, this unresolved grief, rage, and anger became the substratum and operative logic from modernity into postmodernity and supermodernity. Ultimately, feverish, rapid technological development and acceleration challenge the very operative nodes of human experience.

61. N. Katherine Hayles, *How We Became Posthuman: Virtual Bodies in Cybernetics, Literature, and Informatics* (Chicago: University of Chicago Press, 1999), 8.

62. Jed Rasula, *Destruction was my Beatrice* (New York: Basic Books, 2015), xi.

63. Stéphane Mallarmé, *Selected Poetry and Prose*, ed. Mary Ann Caws (New York: New Directions, 1982), 88.

64. Ibid.

65. William Butler Yeats, "The Second Coming," *The Collected Poems of W.B. Yeats*, ed. Richard J. Finneran (New York: Scribner Paperback Poetry, 1996), 187.

66. Mark Fisher, *Capitalist Realism: Is There No Alternative?* (Zero Books, 2010), 65–66.

67. Ibid., 65.

68. Berardi, *The Uprising*, 15.

69. Han, *In the Swarm*, 14.

70. Berardi, *The Uprising*, 7.

71. Ibid.

72. Han, *Psychopolitics*, 48.

73. Ibid., 48.

74. Ibid., 56–57.

75. Ibid.

76. Ibid.

77. Berardi, *The Uprising*, 12.

78. Ibid., 8.

79. For a concise history of AI, see Stuart J. Russell and Peter Norvig, *Artificial Intelligence: A Modern Approach*, 3rd Ed. (New Jersey: Prentice Hall, 2010), 16–28.

80. Ibid.

81. John McCarthy, "What is Artificial Intelligence?" (Stanford: Stanford University, 2007), http://jmc.stanford.edu/articles/whatisai/whatisai.pdf.

82. Ibid.

83. Han, *Psychopolitics*, 88–89.

84. Ibid.

85. Ibid.

86. Ibid., 85.

87. Ibid., 64.
88. Ibid.
89. Ibid., 86.
90. Tzara, "Dada Manifesto 1918," 38.
91. Han, *Psychopolitics*, 88.

Chapter 1

Metaphor and Metanoia
Linguistic Transfer, Cognitive Transformation, and Exclusion

In *Philosophical Investigations* (1953), Ludwig Wittgenstein famously posits the following proposition: "If a lion could talk, we wouldn't be able to understand it."[1] Ultimately, the voice of the unknown reserves its own calculative, optimizing rhetoric for its own self-unknowability. This chapter looks at the structural self-similarity between metaphor as a common way of using language and its effects on the way we experience our everyday lives. Dada asks us to consider how poiesis, literature, and creative destruction may help us confront our exclusion from contemporary algorithmic culture and its attendant psychopolitics, neuro-totalitarianism, and accelerating inhumanism. A leading feature of much modernist literature is the marked emphasis on how we perceive our surroundings over what that environment may objectively be; this preoccupation tends toward reflexivity so that literature inquires into its own function to such a degree that such textual insight into perception may transform the representation of objective environments. Dada attempts to disrupt this reflexivity by aiming to signify nothing. Attempting to negate the reflexivity that constitutes and links all things to the apparatus, Dada both laments and embraces our coming agential exclusion from our poietic role in producing cultural narratives by, paradoxically, both *confronting* and *rehearsing* agential exclusion. To contextualize the modes of reflexivity that merge the mind and language as a closed system, we now turn to cognitive linguistics.

Emerging in the 1980s, cognitive linguistics and its literary branch, cognitive poetics, take the premise that the conceptual structures constituted by the affective materiality of the brain are determined by language; the reverse simultaneously operates. This conceit is shared by phenomenologists of the early twentieth century. Rather than the paradox of infinite regress, a phenomenological criticism of self-representation, this process offers a variety of diegetic level-crossings—between vehicle and tenor, object and percept, language and mind, and levels of narrative—that characterize metamorphosis within the closed psycholinguistic system of psycho-ecology.

Concepts are possible because they are systemically linguistic; language is possible because it is systemically conceptual. Self-reflexive literary experiments are possible, in this sense, because they transform language in a structurally self-similar manner to a transformation in the conceptual system of the mind; or, creative use of metaphor, to speak of one thing using the terms of another, results in metanoia. Metanoia is used here to designate a change of mind. There is a kind of structural and conceptual self-similarity between the reflexivity of modernist literature and cognitive linguistics in the sense that a transformation of language is equated with a transformation not only in perception but in the way one affectively experiences everyday life. That is, language engagement is, at its root, an affective enterprise. In this way, I suggest that modernist literature and the cognitive sciences share the feature of being self-representational; a consequence of this is that these processes are manifest in our everyday experience. Dada wishes to disrupt this as a way of severing these loops and knots. Indeed, Dada shares similarities with questions surrounding listening to the voice of the unknown, the non-articulation of the apparatus, that embed themselves in AI narratives of the early twenty-first century. That is, the overarching question is: how do we access that which lies beyond psycho-ecological loops of language?

As a result, establishing an interpretive mode based on diegetic level-crossing between a work of literature and other self-reflexive conceptual systems should produce novel and unusual results. The human mind is linguistic and language is a product of the human mind. The underlying logic behind this self-reflexive conceit—that we can learn much about the mind by speculating upon language and vice versa—extends itself to interpretive, Dadaist experiments. That is, if the self-similar structures of mind and language reveal much about one another, then it stands to reason that the discombobulation of language and literature with other self-reflexive conceptual systems may yield productive results for *considering the outside*. The interpretive mode here is, akin to Dada, paratactic and synthetic more than it is reductionistic and combinatorial (as is the apparatus). This methodology aims at synthesizing two structurally self-similar systems without claiming any conjunctive permanence. I do not aim to express that, for example, mathematics *and* language operate according to self-similar grammars or conceptual structures at the smallest level suggesting that the two systems share a kind of syntactic relation—in fact, they do not. Rather, the method involves structurally self-similar systems that are juxtaposed—not unlike a collage—upon which one can then meditate and comment. In a sense, it takes for its philosophy the

Deleuzoguattarian maxim to make "use of everything that [comes] within range, what [is] closest as well as farthest away."[2]

THE FLOWER'S COLERIDGE:
PLATONISM AND COGNITIVE LINGUISTICS

In 1945, Jorge Luis Borges wrote a short essay, "Coleridge's Flower," that examines the real and its relation to the imaginary. The piece is suggestive of Platonism: the intellect and imaginative reign over the empirical. Thought belongs to a realm of archetypes; imagination accesses this realm and intelligibility results from accurate translation. For Borges, fine thoughts may be those beautiful expressions that recur in disparate time, location, and media. His interest in the piece is with the possibility that reality may be a reflection of the imaginative. This overturns the more orthodox Aristotelian response to the conundrum: that the imagination is the ornamentation of the real and thought is the effect of sensory stimuli. The piece opens with Paul Valéry's consideration: that the history of literature should be "the history of the Spirit as the producer and consumer of literature."[3] This is echoed by Percy Bysshe Shelley and takes the following shape: "that all the poems of the past, present, and future were episodes or fragments of a single infinite poem, written by all the poets on earth."[4] Heidegger intimates something similar in his 1936 lecture course on Nietzsche: "All great thinkers think the same. Yet this 'same' is so essential and so rich that no single thinker exhausts it."[5] It recurs twenty years later across the Atlantic in Emerson's "Nominalist and Realist": "I am very much struck in literature by the appearance that one person wrote all the books."[6] Borges's speculative project is to carry out a "history of the evolution of an idea through the diverse texts of three authors."[7] He begins with Samuel Taylor Coleridge.

The recurring idea has its first appearance in Coleridge's famous reflection: "If a man could pass through Paradise in a dream, and have a flower presented to him as a pledge that his soul had really been there, and if he found that flower in his hand when he awoke—Ay!—and what then?"[8] The next appearance of Coleridge's flower is in H. G. Wells's *The Time Machine* (1895) in the guise of a wilted flower brought back from a journey into the distant future, a "future flower, the contradictory flower whose atoms, not yet assembled, now occupy other spaces."[9] The flower appears a third time, this time in the work of Henry James. In the unfinished novel, *The Sense of the Past* (1917), James establishes a fantasy that symbolically links the real and imaginary as the present and the past. The flower here has evolved, like the Eloi in Wells's novel, beyond immediate sensibility, yet it remains the flower rationally and imaginatively; now, the flower is an eighteenth-century portrait that puzzlingly has the twentieth-century protagonist as its subject. The hero journeys back in time; he meets the artist, who then paints the subject from the future. What is interesting here is that the protagonist visits the eighteenth century because he is fascinated by the portrait; yet, without his return to the past, the portrait could not exist. So, James—like Coleridge and Wells—reverses the intuitive logic that stimulus precedes imaginative expression; or, as Borges comments, "the cause follows the effect, or the reason for the journey is a consequence of the journey."[10] Significant here is that the quasi-Platonic reason as imaginative archetype enters the world in some form: that Coleridge's flower appears as multiple kinds, in various media, and is relayed recurrently from the imaginative to the real. Rather than an emphasis on the self-reflexivity of text and intertexts—or the failure of language to represent anything outside itself—this dialogue between the two realms proves to be self-reflexive in that the two-directionality of intellect and world engages in a kind of diegetic level-crossing. That is, like Coleridge's dreamer, aesthetic engagements require a movement, in conceptual and narrative terms, between the diegetic space of imagination and an alternate diegetic space of world. The dreamer is stuck in a self-reflexive loop between language and psyche.

This self-reflexive dialogic operates in language itself. Such level-crossing is an inherent quality of the phenomena of self-reference and self-reflexivity. From the work of physicist and professor of cognitive science and comparative literature Douglas R. Hofstadter stem some observations on the self-reference in language. The first four essays in Hofstadter's collection, *Metamagical Themas: Questing for the Essence of Mind and Pattern* (1985), examine self-referential sentences, viral sentences, and self-replicating linguistic structures. For Hofstadter, "self-reference is ubiquitous . . . it happens every time anyone says 'I' or 'me' or 'word' or 'speak' or 'mouth' . . . writes a book about writing, designs a book about book design, makes a movie about movies, or writes an article about self-reference."[11] Many systems inherently represent themselves or refer to themselves within the parameters of their own representation. Some instances of linguistic self-reference are paradoxical as in the case of the Epimenides paradox: "This sentence is false." However, the quality of the paradox here is not axiomatic. Hofstadter provides a series of examples of self-referential and self-replicating sentences, some paradoxical, others not: "I am simultaneously writing and being written";[12] "I am the meaning of this sentence";[13] "Say, haven't I written you somewhere else before?";[14] "I am going two-level with you";[15] or, "This inert sentence is my body, but my soul is alive, dancing in the sparks of your brain."[16] Hofstadter offers a structure to aid in conceptualizing self-reflexivity and self-reference—he calls it the strange loop—in *Gödel, Escher, Bach* (1979). Hofstadter remarks that the "'Strange Loop' phenomenon occurs whenever, by moving upwards (or downwards) through the levels of some hierarchical system, we unexpectedly find ourselves back where we started."[17] He elucidates this abstraction in *I am a Strange Loop* (2007): in a strange loop, "despite one's sense of departing ever further from one's origin, one winds up, to one's shock, exactly where one had started out. In short, a strange loop is a paradoxical level-crossing feedback loop."[18] Ultimately, Hofstadter makes the reader ask amusing questions of the following variety: what is a signifier that can serve as its own referent? What is a destination that can serve as its own departure? What is an effect that can serve as its own cause?

This way of regarding language has fascinating implications. If language and ideas are implicated in a bidirectional, level-crossing loop, the reader is in the territory of, not formalism, but functionalist semantics and linguistic determinism—closed systems that operate, not unlike computers, through indexicalization, self-reorganization, self-reference, and combinatorialism. In the 1920s and 1930s, Polish-American philosopher Alfred Korzybski pioneered the theory of general semantics with the publication of two major works, *Manhood of Humanity* (1921) and *Science and Sanity* (1933). Korzybski's system is a "discipline which explains and trains us how to use our nervous systems most efficiently.... In brief, it is the formulation of a new non-Aristotelian system of orientation which affects every branch of science and life."[19] At the heart of his anti-essentialist project is Korzybski's insistence that structure is the only content of knowledge, that is, we cannot know things in themselves, the human mind—the brain, an organ that abstracts—cannot transcend itself. Language derives from functions of the brain, Korzybski suggests; reciprocally, the brain is a function of language. The following three maxims are most effective for expressing Korzybski's general semantics: the map is not the territory, no map can represent all of its presumed territories, and maps are self-reflexive and can be mapped indefinitely.[20] General semantics is a system of uncertainty that promotes habitual non-elementalism, anti-essentialism, and non-Aristotelian modes of thought. Korzybski's concern is not aesthetic so much as it is the formulation of non-essentialist language use: he wished to eliminate from education the "inadequate Aristotelian types of evaluation."[21] By systematically changing habitual thought and language patterns, general semantics suggests that humans can actively resist the linguistic determinism of an a priori epistemology by actively engaging with the parameters of language use. Korzybski was certainly not advocating for Dada,[22] however. Rather than creative destruction and the drive to signify no thing, Korzybski proved more concerned with rational and logical shifts in language use and the ways such shifts would affect the parameters of thought.

Though Korzybski was to influence many twentieth-century thinkers and artists, the writings of Benjamin Lee Whorf popularized the idea of linguistic determinism and linguistic relativity in the 1940s. Yet, while the hugely influential work of Ferdinand de Saussure—and from Saussure, the work of Roland Barthes and Jacques Derrida, and the psychoanalysis of Jacques Lacan[23]—suggests that there is a historical a priori of language that determines and constitutes thought from within language, what makes Whorfian linguistics striking is its apparent absolutism. In its strong version, the Sapir-Whorf hypothesis—which integrates Whorfian *functionalism* with the linguistic theories of Edward Sapir—claims that language determines thought totally. Perhaps its most controversial suggestion is that of cultural relativism, which argues that communication between different cultures is uncertain due to difficulties in finding common ground through translation. The following is from Edward Sapir and is characteristic of the Sapir-Whorf hypothesis: "Human beings do not live in the objective world alone. . . . We see and hear and otherwise experience very largely as we do because the language habits of our community predispose certain choices of interpretation."[24] Whorf, like Korzybski, was a non-Aristotelian: for traditional Western thought belongs to "materialism, psychophysical parallelism, [Newtonian] physics . . . and dualistic views of the universe in general."[25] Whorf's writing is epistemologically post-Einsteinian; he is concerned with how monistic, holistic, and relativistic interpretations of reality "must be talked about in what amounts to a new language."[26] Speech habits are not personal or subjective, but are rather "systematic, so that we are justified in calling them a system of natural logic."[27] Though provocative, Whorf is certainly productive in his implications: "We dissect nature along lines laid down by our native languages. The categories and types that we isolate from the world of phenomena we do not find there because they stare every observer in the face; on the contrary, the world is presented in a kaleidoscopic flux of impressions which has to be organized by our minds."[28] The Korzybskian and Whorfian self-reflexive loops may be that language determines thought through a system of natural logic while thought expresses itself within and through that logic, determining language habits. The implications for reading literature are fascinating: we simultaneously bring back Coleridge's flower from the dream and create Wells's "flower whose atoms, not yet assembled, now occupy other spaces." Perhaps James's painting is an elegant metaphor for the act of reading.

The influence of functionalism of this variety waned with the rise of formalist and poststructuralist modes of analysis in the 1950s and 1960s. One notable and influential exception is the work of Michel Foucault, particularly in the early work *The Order of Things* (1966). In *Foucault* (1986), Deleuze describes aspects of Foucault's work as "new functionalism."[29] In the preface to *The Order of Things*, Foucault discusses linguistic and cultural relativity; appropriately enough, he writes that *The Order of Things* "arose out of a passage in Borges, out of the laughter that shattered . . . all the familiar landmarks of . . . *our* thought, the thought that bears the stamp of our age."[30]

To demarcate these familiar landmarks of thought, Foucault introduces the *episteme*, an analytical tool for historically demarcating shifts in the constitutive rules of thought. It concerns the historically specific epistemological environments that inform, if not determine, modes of inquiry; or, in his words: "the total set of relations that unite, at a given period, the discursive practices that give rise to epistemological figures, sciences, and possibly formalized systems."[31] What the Borges tale offered to Foucault was a kind of wonderment that recalls Whorf's way of thinking "in what amounts to a new language" and Borges's introduction of a new idea: "The thing we apprehend in one great leap, the thing that, by means of the fable, is demonstrated as the exotic charm of another system of thought, is the limitation of our own, the stark impossibility of thinking *that*."[32] The determinism here is not, of course, bleak; rather, it is productive. The work of Korzybski, Whorf, and Sapir, onward, is something that should be kept in mind when considering modes of resistance to algorithmic determinism, psychopolitics, and neurototalitarianism in the twenty-first century.

In Greek, metaphor means "transfer." Aristotle's definition is descriptive rather than operative: "Metaphor is the application of an alien name by transference either from genus to species, or from species to genus, or from species to species, or by analogy, that is, proportion."[33] Metaphors consist of two parts, one of which is momentarily transformed into the other. Simply put, a metaphor is to speak of one thing using the terms of another; it suggests the separation between demonstration and truth. Thus, the terms fuse and then separate according to a kind of oscillating movement of perpetual transformation. In this sense, a metaphor is the aggregate of a paradoxical and unending operation: one that is self-negating while simultaneously self-propagating through a process of self-reflexive transfer. In short, a metaphor cannot master its reference, yet it operates effectively. This tension is what makes the metaphor a notably fecund analytical model. As a unit of meaning, a metaphor is a closed system that balances itself through the logical recursion of a paradoxical process, yet it is also engaged in systemic level-crossing: the tenor is transformed into the vehicle, which, in turn, is transformed back into the tenor, ad infinitum.

Metaphor is a self-reflexive linguistic unit. The transfer of one conceptual category to another, a kind of oscillating transformation or mutation of meaning, is the semantic trajectory of a metaphor. Its function is not simply ornate, however, but one that is productive in reconfiguring the way we think about and perceive the world. Over the past four decades, the emerging field of cognitive linguistics has been instrumental in creating new ways of studying the level-crossing between language and the mind. In cognitive linguistics, there is particular emphasis placed on the function and operations of meaning, conceptual processes, and experience. Karol Janicki, in *Toward Non-Essentialist*

Sociolinguistics (1990), provides an excellent discussion of the work of both Whorf and Korzybski, with emphasis on the latter, as prototypes for the contemporary scene of non-essentialist linguistics. Concepts, here, are the primary unit of understanding; concepts aid in comprehension and knowledge through systemic modes of categorizing and conceptualizing. Influential within cognitive linguistics is conceptual metaphor theory. Conceptual metaphors are metaphors because their structural logic is based on the association of one domain with another. Rather than being purely linguistic, metaphor is conceptual because the "motivation for the metaphor resides at the level of conceptual domains."[34] Proposed by George Lakoff and Mark Johnson in *Metaphors We Live By* (1980), the fundamental premise of conceptual metaphor theory is that "metaphor is pervasive in everyday life, not just in language but in thought and action. Our ordinary conceptual system, in terms of which we both think and act, is fundamentally metaphorical in nature."[35] In short, Lakoff and Johnson suggest that "metaphors as linguistic expressions are possible precisely because there are metaphors in a person's conceptual system."[36] In this sense, metaphorical linguistic expressions are "reflections of an underlying conceptual association."[37]

Lakoff and Johnson argue that conceptual metaphor theory is primarily concerned with everyday rather than literary language use. The study of poetic metaphor, however, constitutes a particular trajectory of cognitive linguistics: cognitive poetics. In *More than Cool Reason: A Field Guide to Poetic Metaphor* (1989), Lakoff and Mark Turner examine a series of poetic metaphors. These kinds of metaphors are understood through "The Grounding Hypothesis"; here, "metaphorical understanding is grounded in nonmetaphorical understanding."[38] The source term of the metaphor is not understood metaphorically but experientially, that is, the source term is "grounded in the habitual and routine bodily and social patterns we experience."[39] In short, poetic metaphor is not an inaccessible manner of elite expression, but is deictic in the sense that its logical substratum is grounded in common cognitive structures of understanding phenomena; furthermore, poetic metaphor "exercises our mind so that we can extend our normal powers of comprehension beyond the range of metaphors we are brought up to see the world through."[40] In 2002, Peter Stockwell published *Cognitive Poetics: An Introduction* as an introductory textbook to the field. The general aim of the book is pedagogical: to establish modes of association between the study of literature and the study of cognitive linguistics, thus situating literary discourse within contemporary linguistic theories concerned with broad modes of meaning construction. The following year, editors Joanna Gavins and Gerard Steen compiled *Cognitive Poetics in Practice* (2003). A companion piece to Stockwell's introduction, the collection includes a series of ten essays that demonstrate the scope of the field. Perhaps the theme behind cognitive poetics and poetic metaphor can be revealed in the following statement about cognitive linguistics: "Language not only *reflects* conceptual structure, but can also *give rise to* conceptualization."[41]

Incidentally, conceptual metaphor theory complicates the myths of objectivism and subjectivism; these two ways, one typically absolutist while the latter typically Romantic, constitute a conceptual structure that limits categorical modes of knowledge to two constructed ontological polarities. The theory offers a third choice: "an experientialist synthesis." Lakoff and Johnson remark that metaphor unites reason and imagination:

> Reason . . . involves categorization, entailment, and inference. Imagination . . . involves seeing one kind of thing in terms of another kind of thing. . . . Metaphor is thus *imaginative rationality*. Since the categories of our everyday thought are largely metaphorical and our everyday reasoning involves metaphorical entailments and inference, ordinary rationality is therefore imaginative by its very nature.[42]

This is a particularly exciting proposition for the study of literature as it suggests the level-crossing of two diegetic domains, that of language and mind. What is interesting here is how this logic operates when the transfer from the aesthetically treated language is directed to the level of the mind. This logic is semantically accessible and linguistically rational, yet the imaginative dimensions are certainly excessive for artistic effect. The significance here is that, in this self-reflexive loop, literary language can change the very way we perceive and experience the world. The diegetic level-crossing of metaphor is that transformation in language is a transformation of mind; metaphor allows the flower to be held in the reader's hand. Dada knows this and pushes it to extremes.

One strength of the work of Hofstadter, Korzybski, Whorf, and cognitive linguistics is that each, in some way, insists that metaphors as linguistic expressions are possible because there are metaphors in the conceptual system of the mind. This suggests that in any symbolic system, the cause of the system follows its effects; self-reflexive systems operate according to laws of self-similarity. Certainly, the language of literature is not the same as the language of painting or the language of mathematics. Yet, the logic operates according to the laws of structural approximation. As a result, the juxtaposition of one language with another—since both languages must operate according to laws of the mind—should yield productive, if not amusing, results. Vladimir Tasić's *Mathematics and the Roots of Postmodern Thought* (2001) intervenes in the colloquial antagonism between two entities, vaguely labeled "science" and "postmodernism." Tasić avoids broad categories of definition and rather looks into "the possibility of *re*constructing some aspects of postmodern thought ... from a mathematical point of view."[43] What Tasić achieves is a lucid comparison between mathematical developments and the trajectory of thought in the humanities. His principal concern is to suggest that mathematics "*could* have been a formative factor in the rise of postmodern theory."[44] In this speculative examination, Tasić raises notable similarities and discursive cross-currents between mathematics and the major theoretical projects of structuralism, functionalism, and deconstruction. However, there are two points in Tasić's book that are of particular interest here. The first is with Kurt Gödel's self-referential mathematics and incompleteness theorem, and the second with the epistemological intimations that chaos and information theory have on the study of language and literature. These two systems reaffirm the logic of functionalism and, by extension, combinatorialism. Gödel had a considerable influence on the work of Hofstadter, so it is no shock that the incompleteness theorem is itself a mathematical version of a strange loop and self-reflexive grammar; for Gödel, it was not possible "to establish the truth or falsity of the statement 'this statement is false' in terms of computations."[45] The result is an apparent paradox: either mathematics is a contradiction, or the concept of truth cannot be defined mathematically. Unlike truth, Gödel notes, demonstration or mathematical proof can be defined formally. Gödel's conclusion, however, is remarkable: he writes, the "concept of truth of sentences of [a language] cannot be defined in [that language]."[46] Rather than eschewing objective truth and intuition in the formalist fashion, Gödel concludes that mathematical truth is objective and even intuitively knowable, but cannot be fully expressed in language. Tasić's take on this observation is noteworthy: "It seems that Gödel defended a strongly Platonist understanding of mathematics, that is, regarded abstract mathematical objects as objectively existing things and mathematical theorems as expressing objective truths about them."[47] A similar conclusion is made from conceptual metaphor theory. Raphael Núñez, in "Conceptual Metaphor, Human Cognition, and the Nature of Mathematics," writes that "the most abstract conceptual system we can think of, mathematics(!), is ultimately embodied in the nature of our bodies, language, and cognition";[48] and mathematics "is one of the greatest products of the collective human imagination."[49] Whatever truth is, however, it is not the direct referent of mathematics or any other linguistic system.

Much of what formalism and postmodern theory have in common is a denunciation of the Enlightenment conceit that rules are universal. Gödel's findings complicate this dismissal; more recent mathematical developments in chaos theory and information theory disrupt this project to an even more pronounced degree. Chaos theory has been misleadingly labeled as "postmodern mathematics"; N. Katherine Hayles points out this false label in her work on chaos theory and its permeation into literary studies in the 1990s, notably in *Chaos Bound* (1990) and *How We Became Posthuman* (1999).

In *Chaos Bound*, for example, Hayles is both descriptive and prescriptive in her application of the fundamental concepts of chaos theory to the study of literature. The most admirable aspect of Hayles's critique lies in the differentiation between how postmodernist theory and chaos/information theory understand meaning: postmodernism wishes to deconstruct semantic value assumptions inherent in language. In contrast, chaos and information highlight the asemic nature and structure of language. Hayles is always sober in her analysis and is never tempted by overdetermined wishful thinking. Warren Weaver, in "Recent Contribution to the Mathematical Theory of Communication" (1949), remarks that "*information* must not be confused with meaning. In fact, two messages, one of which is heavily loaded with meaning and the other which is pure nonsense, can be exactly equivalent."[50] James Gleick's *The Information: A History, A Theory, A Flood* (2011) examines the theory and history of information theory in lucid depth for the nonspecialist; he is, however, not overly concerned with the implications of information on literary studies. Philip Kuberski in *Chaosmos: Literature, Science, and Theory* (1994), like Hayles, is fascinated by the larger epistemological effects of chaos and information theory on the humanities. Kuberski's study is excellent in its emphasis on the simultaneity of aberrant and deterministic tenets of much postmodernist thought. Like Hayles and Tasić, he traces the paratactic formation of deconstruction and post-Einsteinian science. Kuberski notes a tendency in modernist literature he identifies as chaosmos: a paradoxical venture to achieve a kind of transcendent order by writing intense complexities. Núñez correctly remarks that mathematics, like all conceptual systems, is "not monolithic . . . [and] is every bit as conceptually rich as any other part of the human conceptual system."[51] In this sense, the juxtaposition of one conceptual system with another is speculative and imaginatively productive.

Indeed, chaos and information offer an explicit complication for postmodern thought: points, systems, sets, structures, quasi-teleological infinite limit, and "system states that are described as Platonist points in a Platonist infinite-dimensional universe"[52] are some of the metaphysical idealizations that chaos and information theory pose as major challenges to postmodernist and formalist thought. And with these metaphysical conceits come abstract functions, totalizing logic of identity and grounds of justification, and a multitude of dichotomies. Tasić suggests that the most common version of postmodern thought, as it circulates in both cultural and academic discourse, appears to be a series of permutations on the famous logocentric maxim: "To be is to be the value of a variable."[53] While this play on *copulae* is now random and chaotic, the axiom remains: "Languages speak, structures mean, and changes occur courtesy of a mysterious 'power-in-general' that belongs to no one in particular, which is to say that we are dealing with a kind of functionalism."[54]

This complication intimates a certain heritage of Foucault's work closely linked to his "new functionalism" that Mark G. E. Kelly suggests largely goes overlooked: that of his "happy positivism." If reality is chaotic, the historical habit would tell us that this would be epistemologically incompatible with scientific positivism. Vincent Descombes writes that "on the one hand, Foucault's approach is that of a positivist. . . . Yet, on the other hand, Foucault, as a reader of Nietzsche, does not believe in the positive notion of *fact*."[55] So, Descombes condemns Foucault's work as no more than "a seductive construct, whose play of erudite cross-reference lends it an air of verisimilitude."[56] The accusation that Descombes directs at Foucault's work is that of the classic relativist paradox. Kelly writes,

> the relativist says truth is relative, but then this statement is itself relative—so he cannot be sure of it. Happy positivism avoids this criticism . . . because it asserts the necessity of putting forward underdetermined statements in view of the impossibility of full determination. There is no need for provisos that this is not *really* how things are, since there can be no description which does cleave to how things actually are.[57]

Of course, the relativist paradox is a translation of the Epimenides/liar's paradox; Gödel's incompleteness theorem is brought to mind. Or, as Hofstadter writes, "Gödel's famous Incompleteness Theorem in metamathematics can be thought of as arising from his attempt to replicate as closely as possible the liar paradox in purely mathematical terms."[58] For Gödel, demonstration and mathematical proof can be formally expressed, while truth cannot. For Foucault's "happy positivism," demonstrations likewise can be defined formally, but do not constitute truth. So, language speaks, and structures mean; self-reflexive structures eschew truth statements, yet necessitate diegetic level transfer between subject and object, statement and reference, and so on, as a means to demonstrate operative semantic possibilities. If to be is to be the value of a chaotic variable within the parameters of a determined system, then the cause and effect of the conceptual system is chaotic. To address this, a return to Borges and metaphor is necessary.

In 1951, Borges composed a short piece titled "Pascal's Sphere." He frames the essay with the repetition of a Platonic proposition: "Perhaps universal history is the history of a few metaphors."[59] Borges remarks that one particular metaphor is variously repeated throughout history: the metaphor is an infinite sphere whose center is everywhere and whose circumference is nowhere. Indeed, Borges aestheticizes self-reflexive conceptual systems of metaphor and language; emphasis is placed on two major historical figures and their use and response to the metaphor. For Giordano Bruno, Borges writes, the universe thus became "all center," or "the center of the universe is everywhere and the circumference nowhere." This was a great intellectual and imaginative liberation; the paradox, for Bruno, expressed ecstasy. Yet what proved blissful to Bruno was for Blaise Pascal an abyss. Facing the changing understanding of the cosmos, Pascal felt confusion, anxiety, and isolation. He expressed it as follows: "Nature is a frightful sphere, the center of which is everywhere, and the circumference nowhere." The statement is complex; the concrete subject is an abstraction, which, in turn, is concrete, ad infinitum. That is, a history of a single metaphor expressing a "mysterious power-in-general"; or, the single metaphor is the conceptual system itself. That is, the lost center lamented by the modernists may have *never existed*.

By making the language user the tenor of the metaphor, one finds a remarkably unique analytical mode with which to examine construction/interpretation self-reflexively. So, the working definition of reading here: the language user is an infinite sphere, the center of which is everywhere, and the circumference nowhere. In this sense, the language user, a definite and concretized noun, is abstract, a paradoxical sphere unending its constant force moving outward in any direction, and yet occupying neither space nor time. So, that which is concrete is an abstraction which is self-reflexively concrete. That is, the subject and the predicate, the tenor and the vehicle, negate one another. Whether the subject is the cosmos, Nature, or the language user, the formulation establishes a structural conundrum in which the subject and predicate, tenor and vehicle, concrete and abstract cyclically affirm their constitutive potency through their negation: this statement is false. Thus, the subject is at once present and absent. So, the reading subject is in each of its constituent parts, but cannot be reduced by any of them. Language constitutes the reading subject, and the reading subject constitutes language.

Self-reference and self-replication is thus the nature of metaphor, but so is transformation; the corresponding conceit is that the mind operates accordingly. Language is at the center of the mind, yet its circumference is nowhere; the mind is at the center of language, yet its circumference is nowhere. Linguistic metaphors for conceptual systems are possible because they are structurally self-similar to the conceptual system of the mind. As a result, establishing a literary interpretive mode based on strange loop relations—level-crossing transfer—between a work of literature and another self-reflexive conceptual system should produce interesting conjectures. This logic offers unique speculations through its eccentricity, yet is made possible because the interrelation between one reflexive system (mode of critique) and another (literary work) itself is that of an extended and extending strange loop. Hofstadter, likewise, writes that indirect self-reference, that which involves a kind of transformation, "suggests the idea of *indirect self-replication*, in which a viral entity [the self-reflexive unit], instead of replicating itself exactly, brings into being another entity that plays the same role as it does, but in some other system."⁶⁰ Such odd combinations, made possible through merging reflexive systems, yield interesting speculative results. This mode of analysis reveals how unusual words, syntax, and diegetic structures in literature are made possible by self-similar structures of the mind; simultaneously, it reveals how the self-reflexive transfer of these unusual structural units involves a transformation of mind. In short, new and unusual language yields new ways of perceiving the world but does not permit access to the *outside*.

COLERIDGE'S FLOWER: PHENOMENOLOGICAL ENGAGEMENT

The shift from the embedded Platonism in cognitive linguistics and its predecessors to phenomenology may seem abrupt. Yet, as we have noted, metaphor is a self-reflexive linguistic unit. The movement of metaphor is the transfer of one conceptual category to another: from one level of diegesis to another. Metaphor, in its very emphasis on level-crossing, demands an analogous mode of analysis. We cannot simply assert that language structures mind; we must also approach this conundrum from the perspective of the site of these processes: the body and the sensuous source of self-narration. The operation of this paradoxical interaction is more than structurally elaborate in its strange loopiness, that is, it establishes the strange and tangled path to looking at modernist literature as that which explicitly reconfigures the way we understand the world. This process, then, is one that is active on behalf of the reader—as opposed to the linguistic determinism that seems to lurk not very far beneath the surface of cognitive linguistics—and is intimately bound with the conviction that phenomenological approaches to reading and language engagement foster collaborative, dynamic partnerships about learning itself.

Etymologically, phenomenology derives from the Greek *phainomenon*, to show, and *logos*, reason or study. So, phenomenological investigation is the study of things shown, and it can also be the study of things set before us. From this premise, reading literature through unusual interpretive modes establishes is a dynamic learning experience founded upon authentic participation. More generally, an authentic mode of phenomenological engagement is that in which the external (another level of diegesis) is observed in such a way as to make one's own consciousness emerge as consciousness before oneself. Dan Zahavi writes that the phenomenological line of thought on self-representational consciousness is

> not merely something that comes about the moment one scrutinizes one's experience attentively. . . . Rather, self-consciousness comes in many forms and

degrees. It makes perfect sense to speak of self-consciousness as soon as I am not simply conscious of an external object—a chair, a chestnut tree, or a rising sun—but acquainted with the experience of the object as well, for in such a case my consciousness reveals itself to me.[61]

We must note the distinction between language or an external object being given and where consciousness itself is set before us as a result of linguistic engagement. "In its most primitive (and fundamental form)," Zahavi suggests, "self-consciousness is taken to be a question of having first-personal access to one's own consciousness; it is a question of the first-personal givenness or manifestation of experiential life."[62] And, since we are limiting our discussion to language for now, we may add that this first-personal access follows a conceptual movement that is structurally similar to metaphor: one thing is transformed into another, which, in turn, is transformed back into its original (though now different) state making itself manifest as itself. One virtue of this trajectory of thought is that it insists that metaphor is a fundamental structure that repeats itself, or operates as an effective analog, to the role language and consciousness are distinct and yet the same as diegetic levels. Tim Murphy suggests of Nietzsche's metaphor, *Übertragung* "is not understood as one trope amongst the other traditional tropes . . . *übertragen* is the figure of tropology itself."[63] Again, in a symbolic system such as this, the cause of the system follows its effects; the self-reflexive system functions according to analogy and self-similarity. That is, "unusual impressions . . . produce unusual brain-changes; hence their summary . . . is of unusual kind." In this sense, in examining the texts that follow, it is both fitting that Lakoff and Turner suggest that "to study metaphor is to be confronted with hidden aspects of one's own mind and one's own culture."[64] Indeed, it is, for phenomenologists, this confrontation with that which is hidden that is the source of, not only self-representational consciousness, but the diegetic level-crossing between mind and language that makes this self-manifestation possible.

This shift to an agential engagement with language—a shift that posits the body as the mover of interpretation—is as much engagement with skeptical relativism as it is with phenomenology. Truth or interpretive positivism as an analytical goal is itself a constructed cultural narrative and, therefore, like literature, subject to engaged reconfiguration. Furthermore, modernist skepticism toward both eccentric modes of thought as well as those of the dominant industrial capitalist or military culture of the early twentieth century is integral to the concept of a plastic, agential reader. Indeed, the Platonic desire to subsume the anatomical self to the mind by extending the central nervous system beyond the body finds a parallel in one of Nietzsche's most famous and problematic concepts: the Will to Power. In *Beyond Good and Evil* (1886), Nietzsche writes,

> My idea is that every specific body strives to become master over all space and to extend its force (its will to power) and to thrust back all that resists its extension. But it continually encounters similar efforts on the part of other bodies and ends by coming to an arrangement . . . with those of them that are sufficiently related to it: thus they then conspire together for power. And the process goes on.[65]

For Nietzsche, the Will to Power suggests the fundamental execution of creative forces that drive the individual to their potential greatness. The Will to Power drives the individual, therefore, to "thrust back all that resists" its progress. Ultimately, when various individuals encounter one another in the Will to Power, they come to an "arrangement" and "conspire together for power," whereby all resistance is overruled. For Nietzsche, the Will to Power implies that one must transcend good and evil and proceed resolutely without any heed to ambivalent moral convention. However, we are not concerned here with morality. Rather, what is worth noting is how Nietzsche emphasizes the extension of the self into all space. Here, we see the Will to Power as a counterforce not only against dominant cultural systems but that which moves upward in a paradoxical hierarchy against the means of dominant cultural narrative: language itself. Though Nietzsche implies that not all people acknowledge the Will to Power, the result of those who do acknowledge and proceed with the concepts should not find themselves at odds with one another: they strive for uniqueness and authenticity of experience. Therefore, Nietzsche's philosophical concept gestures toward an expression of order and unity, though one that is bidirectional, loopy, and tangled. Nietzsche intended his concept of the Will to Power to ultimately act as a theory for everything, such as an explanation for the laws of nature (and, thus, the nature of language). Yet, the Will to Power itself is a metaphor, or, *Übertragen*. And if *Übertragen* is the figure of tropology itself, we may remark that metaphor is also the figure of tropology. The tropology here—a multidiegetic one between two levels—is reflexive: the linguistic or narrative space over which the Will to Power wishes to be dominant is that which is simultaneously already embedded within the body (the central nervous system), that is, the movement of the Will to Power-as-extension begins and ends in the same conceptual locale yet is semantically transformed. What is worth stressing, however, is that the extension—unlike that in linguistic determinism—is one founded upon the Will (i.e., agency) of an individual.

One of the major criticisms of linguistic determinism is that the field succumbs to the unqualifiable claim that the role of human agency in thought is secondary and that the thought of an individual is a vehicle animated by language. Such concerns, as we see in Han's psychopolitics and Bifo's neurototalitarianism, are only intensified when we extend this process beyond language to calculation, algorithms, and the apparatus. There is a kind of objectification at work here, that is, linguistic determinism in this sense understands the thinking human being as that which exists as an object galvanized by an a priori linguistic system. Both Whorf and Korzybski, as well as later cognitive linguists with a penchant for the Platonic, suggest that our engagement with language is typically habitual, uncreative, and uncritical. Their solution, in a nutshell, is to learn more languages (alternative grammar and enhanced vocabulary extend the parameters of the determinism) or to at least self-reflexively recognize that the system we use to structure our thoughts is the system that allows such recognition to take place. The drama here, however, is one of the mind: we can extend the mind, but the mind must always be linguistic. The human being in this mode of thought is fundamentally inanimate and is only animated by linguistic systems. The embodied extension of the Will into the space surrounding it—whether physically or intellectual—is, at best, largely not the concern of linguistic determinists. So, the human being exists much in the same way as any other object. Yet, the physical presence of the body existing in the world is an undeniable fact of perception. After all, even the mind-as-brain is, in the most basic sense, a physical structure situated in the material here and now.

This is where we must turn to the work of Martin Heidegger, since his thought permeates this study both implicitly and explicitly. First, for Heidegger, the human being exists *here*. His famous term *Dasein* means being here/there or being in the world. For Heidegger, because we are worldly tuned, self-consciousness or self-acquaintance is that of a self both immersed and embedded in the world. "I neither experience myself as a bundle of experiences and processes," writes Zahavi, "nor as a detached I-object, rather I experience myself in what I do and suffer, in what confronts me and in what I accomplish, in my concerns and disregards. Self-acquaintance is indeed only to be found in our immersion in the world."[66] Human beings, like inanimate objects, exist. However, existing and being are not synonymous. Inanimate objects exist, but they cannot *be*. Individual humans have both existence and being. What makes the human being unique is that, as that which exists, it also has the capability to be; or, the human being can recognize being and engage with what that means. The human has an existential choice in its being in that he or she can recognize that, at some time in the past, their existence was *not yet* and that, at some point in the future, they will no longer be. The finitude of existence is, then, critical to the condition of being able to recognize what it means to be. This process is made possible by thought. Thought, for Heidegger, is intimately embedded within language. Thought makes knowledge possible, and so the human must know what he or she is, what possibilities he or she has for action, and how one may be directly engaged in making choices as a means of affecting reality. Indeed, while Heidegger also suggests that the thought and the mind are both largely linguistic, what makes his oeuvre in contradistinction to linguistic determinism is the marked emphasis on agency and choice. To be self-reflexively concerned with the possibility of choice and the actual choices one makes is to be actively involved in one's being.

The ability to choose, for Heidegger, is more than an instance of selection. Choice is to consider something absolutely. So, the choice to consider being demands that we understand being as a whole. Yet, being is temporal: it once was not and will someday not be. So long as one is alive to consider—to think linguistically—being, one's being is not complete. We are thrown into the world, and we are never completely manifest before ourselves. Instead, we exist as an opening toward existential possibility. This is where temporal directionality comes in: as long as one *is*, one must succumb to the possibility of futurity. As long as one is capable of choice and thought, one is in the strange position of being something that is not yet manifest and therefore is incapable of recognizing being as a whole. The paradox is that to know, to *choose* to know what it means to be, can only be made possible at the moment of death, the point at which being as a whole attests to its finitude. To consider being as a whole, this suggests, can only be understood from outside. The problem, then, is that we are tempted to understand ourselves from the perspective of others. From this logic, we also understand the finitude of existence as that which takes place for other people, and so we are again tempted to treat death as an abstraction from lived experience.

This logic has its analogs: we may also treat language as something abstract from ourselves. That is, this mode of thinking directs human beings toward the acceptance that we are animated and made meaningful only from the perspective of other things, whether people or language. And so existence is not unique but typical: one analogous example among many. So, this assumption of typicality is what seduces the individual into habitual ways of behaving and being. However, Heidegger claims that our temporality directs us to be concerned and to care for our own being: our mode of being is, then, that which must be concerned with our individual being. Like linguistic determinists, Heidegger suggests that the individual must confront unconscious habits. However, unlike the linguistic determinists, he believes that being can be actively engaged and, rather than being understood as something of varying degrees of typicality, is something radically singular. To live habitually—to understand being from the perspective of others—is what Heidegger calls inauthentic.[67] There is a way to live authentically, however, Heidegger claims. That is, there is a way to possess the flower rather than being its possession. To do so is to live toward, to project into the possibility of nothingness and exclusion.

So, the possibility for this authentic understanding of being is intricately embedded within the relation between nonexistence (death) and temporality. Because we are always *not yet*, we are determined not by language but through the possibilities that are set before us in the future. Being is, in a sense, always becoming until the moment of true exclusion; at this moment of nothingness, being can be—though paradoxically—understood in its wholeness. In order to live authentically, then, one needs to understand oneself as temporal, impermanent, and fundamentally transient. In this sense, the past and future take on specific meaningfulness: the past does not determine what one is. Rather, it is our projection of thought and desires into the future that denotes being in relation to the present. The relation between being and time is not one of linear abstraction, of clocks, or lives of others, but tangible and literal transience of our own existence from birth until death and this singular concrete temporality establishes how an individual is radically unique. Death is where the word, and thus agential experience, breaks off. It is strange and unique because it is for the individual the possibility of impossibility: the end of possibility as an absolute negation. In this sense, death is both the limit and the source of possibility. Like Hofstadter's strange loop, we move toward something only to end up at its source: a body without life, a thing without the ability to be. In short, our strange loopy existence is also being-as-time, or, being-for-death.

It is in this context that we understand Heidegger's link between mind and language. To be more specific, the relation of concern here is between thought and language. Just as being is to be fully understood only through the recognition of death—being-toward-nothingness—language becomes a kind of tool for striving for authenticity in being. To be brief, Heidegger claims that we need to learn to think, to let ourselves and others learn. Heidegger suggests that we must encourage ourselves to interrogate those instances of language that he identifies as causing explicit angst: that which tears one from common experience and lays bare one's concerns and prejudices. This experience unveils a new context-specific space of discussion characterized by negotiation and dissent; ultimately, this space is what makes critical investigation possible for both thought and language. Authentic thought, for Heidegger, is that which has yet to be thought in the sense that it allows thought to arrive. This mode of thought is also future directed: toward that which is yet to exist. Yet, the temporal locale of this possibility is, at present, nothing. To think is to think in a kind of openness, to think in nothingness, to think in an abyss. Thoughts come to us, just as the future offers itself to us. Tellingly, Heidegger asks "what could be more worthy of thought for the saying one than the word's being veiling itself, than the fading word for the word?"[68] The fading word for the word is, here, poetry. It is primarily through poetry that the link between language and thinking-in-nothingness can be bridged. It is with poetry that we "let ourselves be told what is worthy of thinking,"[69] and so we can think in a future-directed void: to think with disregard to the habitual use of language and to think possibility. Indeed, he writes that "poetry and thinking belong together. Their coming together has come about long ago. As we think back to that origin, we come face to face with what is primevally worthy of thought, and which we can never ponder sufficiently."[70] Our striving toward the future is, then, also a loop into the past: both are, however, concretely inaccessible. Indeed, a change in language ultimately metamorphoses the way we understand and experience the world: "The word's rule springs to light as that which makes the thing be a thing. The word begins to shine as the gathering which first brings what presences to its presence."[71] So poetic articulation—or what Heidegger calls "saying"—is the key to existing authentically. "The same word," he writes, "that word for saying, is also the word for *Being*, that is, for the presencing of beings. Saying and Being, word and thing, belong to each other in a veiled way, a way which has hardly been thought and is not to be thought out to the end."[72] Indeed, for Heidegger, agency is rather different from Nietzsche's will to power. Yet, there is again a kind of extension of the mind into other spaces. Heidegger, rather than forcing the self to make space for the Will, suggests that we submit and allow thoughts to strike us. We become almost as if we are a medium for poetry and poietic thought. Our extension into unknowable horizons comes to us rather than the other way around. He continues:

> In order that we may in our thinking fittingly follow and lead this element worthy of thought as it gives itself to poetry, we abandon everything which we have now said to oblivion. We listen to the poem. We grow still more thoughtful now regarding the possibility that the more simply the poem sings in the mode of song, the more readily our hearing may err.[73]

We are asked to wait: being-as-patience, being-as-nothingness, being-toward-death, being-as-clearing that accepts and welcomes the radiance of new thought to the openness of authentic existence. So, again in contradistinction to linguistic determinism, Heidegger asks us to submit and succumb to language toward the end of thinking that which cannot be thought in the present because it is always yet to be thought. It is language toward possibility in an existential state of openness and nothingness. Coleridge's flower comes to us, and we endure it; it changes us as an instance of simultaneous submission and choice.

Dada wishes to intensify this. What Heidegger does not discuss, however, is alternative modes of poetry. That is, how does being-as-openness toward poetry endure itself when confronted with an alternative mode of grammar that does not lend itself temporally and cognitively to the primeval reaching-back and stretching-toward futurity? Perhaps Coleridge's flower is of multiple genera. Flusser interrogates this possibility most fully in *Does Writing Have a Future?* (1987). The book engages with methodologies that aim to move beyond teleological approaches to science[74] from the perspective of the humanities. I wish to simply focus on a single though major argument from Flusser's study as it relates to our contemplation of whether it is possible to think the *outside*, listen to the voice of the unknown, and confront the apparatus. For Flusser, a major shift in the horizon of reading and organizing thought will take place with dataism and the gradual dominance of digital code over writing. This transition will revolutionize critique, he argues, by gesturing toward more intense modes of interdisciplinary inquiry. Moreover, it will radically change the way the mind and thought are reflexively structured. "Writing seeks a way out of dizzying circular thinking," he writes, "and into a thinking arranged in lines." He continues:

> Now this can become: out of the magic circles of prehistoric thinking into linear, historical thinking. Writing is a transcoding of thought, a translation from the two-dimensional surface of images into a one-dimensional linear code: out of compact, blurred pictorial codes into clear, distinct written codes; out of the imaginary into the conceptual; out of the scenes into processes; out of contexts into texts. Writing is a method of tearing imaginary things apart and making them clear.[75]

This transcoding of thought is also thought transcoding. Writing fundamentally structures the mind; it is what ultimately leads to fallacies in interpreting the teleological trajectory of methodologies of inquiry like the scientific method. Writing, on the page, is read in linear sequence: it is set before us, and we follow it. It stands to reason, then, that this directionality of the page aims toward an end: the end of a clause, a sentence, a paragraph, a line of argument. In making thought clear, writing is also a great illusionist: the magic circles of prehistoric thought are noumenally still there, hidden behind an artificial system of transcoding:

> the further writing advances, the more deeply the writing incisor penetrates into the abysses of imaginary things stored in our memory, tearing them apart, to "describe," to "explain," to recode them into concept. This advance of writing along lines toward the abysses of memories . . . and toward an objective world, stripped of imaginary things, is what we call "history." It is progressive understanding.[76]

Writing fools us into experiencing progress as something inherent to the nature of thought and knowledge.

Yet, Flusser, like Heidegger, demonstrates that our engagement with language—or codes—is one of active agency so long as we can learn to think in new ways by using codes toward new avenues rather than language and code using us. These avenues, for Flusser, are bidirectional and tangled, however. The means to new thought, he suggests, will be a result of the predominant cultural code shifting from alphanumeric (writing) to digital code and combinatorialism. While writing molds the plasticity of thought patterns toward linearity and progressiveness, digital code, Flusser argues, may someday urge the thinker to interpret in images and nonlinear patterns. He explains that digital code "can proceed in multiple directions"[77] and that we do not read code or a mathematical equation in a linear fashion but in a looping, multi-directionality as we interpret quanta, parts, subparts, and whole.[78] In a sense, digital code allows us to think what is unthought and, yet as Han and Bifo suggest, this unthought of code may eliminate human agency in mental activity. While Han and Bifo are pessimistic about what code can do for thought—that is, both consider code to be rigidly linear rather than multidirectional—Flusser suggests that it permits us to stand on the horizon of nothingness so we may now, not simply learn to think, but learn to think differently. We *may* confront the apparatus by thinking code, but we cannot know it. In his very emphasis on non-teleological modes of thought, however, Flusser is certainly not gesturing toward some kind of utopia of thinking. Instead, while he recognizes the shift from writing to digital code as something profoundly significant, he also, more akin to Han and Bifo, identifies this shift as that which will, though different, lead to similarly biased distortions of experience that we see with writing. He writes, in a comment that confronts all systems of thought that deal with the reflexive relation between mind and representational codes, that "projecting brain function onto apparatuses raises exactly this question, whether this ontological distinction between real and fictional . . . is possible at all and, if it is possible, whether it is meaningful."[79] That is, thought is a simulation of language (or, perhaps in the future, digital codes), and yet language and codes are simulations of brain function. But "simulation is a kind of caricature," Flusser writes, because "it simplifies what is being imitated and exaggerates a few aspects of it."[80] So, if writing exaggerates linearity, then code may exaggerate not only multidirectional modes of thinking but also a new kind of rigidity that is remarkably unlike the poetry that Heidegger suggests is the path to existentially responsible thought. In this sense, electronic literature and the literature of exclusion may capture the multidirectionality of both language and code in its poietic mission.

Digital codes are explicit in the way they address the self-reflexive loops that establish the relation between mind/psyche and systems of representation. "Apparatuses incorporate the 1-0 structure because they simulate the structure of our nervous system," Flusser writes, "there, too, we are dealing with a mechanical (and chemical) turning on and off of streams of electrons between the nerve synapses. From this standpoint, digital codes are a method . . . of giving meaning to quantum leaps in the brain from the outside. We are faced with a self-concealing loop."[81] The self-concealing loops are, indeed, strange loops. They are also indicative of the relation between the mind and any mode of representation—here we are concerned primarily with literature—and the accuracy or fidelity an apparatus has in relation to thought itself. For Flusser, though, new computer codes are unique "because they are using simulated brains [computers] to simulate the meaning-giving function of the brain."[82] In a way, digital code, as rigid as it is at this moment in history, is also analogous to *certain* operations of the brain,[83] Flusser suggests. The brain allows quantum leaps to occur as a means of meaning-making, and the nonlinearity of digital code operates analogously. However, the reorganizing processes of algorithms can skip around via automated self-reorganization in ways that human meaning-making via reading does not. As a result, code "is about to turn this meaning-giving function over to apparatuses of its own accord, then to reabsorb what they project."[84] Code allows for more efficient psycho-ecological reflexivity for better *and* worse. Digital code is set before us and offers itself to us to engage in new modes of thinking the *outside*. Code itself offers narratives unique to its own logic, as does writing. Such narratives, however, are not our own and exclude the linguistic mind from meaningful engagement. Embedded in the dreamer is the flower and, simultaneously, embedded in the flower is the dreamer, that is, thought and language are embodied as a means to embody thought and language. Digital code ultimately resists this as it metamorphoses unpredictability into rigidity.

PSYCHO-ECOLOGY

Our relationship to language is language's relation to ourselves. We have here been calling this psycho-ecology: that multidirectional and tangled series of interactions among thought and linguistic systems of representation that determines the necessity that the totality of the mind lies unpredictably within and without. Psycho-ecologies, like natural ecologies, are remarkable both in their fecundity and in their complexity. And our relationship to these tangled environments is a self-representational relationship. This relationship is, like a natural ecology, also equally intricate in its vulnerability and homeostatic balance. "The environment is that which we experience and we, in turn, are that in which the environment is experienced," writes Flusser. He continues:

> Reality is a web of concrete relations. The entities of the environment are nothing but knots in this web, and we ourselves are knots of the same sort. We are linked to these entities; they are there for us. And the entities are linked to us; we are there for them. Both the environment and the organism are abstract extrapolations from the actuality of their entwined relations. An organism mirrors its environment; an environment mirrors its organisms; and if the arena of their relations is altered in some way, neither the environment nor the organism will be left unchanged.[85]

And so by considering a psycho-ecology, we may add that a reader mimics its texts and the texts its reader; we are linked to text because the text is there for us and there in us. The two levels adapt to one another and, as a result, transform and mutate one another, that is, this double, feedbacking mimesis lends itself to poiesis. Indeed, poetry and literature, as Flusser remarks, "is usually understood as a language game whose strategy is to creatively enlarge the universe of language."[86] If mimesis is imitation, then poietic self-representation is self-reflexive, creative, and mutative. "Poetry in this sense," Flusser continues, "is that source from which language always springs anew and, in fact, overall in literature, even in scientific, philosophical, or political texts, not only in poetic ones."[87] So, the entwined relations that establish mutations between a reader and texts are ubiquitous, though poetry discloses itself only when language and thought spring anew. If we recognize that, like the combinatory possibilities of language, "the agenda of life is inexhaustible," then what "we are appreciating is the blind chance of the 'game of life'"[88] a game that is both biological, unpredictable, flexible, ambiguous, and poetic. Psycho-ecology is the lived experience of reading and thinking language; it is the experience of the very processes that constitute cognitive, mutative plasticity. Such experience discloses itself as temporally finite, yet semantically infinite in permutation: it is paradoxally inward and outward, within and without but with no access to the *outside*: a strange loop. Psycho-ecology is what makes the relation between thought, literature, and poietic possibility possible.

The operations of code and processual proceduralism that operate *behind* digital technology, however, are where the word breaks off. Those literate in coding and mathematical languages, of course, are those with more access to rehearse gazing into the apparatus, therefore creating new openings to alternate psycho-ecologies, instances of new agencies, and revolt against psycho-political neuro-totalitarian exclusion. While these shifts are often discussed as a move toward the posthuman or transhuman, what digital code concerns is the apparatus as the *outside*. However, learning to program the program at once protects against *being programmed*, but also magnifies the immanent parameters of the self-optimizing and self-generating algorithms that make up the apparatus. We have developed an alternate kind of being to operate *for us*, but, as Flusser notes, there is no reason to assume that self-learning and self-evolving algorithms will continue to operate on our behalf. Instead, the apparatus will continue to become something that sculpts us, abandons us, and operates *outside us*. Even modern AI cannot currently bring us closer to the posthuman or transhuman; instead, such processual automata ultimately abandon the human in the service of optimizing the apparatus as the ultimate superidiot: the inhuman as the absolute outsider.

NOTES

1. Ludwig Wittgenstein, *Philosophical Investigations*, 4th edition, trans. by G. E. M. Anscombe, P. M. S. Hacker, and Joachim Schulte (Oxford: Wiley-Blackwell, 2009), 235e.

2. Gilles Deleuze and Felix Guattari, *A Thousand Plateaus: Capitalism and Schizophrenia*, trans. Brian Massumi (Minneapolis, University of Minnesota Press), 3.

3. Jorge Luis Borges, "Coleridge's Flower," *Jorge Luis Borges: Selected Non-Fictions*, ed. Eliot Weinberger, trans. Esther Allen, Suzanne Jill Levine, and Eliot Weinberger (New York: Penguin, 2000), 240.

4. Ibid.

5. Martin Heidegger, *Nietzsche: The Will to Power as Art*, trans. D. F. Krell (San Francisco: Harper & Row, 1979), 36.

6. Borges, "Coleridge's Flower," 240.

7. Ibid.

8. Ibid.

9. Ibid., 241.

10. Ibid., 242.

11. Douglas R. Hofstadter, "Nomic: A Self-Modifying Game Based on Reflexivity," *Metamagical Themas: Questing for the Essence of Mind and Pattern* (Toronto: Bantam, 1986), 7.

12. Ibid., 11.

13. Ibid.

14. Ibid., 12.

15. Ibid., 17.

16. Ibid., 11.

17. Ibid., 10.

18. Douglas R. Hofstadter, *I am a Strange Loop* (New York: Basic Books, 2007), 101–102.

19. Alfred Korzybski, *Selections from Science and Sanity: An Introduction to Non-Aristotelian Systems and General Semantics*, 2nd Edition (Lakeville: Institute of General Semantics, 2010), 7.

20. Robert P. Pula, "A Selection from the Preface to the Fifth Edition of Science and Sanity," *Selections from Science and Sanity: An Introduction to Non-Aristotelian*

Systems and General Semantics, 2nd Edition (Lakeville: Institute of General Semantics, 2010), ix.

21. Korzybski, *Selections from Science and Sanity*, 181.

22. Kozybski's thinking, however, did have a notable influence on surreal science fiction. The work of Philip K. Dick, Samuel Delany, and A. E. Van Vogt, for example, all engage general semantics to varying degrees as a lens through which to examine the parameters of how we experience reality.

23. We will return to these thinkers more explicitly when we consider the digital literature of exclusion.

24. Benjamin Lee Whorf, "The Relation of Habitual Thought and Behavior to Language," *Language, Thought, and Reality* (Cambridge: MIT Press, 1964), 134.

25. Ibid., 152.

26. Ibid.

27. Benjamin Lee Whorf, "Science and Linguistics," *Language, Thought, and Reality* (Cambridge: MIT Press, 1964), 207.

28. Ibid, 213.

29. Gilles Deleuze, *Foucault*, trans. Seán Hand (Minneapolis: University of Minnesota Press, 1988), 24.

30. Michel Foucault, *The Order of Things: An Archaeology of the Human Sciences* (London: Routledge, 2002), xv.

31. Michel Foucault, *Archaeology of Knowledge* (New York: Routledge, 2002), 211.

32. Foucault, *The Order of Things*, xv.

33. Aristotle, *Poetics*, trans. Gerald F. Else (Ann Arbor: University of Michigan Press, 1967), 41.

34. Vyvyan Evans and Melanie Green, *Cognitive Linguistics: An Introduction* (Edinburgh: Edinburgh University Press, 2006), 295.

35. George Lakoff and Mark Johnson. *Metaphors We Live By* (Chicago: University of Chicago Press, 1980), 3.

36. Ibid., 6.

37. Evans and Green, *Cognitive Linguistics*, 295.

38. George Lakoff and Mark Turner, *More Cool than Reason: A Field Guide to Poetic Metaphor* (Chicago: University of Chicago Press, 1989), 113.

39. Ibid.

40. Ibid., 214.

41. Evans and Green, *Cognitive Linguistics*, 101.

42. Lakoff and Johnson. *Metaphors We Live By*, 193.

43. Valdmir Tasić, *Mathematics and The Roots of Postmodern Thought* (New York: Oxford University Press, 2001), 4.

44. Ibid., 6.

45. Ibid., 75.

46. Ibid., 76.

47. Ibid.

48. Rafael Núñez, "Conceptual Metaphor, Human Cognition, and The Nature of Mathematics," *The Cambridge Handbook of Metaphor and Thought* (New York: Cambridge University Press, 2008), 356.

49. Ibid., 359.
50. Warren Weaver, "Recent Contributions to the Mathematical Theory of Communication," *The Mathematical Theory of Communication* (Urbana: University of Illinois Press, 1949), 8.
51. Núñez, "Conceptual Metaphor, Human Cognition," 360.
52. Tasić, *Mathematics and The Roots*, 156.
53. Ibid, 156.
54. Ibid.
55. Mark G. E. Kelly, *The Political Philosophy of Michel Foucault* (New York: Routledge, 2009), 27.
56. Ibid.
57. Ibid.
58. Douglas R. Hofstadter, "On Self-Referential Sentences," *Metamagical Themas: Questing for the Essence of Mind and Pattern* (Toronto: Bantam, 1986), 7.
59. Jorge Luis Borges, "Pascal's Sphere," *Jorge Luis Borges: Selected Non-Fictions*, ed. Eliot Weinberger, trans. Esther Allen, Suzanne Jill Levine, and Eliot Weinberger (New York: Penguin, 2000), 351.
60. Douglas R. Hofstadter, "On Self-Referential Sentences," 60.
61. Dan Zahavi, "Thinking about (Self-)Consciousness: Phenomenological Perspectives," *Self-Representational Approaches to Consciousness*, ed. Uriah Kriegel and Kenneth Williford (Cambridge: MIT Press, 2006), 274–275.
62. Ibid., 275.
63. Tim Murphy, *Nietzsche, Metaphor, Religion* (Albany: State University of New York Press, 2001), 2.
64. Lakoff and Turner, *More Cool than Reason*, 214.
65. Friedrich Nietzsche, *Beyond Good and Evil*, trans. Walter Kaufmann (New York: Vintage, 1989), §636.
66. Zahavi, "Thinking about (Self-)Consciousness," 283–284.
67. Inauthenticity in Heidegger's work does not carry any negative moral assumptions, however. Linguistic determinism, we may suggest, from this point of analysis would be considered inauthentic since it implies that something other than the human being itself provides the possibility for knowledge.
68. Martin Heidegger, "Words," *On the Way to Language*, trans. Joan Stambaugh (New York: HarperOne, 1971), 155.
69. Ibid.
70. Ibid.
71. Ibid.
72. Ibid.
73. Ibid.
74. Similar to Paul Feyerabend's famous *Against Method* (1975), Flusser is highly critical of the teleological claims of science, that is, he is skeptical over the enterprise as one of progress. Furthermore, Flusser's critique aims to identify science as equally a flexible "fiction" or a cultural narrative as it is a methodology of inquiry.
75. Vilém Flusser, *Does Writing Have a Future?* trans. Nancy Ann Roth (Minneapolis: University of Minnesota Press, 2011), 15.

76. Ibid.

77. Ibid., 146.

78. One thing Flusser neglects to examine is digital information illiteracy. That is, nearly a few decades after Flusser wrote his study, digital media has proliferated almost exponentially. While vast number of people use digital interfaces—that operate on digital code—relatively few people are literate in coding and programming. In a sense, the population is being used, coded, and programmed more than they are using, coding, and programming. In recent years, this has become a more pressing concern in media studies, cultural studies, and pedagogy, that is, there is more direct emphasis on making the population of the digital age turn literate in code and programming. Douglas Rushkoff's book, *Program or be Programmed* (2011) is the most concise and penetrating study forcefully and lucidly confronting this conundrum.

79. Flusser, *Does Writing Have a Future?*, 147.

80. Ibid.

81. Ibid., 145.

82. Ibid.

83. This is, however, widely contested by AI researchers.

84. Flusser, *Does Writing Have a Future?*, 145.

85. Vilém Flusser and Louis Bec, Vampyroteuthis Infernalis: *A Treatise, with a Report by the* Institut Scientifique de Recherche Paranaturaliste, trans. Valentine A. Pakis (Minneapolis: University of Minnesota Press, 2012), 31.

86. Flusser, *Does Writing Have a Future?*, 71.

87. Ibid., 71.

88. Flusser and Bec, *Vampyroteuthis Infernalis*, 25.

Chapter 2

The Radical Poetics of Impersonality
The Posthuman, the Inhuman, and Dada

The movement that separates the human capacity to identify with technology is gradual. At present, we are rapidly approaching an encounter with a new kind of human being. If it is indeed the case that we are thoroughly on our way to posthumanism, we should not be surprised that traditional humanist values are increasingly challenged, subject to suspicion, and unaccepted as the standard of epistemological measurement. Posthumanism means many things and is at the heart of a lively, interdisciplinary debate. Here, the term is in accord with that general movement that actively interprets the humanist project with incredulity and ultimately celebrates the rupture with humanism as inevitable and productive. Donna Haraway's *Simians, Cyborgs, and Women* (1991) is among the best, most influential, and most provocative studies of posthumanism. Here Haraway asks, "why should our bodies end at the skin?"[1] and suggests that the gradual merging of the technological and the biological is a formidable and productive moment for feminist commitment. Celebrating the inevitable blurring boundaries between the science-fictional idea of the cybernetic organism and social reality, Haraway ceases upon the metaphor (or literal figure) of the cyborg as a means of thinking differently about gender divisions and boundaries: "the cyborg," she writes, "is our ontology; it gives us our politics."[2] The cyborg actively reinvents nature and, as a result, new lines of relations are established between gender and biology, humans and their environment. Haraway's cyborg manifesto identifies the cyborg as a positive and productive condition for women and a post-gender world. The unique advantage that the cyborg ensures is that of circumventing biological and social narratives that precede. Ultimately, Haraway develops an apparatus of thinking through which she can work beyond the essentialist claims about the distinctions between men and women, human and machine. Moreover, her work dismantles any kind of essentialism.

The cyborg cannot be a determinant, nor can it essentially *be* anything; it is remarkably versatile and can adapt to its situational environment in whatever way suits it best. This coupling of the human being and machine is ubiquitous: from medical technology, industrial production, and techno-warfare, to wearable technology and ubiquitous computers. Indeed, these machines are "eminently portable, mobile"[3] and thus radically transform both ontology and politics. Haraway is familiar with the dangers that inevitably become concrete possibilities in this new ontology. Yet, radical politics remain at the fore, and the gesture is that of dismantling the unified, essential self as envisioned in Western philosophy and society. The cyborg obscures and blurs what would traditionally be identified as distinctions and divisions. It also asks us to consider ourselves as infinitely mutable and plastic: to radically engage with social, historical, and textual norms toward the end of subversion. Accordingly, the posthuman condition is a positive and desirable one. However, the posthuman remains linguistic. Indeed, the cyborg is an intensified and enhanced manifestation of the merger that is already taking place between humans and the apparatus.

A central objection to the narrative of posthumanism is that it asserts extending the human *beyond* the human with a logic of elongating the existence of the human. In this sense, the posthuman and transhuman remain metaphysically inseparable from the human. Both posthumanism and transhumanism seem "to want to get rid of the concept of the human," writes Yuk Hui. "However," he continues, "this gesture is only camouflage. Transhumanism is a quintessentially humanist approach to the world, since all is captured within a metaphysical gaze."[4] We are left asking, at what point does the posthuman become so alien that it no longer shares any qualities that may be identifiable as human, and furthermore, how do such extensions become indistinguishable from the apparatus? At what point does the posthuman become synonymous with that which is alien? The posthuman seems to be that which bridges categories and referents—the cyborg disassembles social and biological essentialism—and yet it stands to reason that the posthuman will eventuate in the inevitable arborescent splitting of lineages that result in a web of complexity well beyond what could be identified to be human ab ovo—though most genealogies are traceable. The inevitability of this trajectory is one whereby the *post* and the *human* are incommensurate in an absolute way. While the posthuman aims at a form of transcending humanism, humanism nevertheless remains a logical constraint through which the transition may be made meaningful. It is this moment of transition that is so contestable, but certainly, there will be a moment when those emerging technological ontologies that make posthuman plasticity possible will surpass humanism and shift the logic of control to the outside. In short, programming—an extension of humanist development—will reach the apogee of complexity whereby it becomes purely self-replicating, self-developing, and self-optimizing. "The invention of digital technology gives us the ability to program: to create self-sustaining information systems or virtual life," notes Rushkoff,

> these are technologies that carry on long after we've created them, making future decisions without us. The digital age includes robotics, genetics, nanotechnology, and computer programs—each capable of self-regulation, self-improvement, and self-perpetuation. They can alter themselves, create new versions of themselves, and even collaborate with others. They grow. These are not just things you make and use. These are emergent forms that are biased toward their own survival. Programming in a digital age means determining the codes and rules through which our many technologies will build the future.[5]

The consequence of the moment at which these emergent programs self-regulate toward the ends of their own interest rather than that of humanism is implicated in the very possibility of a politic: this moment is also the literalization of where word breaks off. If the posthuman is a political and ontological movement, it is so because it is comprised of at least partial human constituency. The logical extension of the posthuman exists in the realm of the *post*. There is a moment when the boundaries between human and technology stop blurring and divide without redress to the biases of preserving the human. Instead, the process will concern itself with itself: the maintenance and optimization of the apparatus itself. Rushkoff writes that "programming is the sweet spot, the high leverage point in a digital society" and that "if we don't learn to program, we risk being programmed ourselves."[6] What Rushkoff identifies here is a kind of evolutionary game of survival: humanism must place an imperative on knowing *how* to program technology in such a way that technology does not program humanism. What is at stake, by extension, is not only the preservation of deliberate and engaged politics of resistance in an era of information illiteracy but also the conservancy of the very enterprise of politics itself. Advanced self-regulating technology, according to ever-elegant algorithms at a certain level of complexity, will have no reason to invest in the social. In short, programs that program are not political or social agents; they are operators of their own functionality. Politics are a human enterprise. When technology is no longer an extension of the human body but instead a self-regulating initiative of its own accord, the very notion of politics is meaningless. So, those suspicious of posthumanism as politically radical are not concerned that "the machine is us, our processes, and aspect of our embodiment"[7] but that the machine is *not* us and is rather its own processes and self-regulating configurations. Programming does not need to navigate negotiations among many groups of differences; it simply reconfigures and maximizes its own efficiency and speed and discards all that which does not facilitate this process.

In his later work, Jean-François Lyotard became increasingly suspicious of technology (particularly techno-capitalism) and posthumanism. Indeed, the position held by Rushkoff (program or be programmed) owes something to Lyotard. In *The Inhuman* (1988), Lyotard, like Flusser, suggests that computers (and, by extension, programming languages) will ultimately surpass humans with the goal of allowing human life to avoid extinction as a result of the heat death of the sun. This question is most explicitly considered in the opening essay, "Can Thought Go On without a Body?" Sufficiently advanced technology can self-regulate, self-improve, self-organize, and collaborate, but its true imperative is solely concerned with its own operational expansion toward the goal of maximum efficiency. Thus, the kind of life that would survive the heat death of the sun would not be human life. It would be posthuman, and as a result, the enterprise of humanism and politics would be supplanted with an enterprise of programming, machinism, and mathematical operations, that is, *replaced* by the apparatus. The urgency behind this anxiety is relative. Absolute extinction of the world as the site of being is quite a way off and perhaps not the concern of philosophy; yet, scientific inquiry—though inevitably stemming from human methodology—vastly opens the scope of contextualization. Ray Brassier contextualizes this vastness and raises the question of urgency for the situation of the human:

> Natural science produces ancestral statements, such as that the universe is roughly 13.7 billion years old, that the earth formed roughly 4.5 billion years ago, that life developed on earth approximately 3.5 billion years ago, and that the earliest ancestors of the genus *Homo* emerged about 2 million years ago. Yet it is also generating an ever-increasing number of "descendent" statements, such as that the Milky Way will collide with the Andromeda galaxy in 3 billion years; that the earth will be incinerated by the sun 4 billion years hence; that all the stars in the universe will stop shining in 100 trillion years; and that eventually, one trillion, trillion, trillion years from now, all matter in the cosmos will disintegrate into unbound elementary particles. Philosophers should be more astonished by such statements than they seem to be.[8]

There are indeed reasons why philosophers may consider this inevitable state of events more seriously. Brassier's concern here, from *Nihil Unbound: Enlightenment and Extinction* (2007), is that "the disenchantment of the world deserves to be celebrated as an achievement of intellectual maturity, not bewailed as a debilitating impoverishment" and that nihilism is "the unavoidable corollary of the realist conviction that there is a mind-independent reality, which despite the presumptions of human narcissism, is indifferent to our existence and oblivious to the 'values' and 'meanings' which we would drape over it in order to make it more hospitable."[9] Brassier's conjecture then—though concerned with a scientific realism of the movement of time indifferent to the human experience—is one that implicitly concerns the confrontation that the project of knowledge will have to think itself without thought.

Or, as Brassier puts it, *"How does thought think a world without thought? Or more urgently: how does thought think the death of thinking?"*[10] A more expansive chronology, Brassier's question overlaps to a degree with Lyotard's suspicion of posthumanism. Both, in a sense, consider how one may think the extinction of *thought as it is*. It seems an intractable question, and yet it astonishes. Lyotard, in the introduction of *The Inhuman*, identifies two nodes of speculation that must come under consideration when thinking of the possibility of the human and the teleology of technology:

> The "talks" collected here . . . have neither the function nor the value of a manifesto or treatise. The suspicion they betray (in both senses of this word) is simple, although double: what if human beings, in humanism's sense, were in the process of, constrained into, becoming inhuman (that's the first part)? And (the second part), what if what is "proper" to humankind were to be inhabited by the inhuman?[11]

For Brassier, extinction is inevitable for human beings as an indifferent unfolding of planetary, solar, and extra-solar forces: nature simply proceeds. Lyotard also seems to hold this position, yet he is also concerned with techno-capitalism and technology. He is concerned, first, with the question as to whether or not humans, in humanism's sense, are in the process of transitioning into the inhuman and, second, whether humanism's primary position will inevitably be subjugated, surpassed, and inhabited by the inhuman. Whether this will happen soon or much later is uncertain. Lyotard, however, is certain that the transition has an expiry date: the point at which the Earth will experience heat death by sun. As the sun runs out of fuel, it will expand, engulfing the inner planets, including Earth. It then experiences a series of massive explosions; these explosive pulsations of solar mass will shatter the surrounding planets. Eventually, the sun will implode into a super-dense white dwarf star. This is the absolute moment at which thought, in one form or another, will either go on or cease.

"Can Thought Go On Without a Body?" is structured around two addresses that fission in apparently incongruous directions and thus establish an intractable divide. The first address is presented by "He" while the second address is given by "She." He eschews the value of philosophy for an optimism rooted in scientific enquiry and the essential need for a bodiless mode of thought that may proceed indefinitely beyond the destruction of the Earth and solar system as a result of the heat death of the sun. She, however, remains skeptical toward He. Rather, She's address reintroduces the significance of emotion, feeling, suffering, and desire into the discussion, arguing that thought cannot be extracted from the body—or, in the case that it is possible, this techno-thought would not be the thought that constitutes philosophy. The two positions thus gesture away from one another: He proceeds toward universalization while She recedes to the increasingly local. What is notable, however, is that Lyotard's choice in having two opposing addresses—neither of which are conclusively triumphant over the other—may prove to be an important structural move in speaking to issues of AI and posthumanism. That is, the paradox of an indexical, self-reflexive, closed system—here, Lyotard's essay—that gestures in opposing directions while simultaneously looping back upon itself invokes certain structural consistencies with scientific speculation on consciousness and AI as intelligent computers. By having the two arguments in conflict with one another, Lyotard's essay displays a similar logic to that underlying AI: in order to create the vastness of genuine intelligence (a move toward the universal), the program must paradoxically recede to the smallest local units through the process of indexical, recursive feedback loops.

The incongruity between the two parts of the essay, however, does not speak to this structural phenomenon directly; rather, the two arguments proceed on their own terms. He's motivation to argue for the necessity of thought without a body is that time is thought's greatest enemy:

> While we talk, the sun is getting older. It will explode in 4.5 billion years. . . . With the sun's death your [the philosopher's] insoluble questions will be done with too . . . You explain: it's impossible to think an end, pure and simple, of anything at all, since the end's a limit and to think it you have to be on both sides of that limit. . . . But after the sun's death there won't be a thought to know that its death took place.[12]

After much apocalyptic speculation, He proposes the obvious technophilic solution to the problem: to "make thought without a body."[13] Quick to distance this argument from metaphysics or theology, He remarks that thought without a body means thought "without the complex living terrestrial organism known as the human body. Not without hardware, obviously."[14] This is He's move toward the universal insomuch as there is no concern for the particular or the individual—rather, thought is to be regarded as an abstract unified principle that is separate from the biological distinctiveness of individual human beings not unlike the transhumanism of Hans Moravec.[15] He is, as a result, not a Platonist but instead an inorganic materialist.

She's assessment of the issue is one of skepticism and protestation. There is incredulity toward the ability of a program—as addressed by He—capable of capturing the connotative, affective, and phenomenological dimensions of intelligence:

> words, phrases in the act of writing, the latent nuances and timbres at the horizon of a painting or a musical composition as it's being created . . . all lend themselves to us for the occasion and yet slip through our fingers. And even inscribed on a page or canvas, they "say" something other than what we "meant."[16]

She is unconvinced that thought can be relocated into any effective programmable software. The dissatisfaction with programs leads She back to the body and unpredictability as a critical aspect of thought. For She "there's a necessity for physical experience and a recourse to exemplary cases of bodily ascesis to understand and make understood a type of emptying of the mind . . . that is required if the mind is to think";[17] furthermore, "suffering," an affect associated with the body as much as with the mind, "is the mark of true thought."[18] Indeed, it is suffering that is most crucial to She's resistance to He's address. Because the optimism of He leads to a rash conclusion, She suggests that "The unthought hurts because we're comfortable in what's already thought . . . thinking, which is discomfort, is also, to put it bluntly, an attempt to have done with it. That's the hope of sustaining all writing . . . : that at the end, things will be better."[19] Since there is no "end," She suggests that He's machines will need to experience discomfort, and will, therefore, need a body as the site of suffering. Finally, She suggests that "the human body has a gender" and that, at least for psychoanalysis, this is "an accepted proposition that sexual difference is a paradigm of an incompleteness of not just bodies, but minds too."[20] She's psychoanalytic concerns with gender are, ultimately, in opposition to He's gesture toward universalization and gender neutralization. Haraway's cyborg, of course, resists this polarization. Lyotard's She, as a result, is an organic materialist; similar to He, however, She is also an anti-Platonist. That is, there is no abstract reality into which the teleology of the mind will transcend.

Resultantly, these two addresses are, though in conversation with one another, gesturing toward the universal, as in the case of He, and toward the increasingly local, as argued by She. To consider Lyotard's essay as a whole, it is certainly more complex than simply offering two positions on a single issue; rather, the essay itself can be thought of as a system where the two arguments, though moving away from one another, paradoxically become entangled in a perpetual cycle of interaction where each repetition comments on both the previous and following cycle in a self-similar and self-generating way. This is more than simply stating that the two addresses in the essay are ever in ineluctable conflict with one another. What is exciting about considering Lyotard's essay in this way is that this looping simulates feedback recursion: a strange loop that attempts to explain self-consciousness and is also instrumental in research on AI.

Hofstadter's strange loop here is, in a way, already nicely intimated in Lyotard's essay, though in different terms:

> [A human being is] equipped with a symbolic system that's both arbitrary (in semantics and syntax), letting it be less dependent on an immediate environment, and also recursive (Hofstadter), allowing it to take into account (above and beyond raw data) the way it has of processing such data. That is, itself.... A human, in short, is a living organization that is not only complex but, so to speak, replex. It can grasp itself.[21]

Therefore, a human being—like an AI and like Lyotard's essay—is not simply composed of parts, but those parts are also in the process of self-consciousness, self-reflexive repetition. The intractable conflict between the two addresses, as they theoretically play out indefinitely in the closed format of an essay, suggests feedback recursion and simulates something akin to a phenomenon theoretically associated with disembodied thought. Above and beyond the raw data, "Can Thought Go On Without a Body?" is an eloquent metaphor in itself that enacts, through language, a rehearsal or simulation of self-generating, self-reflexive electronic data. In short, the essay itself demonstrates not that "thought can go on without a body" (Lyotard seems reticent on this point but does not fully disregard the possibility) but that bodies are still very much here, discourse is still very much human, and that discourse is still *on its way* toward a posthumanism, although that thought—human thought—cannot be expressed through the inhuman. In a way, the essay can be considered as a kind of proto-literature of exclusion in the form of critical theory.

As a result, the essay also expresses anxiety and skepticism toward the prospect of the inhuman since the moment of the inhuman inevitably means the end of human experience. "Development is not attached to an Idea, like that of the emancipation of reason and of human freedoms," Lyotard writes. "It is reproduced by accelerating and extending itself according to its internal dynamic alone. It assimilates risks, memorizes their informational value and uses this as a new mediation necessary to its functioning."[22] The transition from one state to another, it seems, will be slow and gradual but it will ultimately result in absolute incongruity and favor the bias of the inhuman and the apparatus. Lyotard's closing to the book's introduction serves as a starting point for struggle, however:

> Since development is the very thing which takes away the hope of an alternative to the system of thought and actions now turns out to be redundant ... the

question I am raising here is simply this: what else remains as "politics" except resistance to this inhuman? And what else is left to resist with but the debt which each soul has contracted with the miserable and admirable indetermination from which it was born and does not cease to be born?—which is to say, with the other inhuman?[23]

Ultimately, Lyotard writes that it "is the task of writing, thinking, literature, arts, to venture to bear witness" to the debt of what distinguishes the human from the inhuman.[24] It is our task here to look at works of writing and literature that operate as nodes of resistance by setting up substrata of thinking in and amid the shift from humanism to inhumanism, that offer us as readers a sense of illiteracy, powerlessness, alienation, and, ultimately, absolute exclusion. To recognize expressions of what it might be like to experience, despite an innocuous and gradual shift, that moment of schism when the incongruity between human and inhuman takes place. To bear witness such literary sites of radical selflessness, we are asked to at once consider carefully and thoughtfully our present engagement with technology and acknowledge our coming exclusion from such engagement. Indeed, to do so requires the agential negation of agency and an act of self-delimitation in literary production. The literature of exclusion, in this sense, rehearses the inhuman by revisiting and renovating the modernist poetics of impersonality.

DADA AND THE RADICAL POETICS OF IMPERSONALITY

"The revolution of our time is the uncertainty revolution," writes Baudrillard. "Paradoxically, however," he continues, "we attempt to escape from uncertainty by relying even more on information and communications systems, so merely aggravating the uncertainty itself. This is a forward flight: the pursuit race of technology and its perverse effects, of man and his clones, around a track in the form of a Moebius strip has only just begun."[25] However, a century earlier, the Dadaists were already seeking a way off the track as a means of seeking paths to the outside. Indeed, well before dataism began accelerating the expansion of the apparatus while dismantling human agency, Dadaism rallied the call to articulate no thing for a very different type of inhuman. While the former spells uncertainty for the human and optimization for the apparatus, the latter is effectively uncertainty and unpredictability as a revolt against culture *for* a new kind of impersonal mode of being that can oscillate contingently between the human and the inhuman. In many ways a reaction against Enlightenment rationality, the Romantic cult of individuality,[26] bourgeois liberalism, and the cult of progress, a central impulse to modernist aesthetics was to depict the impersonality of the artist or poet. The reasoning behind this shift from agency to automated ventriloquy is varied: from acting as a well-studied medium of history, to surrendering one's agency to the forces of inhuman technologies, to act like a machine that responds rather than creates, to embrace esotericism and occultism, to give oneself over to the unconscious, or to embrace nothingness as a form of stochastic revolt against the slaughter of the First World War. Ultimately, it is the last in this list that best describes modernist poetics of impersonality through the context of Dada. Not simply a movement within and against the arts, Dada was fundamentally motivated by disgust, and the quintessential Dadaist poem is that which is, rather than inspired by a spontaneous overflow of pathos, aleatorically assembled from small bits of text that recursively affirms and negates itself as a kind of paradoxical nihilistic homeostasis. Not only is this poetry meant to change a life, it also responds to changes unique to life in the face of modernity: the sense of absolute subjugation to massive, complex, indifferent (even hostile) technological forces. As the cacophony of the steel, smoke, speed, and industry of the early twentieth century gives way to the digital, instantaneous, and cognitive writing of algorithmic technology of the twenty-first century, the reconsideration of the empirical self as an automated self proves to be more urgent than ever before. Dada, though a modernist movement, prefigured the neuro-totalitarian and psychopolitical dimensions of AI and the apparatus by not solely revolting against the discipline of the body by industrial machines, but also the infections of the mind and psyche by immaterial machines.

Consequently, it is no surprise that the modernist aesthetics of impersonality in the form of a revolt on reason, structure, and rules continue to have a vibrant trajectory. From the Futurists to contemporary remix fiction, the shift toward a poetic impersonality that is both constituted from outside yet reconstructible through practice proves to be of long-lasting interest. These literary practices also have a parallel in music, photography, and film. Just as the Dadaists captured the process of random reassemblage as an act of political resistance, the digital era demands that we either confront the apparatus poietically or be first transformed, then abandoned, by it. The legacy of modernist impersonality, however, is as troublingly fascistic in its psychopolitical and neuro-totalitarian manifestations as it is potentially emancipatory; in its more radical Dadaist form, the assault on rationality and meaning may serve ends as uncertain and incompatible as revolution and nihilism, deliverance and nationalism, and autonomy and algorithmic determination. Ultimately, the process of fragmentation is central to a mode of impersonality crucial to much twentieth-century avant-garde writing; however, it may also offer a way of establishing algorithmic impersonality that confronts and disorders algorithmic automation by resisting psychopolitics and neuro-totalitarianism.

The indeterminacy of this process mimics the way we experience the uncertainty of the present and, yet, is a means by which we can discover surprising instances of poetic insight into supermodern autonomy: a dismantling of the lyrical self toward the ends of setting up a locus whereby one can rehearse possibility and alternatives. The fragmentation and poetry of the literature of exclusion, as intensified Dadaism and hypermodern cut-up (see chapters 5 and 6), can inform a paradoxical engagement with algorithmic determinism *as* resistance against the twilight of autonomy. Indeed, the author is not necessarily dead after all; instead, the literature of exclusion insists that the word can be set free as a precedent for a stochastic agency and that this remains, at least for now, a tangible possibility.

The dismantling of the self is a particularly contentious issue, of course. As a constitutive abstraction, the self is itself comprised of complex level-crossing knots and recursive feedback loops; Dada insists that such pluralism ultimately plays out on the level of mind as much as it does on the body. As a result, the self—an abstract construct—is subject to endless reconfigurations. However, as a kind of meta-commentary on the very idea of a stable mind or identity, Bifo prompts us to consider that "identity [is] a nonsense concept and a psychological trap."[27] The desire to theorize the eschewing identity in favor of poetic impersonality begins with modernism and, in particular, with Eliot and Pound. In *The Poetics of Impersonality: T.S. Eliot and Ezra Pound* (1987), Maud Ellmann writes that "the difficulty is that Eliot and Pound both advocate impersonality . . . yet both resist its implications."[28] Nevertheless, as poets, Eliot and Pound "both efface themselves through masks, personae, and ventriloquy"; as critics, "both suspect that writing is an act of self-estrangement" and "an agon with the other, the unconscious, and the dead."[29] That neither Eliot nor Pound is willing to "dethrone the author without salvaging a good deal of his former privilege,"[30] their contradictoriness is, in itself, indicative of modernist anxieties. If expression rigorously examines and expresses modernity, it cannot cohere. And while the poetics of impersonality can be considered a response to intensified alienation, Ellmann also suggests that the emergence of psychoanalysis engendered a reactionary stance from poets who were "furtive to defend themselves against their readers' scrutiny."[31] Eliot and Pound's identification as expatriates complicates not only the unconscious of the poets but also their language and history; by extension, the poetics of impersonality does not simply guard the poet against being psychoanalyzed[32] by their audience but also aims to free them of the constraints of linear time and space. Like their work, Eliot and Pound offer troubled, collaged identity in place of singular identity.

The politics of modernist aesthetic impersonality are complex and can be mobilized toward revolution and conservatism. While authorial impersonality has precedents that go back to the ancient world in terms of anonymous authorship or the author's adoption of the teacher's or tradition's title, its modern roots interestingly first appear, not in realism, but in the courts that prosecuted the supposed immorality of realist literature. Gustav Flaubert, after being prosecuted in 1857 by Ernest Pinard for the publication of *Madam Bovary* (1856), defended the novel from a misunderstanding public by distinguishing himself from the voice of the novel. Five years earlier on December 9, 1852, in a letter to his mistress, Louise Colet, Flaubert writes that the author, rather than an imperial subject, should act subserviently and analogously to reality itself: "In his work, the author must be like God in his universe: present everywhere and visible nowhere," and yet, "One should sense a hidden and infinite impassibility in its every atom, its every aspect. The effect on the spectator must be a sort of humiliation. He must ask: 'How was that done?' And he must feel crushed because he does not know."[33] Flaubert's insistence on the paradoxical relation between the author as ubiquitous and ambient, yet absent, is a direct affront to the role of authorial agency and, in many ways, marks Flaubert as one of the first modern novelists. However, it is over a half-century later when aesthetic impersonality takes a more radical and technologized turn.

The Italian Futurists were dedicated to an eschatology where humans would evolve *with* and *as* machinic technology. In "The Foundation and Manifesto of Futurism" (1909), F. T. Marinetti discusses how he and some friends were "startled by the terrifying clatter of huge, double decker trams jolting, all ablaze with different-colored lights, as if they were villages in festive celebration"[34] and, after hearing "the sudden roar of ravening motorcars, right beneath [their] windows"[35] Marinetti states that "we're about to witness the birth of a Centaur . . . and soon we shall witness the flight of the very first Angels."[36] While the angels here are both airplanes and a kind of ascendance of agency from Earth/materiality, it is the Centaur that is most revealing. A parody of the human-equine assemblage, Marinetti instead extends this formula to the equating of human with inhuman machinery. And, this is expressed best through words; or, more specifically, expressed through "words in freedom." Marinetti writes that "Words in freedom orchestrate colors, noises, sounds, they mix the materials of languages and dialects, arithmetic and geometric formulas, musical notation, old, deformed or new words, the cries of animals, of wild beasts and motors" and "Words in freedom are a new way of seeing the universe."[37] For Marinetti, however, art is inextricably linked to politics, and, as Ballerini suggests, such activity "involved the human being's totality and resulted naturally from the equation *life = art*."[38] While Marinetti's advocacy of Mussolini demonstrated a "desperate compromise and a blatant contradiction of his aesthetic propensities"[39] and, when the former descended upon Rome in 1922, he "did not do so . . . as an avant-garde poet, but as a pathetically anesthetized member of the Accademia d'Italia."[40] Italian Futurism itself represented a potentiality to resist fascism. However, the technological and machinic extensions or replacements of human agency were, for Marinetti, "no longer appreciated as a powerful opportunity to extend the sensorial and intellectual potential of humans," writes Ballerini. Instead, the transmutation into

> the machine begins to be seen as an ultimate goal in their evolution. This is the modernity of which Marinetti dreams, and he does so without any sense of loss. Man, who has been multiplied by the velocity of the speeding automobile, can now give up his role as the "maker of meaning." He prefers to be subsumed in the "molecular life" of the universe: his aesthetic task will be that of recording not his private lyrical obsession with matter, but the "lyric obsession of matter" itself.[41]

Four years later, outside Italy and as a polar view of modernist political spectra, The Poet in Vladimir Mayakovsky's Soviet Futurist play *Vladimir Mayakovsky: A Tragedy* (1913) also delimits authorship and agency by dismantling the distinction between individuals and environments. The Poet states: "I've wiped out the differences / between faces like mine and those of strangers"[42] and whereby the outside, the inside, and the human are conflated into the quintessential Futurist city, a "projected world [that] is," as Marjorie Perloff writes, "impersonal and faceless."[43] Amid all this, however, is a remarkably important discovery. The Futurists were, Ballerini remarks, "among the first avant-garde artists to see no obligatory connection between communication and information" and "did not construe this form of entropy as a negative condition."[44] That is, the Futurists were able to prefigure a more machinic sense of information in the sense of Warren Weaver and Claude Shannon: one where meaning and content are not primary and that the more disorder in a signal, the more fecund. In this sense, the act of signifying *nothing* is already recognized by the Futurists as being more informationally fecund than possibilities that signify *something*.

Though not a Futurist, Pound was a founding member of a related English movement: Vorticism, a movement in literature, painting, and sculpture, founded in 1914. It was largely dissolved only a few years later due to the way the war unsettled the movement's celebration of speed, technology, and aggression signified by the vortex. Like Futurism, Vorticism expressed a complex relationship between extreme individuality and the reliance on inhuman force and acceleration as a kind of enhancement, extension, or tech-prosthetic to the human. Unsurprisingly, Pound expressed the need for a poetic impersonality through a kind of cyborg-like balance between human and machine whereby agency is not eliminated but, instead, partially galvanized by the inhuman. In his short piece "As for Imagism," published in *New Age*, XVI 13 on January 28, 1915, Pound writes,

> Where the voltage is so high that it fuses the machinery, one has merely the "emotional man" not the artist. The best artist is the man whose machinery can stand the highest voltage. The better the machinery, the more precise, the stronger; the more exact will be the record of the voltage and of the various currents which have passed through it. These are bad expressions if they lead you to think of the artist as wholly passive, as a mere receiver of impressions. The good artist is perhaps a good seismograph, but the difference between man and a machine is that man can in some degree "start his machinery going." He can, within limits, not only record but create.[45]

Pound's insistence on the primacy of the human over the machine only *feels* like Futurism here; in the end, his claim that the main difference between humans and machines is that humans create and start the machines. And, in a material sense, Pound is correct; he is especially correct in the context of industrial machines of the early twentieth century. However, the machines are extensions of the self, and, at some point, one must imagine an instance of singularity in which such technological extension largely severs the author from agential identity altogether. Pound's evaluation will not stand up to the functionalist processes of algorithmic culture a century later where digital processes regularly self-update and self-evolve according to programmed operations. Nevertheless, his work not only intimates the melding of human and technology, but it also complicates the question of authorship in poetry and beyond by setting in motion a transnational (and transtemporal) cosmopolitanism whereby a national poet becomes a citizen of the world throughout history.

The most sustained articulation of modernist aesthetic impersonality, however, is T. S. Eliot's essay "Tradition and the Individual Talent" (1919). Rather than alluding to the machinic, Eliot updates the transformative metaphors of alchemy to the language of chemistry to describe the role of the poet as a catalyst. Here, the poetic process is a chemical reaction and "the more perfect the artist, the more completely separate in him will be the man who suffers and the mind which creates."[46] Eliot calls for a shift away from the Romantic cult of personality for a new modern sensibility as a mode of depersonalized and methodological inquiry: a kind of art that is conceived as a "condition of science."[47] Eliot is not concerned with the Futurist fusing of flesh and engine oil; instead, he calls for an impersonal and objective poetry free from affective expression. Like the Italian Futurists and Pound, however, Eliot's stance was a conservative one, attesting, once again, to the troubled relationship between making it new and proto-fascism. Though an innovator, he aims to capture and promote the resurgence of what he saw as the greatness and unified poetic tradition of pre-Renaissance Europe as emblematized by Dante. While Futurists were to fail as a result of the incompatibility of the desire to destroy the past and usher in an accelerated supercapitalism with Mussolini's fascism that was so heavily dependent on the myth of inherited Roman greatness and Heroic capitalism, Eliot's conservatism—too naïve to be explicitly fascist—solidified an elitism that sought to seize the moment of rapid change by privileging a highly selective historical sense. At a time of traumatically rapid change on all levels of culture and society, Eliot's poetics of impersonality were not so much simply adopting the role of a reagent in a chemical reaction but were as much an opportunity to express deeply held personal cultural biases. The shred of platinum that Eliot evokes in the essay, rather than disappearing, gilds its output, shimmers, and emanates in all directions. After all, the quintessential polyphonic, impersonal mode of poetry is the Epic; and while the classical Epic dismantles the cult of singular authorship, it also has a specific purpose: to elevate a national character and historical myth in a grandiose manner. Both Eliot and Pound's delimiting of authorial agency was, of course, incomplete and hesitant. "Written, the I dissolves into the asemantic play of letters," Ellmann notes. "In Eliot and Pound, speech and writing also come to signify the battle between self and self-oblivion. As much as they denounce personality, they dread its dissolution even more: and the very history that they shore against their ruins conspires in their disremembering."[48] The Dadaists, however, are fully committed to the destruction of rationality, agency, and national identity toward the ends of difference, change, and absolute contingency.

Whereas Marinetti, Mayakovsky, Pound, Eliot, and other major modernist figures envisioned the construction of the new via varying modes of myth-making, Dada aimed to not only destroy the very possibility of myth but also of the lyric agency commonly expected from the construction of rationality, nationalism, subjectivity, and homogenous cultural narrative. And while Dada is often discussed and categorized by the historical locales in which its earliest manifestations took place, this does not necessarily reflect the ethos of the movement. "The story of Dada doesn't conform to the usual narrative arc," writes Jed Rasula, "there's a beginning, sure enough, in Zurich, but there was a prolonged episode in New York around the same time, historically commemorated as Dada even though its participants didn't learn of Dada till later. There's also an apparent end of Dada in Paris, but that didn't deter others from mounting a Dada tour of Holland. There were even Dada start-ups as far afield as Eastern Europe and Japan."[49] Ultimately, it is reasonable that the nomadism of Dada speaks to an internationalism, if not an antinationhood, as a mirror to anti-identity. Tzara, for example, "kept the torch burning, publishing the periodical Dada and fielding a vast international public relations operation on behalf of what he was calling the Dada movement"[50] which is suggestive that Dada's home was not any place but, instead, a lived practice of physical and psychic revolt.

Richter writes that the Dadaists "wanted to bring forward a new kind of human being, one whose contemporaries we could wish to be, free from the tyranny of rationality, of banality, of generals, fatherlands, nations, art-dealers, microbes, residence permits and the past."[51] The emergence of Dada is a tangled story that emerges from a moment of extreme tension, conflict, and change. An intensity of trauma and upheaval—both psychical and physical—splintered confidence in projects of democracy, humanism, and Enlightenment. And certainly, there were very few restrictions put on individuals within the movement, establishing a productive atmosphere of anarchism whereby the aesthetic free-for-all was prioritized over group identity, regulation, and decision making. Tzara's emblematic poem "How to Make a Dadaist Poem" characterizes the aleatoric principles that inform much of Dada's rebellion against reason and the imperial agent:

Take a newspaper.
Take some scissors.
Choose from this paper an article the length you want to make your poem.
Cut out the article.
Next carefully cut out each of the words that make up
   this article and put them all in a bag.
Shake gently.
Next take out each cutting one after the other.
Copy conscientiously in the order in which they left the bag.
The poem will resemble you.
And there you are—an infinitely original author of
   charming sensibility, even though unappreciated by the vulgar herd.

Dada occupies all aspects of life; it is a state of being *and* not being; it is informationally dense nonsense. "Tzara's poem," writes Edward Robinson,

> is significant for a number of reasons, not least of all in that in its suggestion that copying the random phrases yielded by scraps of newspaper makes one "a writer," it prefaces the questioning of the author function. This issue would become, following Michel Foucault's seminal essay, "What is an Author?" (1970), a focal point of both literature and literary criticism in the late twentieth century.[52]

Because *Dada ne signifie rien* (Dada signifies nothing), its richness, like the entropic information understood by the Futurists, offers orderly disorder as the unpredictable catalyst for difference. This asemic being is the new kind of free human being Dada envisions: a random assemblage of everything within reach.

Robinson notes that there is a "clear lineage from the 'simultaneous poem' performed in 1916 by Tzara, Richard Huelsenbeck and Marcel Janco"[53] to the cut-up as both present a semantic nothingness that is rich with possibility. William S. Burroughs is the best known and most influential author of the cut-up technique. He extends the practice of Dada and the poetics of impersonality but in unique ways. However, Burroughs never claimed the cut-up technique to be a novelty of his own invention. He "was keen to stress the way in which the new approach could be applied to specific ends, with specific results."[54] Burroughs's aim was to dismantle the subject so that the self might be emancipated from the constitutiveness of language, politics, heteronormativity, and the "algebra of need." Indeed, the transference of ideas and influence here proves appropriate as nonlocal as it is nontemporal: Burroughs, whose notable cut-up work *Naked Lunch* (1959) was largely written in Tangiers, learned the cut-up technique from his Anglo-Canadian colleague Brion Gysin. Gysin, in the knotted fashion of this tangled lineage, had significant but brief ties to the Surrealists in Europe.[55] Gysin's contribution cannot be considered stream of consciousness, free indirect verse, or automatic writing, Robinson writes. Instead, Gysin's cut-up experiments consist of "the randomised sum of a number of consciously created original parts, drawn out of their original context and placed in a completely new context."[56] Burroughs, however, notes the potentiality of these experiments by focusing on the richness of the original parts becoming previous nonexisting generators of new text (whether meaningful and recognizable or uncanny and asemic). What is particularly important about Gysin and Burroughs's collaboration, however, is the fact that their work together formed another, invisible, author, or a "third mind."[57]

Burroughs and Gysin insisted that this third mind could access a sometimes-occult hermeneutics of the everyday and the cosmic: that these cut-ups revealed "the 'exposure' of a text's true meaning."[58] This is where Burroughs's and Gysin's aesthetics of impersonality differ most explicitly from their predecessors. While many Dadaists turned to Surrealism, "looking to create something new from the collision of images and objects," with the legacy of Gysin and Burroughs, "the aim would be to use the impact to decode what was already there"[59] and was revealed not simply by the text or the author, but a third abstract entity that is the sum of text, cut-up, and reading. As a result, for Burroughs, the readability of the cut-up was a significant issue; the cut-up, as a new form of writing, would require a new way of reading. And, for Burroughs, dissimilar to the radically unedited process suggested by Tzara, "sufficient quantities of the original text remain intact within the composites to allow them to exist in some kind of subliminal capacity."[60] The result is text that is still readable though now emancipated from linearity, dominant history, oppressive contexts, and conscious authorial agency. In this sense, Gysin's and Burroughs's cut-ups are intertextual pieces that enact "fragmentation, genre cross-pollination and the incorporation and adaptation of existing 'texts' informing the formulation of much 'postmodern' work."[61] Yet, Burroughs's and Gysin's "third mind," an autonomous impersonality, aims to draw attention to both the materiality of the cut-up *and* its conceptual effects. Furthermore, Burroughs and Gysin recognized that the cut-up was transferable to all recorded media: literature, film, and recorded audio. That is, authorial impersonality is not simply textual but also in, and on, the air. It is already part of the process of the word breaking off.

Dadaism remains the most violently resistant mode of expression of the desire to escape the trappings of identity and agency. The reimagining of the empirical and political self as an already-constituted automaton or irrational medium brings with it a sense of open-ended, limitless possibility. These practices are expressed as liberating; digital technology today makes these processes widely accessible and limitless in actuality. However, this unlimitedness in the digital era engenders libidinal enthusiasm and thanatotic nihilism simultaneously. This extreme polarization between constructivism and destructivism is perhaps more obvious today than any time prior. In the twenty-first century, for example, the conflation of popular music with the trash bin of consumer imagery makes up the neon anticapitalist aesthetic of vaporwave and other critiques of hypermodernity while meme culture proliferates exponentially and bifurcates endlessly in complex knotted and conflicting apolitical and political ends. Indeed, today it is perhaps the thanatotic psychopathy that is most known for its culture jamming through avant-garde memetics as a means of influencing everything from the normalization of racist, misogynistic, transphobic, xenophobic, nationalist, and fascist ideologies on the deep web to directly influencing the social political process via memetic misinformation. This authoritarian destructivism and pseudo-Dada, then, is ultimately suicidal; it serves the apparatus as it *thinks* it serves psychopathic liberation. Like with all engagements with technology, however, the user is also used by technology in ways that ultimately optimize the apparatus. When Mark Fisher writes that confronting the apparatus "is not a matter of speaking the unspeakable, but of vocalizing the extra-linguistic or the non-verbal, and thereby letting the *outside* in," he also concludes with a warning: "Admit it, count zero, get out."[62] However, once admitted to the apparatus, once accessing the *outside* and both vocalizing and listening to the voice of the unknown, there is no way back. And any encounter with the inhuman will yield inhuman results as we will see in the following chapter.

NOTES

1. Donna Haraway, *Simians, Cyborgs, and Women: The Reinvention of Nature* (New York: Routledge, 1991), 187.
2. Ibid., 150.
3. Ibid., 153.
4. Geert Lovink, "Cybernetics for the Twenty-First Century: An Interview with Philosopher Yuk Hui," *E-Flux* 102 (September 2019), https://www.e-flux.com/journal/102/282271/cybernetics-for-the-twenty-first-century-an-interview-with-philosopher-yuk-hui/.
5. Douglas Rushkoff, *Program or Be Programmed: Ten Commands for a Digital Age* (Berkeley: Soft Skull Press, 2010), 145.
6. Ibid., 139.
7. Haraway, Haraway, *Simians, Cyborgs, and Women*, 180.
8. Ray Brassier, *Nihil Unbound: Enlightenment and Extinction* (Basingstoke: Palgrave Macmillan, 2007), 49–50.
9. Ibid., ix.
10. Ibid., 223.
11. Jean-François Lyotard, *The Inhuman: Reflections on Time*, trans. Geoffrey Bennington and Rachel Bowlby (Stanford: Stanford University Press, 1991), 2.
12. Ibid., 9.
13. Ibid., 13.
14. Ibid.
15. See Hans Moravec's *Mind Children: The Future of Robot and Human Intelligence* (Cambridge, MA: Harvard University Press, 1988) and *Robot: Mere Machine to Transcendent Mind* (New York: Oxford University Press, 1999).
16. Ibid., 18.
17. Ibid., 19.
18. Ibid., 20.
19. Ibid.
20. Ibid.
21. Ibid., 12.
22. Ibid., 7.
23. Ibid.
24. Ibid.
25. Jean Baudrillard. "Superconductive Events." *The Transparency of Evil: Essays on Extreme Phenomena*, trans. James Benedict (London: Verso, 2009), 48.
26. Nevertheless, modernist poetics of impersonality, Ellmann notes, are likely "derived . . . from the very poets they attacked. The Romantic notion of inspiration, for example, implies that the poet is the instrument of forces which transcend his personality." Maud Ellman, *The Poetics of Impersonality: T.S. Eliot and Ezra Pound* (Cambridge: Harvard University Press, 1987), 3.
27. Berardi, *Breathing*, 34.
28. Ellman, *The Poetics of Impersonality*, 2.

29. Ibid., 3.
30. Ibid.
31. Ibid., 5.
32. However, readers and critics were not simply psychologists; one should also count Marxists and poststructuralists here as those that opposed liberal Romantic individualism toward the end of a more heterarchical relationship between reader and text.
33. Pierre Macherey, *The Object of Literature*, trans. David Macey (Cambridge: Cambridge University Press, 1995), 56.
34. F.T. Marinetti, "The Foundation and Manifesto of Futurism," *F.T. Marinetti: Critical Writings*, ed. Günter Berghaus, trans. Doug Thompson (New York: Farrar, Straus and Giroux, 2006).
35. Ibid., 11.
36. Ibid., 12.
37. F. T. Marinetti, "The Free Word Style," *The Untameables*, trans. Jeremy Parzen (København: Green Integer, 2016), 67.
38. Luigi Ballerini, "Italy and/or Marinetti: From Alexandria to Vittorio Veneto," *The Untamables*, trans. Jeremy Parzen (Copenhagen: Green Integer, 2016), 13.
39. Ibid.
40. Ibid., 18.
41. Ibid., 31.
42. Marjorie Perloff, *The Futurist Moment: Avant-Garde, Avant Guerre, and the Language of Rupture* (Chicago: University of Chicago Press, 1986), 153.
43. Ibid.
44. Ballerini, "Italy and/or Marinetti," 26.
45. Ezra Pound, "As for Imagism," *Ezra Pound's Poetry and Prose Contribution to Periodical, Vol II: 1915–1917* (New York: Garland Publishing, 1991), 8–9.
46. T.S. Eliott, "Tradition and the Individual Talent," *The Complete Prose of T.S. Eliot, Volume 2, The Perfect Critic, 1919–1926*, ed. Anthony Cuda and Ronald Schuchard (Baltimore: Johns Hopkins University Press, 2014), 109.
47. Ibid., 108.
48. Ellmann, 17.
49. Jed Rasula, *Destruction was my Beatrice: Dada and the Unmaking of the Twentieth Century* (New York: Basic Books, 2015), xi.
50. Ibid., xiv.
51. Hans Richter, *Dada: Art and Anti-Art*, trans. David Britt (London: Thames & Hudson, 1997), 65.
52. Edward S. Robinson, *Shift-Linguals: Cut-up Narratives from William S. Burroughs to the Present* (Amsterdam: Rodopi, 2011), 7.
53. Ibid., 23.
54. Ibid., 6.
55. Robinson writes that Gysin was as much of a surrealist as he was a Beat. Ultimately, however, Gysin "was an equally independent avant-garde artist who operated free of the constraints of any groups or movements. Having begun his career with the Surrealists, only to be ejected from the group on the eve of a major

exhibition in Paris in 1932, his combining of various media within a single piece of work saw him being briefly aligned with Fluxus and expanded cinema, although ultimately his work defies simple categorization, straddling innumerable boundaries" (*Shift-Linguals*, 23).

56. Ibid., 25.

57. See William S. Burroughs and Brion Gysin, *The Third Mind* (New York: Viking Press, 1978).

58. Ibid., 26.

59. Ibid., 9.

60. Ibid., 18.

61. Ibid., 5.

62. Mark Fisher, "Gothic Materialism," *Pli: The Warwick Journal of Philosophy*, 12 (2001), 242.

Chapter 3

The Divine Neutrality of the Apparatus

The Self-Reflexive Conceptual Horror of B. R. Yeager

In the frequently cited 1917 introduction to his play, *Les mamelles de Tirésias* (1903), Apollinaire achieves two remarkable things. First, he introduces the word "*surréaliste*," and second, perhaps inadvertently, initiates one of the most insightful definitions of technology. "I thought it necessary," he writes, "to return to nature itself, but without imitating it in a photographic manner. When man wished to imitate walking, he created the wheel—which does not resemble a leg. In this way he committed an act of surrealism without knowing it."[1] Not only is this a careful reminder for early-twentieth-century theatre goers that, despite naturalism and realism, the theatre is always separate from actuality; it is a simulation. It will never live up to the capturing of reality that he foresaw in photography and cinema. Rather than faithful representation, Apollinaire aims at "interpretive techniques"[2] that emphasize the metaphorical or analogical ways through which we experience reality. This can only be achieved through surrealist techniques aimed to both capture and initiate an enhanced reality. Representation for Apollinaire is interpretive and conceptual rather than photographically mimetic, but this interpretive activity too often takes place without the acknowledgment of its author. Technology has surpassed the theatre in photorealism since the camera and the cinema are ultimately better vehicles than theatre, marble, or canvas for representation.

As early as 1908, Apollinaire articulates the distinction between the singular realities experienced by the individual from objective reality. However, there is also a desire for transcendence or commune with the outside that accompanies the artist. Artists strive "to become inhuman,"[3] Apollinaire writes:

They painfully search for the trail to inhumanity, a trail found nowhere in nature.
This trail is truth and outside of it we recognize no reality.
But we will never discover reality once and for all. Truth will always be new.[4]

Truth and reality are synonymous, and truth is that which is constantly in flux. However, surrealist art strives for "true inhumanity,"[5] a merger of the nervous system and the body with a nonrepresentational, conceptual aesthetic object. Truth will always be new since a human-inhuman feedback loop undergoes endless configurations, metamorphoses, and mutations. The truth, identity, reality, and art become extensions of one another, bifurcating, knotting, and redefining themselves through perpetual modification. The ontic and noumenal cannot be known; instead, it should be interpreted and conceptualized ad infinitum. In a way, Apollinaire is seeking where the word breaks off but does not necessarily propose an exit strategy from the strange loop. While "Apollinaire's surrealism," Bohn writes, "is depicted . . . as an art which is to nature as the wheel is to the leg,"[6] it is Apollinaire's goal to ensure that we non-habitually commit such acts of surrealism, that is, we must *know* that technology is a nonrepresentational, conceptual work of art and that the inhuman truth/reality is itself a technology. However, the later twentieth-century and early twenty-first-century relationship with technology is amnesiac and automated; the merger with the inhuman has become habitual yet nonrepresentational. In short, it is a conceptual horror show.

The recent work of American contemporary conceptual horror author, B. R. Yeager, is sparse but remarkably promising. His work examines how the nervous system merges with seemingly innocuous technologies of the inhuman and considers the nonintuitive effects this merger yields. He is the author of, along with a number of short stories, two novels, *Amygdalatropolis* (2017) and *Negative Space* (2020), and a narrative deck of cards, *Pearl Death* (2020), a "book in a box" similar in form to B. S. Johnson's *The Unfortunates* (1969). His work is notable for its narrative, formalist, and thematic qualities: fragmented yet coherent, polyvocal yet anonymous, empathetic yet impersonal, domestic yet alien, grounded yet digital, embodied yet nebulous, identifiable but surrealist in Apollinaire's sense of the term. Such paradoxes may suggest cacophony, but Yeager's writing is sharply focused on the memetic qualities of psycho-ecology and the metamorphosing effects that digital technologies and the inhuman have on a sense of self in the early twenty-first century. His insight is nuanced and chilling; the psychopathologies engendered by the reductive zero-sum logic of the digital age in Yeager's work tend toward a conceptual horror whereby there is no way to avoid the merging of the nervous system with new media technologies—that self-reflexive digital labyrinth that self-generates with any hint of offering the human chance for escape or transcendence. His work is horror on a scale that is at once immensely cosmic and intimately private; however, whichever orientation of scale one wishes to pursue—the immense outside or the intimately inward—when digesting his fiction, one finds themselves, to their surprise, right where they began, though different. In a way, Yeager's fiction is the conceptual horror of the self-reflexivity that constitutes the very parameters of thought and being in the digital age. The psychological disruption and physical violence in his work challenge us to consider how the objectives of the mind, no matter how deranged, can make manifest objects in actuality.

Almost as if his work suggests that the digital is itself an occult force parasitically reconfiguring material actualities, Yeager tightens the psycho-ecological knot whereby the *outside* finds its way *inside* and, as a result, the inside (without recognition of this transaction) becomes part of the systematic ubiquity of the exterior. Matt Lee notes that Yeager's fiction is like "a malware carrying the consciousness of Georges Bataille,"[7] and this evaluation, with its emphasis on infection and digital memetics affecting the domain of the flesh, is perfectly on point. At the unique moment in history where the apparatus' functionalism is increasingly replacing agential decisions via automatism and digital autopoiesis, Yeager's fiction considers how human behavior's manifold illogical complexities become ensnared and reconfigured by a logical substratum of rigid, digital automatisms. Such reductionism—from the endless multiplicity of human desire to the rigidity of on-or-off digitality—delimits the libidinal and erotic, even poetic, multiplicity of humanness to the logical consequences of human beings' seemingly endless capacity for thanatotic cruelty. What is most horrific about Yeager's work is perhaps not the physical violence, however. Instead, the horror is conceptual in the sense that it loops back upon itself as an infinite knot, tangling the inside with the outside, and interweaving *as* reality, a reflexive process that Yeager calls "the wound." Robin McKay notes that "unlike the essentially animal responses of fear and terror, horror attaches especially to the conceptual abstraction and reflexivity attendant upon self-consciousness";[8] and, indeed, this conceptual abstraction is at the core of Yeager's work. The outside, the thought, is not necessarily that of the individual but, instead, the force of an abstract system of digitalized code determining an era's ambiance; yet, thinking reinstates the parasitized self as the site of horror. In short, it is the horror of the apparatus and the risk of *something absolutely* replacing the wheel that already replaced the leg.

While both Yeager's novels engage with the collapse of the inside (mind) and the outside (techno-divine, inhuman neutrality), *Amygdalatropolis* meticulously examines the psycho-ecological knotting and recursive, self-reflexive feedback loops of uniquely twenty-first-century cybernetics. Yeager notes that he wrote *Amygdalatropolis* "as a modern Gothic novel."[9] The novel's protagonist is an updated take on the trope of the mad relative hidden away in the attic—although the isolation, in this case, is self-imposed, and the protagonist's mother is tragically pleading for him to come out. There are conversations through cracks in the bedroom door, monstrous births, murder, incest, matricide, disembodied voices (anonymous messageboards), hallucinations, and encrypted languages (darknet encryption). Later, there are ghosts, self-mutilation, metamorphosis, uncanny mannequins (the protagonist, revolted and alienated from the experience of human touch, orders a RealDoll[10]), and oneiric realms (a mysterious online game and even the internet in general). The novel's setting takes place almost exclusively in a middle-class suburban home falling into disrepair: a setting that stands in for the Gothic trope of the ancestral mansion or medieval ruin. Furthermore, in truly Gothic fashion, the house is a metaphor for the world itself, and it houses the protagonist's body while the Computer houses aspects of the apparatus, and the apparatus houses—and eventually replaces—his nervous system. In this sense, it is reasonable to consider *Amygdalatropolis* a work of transgressive, conceptual cyber-Gothic horror.

The novel is formally fragmented and shifts between narrative modes multiple times on a single page throughout the novel. Mike Corrao writes that *Amygdalatropolis* "is a novel of meticulous design, made with a prose structure that can be broken down into three components, which Yeager constantly shifts between. Each page is often occupied by at least two of the different forms of writing."[11] Of these three modes of writing, the first is the most straightforward. It consists of representing the physical world. This is where the protagonist sits in isolation in his filthy room, addicted to messageboards on the deep web, ignores his mother's pleas for him to come out of his room, where he creeps like a worm or a centipede through the empty halls, and enacts forms of violence against himself and others. The second mode of writing is messageboard correspondences, almost exclusively on the protagonist's favorite anonymous forum, /1404er/. This is a space of unfettered psychopathy, hedonism, violence, nihilism, and political reactionism; all users, including the protagonist, adopt a uniquely digital form of authorial impersonality: online anonymity. The messages' content is almost exclusively revolting; however, it is also unclear what messages are naïve nihilist posturing and represent the diegetic level-crossing between online violence and enacted, physical violence.[12] "Yeager utilizes this layer as another author might utilize setting," Carrao aptly notes. He continues, writing that "in the abstract qualities of the voice, in the outward confessions of violent desire, a room is created. One made of mouths or vocal cords. There is always something to be said, regardless of how unimportant or narcissistic it may be. As if these—practically—nameless voices must speak in order to perpetuate their existence."[13] These two modes of narrative, the physical and the digital or virtual stand-in for physical space and, like a strange loop, begin to collapse into one another. The *outside* logic, the rigidity of code, the valueless neutrality of digitality comes to parasitize the physical world (particularly, the protagonist's nervous system). The third mode of narrative, however, is the most elusive and mysterious. Written entirely in italics, Yeager introduces a strange, fragmentary, and poetic "voice" that seems to, in nebulous ways, comment on but also guides the other two conventional modes of narration. Carrao remarks that this third italicized mode of narration is emancipated from time and place and "feels cosmic and unidentifiable" and introduces "a rather abstract space" in which "the voice of the text cannot quite be placed. It is spoken as if by a cleric drifting through the void" with a "distant certainty in the way it speaks."[14] In a sense, Yeager utilizes this third mode to represent the abstract space of reflexivity itself; it is the voice of the unknown and the apparatus' inarticulations. It brings into actuality the posturing of violence, sadism, and psychopathy of the forums, and it makes "The Computer become . . . mundane, pathetic, and grotesque" and shift the book's focus from, as Carraos notes, "exaggerated realism to a metaphysical wandering."[15] And, indeed, the parasitism in the novel is a paradoxical one; this is not simply the voice of the Computer (Yeager uses the uppercase to imply the Computer's pseudo-agency); it is the articulations of a *divine neutrality*. This is the voice, dramatized in Gothic fashion, of the rigidity, neutrality, valueless, absolute inhumanity of the *outside*: the apparatus.

As a result, what we find is a collapse of the materiality of the world with the unconscious chaotics of word *into itself*, resulting in a tumbling, knotting singularity (the invisible, intangible, coded procedures of digital and virtual objects with the wordly realm of mind). Yeager's fiction examines the collapsing distinction between thought and the constitutive parasitism and memetic qualities of code on thought and the intangible, rigid, rule-governed, but inhumanly complex outside. As a result, the role of individual agency is delimited, illusory, or absent altogether, and the force driving the collapsing recursive loop is not human; it is something else beyond an individual's ability for comprehension. Yeager claims that this unknowability is central to his approach to fiction. "I suppose one of my methods for 'making [the book] good,'" he writes, "is incorporating open-ended questions . . . I had a sticky note attached to my monitor that read DON'T EXPLAIN ANYTHING. That's kind of my guiding principle, especially in horror, because nothing is less scary than knowing what's going on."[16] Yeager aims to have this experience link with, or parasitize with, the readerly experience as it denaturalizes the invisible processes affecting neoliberalism's hijacking, shaping, labeling, and limiting of the self. Doing so requires the dictum that nothing is more frightening than not knowing what is going on to be made manifest outside the book's diegetic space.

In a way, the horror of not being able to grasp the constitutive context of a narrative also makes manifest an acknowledgment that the identification one feels with Yeager's horror fiction is indeed that *knowing that you cannot fully know* is the epistemological norm of everyday life. Again, such provocation is not didactic, and Yeager is understandably hesitant to speak of his intent when writing fiction; however, "I don't think that I'm actively generating original concepts," he writes, "and if my books are generating original concepts, I don't think I can take credit for them. That's all on the reader."[17] He continues:

> literature can (should?) act as a catalyst for creating concepts, and I do believe that is something I aim for . . . Not because I feel specifically qualified to create work that catalyzes the creation of concepts, but that tends to be the work that interests and sticks with me. I'm always more interested in art that is more concerned with providing questions than answers; that's evocative rather than explanatory. I like the idea of art as an inductive force, that doesn't carry a direct message, but induces an understanding beyond the author's or even the text's control. That's what I think is most important about highly interpretative work, that the reader is able to have an intensely unique experience, discreet from other readers' experiences.[18]

As indeterminacy acts against standardization, categorization, and quantification of readerly response, Yeager's conceptual horror bifurcates and operates in ways that resist interpretive delimitation. In doing so, his work is contrary to the formative procedures of the neoliberal self. Rather than simply creating genre fiction to escape the everyday, Yeager asks us to also consider the horrific banality of everyday life in the twenty-first century. "The more questions you answer for the reader," he writes, "the more you're pushing the reader out of the experience. There needs to be room for the reader to resolve the questions on their own, for them to bring their own lives and experiences to the work in order for the work to remain interesting."[19] Yeager dismantles authorship's authority toward the ends of emphasizing readerly agency, the very thing which psychopolitics and neuro-totalitarian neoliberal technologies aim to manufacture, standardize, optimize, and mobilize for *their* own ends.

The recursivity of horror in Yeager's fiction is, as a result, not mechanistic but parasitic. "Yeager's . . . straightforwardness with the worst opens before us the abyss of nothingness which we, in turn must open ourselves to," writes Edia Connole in the introduction to *Amygdalatropolis*, "if we are to fully reap the rewards of this brilliant text that attempts . . . to engender in writing and in the reader the dissolution of subject and object that is inner experience.

Through this dissolution communication occurs and a new community emerges ... between Yeager and his projected readers, and more problematically, perhaps, between those readers [and Yeager's protagonist]."[20] Not only does the reader consider Yeager's investigation into the ways that inhuman and incomprehensible forces from outside find their way *in* via the diegetic space of the page, his fiction, instead, pushes this conceit further by asking the reader to consider the degree to which this is a ubiquitous phenomenon in the twenty-first century. This experience is not simply one of interpreting fiction but of fiction interpreting the reader.

When asked about the evocative and striking image chosen for the cover of *Amygdalatropolis*, Yeager remarks that the image is "a public domain photograph of parasitic worms bursting out of some intestines—emblematic of the Wound. I figured people should know what they're getting into."[21] There are a few things worth noting about Yeager's response. First, the fact that the image is public domain is, beyond the obvious choice that so many independent authors and publishers would choose for financial and legal purposes, that its fair use makes it widely available to anyone with access to the internet. Second, this wide availability of both the image and the apparatus which hosts the digital image (the internet) reminds us not only what the reader is getting into but also, according to the logic of the parasite, what is getting into the reader. This bidirectional collapse and rupture, or inwardly and outwardly recursive spiraling, is ultimately a gesture to provoke thinking and interpretation by denaturalizing the internet's ready-at-handness and modern neoliberal technologies of psychical control. This is what Yeager means by the Wound. "Ultimately," he writes,

> I'm concerned with the Wound, and the implications of the Wound, and you can't have a wound without sentient beings... The Wound tends to come from something beyond the self—whether it's a physical weapon, or trauma inflicted by others, or the acquisition of new knowledge (Adam and Eve becoming self-aware, and that self-awareness forcing them to comprehend that the Garden is not paradise, and merely a place they inhabit), etc. And existence (and by extension, modern life) is filled with instruments that cause physical and psychic wounds. What's interesting to me about the Wound is that it forces the subject to adapt to it—it molds the subject in some way.[22]

This violent psycho-ecological merger with something beyond the self, though ripe for abstract philosophical horror in the digital age, is something that Yeager approaches via affect. The Wound, rather than a knowable, observable, or quantifiable phenomenon or process, is, instead, that injurious otherness that is always outside semantic and ontological access. While this may sound like philosophical horror, and he acknowledges his admiration for conceptual horror authors like Thomas Ligotti and Gary J. Shipley, Yeager distinguishes his fiction on the following grounds: "I don't think my writing is originating from a primarily philosophical place or at least a deliberately philosophical place."[23] Instead, Yeager aims for the reader to *feel with* the Wound; moreover, his work suggests that such affect that may contribute a degree of indeterminacy and contingency injected into the contemporary episteme.

Eschewing the philosophical lens of Batailles, Ligotti, and Shipley, Yeager engages with that which is intuitive, hallucinatory, experiential, and affective; indeed, any "philosophical implications," he writes of his fiction, "are only apparent after the fact."[24] Rather than fiction with a thesis, Yeager provokes thinking and interpretation by offering illogical, fragmented, decontextualized patterns that, according to their own operations, will provoke interpretation from others: "what I'm more or less trying to accomplish," he writes, "is document what I've seen, experienced, or felt (even—or especially—if those experiences branch into hallucination) to the best of my ability, and then find the patterns in them. Then—ideally-something else can interpret those patterns, because proper interpretation is beyond my knowledge and ability. It's like I'm trying to create entrails for a haruspex to divine."[25] Because Yeager's work examines the parasitic ways that the digital experience collapses the inside and the outside, writing as the creation of entrails operates as a visceral, affective, and intuitive confrontation with the rigid logic of code and digitality by offering a perpendicular intersection of surreal, occult illogic as confrontation.

In this sense, Yeager's work is a pointed effort at examining "the ways modern technologies—seemingly innocuous technologies—can engender mass and interpersonal violence or disguise mass and interpersonal violence."[26] This claim may seem fundamentally Ballardian because, like Ballard, Yeager aims to bring to light the secret logic of media technologies. While Yeager admits that he cannot claim Ballard as a direct influence and has limited exposure to the latter's work, the Ballardian nevertheless pervades most investigation into the role that media technologies play in what Yeager identifies as "the suffocating sense of inevitable collapse—a collapse that also feels insane because no one seems to recognize it."[27] This collapse can be as broad as a complete social and political collapse and as intimate and private as a complete mental and psychical collapse into inhumanity. While Ballard records the psychical collapse into architecture, freeways, motor car crashes, and twenty-four-hour news cycles, Yeager draws from the twenty-first century's media catastrophes: the recursive and contingent relationship that tightens and accelerates the knot between the psyche and digitality. However, like Ballard, Yeager's fiction has an overwhelming sense, tone, and atmosphere of impending doom to the degree that it implies some kind of looming collapse as an absolute Event. Ballard notes that dissecting bodies as a medical student was one of the most formative experiences in the development of the role secret architectures of the body and mind play in his narratives; Yeager may be more accurately described, not as the autopsist of the twentieth century, but as a twenty-first-century haruspex engaged in extispicy, that is, a digital era mystic rather than a communications era clinician.

Entrails belong on the inside, but fiction as extispicy exposes how the inside can escape, unravel, and reveal. Once the entrails are spilled, the reader-as-haruspex comes to interpret the patterning: the inside escapes, goes outside, and consequently has effects on the minds of others. While new media technologies parasitize the mind, just as worms parasitize the intestines, the process of unraveling the collapse of inner and outer allows readers to experience or see the psychopolitical, neuro-totalitarian, and psycho-ecological knots as they are inherently meaningless but affectively menacing. Yeager offers this occult metaphor as a way of confronting the seemingly innocuous logical protocol of digital culture via illogic, intuition, and irrationality. After all, to examine digital culture by engaging with the procedurality of digitality, one loses the fuzziness of interpretation and, instead, becomes complicit in the calculative, quantitative, and rigid protocols of the digital automation itself.

Part of Yeager's goal, then, is to demonstrate that the self is itself not an inherent entity *in itself*, but instead, the self is perception and the sum of experience that originates without. "A personality," he writes, "emerges by developing a context of both self and the not-self. The person develops an internal experience, and the only way to let that experience outside of their self is to use inadequate and clumsy tools—speech, gesture, text, as well as art. Communication. But communication is not the same thing as the internal experience—it's a crude rendering of internal experience."[28] The crude experience of communication reveals to us that to communicate is to impart information and make it public, to make the inner-thought or the private common, to, as Connole suggests, engage an emerging community. Alongside informing, communication is about uniting and joining together by being informed. To communicate, we become part of the contingency of recursivity, able to affect psycho-ecological loops just as the loops affect us via instantaneous reconfiguration. To communicate is to become common, to become public, and to join with the exteriority of world and word: "We are the sum of our experience," Yeager writes, "and the majority of those experiences come from outside us (and to contradict that somewhat, those experience are also generated by our senses, which exist and act part from our 'self'/consciousness."[29]

Yeager is thus apt to imply that the self is perhaps engaged in a recursive loop that ultimately operates more forcefully and non-agentially from without: "If you think of a person as an antenna," he writes, and they're picking up bits of frequency from all over, and then building a context based from there. That's what the 21st century feels like to me, for better or worse. And there are theories of consciousness that literalize this concept—that consciousness does not emerge from the nervous and endocrine systems, but rather it is received from another source outside of the body. The nervous system merely acts as an antenna.[30]

Yeager's fiction aims to consider the self, indeed the digital and algorithmic self, as a kind of Wi-Fi receiver, and the experience of communication as that which feeds back into the self-optimizing procedurality of Big Data. To communicate, according to the calculative logic of internet technologies—to engender or disguise mass and interpersonal violence—to make public the inner experience, simply optimizes Big Data. Magical thinking, the reader-as-haruspex interpreting in spilled insides, epistemologically reenchants and confronts algorithmic rigidity with illogical excess, desire, and proclamation of alternative forms of agency in an era of, not mechanization, but algorithmic determinism. The magical is akin to the fictive and poetic; it eludes logic, magic's often rigid rules often have no explanation, elude rationality, and strive for multiplicities within an immanent, infinitely non-technological constituent. The magical reenchants the recursivity of horror and loosens the knot that fastens the inside to the outside.

Despite the apparent abstract qualities of Yeager's style and the conceptual qualities of his thematics, his fiction is grounded in narrative and character; he notes that he is "more interested in mood and suggestion than plot and exposition."[31] He continues that he has

> always been interested in storytelling, regardless of the medium. I wrote a lot as a child—short stories but also concepts for movies, video games, and tabletop role playing games. Throughout high school and my early 20s, all my friends were musicians, so I more or less abandoned formal storytelling in favor of being in bands. But even then I was trying (and ultimately failing) to tell stories with the music, or create an atmosphere that suggested a story. I was still writing—mostly poetry and song lyrics, but I didn't fully return to writing fiction until my late twenties (specifically mid-2013). I was always interested in horror—with books it started with R.L. Stine and Christopher Pike, then Edgar Allan Poe, then Lovecraft and so on. But the dam really broke when my mom handed down her copy of [Katherine Dunn's] *Geek Love*. I was maybe 12. That book made me realize that content forbidden in other mediums was permitted—and even celebrated—in literature. That probably set the tone for everything I've written so far.[32]

This permissiveness allows Yeager to examine the generalized submission of the twenty-first-century psyche to the illogical topologies of media technologies and, at the same time, the disrupting and limiting potentialities permitted by the underlying procedurality of, in the twenty-first century, ubiquitous digital media. In a sense, the tension in Yeager's work comes from the struggle between possibility, nonexchangeability, and the bifurcating potentialities of fiction with the regimented and rigid logistics of a society governed and constituted combinatorialism. The poetics of permissiveness behind Yeager's work aim at excess and against delimitation: details fray at the edges as an outside force attempts to shape and contain, potentialities emerge as neoliberal constitutive logic presses back with the tyranny of one-or-zero. The fragmentary style of *Amygdalatropolis* is remarkably effective for this and provides an appropriate mode of representing a supermodern state of mind characterized by the conflict arising from superimposed excess and rigid delimitation. In his experimental novel, *The Atrocity Exhibition* (1970), for example, Ballard discusses how he wanted to present the surrealist logic of the mediascape of the 1960s. Something similar operates in Yeager's work; except here it is not the merging with architecture and centralized, standardizing broadcast media of the twentieth century but, instead, with the ultimate abstract spaces—the "no there there" of Wi-Fi signals and digitality—of the twenty-first century. The internet does not allow for concrete orientation: its pure functionality, inhuman emptying of value, stylistic repetitiveness, and thanatotic abstraction merge with the psyche and create a new kind of human being with novel psychopathologies.

Indeed, *Amygdalatropolis* expresses a digital poetics of impersonality via anonymity. Appropriately so, the fragmented formalism of Yeager's work is in response to his own experience of the internet as an abstract space: with *Amygdalatropolis*, the impersonality and anonymity of the internet affect a notable influence on the thematics of the novels, and he writes that he "feels that the internet is [his] biggest influence, especially on a structural level."[33] Corrao notes that "what fascinates me about [Yeager's] depiction of these spaces is the kind of transcendent atmosphere" that Yeager fills them with;[34] it is this transcendent atmosphere that ultimately lends itself to a complex entrapment-*as*-engagement. Yeager writes that

> my experiences with the internet in my teens (this is a pre-Facebook, pre-MySpace, pre-Friendster, AIM and LiveJournal dominated era) felt incredibly transcendental. I was excruciatingly shy as a teen, lots of anxiety, had a lot of trouble with reading social cues, but I could communicate decently through text, so communicating via anonymous messageboards and instant messenger felt more natural to me. And there was a fantastical element to it, where you could cultivate an aesthetic and identity that felt more in line with how you saw yourself than how you were in defined by flesh and blood . . . these were

intensely important and formative experiences to me, and I try to capture the magical aspect of them as best I can, though it never quite feels sufficient. And I feel like these spaces need to be at least acknowledged, if not explored, if you're writing about the present day.[35]

In the looping, knotted logistics of contemporary experience, it is reasonable to acknowledge such abstract spaces of communication in fiction. The increasingly homogenizing and standardizing social forces of digital media at once reject the very semantics of anonymity while pressing intense profiling of the individual to the degree that they become an anonymous source of metadata. Yeager writes that "I did want *Amygdalatropolis* to somewhat reflect the experience of being online, of scrolling through and between content," noting that "having multiple threads alternating, separated by left and right text alignment, as though they were separate tabs or windows open on a desktop" could intimate this experience.[36] Beyond the disjointed and fragmentary messageboard-style communication, the internet also becomes descriptive of an alternate topology for reality, one with its own calculative, rigid, and inhuman truth. "A lot of *Amygdalatropolis* more or less grew out of observation. When I started writing it, I was pretty immersed in those messageboards, trying to better understand them."[37] Transliterating the online experience to the medium of the novel is consistent with the permissiveness central to Yeager's work. However, the internet in *Amygdalatropolis* does not simply operate as the medium of communication, but itself becomes a world governed by inhuman procedurality of code that *hosts* words but reconfigures language's operating force of constituting mind, identity, and self. The self is, functionally, in the process of self-annihilation.

As a result, Yeager appropriately resists naming the protagonist of *Amygdalatropolis*. In doing so, the protagonist goes under an anonymous pseudonym that conforms to the naming all users of an anonymous messageboard on the deep web: /1404er/: "/1404er/ spent time at a few of the boards, but his favorite was /1404er/. The place he got his name from. Everyone was /named /1404er/ there."[38] The effect of this anonymity is an intensification of the recursive emergence of a new kind of human being. While McLuhan suggests that *Homo electronicus* is the human of the masses—that is, technologies like print, radio, and television help one unite with others at the expense of inner-life and privacy—Han identifies the digital subject, which /1404er/ is exemplary, as *Homo digitalis*. *Homo digitalis*, Han writes, "expresses himself anonymously, as a rule he has a profile—and he works ceaselessly at optimizing it. Instead of being 'nobody,' he is insistently somebody exhibiting himself and vying for attention . . . *Homo digitalis* often takes the stage anonymously. He is not a *nobody* but a somebody—an *anonymous somebody*."[39] Such anonymous somebodies, as in their extreme manifestation in *Amygdalatropolis*, naively imagine their absolute transcendence into the nihilistic neutrality of the digital; a move that is fundamentally naïve as they misunderstand the fact that, once fully merged with digitality, one cannot be an anonymous, impersonal somebody but, instead, will cease to *be* absolutely. "I see /1404er/ and his peers as people clumsily struggling toward this sense of pure nihilism, of this dissolution of the self, but failing miserably," writes Yeager. "Because they're not engaged in a true nihilism," he continues, "they are still concerned with how they are perceived by others (even under the cover of anonymity), chasing this idea of being warriors who lay waste to the weak and what have you, of pushing the world and feeling it push back. A teenage conception of nihilism, which makes sense, given the subjects."[40] Concomitantly, *Homo digitalis*, Han writes, "has 'no character, in the original sense of the word, which comes from the Greek *charassein*, to engrave, to scratch, to imprint'";[41] however, at the conclusion of the novel, /1404er/'s full transformation into digitality results in his becoming digital tendrils of information incapable of imprinting its name.

Prior to the transformation, however, as an anonymous somebody, /1404er/ can carefully cultivate his impersonality by abstracting himself from the material world: "electronic media such as radio *assemble* human beings," writes Han, "in contrast, digital media *isolate* them."[42] In this sense, /1404er/ not only isolates himself but also tightens the knot between his body and his desired digitality: a transition and metamorphosis from the flesh to information but one that will never be fulfilling. Part of the central desire /1404er/ has, however, is ironically shared among others who share the same space and name as him: with the transition away from the body and into information, they wish to eliminate feeling and, in particular, the ability to feel both *as* and *for* others. The transition is a kind of absolute isolation: indeed, /1404er/ attempts to explain his obsession to his mother by referring her to *hikikomori*[43]—individuals in Japan, though also a global phenomenon, who engage in extreme forms of social isolation often accompanied by addictions to media technologies—as a kind of bad faith explanation. His isolation is expressly metaphysical and transformative, and his quest becomes emblematic of self-annihilation toward aggressively dismantling the very possibility of empathy. As a result, /1404er/ is incapable of understanding his mother's constant worry, refuses to visit his father in the hospital as the latter is dying of cancer,[44] and ultimately skips his father's funeral altogether.[45] If he is nobody, he does not need to feel; if he is everybody, he has no unique familial, affective, or ethical relations. "This characteristic of everyone sharing the same name is very reflective of how the anonymous messageboards I observed functioned," Yeager writes. "The anonymity derived from taking an indistinct name is really a practicality—a survival measure—because engaging in aberrant behavior[46] for an extended amount of time can only be done in secret and/or anonymity."[47] Rather than aiming at the transcendence of the body into immateriality whereby the metaphysics of individuality, agency, and humanity become transformed but optimized, /1404er/'s trajectory is ultimately one that puzzlingly aims at self-annihilation *communally* with other self-annihilators: "*We kept separate the names. Names were refused. Names beget annihilation, like how hope ensures castration.*"[48] The teleology here gestures toward some kind of impossible transcendence that leaves no scratch, imprint, or trace behind—an impossibility since, as the reader experiences, his inherited suburban home gradually falls into disuse, neglect, and ruin alongside his self.

So, accompanying /1404er/'s dissolution of body necessitates the gradual replacement of language's sculpting of mind and identity. The delimitation of language and its dissociation for embodied communication completes the absolute psychopathic neutrality of digitality by the subtraction of feeling for another: "*Language formed moat around our commonwealth. Words standing as close enough to nothing; scratches of symbol. Cavernous and quasi sub-masonic. Words not meant for ears, or paper or posterity. That was our strength and right to prosper.*"[49] The status of language on the messageboards, then, is arguably not communicative but, like an extra layer of immaterial skin, defensive. With language, the risk of identity, empathy, poetry, and meaning are too pressing. So, the /1404er/s aim for language divorced from world, duration, and meaning: words standing close enough to nothing. But the power balance between the human and the digital is not equal, and the feedback loop, the recursive input-output process, favors the digital as it neither senses nor rests. What the digital offers /1404er/, however, is a gate to nihilism; yet, his ability to face and merge with *no thing* is met without *experiencing* transcendence. In short, /1404er/ is not prepared for actual nihility—that *no thing* of the apparatus that only haunts the atmosphere and mood of the novel but, appropriately, remains unrepresented.

Yeager distinguishes between the nihilism that /1404er/ seeks on the boards and the digital nihilism that parasitizes him at the novel's conclusion. /1404er/ "transcends his humanity, in that his violent/transgressive impulses (which are incredibly human) give way to a sort of divine neutrality, as he immerses into an existence comprised only of images, without judgment or broader context—here, he is merely being, rather than reacting," writes Yeager. "The self," he continues, "annihilates, and he transcends to reach a true nihilism—that divine neutrality—in contrast to the false nihilism (which was really just reactionism and hedonism) he'd been chasing through the boards."[50] While /1404er/'s reactionism and hedonism yearn for nihilism to be simply an inversion of ethical and social responsibility for the anonymous somebody, the nihilism he encounters—or that fully inhabits him—ultimately configures an absolute, neutral, valueless anonymous nobody. Connole writes that "making present (*poesis, ousia, techne*) of being/structure/self in *Amygdalatropolis* is knowingly—and . . . masterfully—the making of excess and excess which bears a very particular relation to nothingness, and more specially, then, a self-understanding of the standpoint of absolute nothingness."[51] The striving for the point where word breaks off is never fully represented in the novel, of course, but the transformation from human to inhuman necessitates that one signifies nothing. In a quest for transcendence through transgression, /1404er/ becomes procedural neutrality: a concretization of valueless, impersonal functionality.

As an "anonymous somebody" signifying nothing, /1404er/ (alongside all other /1404er/s), however, endeavors to be, at once nobody and everybody, no thing and everything. *Homo digitalis* is not simply nobody and everybody, but also *without* a body and *without* others. For Flusser, *Homo digitalis* is characterized by the shedding of the hands in favor of the fingers. Rather than working with their hands, *Homo digitalis* engages exclusively with digital apparatuses and does not need hands. There is a particular ecstasy to this transcendence for Flusser as it emancipates the individual from manual labor. As a result of this atrophying, fingers will come to replace hands; one will no longer need to handle the physical burden of work but, instead, will be endlessly engaged with immaterial, informational leisure. Yeager takes this further, however. It is not simply his hands that will be replaced by fingers, but the body as a whole: "*If age allowed us a billion years, thick skins would grow over our orifices and our hands would dissolve to stumps. Our blood would shrink so thin as to fall from our pores unbridled. We would grow from pools and breathe fluid through our conjunctiva. The next species may hover, making better use of the air than we could've possibly conceived.*"[52] /1404er/'s cybernetic transfer, however, is never fully realized as transcendence. From the first page of the novel, /1404er/'s becoming *Homo digitalis* is underway: "he always put the Computer to sleep before going to bed. Its boards would click and stir through the night behind its greyed-out face, like a yawn or stretch. He couldn't sleep with it turned off all the way. Now they were both awake."[53] There is an asymmetry here worth noting: while /1404er/ is sleeping, the Computer continues to operate behind its blank monitor. Unlike a human, it does not sleep, dream, and wake; it is either on or off. /1404er/ devoutly aims to merge fully *as* digitality and, given his incessant and aggressive denial of his mother's affection to the degree of plotting matricide, and his fantasies of a digital origin: "/1404er/ was born from video."[54] This digital "birth" then ushers him into the digital realm, and the relations between body and digital information become entangled and confused:

> His way into the threads. His eyes translating light from a stream. Before his eyes translated light from a stream he was only a person. Before the stream

was a stream, it was a file. A VCHD, and prior to that just light reflected and refracted through systems of lenses. A copy of a living thing. Three living things and a fourth, all massed of matter and invisible crackle. But /1404er/ was only around to witness the stream. The stream was a sequence of frames; LED light, flat and stuttered with buffer. Stuttered less than an eye can perceive . . .

The frames floated in the air, through the room. /1404er/breathed in, letting them breach; letting them tumor through his lobes. Adding weight to his gravity. A layer of fat wrapped tight in his chest. A buffer.

He made the stream repeat, over and over, always breathing. Always letting it breach and fill his space, adding meat and corpulence to his form.⁵⁵

The digital stream adds "meat" and "corpulence" to /1404er/'s body as a kind of perversion of common sense: that the body is that which animates the machine. The "layer of fat" in his chest is polysemous: it is at once that which buffers his "heart" from experiencing empathy, *and* it is the digital buffering—the stuttering, pausing playback experienced when playing a file before its download is complete—of /1404er/'s transference into the inhuman. Meanwhile, the *digital itself*—the collective /1404er/—seems to speak of its own parasitic transformation:

> *Bodies and teeth emerged of whatever we gnawed. Our bodies and teeth were nothing before then. No calcium or discernible texture until we learned to devour others' skins, stretching them taught over our gums. The novel tactility. Our outgrowing of biology; splitting tongues and pissing over the last umbilical cords. The ends of grasslands and woods and laws of woman and man*⁵⁶

to that moment when "it didn't matter so much anymore whether the Computer was turned off all the way."⁵⁷ However, this transference of individuality into impersonal procedurality suggests that the psycho-ecological knot's tightening accelerates to the degree that psyche and techne become indecipherable. Such a process is not only preoccupied with the displacement of the body by digitality, but it is also concerned with place and orientation: a process that operates *in* and *as* a digitalized non-place.

Marc Augé's formulation of non-place suggests that it is something outside signification, time, relation, and value: "If a place can be defined as relational, historical and concerned with identity," he writes, "then a space which cannot be defined as relational, or historical, or concerned with identity will be a non-place."⁵⁸ "The hypothesis advanced here," Augé continues, "is that supermodernity produces non-places, meaning spaces which are not themselves anthropological places and . . . do not integrate the earlier places."⁵⁹

Generally, non-places are civic nodes of transfer, logistics, transience, and transport. However, Han writes that

> the world of *Homo digitalis* evinces an entirely different topology. Spaces such as sports arenas and amphitheaters—that is, sites where masses meet—are foreign to this world. The digital inhabitants of the Net do not assemble. They lack the interiority of assembly that would bring forth a *we*. They form a *gathering without assembly*—a crowd without interiority, without a soul or spirit. Above all, they are isolated, scattered *hikikomori* sitting alone in front of a screen.[60]

The topologies of such non-places are quintessentially the spaces that occupy *Amygdalatropolis*: "To Augé's list of non-places we could add cyberspace itself: the internet and other manifestations of networked digital media," write Jay David Bolter and Richard Grusin.[61] "Cyberspace," they continue, "is not, as some assert, a parallel universe. It is not a place of escape from contemporary society, or indeed from the physical world. It is rather a non-place, with many of the same characteristics as other highly mediated non-places."[62] Like the supermodern city, the internet is an inhuman space that does not have a historical referent; humans use it, but it also uses, constitutes, and absorbs the human. Behind the screen, beyond the hardware, a kind of parallel world awaits users:

> the Computer was a lot of things, but for /1404er/ the Computer was mostly the boards. The new town commons, stretched wide enough to fit the Earth's multitudes, though few thousands ever visited. . . . Thousands of boards, comprised of thread. Meccas poured down the Computer's face, and numbers of nameless becoming many and monument. Communion; devotion.[63]

This is a confrontation with time and space *themselves* as preconditions of experience but toward the ends of the preconditions of non-experience. Rather than human desire merging with machine or supermodern architecture, with the supermodern digital, we have the human merging with number, code, algorithms, that is, with monuments and religious devotion to nonmaterial, with *no-thing*, *no-place*, and absolute neutrality—communion and devotion to the divine neutrality of the apparatus.

This absence narratively affects the intimacy the reader experiences with the narrative as much as the narrative itself constitutes an imaginary space. "For me, atmosphere always takes precedence over everything else," Yeager writes. "My favorite books are the ones that induce a sort of psychedelic state, and that's what I aimed for with both [*Negative Space*] and *Amygdalatropolis*."[64] Accordingly, Yeager's work suggests a metaphorical environment that engages metanoia. The work produces diegetic level-crossing of the inside and the outside as the very experience of a fragmented source of identity in the digital age. The psycho-ecological merging of thought and digital spaces ultimately takes place in such a way that the technological embeds itself in consciousness to the most aggressive degree while thought, largely unaware of the self-reflexive process, systemically welcomes it. While the process of the procedurally functional inhabiting the agential largely operates in ways that are at once beneficial and benign (whereby, consequently, the agential feeds back into the procedure to optimize a reflexive relationship between technology and human), there is also the more insidious, even thanatotically transcendent, desire to transfer mind, self, and agency over to inhuman procedurality. While this shift is not transcendent in a literal sense since systematics cannot technically escape systemics, it does disrupt any sense of homeostasis or balance between technology and the sense ratios. In other words, the desire for machinic or procedural transcendence into pure functionality becomes a particularly unique form of twenty-first-century psychopathy. Even more literalized than any Futurist dream of a machinic man, the radical ambivalence of the neurological merging with the inhuman topologies of digitality and the supermodern mediascape of the twenty-first century brings with it a conceptual horror of the liminal whereby human agency asymptotically approaches the inhuman (though, as *Amygdalatropolis* ends, agency merges with the neutral inhuman). Such a shift toward escaping, or finding where the linguistic self breaks off, at once marks the discovery that one cannot shift to the *outside* but instead, like a strange loop, finds that the *outside* is now, in fact, inside.

This marks a specific category of horror: an abstract dread engendered most explicitly by the very fact that it abstracts from the sense ratios the parameters of the sense ratios themselves. Conceptual horror is a kind of cosmic horror in the lineage of H. P. Lovecraft and may be simply summed up with the sentiment, it is best not to know what is *out there*. George Sieg writes that the "purest form of conceptual horror is the realization of inescapable identity with the monstrous perception—the concept—which is both the object and the source of horror. Yet, when that object of horror is also the subject, the instrument of perception, wave upon wave of self-referential, cascading horror is the result."[65] That is, the source of horror and the sense of horror become the same; the fear of the *outside* finds itself, a priori, already *inside*. Such dread ultimately reshapes the will to signify nothing since, to do so, the abyss-as-signified and abyss-as-referent finds itself embedded in the subject rather than in the beyond. The abyss, the void, the beyond, the inhuman, the apparatus—whatever one wishes to call it—is essential to the mood, atmosphere, and topology of Yeager's work. It haunts both the physical and psychical spaces of his fiction's otherwise mundane setting: small American cities and lower- and middle-class suburban domestic settings.

Negative space and black holes seem to lurk in the background (or even *as* the constitutive atmosphere) of both of Yeager's two novels: the two concepts get a special mention in *Amygdalatropolis* (and *Negative Space* is, of course, the title of his second novel). Negative space and black holes serve as productive metaphors for that which is outside epistemology. The black hole, as articulated by Graham Harman, is that immense "absolute object" than can never be known, experienced, or seen directly: a black hole's "gravity," Harman writes,

> is so strong that no information can escape, hence we never see the black hole or have direct access to anything about it. . . . The fact that we cannot encounter the black hole directly does not mean that we cannot speak about it. . . . Numerous properties of black holes can be inferred, despite our inability to receive direct information from them. . . . Even if the effects of the black hole or the object may be what alerts us to their existence, these objects are not identical with their sum total of effects.[66]

The only way it can be said to exist at all is how it affects visible and knowable phenomena around it. Its absolute presence is only meaningful by the absolute absence of experiencing it directly. The haunting of negative space and black holes in Yeager's work attests to his anti-epistemological project. He writes that he has

> a sort of instinctual attachment to the term "negative space," both on a purely aesthetic level as well as to the notion of emptiness, or perceived emptiness, or inverted space . . . I love the idea of the black hole as a metaphor for the forces at work in [*Amygdalatropolis* and *Negative Space*]—forces that can only be "observed" through the effect they have on what is around them. I think something that is often taken for granted is that the sciences are not reality—the sciences only provide models of reality that are inevitably very limited (regardless of how advanced they become). Obviously this does not negate the value of the sciences, but I think it is a common mistake to view scientific knowledge as reality itself, rather than a model of reality . . . my reasoning for having an anti-epistemological slant in these books is . . . to drive that aspect of unknowing even further.[67]

Indeed, the closest thing we get to that the unknowing of the outside are the italicized passages that appear to be the digital itself transliterated into speech and metamorphosing into character:

> *And we and the century became pubescent and scratched out our names with fingernails until our features smeared blank and indiscernible. We printed our*

> dicks out in plastic and chased women from their cities and homes. When our eyes peered their mouths we could process neither tooth nor tongue. Only negative space. A black hole. When we leered at their skin it was flesh of balloon.[68]

At the dawn of the twenty-first century, a new kind of monster is emerging: one that cannot be observed directly but requires human beings for habitation in order to expand its presence as a balloon of flesh. While /1404er/ strives to complete his transformation into an anonymous somebody by scratching out his name until his features are blank and indiscernible, it is, instead, the inhuman *digitality* that itself is procedurally becoming-character by engraving, scratching, and imprinting its names on materiality as if marking is emergence.

Part of the horror that informs Yeager's work is predicated on a capturing and representing a psychogram-as-sigil of the psycho-ecology that merges media technologies and the self in the twenty-first century. However, Yeager notes that just as his work is not explicitly philosophical, it is likewise only contingently political; certainly, he avoids didactics and polemics. This is a particular strength for meditating upon the United States' psychopolitics at the time of the two novels' publication. As a result, Yeager does not explicitly address the rise of the online far-right as the stooges of neofeudalism, neoreaction (NRx), and techno fascism though these tendencies certainly appear in the messageboards of *Amygdalatropolis*. From "general Mussolini worship,"[69] to affectless celebrations of mass catastrophe;[70] from xenophobia and praise for Hitler and Marie Le Pen to anti-scrupulosity and Homophobia ("yeah go kill yourself moralfaggot,"[71] "why are STEM fags so obsessed with colonizing Mars?");[72] from anti-Semitic conspiracies like referring to Google as "jewgle"[73] and referring to physics as "a trick contrived by the jews in order to keep the Aryan people down"[74] to hyperbolic praise for oppressive authorities like security guards using excessive force against the poor;[75] from white supremacy and racial purity ("get all the white people off of here before the whole gene pool gets mudded up")[76] and ceaseless misogyny, incel grievances, and fantasies of rape and matricide. The anonymous messageboards are horrific. However, the messageboards do not necessarily provide insight into whether such vileness is committed or simply nihilistic posturing. After all, *Homo digitalis* carefully crafts their identity. In this sense, Yeager's work captures the effects of neuro-totalitarianism and psychopolitics on developing minds—his central characters are, after all, typically teenage/young adult—engaged in naïve nihilism on anonymous deep web forums. The novels investigate processes of systemic forces—the secret logic of the internet as literal or mystical—and the subsequent effects on individuals.

Consequently, Yeager suggests that a central question behind his work is "how do we reconcile our sense of self with the profound, often destructive forces that are oblivious, or at least uncaring, of our existence, while also dictating the terms."[77] Yeager's religious convictions—hard, contingent deism—play a role in his fiction, and this deism ultimately operates in a technologized manner via systematic and constitutive forces in *Amygdalatropolis*. The novel represents technologies of desire, thanatos, and control. While we think that we use the internet, the internet uses us even more efficiently; we think that we exercise our will on materiality through various practices online but, instead, inhuman, unknown, hypercomplex procedures use humans as operating principles in a project beyond individual cognition and comprehension. In short, while we may experience the effects of such engagements as agential, Yeager's fiction implies that it is the "outside" and the inhuman that ultimately dictate the terms. As a result, his work's political dimension is not explicit, didactic, or polemic; instead, it is implicit and parasitic: something very bad is in the air, and every atom seems to vibrate with a sense of atmospheric collapse and suicidal violence. Yeager writes that "I tend to think that the most effective 'political art' are works with a documentarian objective rather than a didactic objective . . . works about capturing the madness of the time, rather than trying to instil specific lessons or values."[78] Ultimately, Yeager aims at philosophical and psychological investigation rather than political fiction. His concerns examine "the question of whether free will exists within the context of our 'self' and our beliefs, which are at least partially dictated by factors beyond our conscious control—our nervous systems, our endocrine systems, and who knows what else."[79] In this sense, Yeager's fiction is not concerned with questions of policy, governance, and power. Rather, *Amygdalatropolis* addresses the very question of the role that contemporary meta-systematics play in constituting the self, the subject, and individual agency. As a result, his fiction is more concerned with psychopolitical processes invisibly sculpting agency. In short, if "what is *out there*" is horrific in its rigid, procedural inhumanity, the *outside* will—according to psycho-ecological feedback loops—find its way *in*, parasitize, and take control. This is the horror of *Homo digitalis*, a uniquely neoliberal identity.

Here psychopolitics operate as the procedurally active steerers of individual lives in largely invisible ways. Of course, a common trope of conspiratorial horror is the individual's lack of agency once parasitized by a constitutive xenoforce: one is stripped of agency and free will and, resultantly, becomes marionetted in and by a game too complex to be interpreted and too vast for agential intervention. This is emblematized by the game within the novel, a game that takes place online and seems determined, procedural, almost without human origin: "*No one knew who created it or other details of origin.*"[80] In the game, willed mundane acts are met with the actuality that "*your choice will have no effect on the game*"[81] and, again later, even simulated acts of cruelty and violence are not registered as agential: "*Press ALT and bring up the shotgun's crosshairs. Use the arrow keys to line up the crosshair. Press CTRL and HENRY shoots. The dogs turn to wet and red. Killing the dogs has no effect on the game.*"[82] This invisible, constitutive force figures in *Amygdalatropolis* as the systematics of media on the mind and as addiction to the internet *itself* whereby—as the title suggests—the secret logic behind the architecture of the internet becomes the secret logic of the mind itself and vice versa in a recursive, contingent loop. Of course, this is a loop whereby the psychopathology of the inhuman matrices of digital architecture is in a constant level-crossing knot with user behavior. As a horror novel, the users here are the denizens of the deep web—the unconscious of the internet—where the forbidden, excessive, violent, and unknowable fashions itself. Han writes that "Big Data provides the means for establishing not just an individual but a collective psychogram—perhaps even the psychogram of the unconscious itself. As such, it may yet shine a light into the depths of the psyche and exploit the unconscious entirely."[83] *Amygdalatropolis* suggests that such a psychogram is, like the unconscious, horrific and impossible to integrate into the social arena. It represents the absolute return of the repressed and even the systematic acceleration of the repressed in its most optimized and intensified manifestation. *Amygdalatropolis* examines the psychological brood of cybernetics, the ceaseless optimization of input and output, of Big Data. The amygdala-as-city, the constitutive and constituting environs, and the psychogram of *Homo digitalis* are all emblematic of the collapse of the psyche into, and knotted with, *something outside*.

At the conclusion of *Amygdalatropolis*, there is a notable juxtaposition: a messageboard discussion and astrophysics and the world as the site of all perception and knowledge (light coming at Earth via the universe from all directions) with /1404er/'s ultimate merger with *LivePlateau* to see the whole world at once. *LivePlateau* is *"the largest aggregator of live webcams found automatically in search engines from all over the world."*[84] Rather than the limited scope of Earthly perception, /1404er/ becomes an "all-seeing eye." In contrast to the earthly bound human with their limited scope of the cosmos and an overwhelming desire for transcendence, /1404er/ achieves this but *inside-out*. Rather than *transcend*, he *descends* further into the technological and inhabits the negative space of transcendence—annihilation into nothingness, neutrality, mundane inhuman functionality without purpose. Rather than the grandeur of transcendence, there is a kind of pure banality to the digital: "sans-serif lettering printed across the Computer's face. Seventeen-thousand and forty-three cameras. Every aperture a window. Seventeen-thousand and forty-three windows, all stammering arrhythmic. /1404er/ breathed them, one after another. The breaths felt like life become dream; like God alive in the clouds and internal bleeding."[85] The dullness and semantic triviality of /1404er/'s union with the technological, the absolute replacement of his nervous system with rigid functional procedurality, denies any sense of perfection, wholeness, techno-Übermensch fantasy. His metamorphosed ubiquity does not afford him a glimpse into other worlds, the universe, the cosmos, transcendent truth, to divine hedonism. Instead, his all-seeing eye captures "shops and parabolas of Dundee City Square," "empty flurries and stroked peaks of Big Sky Resort," quiet "streets before the city hall in Suensaarenkatu," Buck's Bird Cam, the "perforated white and blue light of Westman Islands," the "empty mustard block and blacked out windows" of Plaza May Albarracín, "Ukkohalla Shi & Sport Resort's greyscale," "Fossen School grounds," "Nagasaki Port," the "Atami-kaigan Expressway," Drachten Animal Hospital Dog Room, the cartilage colored sky of Mashike Harbour, "eleven Ukrainians line dancing to North American pop" at "Metro Club," "straw grass and white bark burning brown old Edmonton," a tired place to die "secluded and comfortable" at "Bristol Head Acres," the "Kamba Waterfall Monkey Park," the "Hiroshima Peace Memorial," "Butterflies snapping frame to frame before Yuki Jinja Shrine," and so on.[86] In short, a series of non-password protected global webcams selected—not as the result of semantic categorization, significance, or importance—but simply because such video feeds are efficiently available online. That is, the coding, the logical substratum, that makes the *LivePlateau* function does not choose; instead, its functionality is without inherent purpose, without value, without intention, and without meaning.

While /1404er/ does transcend his humanity, Yeager notes that "the last thing I wanted was for /1404er/ to go through a redemption arc."[87] The desire for transcendence aspires to bridge the gap between the cosmos with human knowledge, whereas /1404er/'s fate has him continue to unite with the divine neutrality of digitality. Instead of the universe *for* humans, /1404er/ merges fully with the digital's functionality and procedurality; in his merged state, he becomes the optical psychogram of psychopolitics. This is the instant, but not the completion, of the annihilation of the self. He searches "the trail to inhumanity, a trail found nowhere in nature" but, ultimately, he does not find truth. Instead, he merges with the *outside* where "we recognize no reality"; he will never discover reality once and for all since there is no longer a "he" in the procedurality. While for Apollinaire, the truth will always be new, for /1404er/ the truth will always be mundane, without intention, absolutely unconcerned with the anthropic, and entirely inhuman. The transcendence, or the conflation with digital ubiquity, is a merger, in short, with the apparatus. /1404er/ has replaced the wheel that replaced the leg; his self is lost along the way, and, as the qualities of absolute neutrality would dictate, he achieves *nothing and no thing*. Rather than correlating all possible meaning with Godlike, ultra-retinal compound eyes, /1404er/ indeed achieves nothing: divine neutrality.

NOTES

1. Willard Bohn, "From Surrealism to Surrealism: Apollinaire and Breton, *The Journal of Aesthetics and Art Criticism* 36, no. 2 (1977): 203.
2. Ibid.
3. Ibid., 204.
4. Ibid.
5. Ibid.
6. Ibid., 203.
7. B. R. Yeager, "B.R. Yeager Interview," interview by Matt Lee, *Ligeia* (Spring 2020), https://www.ligeiamagazine.com/spring-2020/br-yeager-interview/.
8. Robin McKay, "Editorial Introduction," *Collapse IV*, ed. Robin McKay (Urbanomic, 2008), 6.
9. B. R. Yeager, interview by Andrew C. Wenaus by email, June 8, 2020–July 8, 2020.
10. RealDoll is a life-like, life-size sex doll made with posable inner skeleton and realistic silicon flesh and skin. The dolls are manufactured by, perhaps with unintended irony, Abyss Creations in San Marcos, California.
11. Mike Carrao, "Layers of the Real: On B.R. Yeager's 'Amygdalatropolis,'" *Newfound* 10, no. 1, https://newfound.org/archives/volume-10/issue-1/reviews-amygdalatropolis/.
12. There is one notable and truly horrific exception to this when the digital and the real world do correspond: a confession on the messageboard to a murder that is met with skepticism. However, shortly afterward,

> "the girl with the nose, cheeks and lips all mashed-in with the wine-bottle—or a different girl who bit it the exact same time, the exact same way—went national. (Someone from the boards must of snitched. There was always at least one.) The news sites said a 15 year old was arrested at 6:07 AM on Wednesday June 20th in connection with the murder and rape . . . they didn't release their names because of how young they were and they didn't say anything about their relation. By the time he was charged and his name was released, no one on the boards even cared anymore." B. R. Yeager, *Amygdalatropolis* (London: Schism Press2, 2017), 76.

13. Carrao, "Layers of the Real."
14. Ibid.
15. Ibid.
16. Yeager, interview by Wenaus.
17. Ibid.
18. Ibid.
19. Ibid.
20. Edia Connole, introduction to *Amygdalatropolis*, by B.R. Yeager (London: Schism Press2, 2017), xxxiii.
21. B. R. Yeager, "Digital Native: An Interview with B.R. Yeager on *Amygdalatropolis*," interview by Jacob Siefring, *3:AM Magazine*, February 15, 2018, https://www.3ammagazine.com/3am/digital-native-interview-b-r-yeager-amygdalatropolis/.

22. Yeager, interview by Wenaus.
23. Ibid.
24. Ibid.
25. Ibid.
26. Ibid.
27. Ibid.
28. Ibid.
29. Ibid.
30. Ibid.
31. Yeager, interview by Lee.
32. Ibid.
33. Yeager, interview by Wenaus.
34. B. R. Yeager, "'A Cadaver is Filled with Plenty of Material Activity': Mike Corrao Talks to B.R. Yeager, Author of the Horror Novel NEGATIVE SPACE," interview by Mike Corrao, *Heavy Feather Review*, February 20, 2020, https://heavy-featherreview.org/2020/02/20/yeager/.
35. Ibid.
36. Yeager, interview by Siefring.
37. Ibid.
38. Yeager, *Amygdalatropolis*, 3.
39. Byung-Chul Han, *In the Swarm: Digital Prospects*, trans. Erik Butler (Cambridge: MIT Press, 2017), 11.
40. Yeager, interview by Siefring.
41. Han, *In the Swarm*, 52.
42. Ibid., 11.
43. Yeager, *Amygdalatropolis*, 34–35.
44. Ibid., 77–78.
45. Ibid., 94–96.
46. Yeager acknowledges and supports online anonymity's potential for both good and malice: "I don't think digital anonymity only benefits malicious/antisocial behavior, nor would I advocate for a less anonymous internet. But obviously *Amygdalatropolis* focuses on negative rather than positive aspects of online anonymity, because that's just where I tend to look, at least as a writer." Interview by Siefring. Elsewhere he emphasizes the potentiality of positive action that online anonymity affords:

> "I in no way want to advocate for a less-anonymous internet. The ability to widely communicate under anonymity is one of the greatest benefits of the internet. And I've seen enough to know that toxic behaviour is in no way inherent to anonymity (plenty of people behave in toxic ways without being anonymous). But ultimately, if you want to let the id (or amygdala) run rampant, free of repercussions, you're going to want to do that anonymously . . . I wouldn't say it's a regret, but in hindsight I think one of *Amygdalatropolis*'s weaknesses is that it focuses only on the negative and toxic sides of anonymous message board culture (apart from a few blips at the end). There's a desire to shock and provoke in there (or rather, nuance is undermined by a desire to provoke) that feels somewhat boring to me now. Because while there is plenty of the vile behavior described, there are also examples of disenfranchised people finding support and community that is unavailable

to them in material spaces. Which is what I wanted to convey more in *Negative Space*." Interview by Wenaus.

47. Yeager, interview by Siefring.
48. Yeager, *Amygdalatropolis*, 9.
49. Ibid., 9.
50. Yeager, interview by Wenaus.
51. Connole, introduction to *Amygdalatropolis*, xxxi.
52. Yeager, *Amygdalatropolis*, 94.
53. Ibid., 1.
54. Ibid., 7.
55. Ibid., 7–8.
56. Ibid., 13.
57. Ibid., 104.
58. Marc Augé, *Non-Places: Introduction to an Anthropology of Supermodernity*, trans. John Howe (London: Verso, 1995), 77–78.
59. Ibid., 78.
60. Han, *In the Swarm*, 11.
61. Jay David Bolter and Richard Grusin, *Remediation: Understanding New Media* (MIT Press, 2000), 179.
62. Ibid.
63. Yeager, *Amygdalatropolis*, 2.
64. Yeager, interview by Corrao.
65. George Sieg, "Infinite Regress into Self-Referential Horror: The Gnosis of the Victim," *Collapse IV*, ed. Robin McKay (Urbanomic, 2008), 53.
66. Graham Harman, *Prince of Networks: Bruno Latour and Metaphysics* (Melbourne: re.press, 2009), 184.
67. Yeager, interview by Wenaus.
68. Yeager, *Amygdalatropolis*, 2.
69. Ibid., 3.
70. Ibid., 13.
71. Ibid., 31.
72. Ibid., 58.
73. Ibid., 38.
74. Ibid., 57.
75. Ibid., 52.
76. Ibid., 58.
77. Yeager, interview by Wenaus.
78. Yeager, interview by Lee.
79. Yeager, interview by Lee.
80. Yeager, *Amygdalatropolis*, 17.
81. Ibid., 118.
82. Ibid., 120.

83. Han, *Psychopolitics*, 36.
84. Yeager, *Amygdalatropolis*, 151.
85. Ibid., 151.
86. Ibid., 151–153.
87. Yeager, interview by Wenaus.

Chapter 4

"Something Is Taking Its Course"
Zero-Player Games, Proceduralism, and Samuel Beckett's Endgame

PROCEDURE WITHOUT INTENTION

Yeager's *Amygdalatropolis* pits the madness of the human against the pure indifference of the apparatus; the result is, rather than human transcendence into the digital, /1404er/'s a descent into the banality of the apparatus. In his piece *Trying to Understand* Endgame (1957), Adorno comments that in the work of Samuel Beckett "poetic procedure surrenders . . . without intention."[1] This observation is a remarkable claim about, not Beckett's work, but the effect Beckett's work has on the way we experience intimacy with narrative and can consider how literature thinks. In Adorno's sense, *Endgame*'s poetic procedure establishes a confined and constitutive dwelling from which the language users cannot escape—this dwelling is expressed through the sparse and claustrophobic staging of Beckett's work. However, it also clears the path for the question of what exactly is "taking its course,"[2] a phrase that is ominously repeated in *Endgame*. It opens an interrogation of what is taking its course and how the text proceeds according to its own logic as a kind of automation or zero-player game (a game that proceeds without a player). Adorno suggests that with *Endgame*, "thought becomes as much a means of producing meaning for the work which cannot be immediately rendered tangible, as it is an expression of meaning's absence."[3] He continues: Beckett's text "can mean nothing other than understanding its incomprehensibility."[4] It is here that one may note the distinction between poiesis, thinking, and automated poetic procedure. While the poetic is an intentional act of making something come forth or an act of agential creativity, thinking is an act of submission. A poetic *procedure* (in the sense of a set of logical instructions) as automation or zero-player game, on the other hand, both surrenders and proceeds without intention; in this sense, *Endgame* conflates thinking and poiesis by eliminating the possibility of agential creativity and replaces it with an automated logic that unfolds on its own accord. This is at the heart of Adorno's provocative statement: the poetic should be intentional by definition, thinking should be submissive, but the *procedural* is both without intention and without agency. So, the process that animates *Endgame* is one that ultimately demands of the reader the assumption of an unusual interpretive pose: that of readerly noninvolvement, diminution of agency, and, ultimately, our exclusion from interpretive agency. Indeed, the text provides certain insight into the present shift from the dominance of language to that of code and automation. *Endgame*, in its forceful expression of the exclusion of the liberal subject within a digitally ran apparatus or system, takes its course without recourse to the desire or suffering of the human. As a result, the work encourages speculation on the rapid shift from human involvement with language as alphanumerics to that of code that proceeds according to its own logic indifferent to humanism.

To do so, we must first establish certain premises for this argument:

1. *Endgame* here is an ideal text divorced from materiality or performability (it is, after all, a play); this ideal text is an extended metaphor for code unfolding according to a set of well-formed instructions.
2. The text is a poetic procedure that proceeds without intention.
3. The text continues to take its course without readerly intervention.
4. The reader assumes an imaginary pose: of exclusion and non-agential involvement.

So, what we have here is a thought experiment: a text as an extended metaphor that proceeds without intention and without a reader, a kind of textual automaton. What this thought experiment is asking is: what are the effects of this ideal text? What might it say about our relation to narrative; what is the significance of our exclusion in an era of automation? *Endgame* offers itself to us as a means to meditate on the encroaching shift in the predominant narrative code: the increasing dominance of digital code over alphanumeric-linguistic narrative.

Accordingly, *Endgame* demands that the reader identifies *as* openness and exclusion toward the end of taking up identification with incomprehensibility and become transposed directly into that which is without semantic value. Here, the reader must submit *as* absence or exclusion from the text at hand. The human condition, Heidegger claims, is to *be there/here*. The concern here is with the strange role Beckett asks the reader of the text to assume. What *being-there* means is more nuanced than simply being-in-the-world. This nuance will help bring our thought experiment a little closer to earth. *The effects* of Beckett's text strive for a kind of paradoxical and imaginative rigor rather than for existential exactness. *Endgame* is experimental, and so its effects are experimental: it employs nothingness as a means of making manifest what we wish to forget: meaningless, nothingness, our exclusion from cultural or political narrative. Heidegger writes that "interrogating the nothing—asking what and how it, the nothing, is—turns what is interrogated into its opposite. The question deprives itself of its own object."[5] The task here asks how the textual object may take its course by depriving itself of its questioner, that is, its reader. Our experiment asks of *Endgame* how the determinism of closed systems may be made significant when the text is considered as that which proceeds without intention, takes its course, and is animated without a reader. James Acheson suggests that Beckett's early plays are preoccupied with "the relationship between art and the limits of human knowledge."[6] *Endgame* certainly is a demonstration of this: it pushes this concern to the ends of practicable experience. And yet, this procedure demands that narrative disclose itself *as* narrative simply by taking its course. To do so, the procedure of *Endgame* is that which inverts Heidegger's troublesome formulation of the interrogator investigating nothingness by allowing nothingness to assume the role of procedure and the reader to assume the pose of nothingness.

Endgame takes place in a room with two small windows, a door, a picture hanging near a door, two garbage bins, and, in the center, an armchair on castors. Beyond this room remains more or less unknown: most probably a wasteland. The title of the play derives from chess. It refers to when a game nears its end and only crucial pieces—the two kings—are left on the board. There are four characters. Three are without mobility. Hamm sits in the chair at center stage; he is unable to stand and unable to see. Nagg and Nell, Hamm's parents, are legless and confined to the garbage bins. Clov, the only character with mobility and whose movements are belabored and painful, cannot sit down. The play is characterized by isolation, claustrophobia, loss, nostalgia, and an extremely tight and structured repetitive form.

Early readings of the text are primarily concerned with its relationship to existentialism and postwar trauma's intellectual and cultural influence. Alain Robbe-Grillet suggests that the characters/actors are *there* (on stage) in the sense that they must explain themselves. Martin Esslin's 1961 *The Theatre of the Absurd* also provides an influential and long-lasting existential reading. While compelling, this tradition of reading is reductionistic and, resultantly, by the 1970s and 1980s fell out of favor to nuanced readings focused on language. The play's title influenced critical judgments of the text as "the last part of an on-stage game of chess."[7] The purpose of this chess game is to disrupt a definitive interpretation. Later critics, however, are more concerned with the textual mechanics that make this destabilization possible. More recently, the discussion regarding Beckett's work is concerned primarily with language and performance. Even more recently, there is a marked increase in textual studies of Beckett's work. However, the intervention here concerns *Endgame* as an idealized text and its effects in excluding the reader as a metaphor for the shift from language to code: the coming of information illiteracy and its effects on agency. *Endgame* posits the reader in a movement of diminution. Like Mouth in *Not I* (1972), but to the diegetic level of the reader, Beckett attempts to "supersede anguish" by bringing about the "nihilation of the ego itself."[8] *Endgame* turns the *cogito ergo sum* inside out, demonstrating that something proceeds with no concern to organic intentionality: or, *Endgame* is a procedure, *non sum*. Something is taking its course, but we, as readers, are not in control.

ACTANTS AND PATAPHYSICS: IMAGINING EXCLUSION

In the 1960s, Algirdas Greimas developed the actantial narrative model to analyze narrative processes and functions. Rather than examining the story, plot, or character, Greimas's model suggests that the study of action and operation is the imperative of structural reading. What Greimas provides is the analytical concept of actants.[9] One clarification that needs to be made in regards to actants is that they are not actors. Actants "operate at the level of function," writes Donna Haraway, "several characters in a narrative may make up a single actant," she continues, "the structure of the narrative generates its actants. . . . Non-humans are not necessarily 'actors' in the human sense, but they are part of the functional collective that makes up an actant."[10] On the level of narrative, various elements and essential qualities operate in tandem in such a way as to propel a narrative, to animate it without the agential intention.

Haraway suggests that, in this sense, "action is not so much an ontological as a semiotic problem. This is perhaps as true for humans as non-humans, a way of looking at things that may provide exits from the methodological individualism inherent in concentrating constantly on who the agent and actors are in the sense of liberal theories of agency."[11] While Haraway suggests that action in this sense is more of a problem of sign matrices than of being, Adorno's commentary on *Endgame* suggests that the text may yield some remarkable ontological observations. Not only does the actant as a critical tool provide a means of examining the function of a narrative as it operates without agential intention, this inevitably places the reader in the odd position of false objectivity. "Let us be on guard against the dangerous old conceptual fiction that posited a 'pure, will-less, painless, timeless knowing subject,'" writes Nietzsche, and suggests that "we should think of an eye that is completely unthinkable, an eye turned in no particular direction, in which the active and interpreting forces, through which alone seeing becomes seeing *something*, are supposed to be lacking; these always demand of the eye an absurdity and a nonsense."[12] For the poetic procedures to operate without intention, the reader as an inevitable agential force may aim to imagine their absence, that is, interpretation must take on the conceit of agential exclusion. Though "there is *only* a perspective seeing, *only* a perspective 'knowing,'" suggests Nietzsche,[13] this perspective can only be made more urgent through its temporary eclipse. Such is the oddity the reader/interpreter must face when imagining such an eclipse of semantics and agency. Like the poetic procedure—and *Endgame* as actant—the reader must, then, assume an imagined position: a mode of reading founded upon the principle of imagination and procedure rather than induction. That is, readers must imagine and rehearse their exclusion.

This imaginary positioning is tantamount when considering *Endgame* as that procedure that surrenders without intention. It is a position that is explicitly one of relations among actants, *not* among readers and text. Bruno Latour writes that "there is no other way to define an actor but through its action, and there is no other way to define an action but by asking what other actors are modified, transformed, perturbed, or created by the character that is the focus of attention."[14] In other words, we do not define actors by their agency or intentionality but, instead, on the systemic effects they cause and how these systemic effects precede the very possibility of such causality. One way of thinking about this is by engaging with the text in a pataphysical manner. Alfred Jarry coined the term pataphysics in his posthumous 1911 novel *Exploits and Opinions of Doctor Faustroll, Pataphysician: A Neo-Scientific Novel*: "Pataphysics," he writes, "is the science of imaginary solutions, which symbolically attributes the properties of objects, described by their virtuality, to their lineaments."[15] He continues: pataphysics is

> the science of the particular, despite the common opinion that the only science is that of the general. Pataphysics will examine the laws governing exceptions, and will explain the universe supplementary to this one; or, less ambitiously, will describe a universe which can be—and perhaps should be—envisaged in the place of the traditional one, since the laws that are supposed to have been discovered in the traditional universe are also correlations of exceptions, albeit more frequent ones, but in any case accidental data which, reduced to the status of unexceptional exceptions, possess no longer even the virtue of originality.[16]

While Jarry is at the core of a theatrical movement that Esslin retrospectively christened the Theatre of the Absurd, Esslin's assumption greatly deforms the possibility of Beckett's work. Esslin suggests that "language in Beckett's plays serves to express the breakdown, the disintegration of language" and that his complete oeuvre "is an endeavor to name the unnamable."[17] Esslin remarks that Jarry's pataphysics is "subjectivist and expressionist"[18] and "exactly anticipates the tendency of the Theatre of the Absurd to express psychological states by objectifying them on stage."[19] This is true, but what Esslin disregards, and what is essential in our thought experiment is that pataphysical subjectivism and expressionism need not be projected outward toward some kind of presence on the stage. That is, Esslin is not committed to a pataphysical gesture that would negate the very site of psychological and expressionistic projection. Indeed, as P. J. Murphy suggests, "Esslin's statements epitomize a common tendency to circumvent the full implications of the problem by, at key critical junctures, identifying Beckett's characters as somehow real or human, when it is the rigorous investigation of their very status as bestowed by language that is at the heart of the Beckettian enterprise."[20] Esslin's reading *requires* anthropocentrism, whereas Jarry's, like Adorno's and Beckett's, do not. So, considering Jarry's pataphysics as a guide to Beckett legitimizes the potentialities of imaginative solutions to reading by, paradoxically, imaginatively removing the reader from the procedure at hand. Because, as we saw in Adorno's comment, Beckett's work is by definition exceptional, the readerly position that the reader needs to assume when reading *Endgame* must be exceptional: to assume the pose of virtual disappearance and to allow the constitutive narrative, the actant, to take its course and to attribute the properties of objects to the contours of their operations. Ultimately, reading *Endgame* is pataphysical, and pataphysics proved a presciently twenty-first-century experience.

ENDGAME, EXPERIMENTATION, AND SCIENTIFIC NARRATIVE: EXPERIMENT WITHOUT EXPERIMENTER

Jarry's pataphysics and, by extension, *Endgame*, express the relation between scientific experimentation and literary experimentation: or, the relation between scientific and aesthetic paths to epistemology. Latour remarks that "the accuracy of [a] statement is not related to a state of affairs out there, but to the traceability of a series of transformations."[21] So, when the narrative structure of the scientific method is divorced from the experimenter and object of inquiry, what is revealed is a narrative that confirms itself via repetition and recursion. In this sense, experimentation as a narrative, whether scientific or literary, may be appropriately considered according to the criteria of pataphysics. Experimentation is not that which projects outward; our thought experiment on *Endgame* does not *tell* us something about the world so much as it tells us about analogous methodological procedures. So, whereas Esslin would have experimental modes of theatre perform an expressionistic projection of psychological states, Beckett's text—as it negates the reader as the site of inquiry—projects only its own methodological procedure. That is, experimentation itself, as a kind of narrative, once put in motion also takes its course: science and art, as actants, proceed and surrender without intention. Therefore, the reader's most intense involvement is the pose of noninvolvement, and so the traceability of transformations here is not concerned with the state of affairs of the individual or the world so much as with the effects produced by the transformations within the parameters of methodology as a narrative. "An experiment is a story, to be sure . . . but a story *tied* to a situation in which new actants undergo terrible trials," writes Latour.[22] Something is put in motion by experimentation itself, the experiment takes its narrative course, and ultimately experimentation reveals what it *must* reveal via relations among repetition. However, Endgame will "never end" and "never go"[23] because it cannot accomplish more than the reproducibility of results implicit in the inductive methodology assumed by scientific experimentation. That is, it is bound to the parameters of its functional programming. The text simply refuses to engage our intimacy by prohibiting our involvement.

"The assertions of science are on shaky ground," writes Flusser,

> the puzzle-solving way of reading is a criterion-setting one in disguise, and science establishes values just as politics and art do. Science, like art and politics, is a fiction. It is becoming more and more clear that it is nonsense to try to distinguish sharply between science, art, and politics. We can assume that in science, there are normative-political as well as fictional, artistic, and poetic impulses at work.[24]

Beckett's text may be that which resists the inductive bias behind the scientific project. It is too much to suggest that Endgame's effect is to blur the distinction between science, art, and politics. Instead, what *Endgame* accomplishes through repetition without change is the denaturalization of criterion-setting modes of expectation associated with scientific and experimental narrative interpretation. "Imagine if a rational being came back to earth," muses Hamm, "wouldn't he be liable to get ideas into his head if he observed us long enough."[25] However, Beckett does not allow this rational being to make an appearance, so such a criterion-setting mode of interpretation is excluded, allowing the text to proceed according to its own criteria. It is Hamm who has to provide the voice of this rational being, this extradiegetic entity: "Ah, good, now I see what it is, yes, now I understand what they're at!"[26] For Hamm, this agency of interpretation from without will be that which may justify that his suffering will not "all have been for nothing."[27] Unfortunately for Hamm, *Endgame*, the experiment without experimenter or object of study proceeds according to the criteria of an unseen, programmed procedure that resists rationalization. Whether the course of events is or is not "for nothing" rests outside the methodology of experimentation *as* experimentation. Value judgment *is* interpretation, yet the interpreter is asked by our thought experiment to submit to the pose of nonexistence. The reader, then, cannot "understand what they're at" because to do so is incongruous to the procedure at hand.

In Latour's discussion on Pasteur's philosophy of science, where "the phenomena preceded what they are the phenomena of,"[28] he talks of what he calls the "name of action."[29] The name of action is an expression Latour ultimately uses to describe "strange situations—such as experiments—in which an actor emerges out of its trials";[30] another way of thinking about this phenomenon is when procedure reveals procedure. Here, "we do not know what *it is*, but we know what *it does* from the trials conducted . . . a series of performances *precedes* the definition of the competence that will later be made the sole cause of these very performances."[31] "The actor does not yet have an essence," writes Latour, instead "it is defined only as a list of effects . . . Only later does one deduce from these performances a competence, that is a substance that explains why the actor behaves as it does."[32] The name of action, in short, is what happens when experiment as a narrative unfolds *as* scientific narrative. That is, the methodologies and procedures of scientific experimentation propel themselves by a kind of logical prescription: they are prescribed by their constitutive narrative. *Endgame* follows this process, yet the text excludes the possibility of the later deduction. Instead, the text is the persistent series of performances that precede its causal meaning. In other words, *Endgame* speaks itself; the narrative precedes interpretation and proceeds as an actant. The reader assumes, rather than the privileged position of experimenter-interpreter, an imaginary positioning to the reader-as-text conundrum via exclusion. The name of action for *Endgame*-as-procedure, then, is how the text reveals itself through iteration.

So, the diegetic conundrum in Beckett's text demonstrates, as Latour remarks about scientific experimentation, that "'construction' is in no way the mere recombination of already existing elements."[33] Rather, there is a relationship between the narrative and narrative *as* narrative—both as actants— that *"mutually exchange and enhance their properties."*[34] In this way, we cannot say that Beckett writes as a means of prompting the text to say simply what he wants it to say—that the text cannot simply prompt meaning from the reader—nor can we claim that the reader simply prompts any additional semantic competence from the text or its author. Instead, the three are topologically intertwined and proceed without intention, agential design, or value. Hamm seems aware of not only his lack of agency but also his proxy status as actant indistinguishable from the diegetic determinism of the text:

HAMM:
Clov.
CLOV *(absorbed)*:
Mmm.
HAMM:
Do you know what it is?
CLOV *(as before)*:
Mmm.
HAMM:
I was never there.
(Pause.)
Clov!
CLOV *(turning towards Hamm, exasperated)*:
What is it?
HAMM:
I was never there.
CLOV:
Lucky for you.
(He looks out of window.)
HAMM:
Absent, always. It all happened without me. I don't know what's happened.[35]

That Hamm was never there is a contentious statement. Certainly, he is *there* in Robbe-Grillet's sense: he, as actant, proceeds and repeats like and with the text's narrative. Yet, Hamm is an actant constituent rather than an agent, that is, he is *part* of the text and, therefore, *part* of the textual actant. This, perhaps, is the closest point of identification he can have with the extra-diegetic. Though Clov thinks this exemption is lucky, as if unlike Hamm, he *is there* always, his lot is no different from any*one* or any*thing* constituted by the narrative *as* narrative. "Action is slightly overtaken by what it acts upon," Latour writes,

> an experiment is an event which offers slightly more than its inputs . . . transfers of *in*formation never occur except through subtle and multiple *trans*formations . . . there is no such thing as the imposition of categories upon a formless matter . . . in the realm of techniques, no one is in command—not because technology is in command, but because, truly, *no one*, and *nothing* at all, is in command.[36]

Because nothing and no one is commanding the procedure that animates the actant,[37] there is no reason to attempt communion between diegetic realms. "We have to abandon the division between a speaking human and a mute world," and we must dismantle the assumption that "we have words—or gaze—on one side and a world on the other," writes Latour.[38] Because we need not think of the language of the text as a series of large vertical gaps between things and language, we may instead consider "small differences between horizontal paths of reference—themselves considered as a series of progressive and traceable transformations."[39] *Endgame*, like Latour, aims to move beyond models of interiority versus exteriority, looking for an "alternative to the model of statements that posits a world 'out there' which language tries to reach through a correspondence across the yawning gap separating the two."[40]

The episode, in which Hamm requests a prayer, articulates the drama of incomplete interdiegetic communication, or multilevel interchange. "Let us pray to God,"[41] he suggests. And although he is interrupted by the crisis of a rat in the kitchen, Hamm, Clov, and Nagg do proceed to attempt a petition of observance, first out loud, then in silence, both to no success. With rehearsed and ironic expectation, Hamm asks "well?"[42] only to receive Clov's answer "What a hope! And you?" inevitably abandoning his aspirations for communion; from Nagg, the comical "Wait!" and then "Nothing doing!";[43] and Hamm himself to himself: "Sweet damn all."[44] Their attitude of abandonment is not, however, one of theological crisis. Though Hamm concludes that "the bastard ... doesn't exist,"[45] his remark is not exclusively concerned with God so much as an extra-diegetic *primum movens* of any kind. Here, the absent animator is the reader more precisely than God. The crisis is not religious so much as it is diegetically systematic: the crisis is not cosmic but, rather, one of malfunction in procedural expectation. The text is more indicative of a reiterative, skipping, glitching simulation than a theological cosmology. The reader, in this sense, is the nonexistent bastard, not God. While Hale suggests that Endgame's universe is one "without order,"[46] what unveils itself is that the text is one of strict order. And so the experiment, the name of action, of *Endgame* lends itself to the discourse of computational and calculational procedure just as aptly as it does to procedures of language.

ZERO-PLAYER GAMES AND PROCEDURALISM: *ENDGAME* AS AUTOMATON

The impulse to understand a narrative system that excludes a reader's participation has recently been undertaken in the theory of game and play. At the 2012 *Philosophy of Computer Games Conference* in Madrid, Spain, Staffan Björk and Jesper Juul presented an evocative paper titled "Zero-Player Games, Or: What We Talk about When We Talk about Players." Their argument discloses the biases behind the way we think about games and players. For Björk and Juul, the most frequently cited definitions of games refer to the centrality of players in understanding what games are and what gaming means. Björk and Juul suggest that "many publications from the last few years have tried to argue that it is impossible to discuss games as designed objects, since games only actually exist when played, or *as* played" and that games are objects that "give players the ability to intentionally act towards reaching the goals of a game."[47] In much the same way, we often think of texts as deliberate artifacts that only exist meaningfully when read. Citing the dominant literature on games and players, Björk and Juul find a noticeable bias in the role of player agency, intentionality, and aesthetic engagement.[48] Such features are fundamentally at odds with the procedurality of *Endgame* since the unfolding of the text is, and will be, as Clov remarks, "the same as usual."[49] Linda Hughes (1999),[50] Laura Ermi and Frans Mäyrä (2005),[51] Mia Consalvo (2009),[52] Gordon Calleja (2011),[53] and Miguel Sicart (2011)[54] also privilege the role of the player in understanding games.

While Björk and Juul acknowledge that games are "designed objects"[55] that imply intervention on behalf of a player, they argue "that many common conceptions of players are too vague to be useful"[56] and any definition of a game overly reliant on the player will prove inadequate. To reconceptualize the player, Björk and Juul aim to examine the paradoxical idea of the zero-player game: a game that proceeds without agential intervention and thus an appropriate analog to Beckett's narrative. The critical discussion surrounding the question of what a game is and what a game means is, Björk and Juul suggest, explicitly what they call "player-centric."[57] As a result, extrapolating upon the concept cannot reflexively account for itself as a phenomenon. With the very gesture of the player-centric debate, games are being defined by a subcomponent (the player) assumed to be constituent and thus cannot disclose themselves to themselves as games. The player-centric bias stems from a critical bias; indeed, it is odd to concede that one can consider an object of study without *one considering it*. Yet, what Björk and Juul propose here is not a study that wishes to argue against the significance of the study of players and their role in games but instead to discuss how examining games in the absence of the player concept is productive. With this logic of negation, Björk and Juul are effectively establishing the negative space through which one may consider both games and players *and* games and nonplayers. Here we note the analog to our thought experiment on *Endgame*. Acheson suggests that Beckett undermines "whatever illusion the play might fortuitously create by insisting on *Endgame* as theatre."[58] Yet, we recognize the text as a kind of literary zero-player game in that it operates by a similar conceit: that of an excluded reader[59] and a text that proceeds impartially taking its course.

Yet, in *Endgame*, the role of player/reader is interrupted. Rather than a text that permits the performative expressive acts of play, *Endgame* is a text that reveals itself in the thought experiment as radically unchangeable: the text is the same as usual. Indeed, rather than what Sicart identifies as creative play and agential flexibility, Hamm concurs that, within the parameters of the *Endgame* environment, "there's no reason for it to change" and Clov, always lacking in his faith for any kind of diegetic intervention, utters the significant remark: "all life long the same questions, the same answers."[60] We may suggest that Beckett's play, as a game, is proceduralist rather than player-centric. As a text, it is proceduralist rather than reader-centric. Its central diegetic conceit is, at its most extreme, that the text is a zero-player game.

Perhaps the most well-known kind of a zero-player game is the cellular automaton. Cellular automata "lend themselves to a variety of uses. In some cases, they are used to simulate processes for which the equations that do exist are not adequate to describe the phenomena of interest,"[61] writes Keller. Conventionally cellular automata are implemented as a means of "producing recognizable patterns of 'interesting' behavior in their macrodynamics rather than in their microdynamics."[62] "Cellular automata models are simulators par excellence," she continues, "they are artificial universes that evolve according to local but uniform rules of interaction that have been pre-specified. Change the initial conditions, and one changes the history; change the rules of interaction, and one changes the dynamics."[63] However, these changes can only be initiated *from without* and not from within. In this sense, cellular automata are apt parallel metaphors to the procedural dwelling established in *Endgame* both on the level of agency and setting. Tommaso Toffoli and Norman Margolus write in *Cellular Automata Machines: A New Environment for Modeling* (1987) that

> cellular automata are stylized, synthetic universes . . . They have their own kind of matter which whirls around in a space and a time of their own . . . A cellular automata machine is a universe synthesizer. Like an organ, it has keys and stops by which the resources of the instrument can be called into action, combined, and reconfigured. Its color screen is a window through which one can watch the universe that is being "played."[64]

Keller notes that Christopher Langton, computer scientist and founder of artificial life systems, understands cellular automata as that which could be used to simulate universes or environments for living beings, "where the ultimate goal would be to create life in a new medium."[65] Langton speculates that the simulation of artificial life:

> is the study of man-made systems that exhibit behaviors characteristic of natural living systems. It complements the traditional biological sciences concerned with the *analysis* of living organisms by attempting to *synthesize* life-like behaviors within computers and other artificial media. By extending the empirical

foundation upon which biology is based beyond the carbon-chain life that has evolved on Earth, Artificial Life can contribute to theoretical biology by locating *life-as-we-know-it* within the larger picture of *life-as-it-could-be*.[66]

The means of creating new kinds of life in a process that follows a "bottom-up synthesis,"[67] in which great complexity arises from very simple rules and within determined—limited and local—parameters, has "proved to have immense appeal for people far beyond the world of computer scientists. Perhaps especially, it proved appealing to readers and viewers who have themselves spent a significant proportion of their real lives inhabiting virtual worlds."[68] H. Porter Abbott suggests that what this kind of "formal experimentation requires from the critic is to find ways of talking about Beckett's fiction as an imitation of life without producing those often elaborate structures of meaning, knit from a variety of 'clues,' which have marred so many otherwise excellent discussions of Beckett."[69] When considering *Endgame* as a zero-player game, as cellular automata, we are faced with the potentiality of facing life as we know it and life (or, exclusion from life) as it could be. There are no clues for us here because *Endgame* does not invite the reader to intervene in the procedure. Much like how Langton imagines the significance of computer models of artificial life as creative mimesis, representation that looks-forward and is future-directed, *Endgame* unfolds most intensively in the text. Yet, its effects are felt most intrusively on the extra-diegetic level. The life as it could be, horrific and sterile as it is on the textual level, is life as it is at the extreme of future-directedness: absent.

The most famous example of a zero-player game is Conway's *The Game of Life* (1970). In the October 1970 issue of *Scientific American*, Martin Gardner wrote the piece "The Fantastical Combinations of John Conway's New Solitaire Game 'Life'" in his "Mathematical Games" column, where he discusses John Horton Conway's experimental zero-player game that, at the time, was simply called "Life." The game follows the principles of automation expressed in the work of game theorist and mathematician John von Neumann. "A mathematical simulation of cellular genetics," writes Justin Parsler, the game is more of an "intellectual puzzle" than a traditional game. In this sense, the game follows in the same spirit as *Endgame*, a text that Acheson identifies as "a puzzle."[70] *The Game of Life*, like *Endgame*, plays out on a metaphorical checkerboard.[71] The squares on the board are representative of a cell that is either dead or alive. With each turn, "cells either die or come to life, depending on the number of living neighbors they have: a cell with two live neighbors dies, one with more than three dies, one with three stays stable. A dead cell with three live neighbors comes to life."[72] The game is, in essence, a Universal Turing Machine. First conceptualized in 1936 by mathematician and cryptologist Alan Turing, the Turing Machine can simulate any well-formed instructions. In other words, the Machine can be modified in such a way as to process the logic of any computer algorithm. The game also establishes a logic of complexity from simplicity: "The rules," Gardner suggests, "should be such as to make the behavior of the population unpredictable."[73] And the rules are quite simple.[74] Once the pieces on the board are set up, there is no direct engagement by the player. "The initial setup of the game board," writes Parsler, "constitutes 'playing' the game, even though there are no set goals, nor any winner";[75] in this sense, the processes that follow from the well-formed instructions unfold as a series of deterministic nodes of mutation and change upon which the instigator may consider. In other words, like *Endgame*, *The Game of Life* proceeds without intention and can operate as an expression of meaning's absence and its paradoxical dislocation from agential engagement.

Similar to simple systems of chaos and unpredictability, Conway's *The Game of Life* demonstrates that even within the confines of determinism, even simple determinism, the emergent complexity and variability of possible results are staggering. Hayles writes that

> emergence implies properties or programs appear on their own, often developing in ways not anticipated by the person who created the simulation. Structures that lead to emergence typically involve complex feedback loops in which the output of a system is repeatedly fed back in as input. As the recursive looping continues, small deviations can quickly become magnified, leading to the complex interactions and unpredictable evolutions associated with emergence.[76]

Gardner discusses this emergence further: "You will find the population constantly undergoing unusual, sometimes beautiful and always unexpected change." He continues, "most starting patterns either reach stable figures—Conway calls them 'still lifes'—that cannot change or patterns that oscillate forever. Patterns with no initial symmetry tend to become symmetrical. Once this happens the symmetry cannot be lost, although it may increase in richness."[77] And here, with the "still life" is where we find *Endgame*. Itself a kind of zero-player game, a diegetic automaton, a procedure that cannot change, is skipping, and endlessly oscillating. Hamm's repeated phrase "don't stay there, you give me the shivers"[78] thus signifies something structurally metonymical: his shivers are the shivers of the simulated, still life universe. He is not commanding Clov to cease standing because of the ominous sense it causes him to experience. Rather, it becomes indicative of the text itself and its recognition thereof: Hamm addresses the simulated universe as much as he addresses Clov. The shivers are the oscillating vibrations of still life, the characters' recognition of the constitutive procedural apparatus in which they dwell. "Well, you'll lie down then, what the hell!" expresses Hamm, "Or, you'll come to a standstill, simply stop and stand still, the way you are now. One day you'll say, I'm tired, I'll stop. What does the attitude matter?"[79] The attitude does not matter; one may say that they are tired and will stop, but this termination of forward movement is not an end but an oscillation. The standstill, the simple stop, shivers, and oscillates. The text itself takes on "nice dimensions, nice proportions."[80] The text's procedurality, assuming symmetry that cannot be lost, thus bars the possibilities of agential poiesis through language. While Heidegger differentiates poiesis from thinking in that the former is creative and the latter is submissive, the procedurality in Beckett's text *constitutes* rather than creates. Its requirement of submission is axiomatic, not a willed opening to a clearing.

So, when Hamm demands to know "what's happening,"[81] Clov's response that something is taking its course is indicative of the proceduralist rhetoric as it is an accurate description of the diegetic motion of the text. "Proceduralists claim that players, by reconstructing the meaning embedded in the rules, are *persuaded* by virtue of the games' procedural nature," writes Sicart.[82] We are particularly concerned with how the narrative-as-game may disclose certain operations of reading *Endgame* on the extra-diegetic level. The work of Ian Bogost in his studies *Unit Operations: An Approach to Videogame Criticism* (2006) and *Persuasive Games: The Expressive Power of Videogames* (2007) are major contributions to proceduralist criticism in both academia and industry: "It is the success of Bogost's arguments not only across the academic body," Sicart writes, "but also in the games industry what makes proceduralism a popular way of conducting computer games scholarship."[83] Sicart continues:

> What proceduralism . . . [argues is] that computer games present a technological and cultural exception that deserves to be analyzed through the ontological particularities that make computer games unique, in this case, the fact that they have a "procedural nature." The proceduralists take their starting point in [the][84] statement that digital games are unique, among other things, because of their procedural nature . . . that is, because they are processes that operate in [a] way that is akin to how computers operate.[85]

With *Endgame*, the conceit of proceduralism is carried to an extreme. The text itself embodies a diegetic value in its design, and this value is reconsidered as that which operates and proceeds without intention like a cellular automaton. The demonstration at play is a text that proceeds without semantic value. Value here is the status of meanings in relation to one another: value is the intentionally structured hierarchical merit of one term in semantic exchange with others. To be without semantic value is to be semantically procedural and heterarchical. That is, *Endgame* expresses its value as a procedure signifying that without value. Hamm asks what is happening, but he must already know (if knowledge is constituted and programmable) as unseen procedures and rules move him. We do not "play" the players in the text. Rather they are played by the valueless process, the design, of the play itself: "Me—*(he* yawns)—to play," Hamm notes, his yawn expressing inevitable compliance and agential disjunction more so than ennui. The disjunction being between "me" and "to play," that is, rather than indicating that he "plays" and therefore "is," Hamm's yawn signifies a vocalized gap that separates agency from procedure. Hamm, though without diegetic agency, is not without an acute sense of anxiety. There is embedded in *Endgame* the sense that the game itself hesitatingly wishes to transcend its own process. The desire to exceed what Ruby Cohn calls the "claustrophobic boundaries"[86] of the room's walls that both constitute and signify the architecture of procedurality is the straining to escape the valueless processes. This, however, seems impossible.

The limits of proceduralism unsettle not only the status of narrative but also the status of language in *Endgame*. In his discussion on *Endgame*, Benjamin H. Ogden suggests that Beckett's language is one that forgoes any attempt at an ideal abstract language of the kind Wittgenstein proposed in *Tractatus Logico-Philosophicus* in favor of a language that is understood to be explicitly concerned with, following Stanley Cavell, natural concretisms. Ogden suggests that "in order to speak a language properly, then, one cannot just know the dictionary or formal definitions of words (its 'ideal' generative grammar), but must understand the 'natural environment' in which phrases and words are logical or appropriate."[87] The act of reading literature, Cavell suggests, is a process of "naturalizing ourselves to a new form of life, a new world" and that by doing so it is essential to focus upon the inhabitants of the fictional world.[88] Ogden, however, seems to be gesturing more toward the sort of reading position with which proceduralists would agree. He finds Cavell "too eager to 'hear' things in the text, to discover the cleverest readings rather than to permit the text to yield its unique, multiform logic" and, so, Ogden opts to "allow *Endgame* to speak for itself."[89] The play's wording must not speak *to* but rather speak *for itself*, to proceed without intention. The wording of Hamm's request for his dog is, then, worth noting for its indeterminacy: "Is my dog ready?"[90] Clov's responses, that the dog "lacks a leg" and that he is "a *kind* of Pomeranian,"[91] are equally telling; the animal is, after all, a "black toy dog" with "three legs."[92] Here we cannot read *Endgame* literally because we assume that the text proceeds on its own; the zero-player games move itself and speak itself. So, not only is the dog a simulation, but it is one that reveals itself as an imperfect simulation demonstrative of a debilitating mutation of the appendages of agential mobility. Indeed, the lifeless dog becomes metonymical of both the status of language and the text itself:

CLOV:
Your dogs are here.
(He hands the dog to Hamm who feels it, fondles it.)
HAMM:
He's white, isn't he?
CLOV:
Nearly.
HAMM:
What do you mean, nearly? Is he white or isn't he?
CLOV:
He isn't.
(Pause.)
HAMM:
You've forgotten the sex.
CLOV *(vexed)*:
But he isn't finished. The sex goes on at the end.
(Pause.)
HAMM:
You haven't put on his ribbon.
CLOV *(angrily)*:
But he isn't finished, I tell you! First you finish your dog and then you put on his
ribbon!
(Pause.)
HAMM:
Can he stand?
. . .
CLOV:
Wait!
*(He squats down and tries to get the dog to stand on its three legs, fails, lets it go. The
dog falls on its side.)*
HAMM *(impatiently)*:
Well?
CLOV:
He's standing.
HAMM *(groping for the dog)*:
Where? Where is he?

(Clov holds up the dog in a standing position.)
CLOV:
There.
(He takes Hamm's hand and guides it towards the dog's head.)
HAMM *(his hand on the dog's head)*:
Is he gazing at me?
CLOV:
Yes.
HAMM *(proudly)*:
As if he were asking me to take him for a walk?
CLOV:
If you like.
HAMM *(as before)*:
Or as if he were begging me for a bone.
(He withdraws his hand.)
Leave him like that, standing there imploring me.
(Clov straightens up. The dog falls on its side.)[93]

While Clov is only partly committed to the farce—he refers to the dog in the plural, concedes that the black dog is "nearly" white, only to, upon interrogation, admit that the dog, in fact, "isn't"—he does seem to demonstrate a recognition of the proceduralism of the narrative as metonymically expressed by the dog. His response to Hamm's accusation that the maker has forgotten the dog's reproductive organs is indicative of the diegesis itself as an iterative procedure that is at once static and sterile. The dog "isn't finished," and, until the end, the dog will be without genitalia. However, there is no end to *Endgame*; the procedure forbids it. *Endgame* is, rather, taking its course, and will continually do so ad infinitum. The dog cannot stand and, therefore, cannot—like Hamm, Nagg, Nell, and the narrative itself in our thought experiment—have or be engaged by any agential mobility. Like the dog, the text can only demonstrate the *as if* it were being asked to be taken for a walk; or *as if* the intervention of agency and intentionally could provide alternatives to the strict design. That the narrative can "go on" differently from the procedural patterns determined by the text's design is impossible: an attempt at intentional intervention will, like the dog, fall flat. Indeed, while both Hamm and Clov indicate awareness of the proceduralism that governs the course of the text, here it is Clov who euphemistically expresses that the text is "not a real dog, he can't go."[94] Indeed, like the dog, the play's diegesis is a simulation: it is "not even a real dog!"[95] It is not a real diegetic environment; it is not a game with a player; it "can't go"; it simply takes its course.

SIMULATION FEVER: *ENDGAME* AS ZERO-PLAYER SIMULATION

That *Endgame* is not a real diegetic environment suggests its status, not only as a zero-player game but also as a simulation. Keller identifies simulation as follows: "simulo *v.* 1. *To make* a thing *like* another; *to imitate, copy* . . . 2. *To represent* a thing as being which has no existence, *to feign* a thing to be what it is not."[96] So, simulation is simultaneously openly mimetic and artificial. In *Unit Operations* (2006), Ian Bogost employs the concept of "simulation fever" as a means of discussing the implications of procedurality on the relation between the system and its player. "Working through simulation fever means learning how to express what simulations choose to embed and to exclude," he writes.[97] The player thus becomes integrated into his or her relation to the processes determined by the game. Working through simulation fever involves recognizing how one is embedded within and how one is excluded from the procedurality of the game. Thus, this mode permits flexibility in the player's agency in understanding the game while simultaneously remaining implicated in and determined by the game processes. Bogost suggests that certain kinds of interpretation may achieve a point through which one may understand the system from within and without: this

> would encourage player critics to work through the simulation anxiety a simulation generates. Part of this process takes place within the gameplay, as the player goes through cycles of configuring the game by engaging its unit operations. Another process of configuration has to do with working through the play's subjective response to the game, the internalizations of its cybernetic feedback loops.[98]

What Bogost identifies as the working through of simulation anxiety is, in fact, a kind of anxiety itself. That is, the anxiety of undergoing an experience with simulation is that which discloses anxiety to itself. The experience cannot be governed by anxiety, but instead, anxiety is that disposition that reveals anxiety. Anxiety is that which helps the player both recognize how he or she is embedded within the systemic procedure of *Endgame*. Yet it also forces the system's indifference to that recognition by unveiling how one's intentionality is ultimately, and paradoxically, excluded from the operation. The concept of simulation fever, then, is a means of making meaningful the constitutive system while at the same time attempting to express how the player or reader experiences the system.

The player is, as a result, both embedded and excluded. Yet, this balance is, unlike almost every other element in Beckett's text, hardly symmetrical. Hamm and Clov are ultimately forced into this paradoxical stance. They seem largely aware of the procedurality of the text—of the parody that mocks the possibility for them to live authentically or make a meaningful and meditative choice—and, yet, are unable to affect the very procedurality that determines the reiterative narrative. So, when Hamm, for example, remarks that "nature has forgotten us,"[99] and Clov responds that "there's no more nature,"[100] the two are simultaneously recognizing the text itself as a kind of simulation as well as that constitutive environment, nature itself, being excluded from the artificial system in which they take their course. "No more nature! You exaggerate,"[101] Hamm repudiates suggesting that there is at least something that resembles nature—the artifact, the text as simulation—but Clov is steadfast: there is no more nature "in the vicinity."[102] That is, simulation is an approximation but not a spatial proximity; Hamm and Clov are, as a result, both embedded and excluded from the system. Again, Hamm and Clov do not fully correspond with Bogost's player; instead, it is the reader of *Endgame* who is most intimately embedded, and yet taking the conceit of the text as a case of radical procedurality—the zero-player game—the reader is, paradoxically, excluded from the text by being embedded in the text. While simulation fever allows, Sicart writes, for games to "convey messages and create aesthetic and cultural experiences by making players think and reflect about the very nature of the rules,"[103] this reflexivity is one that gestures more intensely to that which is excluded rather than that which is embedded. If Hamm and Clov were fully embedded in the text, one could suppose some degree of agency from them. Because they are not, one sees that they often do think and reflect about the nature of the rules, but the nature of the rules is not natural; they are artificial, simulated, and programmed. The procedurality here does not establish a delicate balance between agency and absence; rather, the text is one that gestures more toward that which expresses diminution of choice to the point of absence, nothingness, exclusion: zero. "Both mental modeling and cognitive mapping show how the interpretation of a game relies as much or more on what the simulation excludes or leaves ambiguous than on what it includes" writes Bogost.[104] In a strange turn for this logic, our zero-player game embeds the reader by readerly exclusion. Like Björk's and Juul's examination of what the player means to gaming in zero-player games, *Endgame* raises the question of what a reader means with a text *as* zero-player game. The simulation generated for the reader is at once that which intensifies self-awareness only toward the recognition of exclusion and conditionality of the reader.

As a demonstration of exclusion, the text's diegesis cannot signify, it calls forth, encourages, and summons the reader to identify with that which minifies beyond the elemental: an identification with the abyss, to encourage a narrative that proceeds on its own. By dramatizing the reader's exclusion, the text operates in such a way as to make the narrative appear before itself as narrative. It does this by suggesting the absence of the extra-diegetic: an audience or reader. This procedure discloses itself most tellingly in the short episode where Clov turns a telescope, first on a window and then on the auditorium. This move operates in two ways when considering the text as a kind of zero-player game. First, it reveals its diegetic level as something distinguished from, though somehow connected to and dependent upon, that which is *without* the text. Second, by emphasizing extra-diegetic misplacement, Clov unveils that the link that establishes readerly agency has been severed.

CLOV:
(He gets down, picks up the telescope, turns it on auditorium.)
I see . . . a multitude . . . in transports . . . of joy.
(Pause. He lowers telescope, looks at it.)
That's what I call a magnifier.
(He turns toward Hamm.)
Well? Don't we laugh?
HAMM *(after reflection)*:
I don't.
CLOV *(after reflection)*:
Nor I.
(He gets up on ladder, turns the telescope on the without.)
Let's see.
(He looks, moving the telescope.)
Zero . . .
(he looks)
 . . . zero . . .
(he looks)
 . . . and zero.
HAMM:
Nothing stirs. All is—
CLOV:
Zer—[105]

The "zero" to which Clov refers is not simply the enigmatic nothingness that lies beyond the room. There is, at once, a reader beyond; however, the conceit demands the reader amounts to zero. The hiddenness of the reader, that is, announces itself via its exclusion from the automaton at hand. The reader is, in a word, zero. And yet, as Heidegger suggests, this kind of formulation deprives itself of its own object. A little later, at what seems to be a moment of intense anxiety in the text, Hamm attempts to initiate an intervention into the unfolding procedure, to bring something unthought, unknown, or unprogrammed into being: "Think of something,"[106] he requests.

THINKING EXCLUSION: *ENDGAME*, FLUSSER, AND INFORMATION ILLITERACY

This formulation, of course, is all very strange for the reader. After all, the reader is to take the submit to the conceit of exclusion. How then, if the characters of the play are incapable of action or thinking, is the reader to undergo experience while accepting the position of that which negates experience? This is perhaps our paradoxical intimacy with a text that resists intimacy. If we are to learn, we must dispose of everything we do so that we may be open to the essentials of the text given to us at any given moment. We learn to think by giving over our minds to nothingness: to give our minds over to the demonstration of nothingness, that which there is yet to think about and that which there is to think through. Like our idealized text, we must allow something to take its course, to surrender to a poetic (or should we say procedurally programmed) procedure. "We never come to thoughts," writes Heidegger, "they come to us."[107] Thoughts here, in a traditional sense, however, cannot truly arrive. Events are "the same as usual,"[108] remarks Clov, while Hamm concurs: "there's no reason for it to change"[109] because *telos* in our thought experiment is impossible. There is no end-point, only a suspended endgame, a still life. Hamm wishes for a terminus, "old endgame lost of old," he muses, "play and lose and have done with losing,"[110] but he cannot escape the patterns which oscillate and shiver forever. Clov, perhaps hopefully, remarks that "it may end. *(Pause.)*," yet remains partially practical: "all life long the same questions, the same answers."[111] Yet, each knows that the latter bit of Clov's remark is accurate, and his hopefulness is procedural and without opportunity. "That's always the way at the end of the day, isn't it, Clov?" Hamm remarks, and Clov, astutely: "Always."[112] And this is, in itself, the revelation—a rerevelation—of infinite iterations: "it's the end of the day like any other day, isn't it, Clov?"[113] The infinite repetitiveness that constitutes them is not only temporal. It is also potential and conceptual: it is a procedure that proceeds without value. Hamm and Clov experience that which is both strange and intimate to the reader: the experience of the disappearing influence of alphanumeric language and narrative replaced by automation, digitization, and proceduralism.

What proves significant with undergoing this paradoxical experience with *Endgame* is the manner through which this undertaking proves remarkable. "To undergo an experience with something," writes Heidegger, "means that this something befalls us, strikes us, comes over us, overwhelms and transforms us. When we talk of 'undergoing' an experience, we mean specifically that the experience is not of our own making; to undergo here means that we endure it, suffer it, receive it as it strikes us and submit to it. It is this something itself that comes about, comes to pass, happens."[114] And yet, here, with each pass, something takes its course. *Endgame* does not permit an experience beyond what appears as the text itself. Clov and Hamm experience what comes about, what comes to pass, and what happens: they experience proceduralism. But this, for them, is what must always constitute experience. For the reader, however, *Endgame* establishes a textual conundrum through which he or she succumbs to the twofold nature of undergoing an experience. The narrative delimits experience to something confined and defined, that is, the narrative of *Endgame* is a procedural gesture. However, the experience of the reader—as a witness to a zero-player game—thus undergoes an experience that is not his or her own making. One must endure it, suffer it, and receive as it strikes us. *Endgame* is a text to which we must submit if we wish to learn, confront, and think in new ways in an era that increasingly relies on code that proceeds on its own and is indifferent to the liberal subject.

Experience is and has been for the liberal subject textual, linguistic, and agential; however, future experience suggests something governed by the programmatic and procedural. "To undergo an experience with language . . . means to let ourselves be properly concerned by the claim of language by entering into and submitting to it,"[115] writes Heidegger. He continues, "man finds the proper abode of his existence in language"[116] and, therefore, any "experience we undergo with language will touch the innermost nexus of our existence. We who speak language may thereupon become transformed."[117] If language is indeed the "house of being," then the architecture of digital code anticipates very alien dwellings. That Clov is "doing his best to create a little order" indicates his struggle with this procedure. Moreover, this struggle against the constitutive process shows that Clov's behavior is futile. He cannot submit and allow the experience to come and pass because he is bound to the procedure by a different, unrelenting logic. "A *program* is to be understood as writing directed not toward human beings but toward apparatuses," writes Flusser.[118] "Here no human beings require instruction," he continues, "instructions can instead be issued to apparatuses. In this way, it becomes clear that the goal of instruction," that is, proceduralism, causes subjects—or simulations of subjects—to "behave as they should automatically."[119] Heidegger's gesture toward the authenticity of an experience with language is indeed that which makes more striking the impossibility for thinking or experience on the level of *Endgame* as conceived in our thought experiment. Indeed, the manner we experience alphanumeric language differs radically from the way we experience programs.

"Scientific and philosophical information about language is one thing; and experience we undergo with language is another," Heidegger suggests, "whether the attempt to bring us face to face with the possibility of such an experience will succeed, and if it does, how far that possible success will go for each one of us—that is not up to any of us."[120] And while the possibility of any experience is something that proceeds outside agency, the possibility and value of experience in *Endgame*'s proceduralist simulation are strikingly demoted. Indeed, for Heidegger, information about language—a text-as-simulation—thus produces something radically altered from an experience with language. Does *Endgame* as a text that simulates the effects of our information illiteracy become a space or gesture of cruelty? Hamm's constant physical discomfort, and his addiction to painkillers, suggests a kind of simulation whereby this discomfort proceeds pitilessly as if inflicted by the something that is taking its course, that a constitutive narrative unfolds then repeats relentlessly and indifferently. The demonstration at play is a text that proceeds without intention. What is uncomfortable for the humanities is that we, as readers and theorists of narrative, are left out of the equation. On six occasions, Hamm asks for his painkiller.[121] Hamm, with his programmed addiction, expects that there should be relief. "There's no more pain-killer,"[122] Clov finally responds, therefore assuming that, at this final yet endless recursive iteration, there never was and never will be painkillers for Hamm. Hamm's response, "Good . . . !,"[123] is not so much one of reserve or coming-to-terms as it is an approval that, as always, something is taking its course as it should. That is, he responds not to the nonexistence of the painkiller so much as to the functional accuracy of the diegetic actant proceeding recursively and unintentionally as it *must*. Indeed, "in logically constructed computer programs," writes Flusser, "there is no symbol for *should*."[124] The textual simulation, the procedural actant, is another thing entirely from an experience with language. There is no symbol for *should* and, resultantly, to assume *Endgame* as a cruel simulation is to approach the situation before us with misleading criteria. The zero-reader text does not invite intimacy: instead, it excludes. Digital narrative is something very alien, something that proceeds with indifference. We can talk *about* it with critical biases. However, we cannot fully engage *with it* in traditional ways because there is a fundamental change in the predominant code underlying knowledge (which is embedded in knowledge production and knowledge mobilization) currently taking place. The apparatus is always *outside*.

Then, the procedural indifference plays out in a slightly different way on the level of the reader: it is not painful as much as anxious and uncomfortable. Though the conceit of our thought experiment is that *Endgame* is a zero-player game, the text is nevertheless expressed through language. Oddly enough, though, we must imagine that the language negates itself by posing as something like programmed code for our thought experiment. "When the issue is to put into language something which has never yet been spoken, then everything depends on whether language gives or withholds the appropriate word," writes Heidegger.[125] That which has never been spoken, in the case of *Endgame*, is the use of language for the conceit of absolute procedural narrative motion: digital code is not fully informed by our thinking, yet there is evidence that it may gradually constitute our thinking. Like the reader, *Endgame* proceeds to put into motion that which is already in motion, to endure the diegesis but also submit to its absence from its very proceduralism. The experience of *Endgame* is, then, where experience breaks off just as, for those who are not code literate, our experience with the coming dominant cultural code breaks off. "Where something breaks off, a breach, a diminution has occurred. To diminish means to take away, to cause a lack," Heidegger notes.[126] He goes on: "no thing is where the word is lacking,"[127] that is, no thing—simulation—is where code determines. Furthermore, the reader, being where the word is lacking, poses as an absence. This absence, though, is not renunciation; indeed, it would be absurd to push the conceit so far. Instead, the sense and ability to think about no-sense and unthinking opens the possibility for the simultaneity of experience and nonexperience: code, simulation, and proxy are the best sites for this procedure. Not only is the text a demonstration of meaninglessness, but its effects also operate to dramatize the diminution of the self. It provides the analgesia that is forbidden to Hamm; if we submit, it reveals the threshold of experience.

In the years since Beckett's death in 1989, developments in the instruction of digital code have rapidly taken root. Ultimately, the pose the reader must assume when reading *Endgame* interrogates a fundamental conundrum at the center of reading today, a conundrum that goes beyond Beckett. Jonathan Boulter writes that one of the fundamental themes of Beckett's work is "the agonizing fact of being in a language that endlessly composes and decomposes the subject. Being in Beckett means existing, finally, and forever, in a language."[128] For Heidegger, Being is Dasein; more specifically, being is an openness and submission to linguistic and poetic experience. The language of *Endgame* is that which asks the reader to assume the submission to its proceduralism: our thought experiment asks of us how *Endgame* also makes manifest the agonizing fact of being in a world increasingly organized, mobilized, and run by digital code. Ogden suggests that the language of *Endgame* "might justly be considered a dialect, a language that shares an alphabet and lexicon but that differs grammatically and syntactically to such a degree that communication can effectively break down between those speaking the dialect and those speaking the language from which it derives."[129] But Beckett goes even further than this. He establishes a textual logic in which the text *must* speak itself. Flusser suggests that the transition from alphanumerical language to digital code will have a radical impact on the very nature of critique. With this transition, "critique becomes a synthesized practice, based on knowledge that is interdisciplinary and part of a network of knowledges."[130] The transition to learning digital code, for Flusser, is a way to relearn thought:

For us, thinking was, and still is, a process that moves forwards, that frees itself from images, from representations, that criticizes them, thereby becoming increasingly conceptual. We have the alphabet to thank for this understanding of thought and this understanding of thought to thank for the alphabet (feedback). The new digital codes arose from the new understanding of thought, and feedback is making us think in quanta and images more clearly the more we use the new codes.[131]

Assuming a more intense degree of intentionality than Heidegger's openness, Beckett's negation, or Bogost's proceduralism, Flusser does, however, anticipate a kind of productivity to this shift. Perhaps the endgame is alphanumeric language itself. That which will ultimately be lost of old will indeed play and lose and have done with losing. The alternative in this instance is digital code; while it offers alternatives, it nevertheless also attracts the alternatives of the zero-player game, of a different order of proceduralism, a new kind of poetic submission. While Murphy suggests that, in Beckett, "expression necessarily precedes existence,"[132] here we suggest that being submits to procedure and precedes the codification of existence. The engagement with digital code for most readers, however, is of a different order of reader negation: information illiteracy. The reader's proof of existence is made manifest via the pose of absence: the anxiety here is the intense non-self-awareness or intense self non-awareness. We are not compelled to repeat so much as we are compelled to recognize that repetition, oscillation, and still life are apt metaphors for how closely we can truly identify with the stories—and the technical means upon which they are made possible—that we rely upon. The reader's inability to identify on an intimate level with the text is an expression of the inability to engage with the zero-player automaton; moreover, though, our exclusion is an experiment for the traditionally literate to experience the coming information illiteracy. Not only does the effect of *Endgame* allow us to imagine a zero-player/reader text in the sense that it calls for the clearing for thinking, it is the zero-player game whose central conceit is bringing to light our absence from the coming thought of a new competence via a new language: the processes of code.

So, it is appropriate to recognize the ontological puzzle that Beckett expresses as one that is in itself linguistic, poetic, and procedural. Yet, *Endgame*, in our thought experiment, expresses most intensely the poetic procedure: that which calls for surrender and proves a demonstration of meaninglessness. Without meaning, the semantic force of language, we experience anxiety. The removal of self in this thought experiment demands the reader assume the role of thinker. To think of nothingness is to dedicate a concept or referent to *nothing*, thus negating its very status as that which it is, which is the *is not*. We must assume nothingness as a means of being open to its valuelessness, to submit and surrender to its procedure. In this way—though difficult and in many ways at the parameters of articulation—*Endgame* discloses a remarkable opening for thought. By deconstructing the biases of perception, *Endgame* projects, to borrow a phrase from Paul Éluard, a "vision beyond this crass, insensible reality which we are expected to accept with resignation, [and] conducts us into a liberated world where we consent to everything, where nothing is incomprehensible"[133] Our thought experiment demands that we must take seriously the idea that the text takes its course and that our identification with nothingness is the very path to considering how we may go on when we can no longer go on. Topsfield is correct to remark that, despite the relentless logic of diminution and negation in Beckett, "the 'message' of *Endgame* is positive."[134] Our nonengagement is our path to engagement with the procedure, and "since that's the way we're playing it," Hamm determines, "let's play it that way and speak no more about it."[135] With this inability to speak and think from nothingness, whether our illiteracy is linguistic or digital, *Endgame* becomes the path for a potential revelation through the surrender and submission to new and unconventional procedures of perception. Like Hamm's experience, the effects of *Endgame* ask us to acknowledge the procedures that surrender without intention: the effects ask us to be nothing, to urgently *think of something*. Ultimately, what these effects offer us is an instructional unfolding of the minimizing of the self, the recognition that radically different narratives are on the horizon, and that something unarticulated is always innate. If digital code has something of a narrative embedded in it, it will be alien indeed.

NOTES

1. Theodor Adorno, "Trying to Understand *Endgame*," trans. Michael T. Jones, *New German Critique* 26 (1982), 119.
2. Samuel Beckett, *Endgame, A Play in One Act, Followed by Act Without Words, a Mime for One Player*, trans. Samuel Beckett (New York: Grove Press, 1958), 13, 32.
3. Adorno, "Trying to Understand *Endgame*," 120.
4. Ibid., 120.
5. Martin Heidegger, "What is Metaphysics?" in *Basic Writings,* ed. David Farrell Krell (London: Harper Perrenial, 2008), 96.
6. James Acheson, *Samuel Beckett's Artistic Theory and Practice: Criticism, Drama, and Early Fiction* (Houndmills, Basingstoke, Hampshire: Macmillan, 1997), 141.
7. Ibid., 150.
8. Ibid., 217.

9. Greimas categorizes actants into six categories of three oppositions: (1) the axis of desire: subject/object; (2) the axis of power: helper/opponent; (3) the axis of knowledge: sender/receiver. See A. J. Greimas, *Structural Semantics: An Attempt at a Method*, trans. Daniele McDowell, Ronald Schleifer, and Alan Velie (Lincoln: University of Nebraska Press, 1983).

10. Donna Haraway, "The Promise of Monsters: A Regenerative Politics for Inappropriate/d Others," *The Haraway Reader* (New York: Routledge, 2004), 115.

11. Ibid., 115.

12. Friedrich Nietzche, *On the Genealogy of Morals*, trans. Walter Kaufmann and R.J. Hollingdale (New York: Random House, 1967), 119.

13. Ibid., 119.

14. Bruno Latour, *Pandora's Hope: Essays on the Reality of Science Studies* (Cambridge: Harvard University Press, 1999), 122.

15. Alfred Jarry, *Exploits and Opinions of Doctor Faustroll, Pataphysician: A Neo-Scientific Novel*. Vol. 2 of *Collected Works of Alfred Jarry: Three Early Novels*, ed. Alastair Brotchie and Paul Edwards, trans. Alexis Lykiard, Simon Watson Taylor, and Paul Edwards (London: Atlas Press, 2006), 145.

16. Ibid.

17. Martin Esslin, *The Theatre of the Absurd: Revised and Enlarged Edition* (Harmondsworth: Penguin, 1968), 85.

18. Ibid., 351.

19. Ibid.

20. P. J. Murphy, "Beckett and the Philosophers" in *The Cambridge Companion to Beckett*, edited by John Pilling (New York: Cambridge University Press, 1994), 222.

21. Latour, *Pandora's Hope*, 123.

22. Ibid.

23. Beckett, *Endgame*, 81.

24. Flusser, *Does Writing Have a Future?* 83.

25. Beckett, *Endgame*, 33.

26. Ibid.

27. Ibid.

28. Latour, *Pandora's Hope*, 118–119.

29. Ibid., 119.

30. Ibid., 308.

31. Ibid., 119.

32. Ibid., 308.

33. Ibid., 124.

34. Ibid.

35. Beckett, *Endgame*, 74.

36. Latour, *Pandora's Hope*, 298.

37. Beckett, as author, certainly commands the text. However, the thought experiment here asks that we suspend this kind of judgment. Beckett's presence in this kind of formulation is that of one who establishes the initial setup of the actant. He puts the automaton in motion, but it is the automaton that takes its course.

38. Latour, *Pandora's Hope*, 140.
39. Ibid., 141.
40. Ibid.
41. Beckett, *Endgame*, 54.
42. Ibid., 55.
43. Ibid.
44. Ibid.
45. Ibid.

46. Jane Alison Hale, "*Endgame*: 'How are Your Eyes?'" in *New Casebooks: Waiting for Godot and* Endgame, ed. Steven Connor (Houndmills, Basingstoke, Hampshire: Macmillan, 1992), 83.

47. Staffan Björk and Jesper Juul: "Zero-Player Games. Or: What We Talk about When We Talk about Players" (presentation, *The Philosophy of Computer Games Conference*, Madrid, 2012), http://www.jesperjuul.net/text/zeroplayergames/.

48. My survey of the critical literature is indebted to research compiled by Björk and Juul "Zero-Player Games. Or: What We Talk about When We Talk about Players." See note 47 above.

49. Beckett, *Endgame*, 4.

50. Linda Hughes, "Children's Games and Gaming," ed. B. Sutton-Smith, in *Children's Folklore: A Source Book* (New York, NY: Routledge, 1999).

51. Laura Ermi and Frans Mäyrä, "Fundamental Components of the Gameplay Experience: Analysing Immersion," in *Proceedings of DiGRA 2005* (2005).

52. Mia Consalvo, "There is No Magic Circle," *Games and Culture* 4, no. 4 (2009).

53. Gordon Calleja, *In-Game: From Immersion to Incorporation* (Cambridge, MA: MIT Press, 2011).

54. Miguel Sicart, "Against Procedurality," *Game Studies* 11 (2011).

55. Björk and Juul.
56. Ibid.
57. Ibid.

58. Acheson, *Samuel Beckett's Artistic Theory and Practice*, 152.

59. Here the reader could conceivably constitute a traditional reader, theater spectator, or stage actor responding to textual prompts. For this discussion, however, we will limit the inquiry to the scope of this project: the reader in the conventional sense, a person who reads text from a printed book. There is much discussion regarding Beckett's intertextuality, that is, the relational role of text-as-text. For an introduction, see Michael Worton's "*Waiting for Godot* and *Endgame*: Theatre as Text," in *The Cambridge Companion to Beckett* (New York: Cambridge University Press, 1994).

60. Beckett, *Endgame*, 5.

61. Evelyn Fox Keller, "Marrying the Premodern to the Postmodern: Computers and Organisms after World War II," in *Mechanical Bodies, Computational Minds: Artificial Intelligence from Automata to Cyborgs*, eds. Stefano Franchi and Güven Güzeldere (Cambridge: MIT Press, 2005), 205.

62. Ibid., 205.
63. Ibid., 207.

64. Tommaso Toffoli and Norman Margolus, *Cellular Automata Machines: A New Environment for Modeling* (MIT Press, 1987), 1.

65. Keller, "Marrying the Premodern to the Postmodern," 209.

66. Christopher Langton, "Artificial Life" in *Artificial Life: Proceedings of the Santa Fe Institute Studies in the Sciences of Complexity*, Vol. 6 (Redwood City, CA: Addison-Wesley, 1989), 1–2, https://archive.org/details/artificiallifepr00inte/page/n3/mode/2up.

67. Keller, "Marrying the Premodern to the Postmodern," 210. The virtual worlds to which Keller refers are extended here to those which range from various forms of social media to our engagement with aesthetic artifice.

68. Ibid., 210.

69. H. Porter Abbott, *The Fiction of Samuel Beckett: Form and Effect* (Berkeley: University of California Press, 1973), 8–9.

70. Acheson, *Samuel Beckett's Artistic Theory and Practice*, 204.

71. Conway's *The Game of Life* can, however, also be played on an actual checkerboard.

72. Justin Parsler, "Life," in *Encyclopedia of Play in Today's Society*, ed. Rodney P. Carlisle (SAGE Publishing, 2009).

73. Martin Gardner, "The Fantastical Combinations of John Conway's New Solitaire Game 'Life,'" *Scientific American* 223 (October 1970), 120.

74. In fact, Gardner identifies only three rules: first, "there should be no initial pattern for which there is a simple proof that the population can grow without limit," second, "there should be no initial patterns that apparently do grow without limit," and finally, "there should be simple initial patterns that grow and change for a considerable period of time before coming to end in three possible ways: fading away completely (from overcrowding or becoming too sparse), settling into a stable configuration that remains unchanged thereafter, or entering an oscillating phase in which they repeat an endless cycle of two or more periods" (Gardner 120).

75. Parsler, "Life."

76. Hayles, *How We Became Posthuman*, 225.

77. Gardner, "The Fantastical Combinations of John," 120.

78. Beckett, *Endgame*, 32, 65.

79. Ibid., 37.

80. Ibid., 2.

81. Ibid., 13.

82. Sicart, "Against Procedurality."

83. Ibid.

84. See Janet H. Murray's *Hamlet on the Holodeck: The Future of Narrative in Cyberspace* (New York, NY: The Free Press, 1997).

85. Ibid.

86. Ruby Cohn, *Just Play: Beckett's Theatre* (Princeton: Princeton University Press, 1980).

87. Benjamin H. Ogden, "What Philosophy Can't Say about Literature: Stanley Cavell and *Endgame*" in *Philosophy and Literature* 33, no. 1 (2009), 127.

88. Ibid., 127.

89. Ibid. 136.
90. Beckett, *Endgame* 39.
91. Ibid., 39, emphasis added.
92. Ibid., 39.
93. Ibid., 40–41.
94. Ibid., 56.
95. Ibid., 69.
96. Keller, 203.
97. Ian Bogost, *Unit Operations: An Approach to Videogame Criticism* (Cambridge: MIT Press, 2006), 109.
98. Ibid., 108–109.
99. Beckett, *Endgame*, 11.
100. Ibid., 11.
101. Ibid., 11.
102. Ibid., 11.
103. Sicart, "Against Procedurality."
104. Bogost, 105.
105. Beckett, *Endgame*, 29.
106. Ibid., 46.
107. Martin Heidegger, "The Thinker As Poet," in *Poetry, Language, Thought*, trans. Albert Hofstadter (New York: Harper Perennial, 2001), 6.
108. Beckett, *Endgame*, 4.
109. Ibid., 5.
110. Ibid., 82.
111. Ibid., 5.
112. Ibid., 13.
113. Ibid., 13.
114. Martin Heidegger, "The Nature of Language," in *On the Way to Language*, trans. Peter D. Hertz (New York: Harper One, 1971), 57.
115. Ibid., 57.
116. Ibid., 57.
117. Ibid., 57.
118. Flusser, *Does Writing Have a Future?*, 56.
119. Ibid., 56.
120. Heidegger "The Nature of Language," 59.
121. Beckett, *Endgame*, 7, 12, 24, 35, 48, 71.
122. Ibid., 71.
123. Ibid., 71.
124. Flusser, *Does Writing Have a Future?*, 57.
125. Heidegger, "The Nature of Language," 59.
126. Ibid., 60.
127. Ibid., 60.
128. Jonathan Boulter, "'Speak No More': The Hermeneutical Function of Narrative in Samuel Beckett's *Endgame*," in *Samuel Beckett: A Casebook*, ed. Jennifer M. Jeffers (New York: Routledge, 1998), 133.

129. Ogden, 135.

130. Anke Finger, Rainer Guldin, and Gustavo Bernardo, *Vilém Flusser: An Introduction* (Minneapolis: University of Minnesota Press, 2011), 74.

131. Flusser, *Does Writing Have a Future?*, 145.

132. P. J. Murphy, "Beckett and the Philosophers," in *The Cambridge Companion to Beckett*, ed. John Pilling (New York: Cambridge University Press, 1994), 222.

133. Paul Éluard, "Beyond Painting," in *Beyond Painting* (Solar Books, 2008), 158–159.

134. Valerie Topsfield, *The Humour of Samuel Beckett* (Houndmills: Macmillan, 1998), 112.

135. Beckett, *Endgame*, 84.

Chapter 5

Blossoming Ghost

Memetic Engineering, Hauntology, and Metamorphiction in Jeff Noon's Falling Out of Cars

Contemporary British novelist and playwright Jeff Noon is most often celebrated for his poetic and iconoclastic award-winning debut novel, *Vurt* (1993). His stylistically masterful surrealist fiction reads like a hybrid of Lewis Carroll, Jorge Luis Borges, Italo Calvino, Georges Perec, William Gibson, George Elliot, and the latest release from Warp Records. That the preceding list could go on for pages is central to his work: Noon remixes cultural and subcultural canons into new carefully crafted, poetic, and dreamlike works of fiction. After the unexpected international success of *Vurt*, Noon published three more novels loosely connected to it. Afterward, his work took a more avant-garde turn: a work of experimental writing in the style of a novel-length pop song (accompanied by a recording collaboration with David Toop), a collection of remix short stories, stage and radio plays, an *avant texte* work of fiction, an online hypertext writing game in collaboration with Steve Beard, Susanna Jones, Alison MacLeod, and William Shaw. A further collaboration resulted in Noon's 2010 story "Artwork 2058: Probability Cloud," published "at the request," he writes, "of Dominique Gonzalez-Foerster, to accompany her exhibition in the Tate Modern's Turbine Hall."[1] Nine years after the publication of *Vurt*, Noon would publish *Falling Out of Cars* (2002), a novel that replaces the frenetic punk and techno energy of the earlier work with a subdued, disorienting, hypnotic balancing act of delicacy and unease. A year after *Falling Out of Cars*, Noon wrote the play *The Modernists* (2003). However, after *The Modernists*, Noon did not publish another work of long fiction for nearly a decade. In 2012, he published the DRM-free novella *Channel SkIn*, while in 2016, Noon's ongoing collaboration with Beard blossomed into the wonderful collaborative novel *Mappalujo*. Noon is now publishing more regularly with his labyrinthine, hypnogogic Nyquist mysteries detective series: *A Man of Shadows* (2017), *The Body Library* (2018), and *Creeping Jenny* (2020). Noon's distinct experiments in form, remix, memetics, and hauntology, however, are at their most striking in *Falling Out of Cars*.

While Noon's handle on the English language is nothing short of virtuosic, *Falling Out of Cars* is arguably his most elegant piece of writing. For many, it is also his most challenging piece. *Falling Out of Cars* occupies the instance of the word breaking off in a literalized sense: England has been infected with a mysterious "illness" called "The Noise" that is, quite literally, disrupting perceivers' ability to correlate meaningful chains of signification. At once a celebration for the radical possibilities of experimental prose and a lament for lost futures, *Falling Out of Cars* is a novel that expresses the instance when language as the dominant creator of cultural concepts is being replaced by information and automated combinatorialism as a moment so abstract and inhuman that it forces its characters to exist in a world where meaning and value are at risk of disappearing absolutely while, simultaneously, possibilities proliferate. As ambient as it is ambivalent, *Falling Out of Cars* inhabits this moment of confronting of exclusion. However, unlike Yeager or Beckett's work, Noon considers the encounter with the apparatus as both a site of loss *and* an opportunity for poiesis. Just as the protagonist of *Falling Out of Cars* both mourns the loss of her daughter and confronts the anxiety of losing the very memories of her child, the novel also observes such grief as activated by the encroaching inhuman forces of neoliberal capital. "The Noise" in *Falling Out of Cars* operates in characteristically Noonian fashion at both the level of content and form as the novel takes the reader on a journey of grief, mourning, and, finally, resignation. Yet, the resignation expressed by this melancholic novel ultimately concludes with the ambiguous potentialities of ambivalent optimism: if all is lost, perhaps a patient new beginning for an alternative future *is* possible.

Falling Out of Cars is characterized by a recurring series of textual samples—many recognizably from canonical literature—mutated *almost* beyond recognition. The result is an intense sense of textual haunting in the literal sense: the past, in the nebulous form of mutant intertextualities, habitually frequent the present. Upon its publication, the novel's reviews were largely enthusiastic, yet it did not generate the same explosive effect as did Noon's work in the 1990s. This is likely partly to do with the tone of the novel: whereas Noon's work in the 1990s scintillated with the accelerated superabundance of musical genres IDM, dub, punk, jungle, and drum & bass (all genres that influence Noon's remix approach to fiction), *Falling Out of Cars* has a literary affect more analogous to Henry Purcell's "When I am Laid in Earth" fused with John Coltrane's *A Love Supreme*. Tomas L. Martin writes that "Noon's prose is sublime," and that it "could be the most impressive stylistic novel of recent times";[2] John Berlyne remarks that the work is "an extraordinary piece of writing ... a prose poem rather than a novel ... filled with Pinteresque dialogue, peppered with non-sequiturs and eerily disturbing scenes that read like a literary puzzle";[3] Tony Chester adds that "Noon has proved once again that he is at the forefront of literary innovation."[4] Tomas Vergara, in his excellent Deleuzoguattarian reading of the novel suggests that, by positing catatonia as the equivalent to the cultural logic of late capitalism, "*Falling out of Cars* forces readers to reassess historical tendencies in global capitalism and poses multiple challenges to cultural studies on postmodern schizophrenia," while the novel also "provides an alternative to postmodern accounts on cultural schizophrenia by provides how capitalism's organisation of social practice is experienced according to negative affects—melancholy, dissociation, anxiety and disorientation."[5] Ultimately, Ismo Santala succinctly explains that "*Falling Out of Cars* is a poetic essay on perception, memory and the arts."[6]

Rather than the posthuman, thanatotic, accelerationist tendencies behind so many cyberpunk novels, including Noon's own early work, *Falling Out of Cars* is notable for its dreamlike, fluid pacing and emphasis on the subtleties of grief, uprootedness, and loss. In his notes on the novel, Noon writes, "I like to call *Falling Out of Cars* a transcendental road novel. A journey through a strangely transformed, diseased, England ... the quest is not the governing force behind the novel; these people are ... lost."[7] As the novel unfolds, the conflation of the quest with the theme of loss intensifies to the point of implosion. Indeed, the reader gets the mystifying sense that the journey is at once progressing through a diseased England while also confronting the grief of losing even the *very meaning of* loss and mourning.

The difficulty of *Falling Out of Cars* is at once its attraction. The piece is, as Berlyne notes, "plotless"—at least in the traditional sense of plot—yet, the intertextual, sampled, and remixed nodes in the novel are abundant. The fragmented nature of the work gives the impression of a vaporous whorl constituted by one's memories of having read *a lot*; the reader's experience of the uncanny, the "I feel like I know this from somewhere," itself enacts on an extra-diegetic level the unfolding amnesia in the novel thus placing the reader in a self-reflexive relationship not only with the book but with *narrative itself*. Claude Lalumière notes that "the narrative ... gets increasingly fractured into nearly incoherent fragments whose meaning is elusive yet tantalizingly almost graspable" and that it "shimmers with unexplained and intriguing mysteries."[8] Indeed, the novel can feel like life itself is like one of Tzara's Dadaists poems. However, this semantic elusiveness is achieved by merging cultural narrative, not with dream theory or absurdism, but with the science of information theory: a science unconcerned with semantic value and instead focused on the relationships between pattern and noise.

The illness—The Noise—that flattens and abandons the relationships between absence and presence, so central to *meaning-generation*, ultimately operates as a metaphor for the emotional state of loss and mourning. Yet, despite its emotionally turbulent subject matter, *Falling Out of Cars* is executed with tranquility and control; the noise here is randomness, static, and stochasticism, *not* bombastic velocity and amplitude. While much of Noon's earlier work balances the melancholic and elegiac with the energetic, humorous, and zany, *Falling Out of Cars* exclusively expresses a sense of melancholic quietude and elegance. Santala writes that "as Noon's characters are searching for the right words, searching for ways to reach out, their speech at times lapses into banality, into noise. On the other hand, the prose is highly controlled, a signal pregnant with meaning. . . . Soon, the reader picks up a clear, vibrant pulse. It's the heartbeat of literature."[9] Moreover, it is this literary pulse that Noon wishes to stimulate as a kind of resistance to the banality of fiction in the face of the encroachment of constitutive media technologies and neuro-totalitarianism. A kind of Dr. Frankenstein for the information age, Noon wants to give life back to dear, disparate, and discarded experience. A year before the publication of *Falling Out of Cars*, Noon wrote in his "Post Futurism Manifesto," in which he writes that "if the English novel is truly dead, we should place a flower on its grave, trample down the dirt. Now is the time to raise up the fragile, blossoming ghost." *Falling Out of Cars* is that fragile, blossoming ghost. Noon's haunted writing ultimately intimates the anxious and yet celebratory engagement with the gradual evaporation of print culture and, with it, the traditional literary arts.

In Noon's work, the representation of loss and mourning is intimately linked with his remix techniques. While in *Falling Out of Cars* this loss is concretized in the form of the death of a child and encroaching amnesia, it is also indicative of a broader cultural zeitgeist at the turn of the millennium that has become pathologically obsessed with the hauntings of the past in place of dreams for the future. "Instead of being about itself," writes Simon Reynolds, "the 2000s has been about every other previous decade happening again all at once. . . . Instead of being the threshold to the future, the first ten years of the twenty-first century turned out to be the 'Re' Decade. The 2000s were dominated by the 're-' prefix: *r*evivals, *r*eissues, *r*emakes, *r*e-enactments. Endless retrospection."[10] Responding to this zeitgeist, the mode of haunted, ghostly, and endlessly *r*eturning writing (i.e., Noon's "metamorphiction") is as much a process as a product of this cultural act of failed mourning. As a process, metamorphiction, Noon writes, "imagines text to be a signal, which can be passed through various FILTER GATES, each of which has a specific effect upon the language. Each gate allows the writer to access different creative responses within his or her imaginations. . . . This process is entirely dependant on the user's inspiration, moment to moment, as the text makes its journey."[11] In this sense, metamorphiction is a hesitant form of authorial impersonality. An essential aspect of metamorphiction operates by using samples, that is, an excerpt of either canonical or original text is subject to imaginative manipulation and mutation. The product of this metamorphosis is the finished text. Metamorphiction is in the lineage of Tzara, Burroughs, and Gysin; however, Noon cautiously and meticulously reclaims the role that authorial agency *can* play in the face of the aleatory or the inhuman.

Another way of understanding the retrospective impulse of metamorphiction is as a process similar to remix techniques of electronic music.[12] His work of avant-garde, concrete remix poetry, *Cobralingus*, demonstrates the process of metamorphiction by including all the preparatory materials, the mutation of those materials, and the result. In short, the work *shows* the process with the implication that the process is integral to the final product, and so *Cobralingus* is a work that includes its own *avant texte*. This emphasis on process and transformation is crucial to understanding so much of Noon's work, and *Cobralingus* offers insight into his technique. While he is concerned with the novel's possible disintegration as an aesthetic medium, his writing expresses an anxious enthusiasm for the reconfiguration and mutation of textual fragments. His work constitutes an ecology of narrative and storytelling: that our stories are alive, breeding, adapting, and adopting in a process he cheekily calls "nymphomation." Nymphomation is "sexy information" and accounts for the ways that stories mutate in a process akin to the ways organisms adopt and adapt to changes in their environments. If the apparatus is replacing human agency in storytelling with technological automation, Noon's metamorphiction has the author, like a genetic engineer *intervening* in biological selection, employ writerly poiesis as memetic engineering.

IMPERSONAL MEMETIC ENGINEERING AND METAMORPHICTION

Unlike Tzara, Burroughs, and Gysin's cut-ups, Noon's metamorphiction is concerned less with print culture's materiality and more with *stories themselves* and their memetic infectiousness. A meme is a cultural analog to a gene—a unit of information that changes, mutates, and adapts with each reproduction and reiteration. Memetics operate by jumping differing psycho-ecological levels by establishing topological distinction between meme and mind. These topologies as conceptual metaphors establish a kind of geometrical grid that permits the visualization of diegetic matrices that facilitate interdependent relationships between the concrete and the abstract. In 1965, American neurophysiologist, neurobiologist, and Nobel laureate, Roger Sperry, intimates a kind of abstract topology for the diegetic level of ideas in his 1966 paper "Mind, Brain, and Humanist Values." Sperry suggests a self-similarity between the two different levels: neurons and the ideas that these neurons make possible. The suggestion is one of ontological significance in that Sperry suggests that neurons and ideas may coexist on the same level of reality, that is, the relation between the brain and ideas is heterarchical or, at least, a tangled hierarchy. "Ideas cause ideas and help evolve new ideas," Sperry writes, "they interact with each other and with other mental forces in the same brain, in neighboring brains, and thanks to global communication, in far distant, foreign brains. And they also interact with the external surroundings to produce in toto a burstwise advance in evolution that is far beyond anything to hit the evolutionary scene yet."[13] Ideas, like organisms, are apt to mutate and adapt to their environment. The primordial ooze of nature is, in this sense, analogous to a kind of primordial infosphere where organisms and ideas, materialism and abstractionism, and brains and semiotics are all subject to the same systemic parameters of dynamism and plasticity. James Gleick writes that

> Atoms of hydrogen, oxygen, carbon, and iron could mingle randomly for the lifetime of the universe and be no more likely to form hemoglobin than the proverbial chimpanzees to type the works of Shakespeare. Their genesis requires energy; they are built up from simpler, less patterned parts, and the law of entropy applies. For earthly life, the energy comes as photons from the sun. The information comes via evolution.[14]

Like Borges's "Library of Babel" (1941), the biosphere constitutes infinite combination just as on the scale of infinite ideas all possible ideas find their home among the semantic vortex of endless combination. Where there is possibility in noisy, looping relationships among multiple levels, there is the possibility of knowledge by constant reorganization of semantic extensions of the mind. Likely the former is why so few have undertaken the task of theorizing a kind of selection of ideas. For many scientists, it is tempting to shy away from such poetic conceits—the cognitive fecundity of conceptual metaphor—in favor of a materialism indifferent to the medium of communication: linguistic potentiality. That Sperry and others take the pains to entertain this diegetic topology, however, is telling.

Likewise, French Jesuit paleontologist and philosopher Pierre Teilhard de Chardin[15] established an analogous conceptual topos to describe the infosphere: the noosphere. "Similar to the atmosphere and biosphere, the noosphere is composed of all the interacting minds and ideas on earth," writes Morville, "it's a provocative and romantic concept. But is the noosphere real? Or, is it just a metaphor, a figure of speech for relating one experience of the physical world to the ethereal realm of knowledge?"[16] Indeed, de Chardin's work had a major impact on media studies. Tom Wolf, for example, describes the profound effect that Teilhard's work had on McLuhan:

> technology was creating a "nervous system for humanity, "[Teilhard] wrote," a single, organized, unbroken membrane over the earth," a "stupendous thinking machine. . . ." That unbroken membrane, that noosphere, was, of course, McLuhan's "seamless web of experience." And that "one civilization" was his "global village." We may think, wrote Teilhard, that these technologies are "artificial" and completely "external to our bodies," but in fact they are part of the "natural, profound" evolution of our nervous systems. "We may think we are only amusing ourselves" by using them, "or only developing our commerce or only spreading ideas. In reality we are quite simply continuing on a higher plane, by other means, the uninterrupted work of biological evolution." Or to put it another way: "The medium is the message."[17]

Though Morville rightly suggests that this conceit is both provocative and romantic, the ramifications of the noosphere being "just a metaphor" are somewhat misleading. That is, for both Teilhard and McLuhan, what the noosphere represents is a process of transformation whereby thought—or the central nervous system—crosses from one level of narrative to another through a process of transformation. These levels are not simply deceptively stacked; instead, they prove to be embedded within one another.

Teilhard suggests that "the further the living being emerges from the anonymous masses by the radiation of his own consciousness, the greater becomes the part of his activity which can be stored up and transmitted by means of education and imitation."[18] For Teilhard, the noosphere is a topological space where thought is born and proceeds according to the processes of evolution:

> The recognition and isolation of a new era in evolution, the era of noogenesis, obliges us to distinguish correlatively a support proportionate to the operation—that is to say, yet another membrane in the majestic assembly of telluric layers. A glow ripples outward from the first spark of conscious reflection. The point of ignition grows larger. The fire spreads in ever widening circles till finally the whole planet is covered with incandescence. Only one interpretation, only one name can be found worthy of this grand phenomenon. Much more coherent and just as extensive as any preceding layer, it is really a new layer, the "thinking layer," which, since its germination . . . has spread over and above the world of plants and animals. In other words, outside and above the biosphere there is the noosphere.[19]

This conceptual space above and outside the biosphere is also the diegetic space where memetic influence takes place. Subtle coercion dramatizes the cognitive processes of crossing levels of tangled narrative levels and, as Teilhard suggests, "from this point of view man only represents an extreme case of transformation."[20] This transformation is one which the reader experiences in a manner that is both intellectual as well as affective: transfer to and from "the noosphere tends to constitute a single closed system in which each element sees, feels, desires and suffers for itself the same things as all the others at the same time."[21] The empathetic unity here in both Teilhard and McLuhan's work is largely informed by their Catholicism: the merging of all human nervous systems *into* and *as* the noosphere attests to the teleology of the mystical body of Christ. In this sense, their conception of the noosphere is markedly different from that of the indifferent, superidiotic, self-optimizing apparatus. Ultimately, Teilhard's conceptual map is fascinating, yet it does not account for a theory that describes the means through which the substance of level-crossing may operate through the impersonality of memetics.

Parisian biologist and Nobel Prize winner Jacques Monod, however, did theorize a way to conceptualize the transfer and transformation of ideas in the age of information. Monod's proposal was that analogous to the biosphere, which "stands above the world of nonliving matter,"[22] another conceptual level of abstractions—of ideas—can exist beyond the biosphere: "Ideas have retained some of the properties of organisms. Like them, they tend to perpetuate their structure and to breed; they too can fuse, recombine, segregate their content; indeed, they too can evolve, and in this evolution selection must surely play an important role."[23] This topology is a conceptual space of remarkable fecundity that ultimately blends sense ratios, emotional ambivalence, meaning, and information. Dawkins, six years later, comes to a similar conclusion through a study of genetics. Dawkins remarks that genes are the units of natural selection:

> They are past masters of the survival arts. But do not look for them floating loose in the sea; they gave up that cavalier freedom long ago. Now they swarm in huge colonies, safe inside gigantic lumbering robots, sealed off from the outside world, communicating with it by tortuous indirect routes, manipulating it by remote control. They are in you and in me; they created us, body and mind; and their preservation is the ultimate rationale for our existence. They have come a long way, those replicators. Now they go by the name of genes, and we are their survival machines.[24]

From this position, Dawkins speculates on an analogous unit to the gene and thus coins the term "meme." The origin of memes, for Dawkins, is in the brain of the individual. Memes are kinetic and travel along certain trajectories; the specifics of these trajectories are unique to the type of thought with which the meme corresponds. What is crucial, however, is that the meme always gestures outward yet is, at the same time, embedded within the brains of individuals: memes are memories reflexively slipping from one mind into another and mutating ad nauseam.

Regardless of its specific qualities or content, a meme always travels away from one mind toward another mind. In this sense, a meme is both a unit of thought constituted within the brain of an individual and simultaneously that which crosses diegetic levels: springs from the material brain to the abstract ambiance of tangled trajectories that link cognitive terminals and into another material brain. Gleick clarifies that memes travel outward and away from the brain

> establishing beachheads on paper and celluloid and silicon and anywhere else information can go. They are not to be thought of as elementary particles but as organisms. The number three is not a meme; nor is the color blue, nor any simple thought, any more than a single nucleotide can be a gene. Memes are complex units, distinct and memorable—units with staying power. Also an object is not a meme. The hula hoop is not a meme; it is made of plastic, not of bits. . . . The hula hoop is a meme vehicle . . . the meme is not the dancer but the dance.[25]

Memes, like Dada and poetic impersonality, are both process and effect. Gleick and Dawkins suggest that memes are not conscious and active agents; rather, they are abstract units whose only procedure is to further their replication in the cultural environment. "[Memes'] interests," Gleick remarks, "are not our interests";[26] yet, "awareness of memes [foster] their spread."[27] This recalls the complexity of thinking about information in relation to meaning: the asemic quality of mathematical information guarantees the possibility for the manifestation, and gradual reconfiguration, of any number of semantic patterns. In order to do so, however, requires a shift from one topology to another. "A gene might maximize its own numbers by giving an organism the instinctive impulse to sacrifice its life to save its offspring," Gleick writes, "the gene itself, the particular clump of DNA, dies with its creature, but copies of the gene live on. The process is blind. It has no foresight, no intention, no knowledge. The genes, too, are blind."[28] Just as the genes have no foresight, no intention, and no knowledge, the same can be said of memes. Memes emerge from the brain, yet they proceed without intention and meaning; adding violence or extreme affect to a meme, however, adds an emotional force that is otherwise absent in the actual course of memetic transfer and transformation. Just as "the gene is not an information carrying macromolecule" but rather "is the information,"[29] memes are not information carrying conceptual units but rather *are* information. This distinction helps distinguish memetic dissemination from, for example, allusion, homage, or intertextuality. Rather, this mode of conceptualization allows for certain valueless processes to propagate and proceed according to their own logic in conjunction with the logic of the cultural environment in which they are situated. Memes, like genes, like the impersonal remixing of texts, adapt to new environments; they are both the process and the effect.

Adaptation has a biological connotation associated with processes of evolution and mutation and, therefore, a different kind of metamorphosis of form than that which is associated with the revelation of underlying metaphysics of language. Linda Hutcheon's *A Theory of Adaptation* (2006) examines the processes in which narratives continually reappear—that is, are adapted—from one form or medium into another. Crucial to Hutcheon's analysis is Dawkins's concept of the meme. What is noteworthy about this gesture is that Hutcheon sets up an analytical model where cross-media adaptations can be examined beyond reader/audience expectations regarding formal and semantic fidelity to its original. Instead, she redirects the focus to the necessity for change, sometimes radical, when considering adaptation. In short, there is a shift away from agency: memetic adaptation is blind, has no foresight, no intention, and no knowledge of its origin and its plasticity. Like in biological reproduction, the adapted text must have some copying fidelity, but what is even more crucial is that the texts-as-memes must, in Dawkins's words, "exploit their cultural environment to their own advantage."[30] Hutcheon agrees: a form "adapts to its new environment and exploits it, and the story [or form] lives on . . . the same and yet not."[31]

The processes of environmental engagement—cross-diegetic mutations—prompt the question as to whether we can "look for selfish or ruthless memes."[32] Dawkins's answer is "that we might, because there is a sense in which [memes] must indulge in a kind of competition with each other."[33] Dawkins continues: "The human brain, and the body that it controls, cannot do more than a few things at once. If a meme is to dominate the attention of a human brain, it must do so at the expense of 'rival' memes."[34] This is where Dawkins's argument complicates the role of agency. For Dawkins, the brain is in control; perhaps it is over-occupied by a particular meme—establishing competition with rival memes—but the multilevel diegetic topos between ideas and the brain is, in general, ambient. "In the competition for space in our brains and in the culture," suggests Gleick, "the effective combatants are the messages. The new, oblique, looping views of genes and memes have enriched us. They give us paradoxes to write on Möbius strips."[35] While Dawkins suggests that one meme—a single reading of the sentence—must dominate another reading, an effective manner of experiencing the memetic Dada would be to read both simultaneously. Phrases, language, and memes certainly are in selfish or ruthless competition, though a single mode of reading cannot dominate the text itself but rather only momentarily dominate the reader's mind. To the reader's surprise, one possible meaning will slip and loop upward or downward to another semantic possibility; a myriad of other readings—both semic and asemic, emotionally ambivalent, and chronologically linear or nonlinear—will also struggle for linguistic and informational authority.

Dawkins reminds us that "we must not think of genes as conscious, purposeful agents. Blind natural selection, however, makes them behave rather as if they were purposeful, and it has been convenient, as a shorthand, to refer to genes in the language of purpose."[36] Here is an explicit example of conceptual metaphor: a mode of language employed to transform asemic and valueless processes into meaning. That this mode of language seems to provide agency to those chemical—or linguistic—processes is indicative of how the mind itself is engaged in a bidirectional relationship of semantic formation with phenomena. Dawkins employs the following example: "When we say 'genes are trying to increase their numbers in future gene pools,' what we really mean is 'those genes that behave in such a way as to increase their numbers in future gene pools tend to be the genes whose effects we see in the world.'"[37] That this mode of utilizing conceptual language or agential metaphors, describing valueless processes in terms of those which may be the effects of willed action, is convenient according to Dawkins:

> Just as we have found it convenient to think of genes as active agents, working purposefully for their own survival, perhaps it might be convenient to think of memes in the same way. In neither case must we get mystical about it. In both cases the idea of purpose is only a metaphor, but we have already seen what a fruitful metaphor it is in the case of genes. We have even used words like "selfish" and "ruthless" of genes, knowing full well it is only a figure of speech.[38]

Yet, figures of speech are indeed the modes of accessing, evaluating, and transforming reality; language, like scientific modes of symbolic notation, is not numinous but is itself metaphoric and metanoiac. The claim that these agential modes of language are *simply metaphor*, however, is misleading. Dawkins suggests that memes are living structures; the "life" or "living" of these linguistic modes is, in fact, not at all mystical—that is, transcendent—but are instead immanent extensions of the infosphere that changes and adapts with its constitutive ambient media ecology.

Something is at stake here, however, at least on a material analytical level. Thinking about memes, or metamemetics, disrupts certain distinctions between the material and the conceptual; there is an ontological level-crossing that brains (material structures) are structurally reconfigured by ideas (conceptual abstractions). Gleick records evolutionary psychologist Nicholas Humphrey's response to Dawkins's meme as that which should not simply be considered metaphorically, but rather, technically: "When you plant a fertile meme in my mind," Humphrey writes,

> you literally parasitize my brain, turning it into a vehicle for the meme's propagation in just the way that a virus may parasitize the genetic mechanism of a host cell. And this isn't just a way of talking—the meme for, say, "belief in life after death" is actually realized physically, millions of times over, as a structure in the nervous systems of individual men the world over.[39]

Humphrey's emphasis is that certain ideas or memes have *physically* and *technically* become manifest in the nervous systems of individuals all over the world. This is another instance of hierarchical level-crossing ad infinitum. The haziness here is between the conceptual and the material, though the two are self-reflexively intertwined in ways that suggest a complexity that disorders such a hierarchy: a paradox of transcending incompleteness.

Yet, this gesture does not explicitly suggest that the organic or the cognitive is undergoing a mutation to the material, so much as the inanimate is most effectively conceptualized as *alive*: as living structures. Dawkins engages in a kind of Darwinian structuralism, or what he refers to as "Universal Darwinism."[40] From this position, he suggests that "all life, everywhere in the universe, would turn out to have evolved by Darwinian means."[41] That Dawkins recognizes this conceit as one that is "general," rather than as a concise argument "based upon the facts about life as we know it," suggests that this approach is one that proceeds in principle and without intention. "In principle arguments such as mine," he writes, "can be *more* powerful than arguments based on particular factual research. My reasoning, if it is correct, tells us something important about life everywhere in the universe. Laboratory and field research can tell us only about life as we have sampled it here."[42] This universalist claim is not so much philosophical arrogance so much as it is an intellectual conceit from which Dawkins can make further claims, not only regarding natural selection on the genetic level but also in regards to analogous parallelisms. Therefore, Dawkins is capable of making provocative claims like: "Memes should be regarded as living structures, not just metaphorically, but technically."[43] Here is Dawkins's apology: "DNA is a self-replicating piece of hardware. Each piece has a particular structure, which is different from rival pieces of DNA. If memes in brains are analogous to genes they must be self-replicating brain structures, actual patterns of neuronal wiring-up that reconstitutes themselves in one brain after another."[44] That is, memes, or ideas, restructure the patterns of the brain, and according to Dawkins, physically rearrange brain structures.

Like all replicators, memes are "survival machines," a term Dawkins employs to denote both the material and the processes through which replicators mutate for survival. The brain and culture form a kind of closed, dynamic ecology. The "messages" in Noon's metamorphictional memetics—the linguistic and cognitive processes that instigate change among the respective diegetic levels as a means toward the survival of human stories—become the constitutive and ubiquitous structure through which "survival machines" can continue to operate culturally in the face of the apparatus. In his 2011 essay, "The Ghost on the B-Side," Noon provides an updated and concrete description of his technique and methodology in remixing narrative. Unlike the Cobralingus Engine, what Noon describes here explicitly involves using randomizing algorithms as digital cut-up machines. He writes that this "technique can be used to produce new, standalone stories or poems. It also works to create a second text that works in conjunction with an original piece. In this sense, it acts like a musical remix or an old-school B-side dub mix."[45] In the essay, Noon systematically goes through a remix of his own. The example he provides involves the remixing of two texts, one of his own, and a much shorter sample from a secondary source. The Second source material "is there only to bring in a bit of leftfield mystery."[46] The primary text is a random sample from Noon's files:

> These strange children with their marked skin, with their eyes always half-closed. These youngsters, outsiders, freaks of the shanty towns, silent and bowed, hands atremble with secret messages, codes of the new dance, moon-feverish. These kids of the wanderzones, magnetic units of flesh and blood and dark-hearted desires drawn to the duskline.[47]

For the secondary text, Noon samples a fragment of David Bowie's 1972 song, "Starman": "Come back like a slow voice on a wave of phase, / That weren't no D.J. that was hazy cosmic jive."[48] The next stage is to combine the two texts in a word processor and then proceed to cut-up the text in an online cut-up machine or, in the more traditional manner, with paper and scissors. From this, Noon proceeds to demonstrate how one may go about remixing the narrative. Providing five distinct stages of the remixed sample texts and, finally, the completed work of dub fiction, Noon explains and gives methodological suggestions on how to deal with the often surreal and nonsensical results. Ultimately, Noon demonstrates memetic engineering as both a technical practice—the impersonal and processual employment of randomizing algorithms—*and* an eminently poietic practice.

Perhaps the best examples of metamorphiction in *Falling Out of Cars* occur when the sample text haunts the finished product forcefully. As Noon's novel nears its end, the protagonist, Marlene, resolves to abandon her quest. The episode in question is a remix of a passage from Nabokov's *Lolita* (1955). Here, the despairing Humbert Humbert, after the murder of playwright Clare Quilty, is thwarted by police and gently drives his car into a tree:

> The road now stretched across open country, and it occurred to me . . . that since I had disregarded all laws of humanity, I might as well disregard the rules of traffic. So I crossed to the left side of the highway and checked the feeling, and the feeling was good. . . . Then in front of me I saw two cars placing themselves in such a manner as to completely block my way. With a graceful movement I turned off the road, and after two or three big bounces, rode up a grassy slope, among surprised cows, and there I came to a gentle rocking stop.[49]

Discarding the bombast that may follow a car chase episode, Nabokov shifts the defeat to be one of gentle despair. The node that Noon finds between *Lolita* and *Falling Out of Cars* is that of the loss of a child; though, in the two works, this love is of a drastically different kind: for Humbert, the loss of his victim, Lolita, while for Marlene, the double loss of the very memory of her deceased daughter. Here is Noon's remix of Nabokov:

> Time was a slow liquid through which we moved, now swerving towards the trees. A bank of earth slowed us even more, and we crested the rise at an easy pace and then slid to a halt against an old, blackened tree trunk. The seat belt embraced me round the heart, so gently. I felt that we had caressed the tree, rather than hitting it. A scuffle of birds flew away through the branches, and then all was still.[50]

Nabokov's road stretching "across open country" becomes Noon's time like "slow liquid" that swerves "towards the trees"; Nabokov's "feeling was good" morphs into a "seat belt [embracing Marlene] round the heart, so gently"; the "two or three big bounces" in Nabokov's text melt to become the "bank of earth"; Humbert comes to a "gentle rocking stop" while Marlene's car caresses "the tree, rather than hitting it." There is a strange bidirectionality to metamorphiction when done well. Nabokov haunts Noon, yet Noon haunts Nabokov: it becomes increasingly difficult to imagine this episode in the open American countryside without a scuffle of English birds.

Metamorphiction and memetic engineering here, then, is both processually technical and impersonally poietic. Noon disassembles and reconfigures the text using aleatoric modes as a means of revealing hidden truths of/in language, just as did his predecessors; however, while Tzara, Burroughs, Gysin, Stewart Home, Kathy Acker, Kenji Siratori, and Lee Kwo are interested in linguistic iconoclasm, Noon's project gestures in a different direction. "The most important point," Noon writes, "is that the actual cut-up engines are a tiny part of the method. They offer random inputs at two key stages: one to start the remixing process; the second to rearrange the almost finished piece."⁵¹ He then engages with extensive editing to create a writing that is poetic and semantically dense, as exemplified in the remix of Nabokov. "I now treat [the cut-up text] as a bank of potential images," writes Noon, "I go through the text, taking each group of words in turn as a self-contained unit. You will find that groups of words operate as phrase fragments. These phrases considered in isolation might well make a kind of everyday sense, but more often they work as surreal or nonsensical or poetic images."⁵² What Noon is aiming at is the potential of chaos in the face of reductionistic, quantitative combinatorialism and the possibility of *human—not apparatus—selected pattern* in the face of randomness; he focuses on the beauty and complexity of disorder, rather than cacophony, as a productive force:

> remove any words that just look plain ugly . . . look for the secret codes, the shadows of meaning. . . . Continue until the piece has coherence, structure and narrative flow, however those values may apply in the circumstances. . . . During this final stage, keep in mind the original source material, so that the remix mirrors it in some way.⁵³

That the remix is meant to mirror the original suggests a kind of fiction through the looking glass, a bidirectional haunting. Noon sees this "kind of dub fiction as a way of creating a more atmospheric or experimental or abstract or lyrical version of the original."⁵⁴ Indeed, he is suggesting a similar theory of remix as Paul D. Miller, aka DJ Spooky, suggests in *Rhythm Science* (2004): "Rhythm science . . . Think of it as a mirror held up to a culture that has learned to fly again, that has released itself from the constraints of the ground to drift through dataspace, continuously morphing its form in response to diverse streams of information."⁵⁵ Metamorphiction explicitly addresses the troubled status of literature in the digital age; it also suggests an urgent need to place the role of literature and poetry at the vanguard of imagining the future since narrative poiesis is resistance again algorithmic culture. While Noon's metamorphictional writing can be understood as the "ghost . . . haunting the original text," it may also be understood in a more abstract context as that methodology which aesthetically and critically addresses the mirroring effect of chronology regarding the past, present, and future's tendency to loop back into themselves, tangle, and become part of the system they are meant to signify sequentially.

For Noon, there is an intimate link between ghosts, remix, and logical sequentiality. One particular aspect of Noon's writing is his ability to exhaust any variety of semantic connotations to a given word or phrase. Ghosts, in *Falling Out of Cars*, are, on the one hand, explicit: a loss of narratives, a loss of literary tradition, the gradual disappearance of print culture, a parent's tragic loss of a child. Yet, Noon aims to harness any potential opportunity for optimism and solace in disintegration. The gesture of information technologies for the writer is that even the prospect of the material solidity of printed texts transition, at an increasingly rapid rate, into a state of fluent aberration. Marx's phrase, "all that is solid melts into air," is axiomatic in the digital age. The complete statement, however, nuances the intense ambivalence that this mutation implies. Elegance and disorder are the foggy by-products of a hastily evaporating material culture. So that "all that is holy is profaned, and man is at last compelled to face with sober senses his real conditions of life, and his relations with his kind."[56] Marx and Engels, however, could not foresee that the information age will be one long carnival that struggles to produce new order. As material culture melts into air, so do text and self evaporate, "Our souls—which to advance their state, / Were gone out,"[57] as Donne writes, and the ecstasy may or may not ever come to a halt, script and serotonin rapidly depleting with altitude. DJ Spooky suggests that

> An intangible sculpture that exists only in the virtual space between you and the information you perceive—it's all in continuous transformation, and to look for anything to stay the same really is to be caught in a time warp of another era, another place when things stood still and didn't change so much. . . . [Today, we must] think as the objects move, to make us remember that we are warm-blooded mammals and that the cold information we generate is a product of our desires, and that it manifests some deep elements of our being.[58]

With this fluidity comes unpredictability; "as we flow across the page in the here and now, and as you process the words as you read them, remember this: They process you as well."[59] Word processing is world processing, information is the exhaust of our desires, and early in his oeuvre, Noon establishes this enchanted dissatisfaction beautifully: "Everything going wrong and the far-off call of the owl. If they can remix Madonna after she's dead, why can't they remix the night?"[60] Where there is unpredictability, there are opportunities for pattern; Noon asks us to find our own narrative patterns amid the noise: illogical, surreal, dreamlike, excessive patterns that resist the delimiting and standardizing processes of the apparatus. Where there is loss, there is something else to be discovered.

HAUNTOLOGY AND THE SPECTER OF THE NOVEL

This kind of optimistic ambivalence toward loss is mediated through the virtuosic wordplay at the center of Noon's aesthetic. Words, like information, can combine, disintegrate, and breed: nymphomation. Polysemy and ecstatic semantic instability drive the syntactic and poetic trajectory of Noon's work; it is his merging of human and technology in the writing process that largely accounts for his ability to confront the *without* through permutation. "The future of language," Saul Williams suggests, "would involve our getting closer and closer to being able to articulate the unspoken. Consciousness, like technology, evolves in the same way that there are advances in technology that may take a decade or more before they reach the public, there are also shifts in consciousness that gradually becomes understandable to the masses."[61] This gesture toward the future, of possibilities and the unspoken, links to increasing instability in the status of memory in the digital age. Williams is optimistic that the analogous mutations of word processing and world processing will eventually find a kind of stability or understandability. That some nonconceptual textual form—nonconceptual because the body of knowledge will be more akin to clittering cacophony than canon—of cultural and textual memory can gradually be intelligible by the masses is complicated by two notions. First, the structural logic of the masses cannot be made sensible in a culture where social and emotional relations are utterly pliable. Second, DJ Spooky writes that "silence is one of contemporary culture's rarest commodities,"[62] and speculating on the past necessitates stillness and silence from the present, but there is no indication of the deceleration of information. "There's a famous story about the artist Marcel Duchamp," DJ Spooky narrates,

> No one knows if it's really true, but that's how stories work. Sometime over a period of years in the mid-twentieth century, he decided to stop painting, saying he stopped simply because he had started to just "fill things in . . . ." This is what's going on now. When I talk about the crowded spaces of infomodernity—I'm talking about a world filled with noise, and if there's one thing we learned from the twentieth century, it's this: noise is just another form of information.[63]

Whether writers, poets, artists, composers, and so on, are currently filling in our memories or whether they are filling in the stuff of an ever becoming present makes for a complicated distinction. What may be most arresting about Williams's suggestion is the curtailed emphasis on the "future" and "unspoken"; this asks what division can be meaningfully made between past and future that are equally unspoken. In a culture of noise and ever-rapid infoproduction and info-recirculation, the past frequents the present, the present retrospectively mutates perception of the past, and both haunt a future that never seems to arrive. Noise and information are, like artists, filling things in; the discrepancy is that the artist wills this filling while information fills without intention. These are the ghosts of which Noon is concerned, those of human memory and self-generating, rapidly updating information technologies. *Falling Out of Cars*, then, is intimately invested in the artist as concept and meaning generators while, simultaneously, information technologies and noise uncompromisingly occupy the same cultural role. "Once you get into the flow of things," writes DJ Spooky, "you're always haunted by the way things could have turned out."[64] Haunting, in Noon's fiction, is chronologically absolute; it is ecstatic. The past haunts the present, the present haunts the past, the future haunts the present: "The haunting is calling you; come up, come up! Let me take you higher."[65]

As a result, what is particularly fecund in Noon's assertions regarding metamorphiction is how this kind of writing seems intensely invested in the notion of spectrality. The way Noon seems to posit the material print culture of literature in a kind of non-opposition with that of info-culture is telling. This is a kind of Derridean enterprise. Indeed, that Noon's collaborator on *Mappalujo*, Steve Beard, references Derrida's "hauntology" explicitly in an interview with D. Harlan Wilson is telling.[66] The source of hauntology is Derrida's *Spectres de Marx/Specters of Marx* (1993). Those familiar with Beard's fiction will attest to his explicit engagement with critical theory for aesthetic guidance. For Noon, however, the references to critical theory are obscured for the sake of privileging phonology and poetry. Furthermore, as the style and tone of "The Ghost on the B-Side" suggests, metamorphiction is for all, in terms of both consumption and production, something that sets his theorizing in notable contrast with the more intensely involved critical work of Beard and DJ Spooky. "Repetition and first time" writes Derrida in *Specters of Marx*,

> this is perhaps the question of the event as question of the ghost. . . . Is there *there*, between the thing itself and its simulacrum, an opposition that holds up? Repetition and first time, but also repetition and last time, since the Singularity of any first time, makes of it also a last time. Each time it is the event itself, a first time is a last time. Altogether other. Staging for the end of history. Let us call it a hauntology.[67]

The ontology of the ghost, for Derrida, is one of undecidability. That is, the ontological status of a ghost is that which represents the non-opposition between "the real and the unreal, the actual and the inactual, the living and the non-living, being and non-being."[68] Hauntology, a portmanteau word comprised of haunting and ontology, conflates the ghost with the question of existence; in this way, meditation on the undecidability of the ghost poses fascinating questions regarding the existence of that which has no presence. Commonly, ghosts are considered to be from the past, haunting the present; these ghosts may be deceased individuals, memories, individual or cultural traumas, the revisiting of something lost to the present. What is significant here is that ghosts intimate something, like the past, that is absent from the present yet still believed to exist in some sense.

For Fisher, hauntology is another way to consider the cultural effects of neoliberalism and should be distinguished from Linda Hutcheon's description of parody or Frederic Jameson's pastiche as the dominant modes of postmodernism. Fisher is particularly concerned with the disappearance, beginning in the 1980s but culminating in the first decades of the twenty-first century, of a kind of postwar popular modernism that fostered experimentation and innovation. For example, it is almost impossible to mistake, say, the popular music of the 1960s for the 1950s or the 1970s for the 1960s. By the 1980s, the emerging nostalgia industry begins to replace and calcify the popular imagination and shifts instead toward endless repetitions of the past. This process is, similar to Derrida's sense, knotted with politics. "If the conditions for this 'popular modernism' were provided to a large extent by social democracy," Fisher writes,

> its aspirations were not confined to a hope that social democracy would simply continue. The radical dimension of social democratic culture, in fact, consisted in the way it produced a longing for its (self-) overcoming, that it was premised on the movement toward a scarcely imaginable future. . . . The actual future [however] would not be popular modernism, but populist conservatism: the creative destruction unleashed by the forces of business on the one hand, the return to familiar aesthetic and cultural forms on the other.[69]

This repetitive, compulsive returning to cultural artifacts of previous decades becomes the popular mode of narrating the present and is indicative that the future that was promised did not, and under such conditions, cannot arrive. We were promised flying cars, but we got Trump; we were promised a lineage from Autechre and David Cronenberg but got the Arctic Monkeys and more *Star Wars*; we were promised a literary heir to Octavia Butler but got *Harry Potter*. Fisher identifies two bifurcating tendencies of hauntology: the first "refers to that which is (in actuality is) no longer, but which is still effective as virtuality (the traumatic 'compulsion to repeat,' a structure that repeats, a fatal pattern)"[70] while "the second refers to that which (in actuality) has not yet happened, but which is already effective in the virtual (an attractor, an anticipation shaping current behavior)."[71] Rather than simply nostalgic, however, hauntology is also mournful and melancholic. The attractor here, in the second sense of hauntology, is of particular importance in its relation to the failed mourning that characterizes Fisher's vision of the early twenty-first century. The hauntological condition is the desire or compulsion to repeat endlessly, sample, or relive the past. It is also a constitutive condition of replacing a culture once governed messily by human agency and innovation to that governed ultra-efficiently by reductive and predictive algorithmic calculation; endless upgrades of the same have replaced innovation. Hauntology is also, as Katy Shaw remarks, a "peculiarly English phenomenon,"[72] and, as a result, it is appropriate the narrative of *Falling Out of Cars* takes place in an England infected by spatial, temporal, and mnemonic disorder.

In the novel, that which determines the shaping of the future is expressed as The Noise—where past, present, and future are difficult to disentangle and where the future could as easily be the shaper of the present as the past is to the future—and it is this informational threshold where the word breaks off and meaning is nebulous. In many ways, Marlene's quest is not only one to preserve the memories of her daughter or to find solace in her grief, but to hold on to language as a confrontation to hypercomplex algorithmic culture. Noon's experimentalism is itself complex territory, but his whole project beginning in the early 1990s is an ongoing quest for a kind of modernist spirit of possibility, conceptual expansion, and innovation. The Noise, after all, is informational and is at once a calculable process independent of human agency and beyond semantic or poietic delimitation; however, information is also characterized by its fecundity as possibility for endless alternatives. In a sense, the mourning in *Falling Out of Cars* is a resistance to the attractor force of calculation's inscrutability via its replacement by articulation. As a kind of inversion of the grand romantic trope of the genius confronting the sublime, *Falling Out of Cars'* soft and delicate, staticky noisiness offers the meaningfulness of small articulations in the face of, not nature, but the radically inhumanness of procedural, algorithmic culture. Indeed, writing itself is haunted by the uncanny, strange-loopy, self-reflexive spectral future of writing haunting the present.

THE SPECTRALITY OF EPISTOLARY WRITING AND THE CHAOTICS OF MEMORY

Another way of linking hauntology to metamorphictional writing is to consider Kafka's commentary on epistolary writing's spectrality. "Letter writing, according to Kafka," John Zilcosky notes, "depends on two specters: the absent self and the absent interlocutor. Beyond these two, there is a vast community of ghostly offspring watching, listening, and devouring. . . . Letter writing is thus never a private exchange; it is staged before a voracious and ever-proliferating group of ghostly readers."[73] The absent author and excluded interlocutor are offered treatment in *Falling Out of Cars*, itself an epistolary novel; however, what is most pressing here is the idea of not only letter writing but literature itself as a non-private exchange.

For metamorphiction, both original writing and print culture haunt the present; literature is not only consumed by a voracious and propagating group of ghostly readers, but is also subject to mutation and production by those readers. For Derrida, the haunting of non-private exchange is heightened by information technology: "What Kafka says about correspondence, about letters, about epistolary communication, also applies to telephonic communication . . . I believe that ghosts are part of the future, and that the modern technology of images, like cinematography and telecommunication enhances the power of ghosts and their ability to haunt us."[74] Just as spectrality obliterates privacy in epistolary writing, information technologies offer an entirely new forcefulness to ghosts: both the sender and the receiver experience an absence, and beyond these two is the possibility of a near-infinite interference of ghostly progeny. The ghosts of metamorphiction are those samples of the literature haunting the present. Yet, simultaneously ghosts are part of the future, the remixed texts that are—though in the present nonexistent in the form of textual and cultural noise—nevertheless the subject of an undecidable reality status: the possibility of future manifestation. Indeed, information technology is central to Noon's formal conception of *Falling Out of Cars*.

The narrative of *Falling Out of Cars* is presented as a series of diary entries by Marlene Moore, a middle-aged journalist:

> My name is Marlene Moore. This is my book.
>
> It's the kind of notebook a teenager might buy, with the picture of a tiger on the cover. A tiger with blue stripes. Inside, the paper is thin, almost translucent; the ink from my pen seeps through. All these lines of writing. Shadows, glances.
>
> This is the story. These are all the various things that have happened to me in the last few weeks. But now, as I flick through the book, I see only the mess I have made. Words, sentences, paragraphs, whole pages, scoured with black marks. Mistakes. The noise gets in everywhere. Pages are ripped, or torn out completely; some discarded, other taped into new positions.[75]

The reference to the tiger with blue stripes recalls Jorge Luis Borges's short story "Blue Tigers" (1983). "Blue Tigers," like *Falling Out of Cars*, examines the thresholds of human understanding when faced with the infinite, incalculable, or inhuman. And the incalculable disrupts the significance of memory; recall is a mess when noise is ubiquitous. However, Noon desires to offer metamorphictional homage to Borges and include Borges among the various other literary nodes informing the novel. The reconfiguration of samples—there seems to be an explicit reference to cut-ups here in the form of ripped pages taped into new positions—as textual samples also function as the ghosts of literature that Noon wishes to resurrect in contemporary writing.

Marlene is on a quest by car—commissioned by a mysterious and ailing elderly man, Kingsley—for fragments of a broken mirror that have been scattered across a dystopian England. The shattered mirror in the work is presumably the same mirror through which Alice had traveled in Carroll's *Through the Looking-Glass*. Along the way, Marlene picks up three companions: a young woman who practices tai chi, Henderson; an ex-soldier, Peacock, who has "got a gun";[76] and a teenage girl, Tupelo, a hitchhiker who is picked up from the side of the road, holding a sign that reads "wherever."[77] England has been infected with an illness known as "The Noise." The origin of this illness is never explained; this proves to be narratologically necessary. While its symbolic status is marked by the reader's acceptance of the relationship between the illness and loss, on a textual level, however, mourning and loss are made manifest *as* the illness. Grimwood explains the symbolic significance of the covered mirrors: "No sufferer from the virus may look in a mirror, so looking glasses are painted over or turned to the wall, as though the whole country had gone into high-Victorian mourning for a lost way of life."[78] Marlene records that "the noise is a dark hand, a soft hold, slow poison, sickness, it will not leave me go. And yet I will have such moments of lucidity, a sudden pain of memory, whole and vibrant; a fleeting glimpse that must be caught hold of immediately, or else be lost for ever."[79] Her notebook, and the novel itself, replace her memory: "I have to keep writing. There is no other escape, especially now that I seem to be getting worse . . . This is the book."[80] Marlene, Henderson, and Peacock are suffering from the illness, and, consequently, also suffering from individual sorrow. Tupelo, on the other hand, is immune to the illness; though it is important to note, she is not immune from mourning. Furthermore, Marlene has lost her daughter to the illness, a back story which, along with Marlene's abandoned marriage, allows Noon to engage in the meditation on loss and memory. The Noise can be provisionally treated with a government distributed drug, "Lucidity" or "Lucy." These are the basic plot elements with which Noon engages as the substratum of a series of metamorphictional meditations upon the evaporating state of literature.

The narrative of noise and haunting occurs in non-space: the "no there there" between a transmitter and a receiver of a communication circuit. Before the first chapter, Noon establishes this non-space by having a page with the word "Transmission" at the top of the page, and the word "Reception" near the bottom, while two questions are situated in between: "Where do you come from? / And where are you going?"[81] The novel and its components are not a vacuum, but rather a signal passing through noise governed by the semiotics of chaos where, as in *Cobralingus*, all meaning appears provisional; the signal flickers, is distorted, feeds back, and mutates. Noon establishes this narrative non-space where semiotic relations, the mirror and its image, the writer and the interlocutor are subjected to chaotic flux. For Noon, however, the chaotic pathway from a transmitter to a receiver, destructive and disorderly as it may appear, is the narrative space in which fertile experimentation occurs. This is expressed in Noon's conclusion to the novel:

> In these days of chaos, possibilities abound.
> I shall leave this book on the nightstand, in between the traveler's bible and the telephone directory. These pages of smoke. They have their own conclusion. I can only hope that some other sweeter device or agency will cast its spell upon them, making them clean, and the world alongside.
> Listen now. Whoever you are, with these eyes of yours that move themselves along this line of text; whoever, wherever, whenever. If you can read this sentence,[82] this one fragile sentence, it means you're alive.[83]

The past haunts the present, the present haunts the future that refuses to arrive, and both present and future simultaneously haunt, even determine, the past. Here, Noon establishes the relation between the past, the dissolving of cultural and personal memory, and the desire for a future where possibilities abound; equally delicate is the status of the present, only legitimated by the ability to decode one fragile sentence.

We can also consider *Falling Out of Cars* as a general communication system with five constitutive parts as mapped out by Claude Shannon. This consists of the information source, the transmitter, the channel, the receiver, and the destination. Shannon explains the information source as that "which produces a message or sequence of messages to be communicated to the receiving terminal."[84] The transmitter also functions in a rather straightforward way: it "operates on the message in some way to produce a signal suitable for transmission over the channel."[85] The channel is simply the medium between the transmitter and receiver, whether it is a set of wires, a band of radio frequencies,[86] or, in the case of Noon, literature. Shannon explains that "the receiver ordinarily performs the inverse operation of that done by the transmitter, reconstructing the message from the signal"[87] and consequently provides a received signal similar to its original manifestation. The final part of the system, the destination, is essentially "the person (or thing) for whom the message is intended."[88] In terms of Noon's metamorphiction, the sample text may be thought of as an information source, the transmitter as the metamorphictive process which transforms the inlet text into a poetic signal appropriate for transmission, the channel is the *avant texte*, the mutated text is the reconstructed message, and the destination might be considered to be the book itself and—by extension—its readership. However, the destination has a second significance: it is, unlike a receiver that aims to delimit and control the message, radically unpredictable and represents an open, rather than a determined, endpoint. This trajectory is what Noon wishes to intimate in *Falling Out of Cars*.

Taking the general communication system as a model, noise may affect the signal anywhere between the transmitter and the receiver. With *Cobralingus*, for example, the reader may delight over the chaotic mutation and semantic flux that the texts undergo along the signal pathway. These instances constitute some of the most pleasurable moments in *Cobralingus*; yet, the significance of this enjoyment is related to the metamorphictive process as a whole. *Falling Out of Cars*, when considered in terms of a general communication system, may be regarded as an extended narrative that occurs in this conceptual space and time. In other words, the narrative of *Falling Out of Cars* is an extended interim stage of metamorphiction: a constant grasping at samples, memories, and reiterative behaviors while struggling to allow the past to be the past as a means to accept loss and move on to the uncertainty of the future. However, this interim stage does not refer to an original transmission, which would arguably be Marlene's extra-diegetic experience. Ultimately, Noon expresses a narrative as a nonspatial and paratemporal pulsation situated between a transmitter and a receiver—where and when a signal is most susceptible to noise. What remains is a nonspatial and paratemporal narrative that is constantly at odds with itself yet elegant in its balance, a structure both exemplifying and permissive of metamorphictional experimentation. Weaver explains that when "noise is introduced . . . the received message contains certain distortions, certain errors, certain extraneous material, that would certainly lead to what the received message exhibits, because of the effects of the noise, an increased uncertainty."[89] In *Falling Out of Cars*, however, the correlation between noise and uncertainty conveys the necessity of both the desirable and undesirable implications of information. Noon is quite explicit as to the desirable influence noise may have on the arts.

Alternatively, the ubiquity of noise evokes the metaphor of an illness that disrupts all meaningful categories of communication and identity for the novel's characters. Indeed, this radical uncertainty ultimately results in death, as in the case of Marlene's nine-year-old daughter, Angela, who was, as Marlene laments, "drowned by her own heart."[90] Angela's death is an "error" from Marlene's perspective; yet, the mother must nevertheless learn to accept the reality of her daughter's death. Likewise, culture must accept the loss of innovation to algorithmic combinatorialism in order to reinvigorate *the new*.

Like Marlene's mourning, the narrative itself is in continual mutation due to signal interruption and noise. In this sense, the characters' inner lives may be understood as metasignals within a larger constitutive signal, consequently subjected to emotional and philosophical distortions, turbulence, errors, and noise. The character-as-metasignal caught between a transmitter and a receiver is part of Noon's fascination with perception, a philosophical meditation at the heart of *Falling Out of Cars*. Indeed, the epistolary form of the novel allows the reader to follow, as Santala explains, the "dreamlike, languid downward spiral into the increasingly unstable mind of Marlene."[91] Marlene as narrator, in short, is a metasignal, and the diseased England is a nonspatial and paratemporal locale between two metaphorical poles of a communication system. The environment in which Marlene is situated is subject to the interference of the noise insomuch as it infects the English landscape while she, as epistolary narrator, amplifies the discordant confusion through her diary entries; she is, in this sense, both subject to the noise and has the noise as her subject.

The metaphor of noise as an illness is ambient and ubiquitous; both the perceiver and the percept are affected and contaminated. While the reader must be suspicious of Marlene's apprehension and interpretation of events, the phenomenological objects themselves are infected. This, of course, is ontologically confusing. On the one hand, the material landscape constitutes the fictive world of the novel; yet, this landscape is to be understood as a disrupted signal. The signal, however, is a metaphor for malleable and chaotic text. Consequently, the very architecture of both utterance and perception is deranged. What follows is a narrative game with the nature of perception that emphasizes the narrator's ghostly status. So, Marlene's diary entries are subjected to the chaotics of communication—flux, dislocation, disorder—therefore radically altering the dramatic and ontological immediacy of *Falling Out of Cars*. She herself becomes an infected metasignal within an immanent paraspace affected by the same disease.

Like Kafka, Marlene becomes as ghostly as the interlocutor. An episode of interest is Marlene's description of a "machine" that can be used to simultaneously look at a mirror and read a passage of a text—both tasks being of exceptional difficulty and danger to a sufferer of the illness. The machine is comprised of seven parts: a silver coin; a single blade of a pair of scissors; a small battery; a compact disc of *Tomorrow Is the Question*, by Ornette Coleman that is "broken, one shard missing";[92] a piece of string; a bottle top; and a page torn from *The Diary of Samuel Pepys*.[93] Marlene explains how the machine works:

> First, choose a location approximately one metre from the water's edge, with the tide incoming; here the blade of the scissors is buried halfway in the pebbles, with the sharpened point showing; the compact disc is placed horizontally on the blade, with the point of the blade pushed securely through the hole provided; please note that the labelled side of the disc must be facing downwards, and that the disc should be tilted at a slight angle, towards the operator; a knot can now be tied in one end of the piece of string; the other end is tied round the battery. The battery is placed on the pebbles close by the compact disc, with the page

of the book held in place beneath the battery . . . finally, the knotted end of the string is placed within the broken part of the compact disc, in such a way that the string is held there. . . . The operator should place themselves in such a position that they can both read the text and see their own face reflected in the mirrored surface of the compact disc. The eyes glance back and forth between the text and the mirror, as the text is read aloud. . . . And the mirror holds the face, gently.[94]

Marlene explains that "all that matters is the text and the mirror, the joining of the two, and that the text be read aloud to the final word whilst the eyes stare back at themselves, examining."[95] She adds that "the fact that nobody has yet managed this task, not completely, should not discourage us."[96] The machine serves Noon well; it opens a passage examining the correlation between the infected perceiver and the phenomenological object.

The strange episodes that follow Marlene's gaze into the machine signify one of Noon's most profound narrative examinations: that of the failing distinction between the perceiver and the perceived and the paradox of subject position in non-space. The episode opens with Marlene recognizing another subject:

> I saw somebody. I saw a person that I recognized, or thought I recognized. In the crowd. A sideways glance of somebody known briefly, or well known, a long time ago or recently. A woman. In the crowd that moved along the beach path, she walked there, below the promenade . . . I followed her. I pushed through the crowd, trying to keep the woman in sight. Sometimes she would seem very near to me, and then further away, and sometimes she would vanish altogether, drift away and then reappear some distance off, and always moving.[97]

Marlene calls out to the woman and is surprised by her own utterance: "My name. My own name," Marlene writes, "we have the same name. The woman stands there quite still, with her back towards me, as I approach."[98] The distinction between Marlene and the other woman becomes increasingly strange as the narrator is uncertain who—Marlene or the woman—is speaking: "'Marlene? Is that you?' Someone speaks. The woman turns round . . . I have to move close myself, one step, one more, to let the face reveal itself. And with these eyes, those lips, this mouth, that strand of hair falling, these bones, that skin so pale, these hands that reach forward."[99] The constituent and constitutive noise dissolve the boundary between Marlene the perceiver and the other woman as perceived. This blurring culminates with the alternation between the proximal and the remote, "this" and "that," indicating the two bodies' perceptual merging. That is, the noise affects the perceived exterior—the signal, the woman—and the perceiving interior—Marlene, the infected metasignal—to such a degree that the two become indistinguishable.

CHARACTERS AS METASIGNALS AND WRITING PATTERN FROM RANDOMNESS

Fictional characters may be understood as proxies with a likeness to actual individuals, that is, characters-as-characters. On another ontological level, a character is textual, existing within a linguistic system, a character-as-text. Because *Falling Out of Cars* is considered here as a disrupted signal situated in the non-space between a transmitter and a receiver, the characters are ultimately subject to the same ontological analogy: on the one hand, they are characters-as-characters within the novel. On the other, signals within a signal, thus characters as metasignals. Because the text of *Falling Out of Cars* is a disrupted signal, it follows that the textual characters must also be manifestations of that disrupted text. If the characters are to function iconically—that is, according to a likeness or similarity to nonfictional perceiving individuals in a chaotic environment—we may assume that, by analogy, they perceive a chaotic landscape as chaotic perceivers. In *Falling Out of Cars*, the text is chaotic and noisy; therefore, the characters perceive chaos and noise. These ontological distinctions are deliberately blurred by Noon, producing an effect that is simultaneously consistent and recognizable, yet alienating. In the subsequent episode, there is a narrative shift away from Marlene's first-person diary entries. However, the scene is still to be considered an excerpt from Marlene's diary, and therefore the unnamed narrator is, in fact, the woman who pulled Marlene toward her: a paradoxical third-person Marlene, posterior to the previously established locale of perception. This shift in perceptual locale ultimately marks the intersection between perception and memory.

As Marlene-the-metasignal is relocated into the position of the perceived, she fears the loss of her memory. Much earlier in the novel, Marlene explains that "there seems to be no ruling to how my memory works; certain events will stay with me, free as yet from infection, but lately, and more and more, I can feel the past drifting away. Beyond hold. The weeks, the years gone by, one by one, all drawn over by confusion."[100] Her anxiety about memory loss is the product of Marlene's translation/translocation from her position as a metasignal/character to the infected signal itself, that is, dissolving into the environment of noise and information as an absolute extension of being. The ubiquity of noise in the principal signal threatens the "events" and memories that are "free as yet from infection." Of course, the memory Marlene holds most precious is that of her dead daughter, Angela. An unnamed narrator tells the episode describing Marlene's feverish attempt to write Angela back into existence:

> Black marks, wetness, scratches. In the darkness, a pen moving across skin, across a young girl's skin. Words being put there, on the skin, with Marlene's

own hand doing the writing. Words, these words, being written on the skin and Marlene thinking to herself that only by covering the body with words, entirely, will the young girl be saved. And then feeling the sharp, polished nib of the pen cutting into the skin, pushing the ink through into the body of the girl, pushing the words deep into the veins; Marlene realizing that the words, these very words, they will either enliven the girl, or kill her. Only by putting the correct words down, in the correct order, will the girl be roused again.[101]

This episode suggests that "Marlene the third-person narrator" now belongs to a realm paradoxically removed from "Marlene the first-person narrator," that is, there has been a diegetic translocation from a metasignal to the infected signal, or from the perceiver's diary toward the perceiver's phenomenal environment. Marlene's desperate attempt is marked by her efforts to save the memory of her daughter from drifting away by transforming text into body by transcoding Angela back into a character-as-metasignal. By providing a third-person narrative from the infected signal's position, Noon demonstrates Marlene's desire to reconstitute Angela, thus giving Angela presence in both memory and physicality.

However, Marlene's desire to write her daughter back into existence proves impossible and is thoroughly hauntological. Moreover, the act of writing takes a disconcerting turn as, rather than giving the daughter presence, it literally tortures Angela and figuratively damages her as she exists as a memory for Marlene. The third-person Marlene explains the absurdity of this task:

> The soft wetness, shreds of skin, scratches, the black ink. Tiny cries of pain, the darkness. Marlene knew that she was failing, she was failing in the task. The writing was a poison. But still, she could not lift the pen away from the flesh. Marlene could not stop writing. And then from nowhere came the idea that all she had to do, to stop herself from writing, was to wake up. She had to wake herself up from this dream, that was all . . . to lift the pen from the body of the young girl, to let the eyes come open finally, blinking at the light that burned into them.[102]

This passage is almost certainly a remix of Kafka's "In the Penal Colony" (1948). The theme linking the two stories is the metamorphic relation between body and text. In Kafka's story, the sentence of the Condemned man is inscribed—with the use of needles—upon his body by an elaborate torture device, operated by an Officer. Upon the completion of the inscription, the Condemned, though enlightened, dies. Of particular importance is the idea of transforming the Condemned—by an inscription upon the body—into text, that is, from body to sentence, both in its legal and grammatical sense. Marlene's intention is based upon the same idea, though inverted. Her desire is to, by writing upon the body of Angela, resurrect her, that is, rather than transform body into text, Marlene attempts to metamorphose text into body and information into materiality: an impossible transformation of informational randomness to material presence. Although Marlene desires to rescue the memory of her daughter and to give her presence as a means of bringing about a promised future through the act of writing, the outcome ultimately proves to be similar to that in Kafka's tale: to torturously inscribe the guilt and sentence onto the flesh of the condemned. Like the execution device in Kafka's story, Marlene's body is described as an organic automaton, "a slow machine, with only the brain and the hand at work, the writing hand."[103] Here, however, the guilt being inscribed on Angela's body is not that of the daughter, but Marlene: the guilt and sentence are derived from the mother's sense of debilitation and helplessness. While the turn of fate in the Officer's resolve upon himself subsequently leads to a mechanical malfunction that immediately places a death sentence upon the Officer, Marlene is left to recognize that inscribing the body of her daughter is, in fact, a painful act of self-reflexive guilt, rather than one motivated by the desire to resurrect Angela through writing.

THE CHAOTICS OF MEMORY, NARCOSIS, AND CONTINGENT CONSOLATION

Upon Marlene's awakening from the "dream," the narration shifts back to the first-person Marlene, realizing her failure to give Angela physical presence: "Where was I? Painful, curled up on the back seat of the car, coming to, awakening. Alone."[104] For Marlene, the consolation for her loss cannot be obtained through an information-to-body metamorphosis of her daughter. Rather because *Falling Out of Cars* is conceived as a signal situated between a transmitter and receiver—and therefore constantly subject to noise—the process of mourning is, like everything else in the novel, chaotic. The success of consolation between Marlene's dissolving perception and her memories is subject to, even subjective as, uncertainty and instability. Ultimately, chaos operates as a metaphor for the incomprehensibility, despair, and anxiety ineluctably fused as loss and mourning; a chaotic confusion of perceiver and percept confirms the mourner's inability to achieve emotional closure.

The novel's conclusion resists reconciliation between Marlene's memory and perception. After abandoning her fellow travelers, Marlene takes the car and continues on her journey across the infected English landscape: "It wasn't that long a time since I'd last driven the car, a week perhaps two, but it felt like some months had gone by, and I had changed since then, grown worse in the sickness, and the car the same. We were bound together, held one within the other."[105] The wretched Marlene continues on her journey, alone:

> I moved on. Open country, slowly giving way to trees, and the pale sun climbing. I would pass the occasional other vehicle, or a man walking the roadside, or people working the farmlands. And then the forest closed in and I saw nothing but the trees themselves, still in leaf.
> Driving, only driving; only drifting.
> The car started to move across the road from side to side, without my command, the wheel slipping in my hands. I should have stopped then; I thought of stopping but then the car would right itself, giving control back to me. The journey was not quite done.
> From the radio, only sighs of breath.
> ... I took my hands off the wheel.[106]

Marlene is reluctant to admit her despair and the apparent defeat of her perception and memory. She protests that the "journey was not quite done," though she admits to "only driving; only drifting." The agency of the journey shifts from Marlene to the car: she admits that she should stop the car, but that the car "would right itself." A kind of techno-pathetic fallacy follows: the car responds to Marlene's projecting of the journey's impetus onto the vehicle with no more than "sighs of breath." The car is not simply a projection on Marlene's behalf, but takes a conscious and active role in the narrative. Ultimately, Marlene and the car abandon the quest. Marlene removes her hands from the wheel, and the car and its passenger glide softly into a tree; this marks the Nabokovian remix discussed earlier. The car continues to take an active role in sympathetically guiding Marlene toward confronting her grief. The nominative plural pronoun "we" establishes the active relationship between Marlene-as-perceiver and the car-as-animated-object. Indeed, the car takes an active role in compassionately approaching Marlene's guilt: its seat belt embraces her heart and caresses the tree "rather than hitting it." Marlene, on the other hand, passively allows the impact to occur in acceptance that her quest is ending in defeat while the subsequent episode clarifies the significance of the novel's title: "Everything seemed to be fine, until I opened the door and tried to climb out of the car. A dizziness came over me, and I fell to the ground, the air singing around me. And I lay there in the grass for a time, a good time, I don't know how long a time, just lying there."[107] Here, Marlene literally falls out of the car, an act which symbolically permits her to confront her mourning and sense of guilt by ending her delusional quest. Marlene is roused by a snake "curling and uncurling"[108] around her hand, a scene evocative of postlapsarian guilt. Collecting the items from the wrecked car—her bag, the notebook, the photograph of Angela, and some clothes—she continues into the forest on foot.

In this scene, Noon includes three further polysemous signs: an ivory-coated horse with a "gleaming eye of the deepest blue,"[109] mirrors, and a river. Whether the symbols function together according to a self-contained logic is unclear. Noon's interest in and understanding of mythical symbolism—most evident in his novel *Pollen* (1995), but pervasive throughout his oeuvre—is accomplished. In this episode, however, the symbols are so overdetermined with meaning that they may function as a kind of symbolic noise. For Marlene, this excess of dissonant symbolic information ultimately functions as an expression of the culmination of her struggle. The symbolic and semantic abundance of this episode effects a kind of catharsis whereby Marlene, although incapable of deciphering the symbolism, is led through a series of ritualistic motions. First, she is led by the horse deeper into the forest until she reaches a river:

> The horse walked ahead of me, weaving a pathway. The further we went, the more I seemed to lose all sense of myself, and my surrounding. Now, in recollection, I can use these various words: horse, tree, gun, flower, clock, Marlene. But just then I no longer knew the name of the creature that roamed ahead; I no longer knew the name of the strange objects that grew all around me. I no longer knew what it was I should call myself, not even this; neither my being, my species, nor my given name.
>
> Presently, seen first only as flashes of light, of reflection, the forest gave way to a body of water.[110]

While the symbolism here is profuse, it is evident that the horse functions as a type of surrogate for the car, which leads Marlene into an existentially threatening environment, the forest, where she must lose herself in numbness in order to find a new self in a scene reminiscent of the Narcissus myth. Indeed, Marlene's inability to recognize herself allows her to purge her anxieties concerning her loss of memory momentarily. At the moment of her inability to identify her reflection, she becomes emotively and philosophically equipped to confront and consolidate undesirable affect without the angst caused by her traumatic amnesia.

Narcissus, in this episode, is particularly McLuhanesque. In "The Gadget Lover: Narcissus as Narcosis," McLuhan famously argues that technologies are extensions of the self, that we mirror the effects of technologies, and that we need to become aware of this. Centering the discussion around the Greek myth of Narcissus, McLuhan reminds us that the myth is not about vanity (the way the term narcissism is used popularly) but about narcosis: numbness. This numbness can then be considered a kind of "autoamputation" of the body:

> The Greek myth of Narcissus is directly concerned with a fact of human experience, as the word Narcissus indicates. It is from the Greek word narcosis, or numbness. The youth Narcissus mistook his own reflection in the water for another person. This extension of himself by mirror numbed his perceptions until he became the servomechanism of his own extended or repeated image. The nymph Echo tried to win his love with fragments of his own speech, but in vain. He was numb. He had adapted to his extension of himself and had become a closed system. Now the point of this myth is the fact that men at once become fascinated by any extension of themselves in any material other than themselves. . . . This is the sense of the Narcissus myth. The young man's image is a self-amputation or extension induced by irritating pressures. As counter-irritant, the image produces a generalized numbness or shock that declines recognition. Self-amputation forbids self-recognition.[111]

In this sense, narcissism is about the fascination we have with extensions of the body (i.e., technology or medium/media). However, such extension brings with it an anxiety or irritant: the wheel as an extension of the foot produces a strange effect on the isolated or disregarded use of the actual feet—the foot feels numb or useless and, therefore, it is auto-amputated. Giving over one's own willed bodily motion to that of the machine (whether the car or the horse) is met with numbness or shock. If one can accept autoamputation or forget their relationship with technology, one becomes blind to the changes in sense ratios due to forgetting one's extensions.

Marlene, ultimately, finds herself integrated into this process of narcosis. She responds to the numbness and shock by forbidding self-recognition, whereby autoamputation becomes a kind of survival mechanism in the face of increasingly rapid technological change. Indeed, narcissism is not about vanity. It is about giving over entirely to a technology or medium/media and losing self-recognition along the way. McLuhan reminds us that technologies, media, devices, gadgets, and so on, are not just tools for us to use or not use. Instead, they become extensions of the body and mind: they are *part of ourselves*. We cannot just get rid of technologies and go back to living in a mythical forest. Even if we did, like Narcissus, there are technologies all around and indivisible from the human experience. With technology, McLuhan writes, "man extended, or set outside himself, a live model of the central nervous system itself. To the degree that this is so, it is a development that suggests a desperate and suicidal autoamputation, as if the central nervous system could no longer depend on the physical organs to be protective against the slings and arrows of outrageous mechanism."[112] That is, our dependence on tech is much more serious than we often acknowledge. Technology is indivisible from us. We shape it but are also shaped by it; and, we generally forget or lose track of this. However, McLuhan asks us to look *beyond the obvious* effects. Considering McLuhan's analytical approach, though, we want to consider this *narcissism* as *narcosis* (numbness or autoamputation) rather than vanity. The narcissism of Marlene's experience is, of course, not one of egotism. Instead, it is one of narcosis: she is at risk of becoming completely numb and anesthetized to the material actualities and the internal sense of self by becoming displaced in a virtual realm whereby the informational image of the self risks replacing the embodied self and, by extension, eventuates in the absolute loss of the daughter.

Once she arrives at the river, she recollects "another person, sitting as [she] was, partially hidden behind the flowers and the weeds. The figure could not be made out clearly."[113] The person across the river is probably some manifestation of Marlene herself; the figure functions as a mirror image. As if she understood the ritual—"the idea came to me"[114]—Marlene begins to place the mirror's collected fragments into the river; the woman on the opposite bank acts accordingly. Upon gazing at the submerged mirror fragments, Marlene sees herself: "Seeing myself. The face that was held beneath the surface, a drowned woman, staring back at me."[115] The motif of the drowned woman takes on a dual significance. On the one hand, it indicates Marlene's contemplation of suicide by walking into the lake: "All of the troubles endured since Angela's passing, they would melt away in the cold depths, and be laid finally to rest."[116] Yet, it also facilitates for Marlene a philosophical shift permitting her to surrender her desire for reconciliation between her failing memory and her emotional preoccupation with Angela's presence. That is, Marlene comes to learn that the relationship between perception and memory is based on principles of immanence rather than presence:

> This was it. I could not turn away from the drowned woman, this one temptation, and, reaching forward, I let my fingers play amongst the contours of the face. I felt I had dipped my hand in mercury. The image rippled, becoming lost, and then slowly re-forming itself. And I found in there, in place of my own features, the now clearly seen lines of my daughter's face; as though the one contained the other.
> Which it did, which it did.[117]

Marlene resigns herself because the relationship between perception and memory, although precarious, is inherently meaningful even in the face of constitutive informational forces, that is, love persists in memory and language. While she may become increasingly incapable of retrieving orderly, patterned memories of Angela, this immanent relationship between the mother and the memory of her daughter affords Marlene provisional consolation and enables her to refuse suicide:

> My hand slipped deeper into the water, without my choosing. The face closed round my wrist. Something stirred within me. A beating heart. It was not of any great notice, all told; a small releasing and nothing more. A simple refusal.
>   No. It would not end here, and not in this way.
>   Nothing more. But such a moment; so pure, and so forgiving. The water glistened. The snake uncurled itself. The violet snake shifted on my skin, and was then washed clean, its thin transparent body drifting away through the shallows.[118]

Marlene's rejection of suicide is far from cataclysmic; it is a "small releasing" and a "simple refusal." Though subtle, her epiphany leads to self-forgiveness: the snake, as a symbol of her guilt, is "washed clean," its body is transparent and drifting away as her sense of remorse fades. In her increasing failure to retain memory, Marlene recognizes that her recollection of Angela is subject to the logic of chaos. Angela is the inherent order in the increasingly disordered mind of Marlene. Ultimately, by falling out of the car and pursuing the ritual that follows, Marlene is fleetingly made capable of quelling her anxieties by comprehending the significance of her loss. While Marlene cannot experience the future promised by her child's birth, she can hold on to the concept-creating potentials of language as a mode of resistance to and the intentionless noise of the apparatus.

The final fragment of the novel suggests Marlene's recognition of the fragility of her mourning. Her solace lies in the fact that the memory of Angela is immanent even if it is not necessarily lucidly retrievable:

> Only the photograph. The one thing left to me. How it blossoms in my sight. It burns. Or else clouding over, a murmur of scent arises. In scarlet and blue it cradles; in crimson and gold it may scatter and swirl, unfold, dispersing itself. Now, let these colours cascade. Let these whispers awaken; let these sparkles compose, gleam forth, froth and foam, fizzle, burst, enclose and caress themselves, speaking themselves. Now let this tongue emerge from the light that fell once on a garden, on a child's face, on chemicals. Let the picture overflow from itself, spilling itself. It spills over and spells out the word of itself, and then dispelling itself, making a game of itself, a flame of itself, the blossom and bloom and perfume of itself. Only the photograph. This word, this tiny word, almost known. Almost spoken. Louder now, softer. I will wait. Now let me wait.[119]

Marlene is left to remember her daughter abstractly. The photograph no longer functions as a surrogate for the absent Angela but rather as a fissioning signifier of chaos and immanence. No longer is Angela simply represented by the photograph, but her image blossoms, burns, clouds over, cradles, scatters, swirls, unfolds, and disperses. Akin to the novel's artistic statement—"In these days of chaos, possibilities abound"[120]—Marlene's comfort is to be continually sought after in the paradox of order inherent in chaos and the interplay of pattern and randomness. Grimwood observes that "Marlene hunts because hunting gives her life what little meaning it still contains."[121] Noon experiments to illuminate in contemporary literature what meaning he feels the artform still contains and whether literature and poiesis can be acts of melancholic resistance against the replacement of semantic value by information. In this sense, *Falling Out of Cars* may be read as Noon's impassioned expression of the conflict inherent in the "post futurist" novel: it is an act of at once mourning the loss of literary traditions and celebrating the resurrection of these forms in spectral fiction. Indeed, *Falling Out of Cars* itself is mist: a multiplicitous and mutating set of allusions to the poignant images and ideas of great authors. Yet, Noon wishes to do more than merely acknowledge; rather, he aims to transform fiction into a ghostly new literary manifestation. Marlene's consolation, initiated through her commemoration of Angela via radically new spectral abstractions, ultimately becomes a metaphor for Noon's entire literary project: to raise the fragile, blossoming ghost of the novel.

NOTES

1. Jeff Noon, "Artwork 2058: Probability Cloud," in *Unilever Series: Dominique Gonzalez-Foerster TH.2058* (London: Tate Modern, 2008), http://blog.tate.org.uk/unilever2008/.

2. Tomas L. Martin, review of *Falling Out of Cars*, by Jeff Noon, *Science Fiction Crowsnest*, https://web.archive.org/web/20080509184449/http://www.sfcrowsnest.com/sfnews2/03_dec/review1203_23.shtml.

3. John Berlyne, review of *Falling Out of Cars*, by Jeff Noon, *SFRevu* (November 2002), http://www.sfrevu.com/ISSUES/2002/0211/Book%20-%20Falling%20Out%20of%20Cars/Review.htm.

4. Tony Chester, review of *Falling Out of Cars*, by Jeff Noon, *The Science Fact & Science Fiction Concatenation* (2002), http://www.concatenation.org/frev/falling.html.

5. Tomas Vergara, "Catatonic Futures and Post-Apocalyptic Capital," *C21 Literature: Journal of 21st-Century Writings* 8, no. 1 (2020), https://c21.openlibhums.org/article/id/970/.

6. Ismo Santala, "Jeff Noon – Works: *Falling Out of Cars*," *The Modern Word* (October 14, 2003), https://web.archive.org/web/20060329141101/http://www.themodernword.com/SCRIPTorium/noon_works.html#Anchor-Falling-35326.

7. Jeff Noon, "*Falling Out of Cars*: Extra Content," *Metamorphiction – Roots* (2002), https://web.archive.org/web/20130121004708/http://www.metamorphiction.com/index.php/printed/falling-out-of-cars/.

8. Claude Lalumière, review of *Falling Out of Cars*, by Jeff Noon, *Infinity Plus*, http://www.infinityplus.co.uk/fantasticfiction/fallingoutofcars2.htm.

9. Santala, "Jeff Noon – Works."

10. Simon Reynolds, *Retromania: Pop Culture's Addiction to its Own Past* (London: Faber, 2012), p. xi.

11. Jeff Noon, *Cobralingus*, illus. Daniel Allington (Hove: Codex, 2001), 13.

12. See Noon's essay "Origins of a Dub Fiction," *Codex Books*, https://web.archive.org/web/20050215083945/http://www.codexbooks.co.uk/origins.html.

13. Roger Sperry, *Science & Moral Priority: Merging Mind, Brain, and Human Values* (New York: Praeger, 1985), 36.

14. James Gleick, *The Information: A History, A Theory, A Flood* (New York: Pantheon, 2011), 292.

15. In his 2004 article, "McLuhan's New World," Tom Wolfe writes, "here we see the shadow of the intriguing figure who influenced McLuhan every bit as much as Harold Innis but to whom he never referred: Pierre Teilhard de Chardin . . . His mission in life, as he saw it, was to take Darwin's theory of biological evolution, which had so severely shaken Christian belief, and show that it was merely the first step in God's grander design for the evolution of man. God was directing, in this very moment, the twentieth century, the evolution of man into a noosphere . . . a unification of all human nervous systems, all human souls, through technology. Teilhard . . . mentioned radio, television, and computers specifically and in considerable detail and talked about cybernetics. . . . He died in 1955, when television had only recently come into widespread use and the microchip had not even been invented. Computers were huge machines, big as a suburban living room, that were not yet in assembly line production. But he was already writing about 'the extraordinary network of radio and television communication which already links us all in a sort of etherised human consciousness, and of those astonishing electronic computers which enhance the 'speed of thought' and pave the way for a revolution in the sphere of research.'" Tom Wolfe, "McLuhan's New World," *The Wilson Quarterly* 28, no. 2 (Spring 2004), 22.

16. Peter Morville, *Ambient Findability* (Sebastopol: Farnham, 2005), 33.

17. Tom Wolfe, "McLuhan's New World," 22–23. See note 14 above.

18. Pierre Teihard de Cardin, *The Phenomenon of Man*, intro. Julian Huxley, trans. Bernard Wall (Toronto: Harper Perennial, 2008), 225.

19. Ibid., 182.

20. Ibid., 225.

21. Ibid., 251.

22. Gleick, *The Information*, 310.

23. Ibid., 311.

24. Richard Dawkins, *The Selfish Gene* (Oxford: Oxford University Press, 1989), 19–20.

25. Gleick, *The Information*, 313–314.

26. Ibid., 314.

27. Ibid., 318.

28. Ibid., 304.

29. Ibid., 308.

30. Dawkins, *The Selfish Gene*, 199.
31. Linda Hutcheon, *A Theory of Adaptation* (New York: Routledge), 167.
32. Dawkins, *The Selfish Gene*, 196.
33. Ibid., 197.
34. Ibid.
35. Gleick, *The Information*, 322.
36. Dawkins, *The Selfish Gene*, 196.
37. Ibid.
38. Ibid.
39. Gleick, *The Information*, 315.
40. Dawkins, *The Selfish Gene*, 322.
41. Ibid., 322.
42. Ibid.
43. Ibid., 192.
44. Ibid., 323.
45. Jeff Noon, "Ghost on the B-Side: Remixing Narrative," *Metamorphiction*, 26 (November 2011), https://web.archive.org/web/20161206185549/http://www.metamorphiction.com/index.php/the-ghost-on-the-b-side-remixing-narrative/.
46. Ibid.
47. Ibid.
48. Ibid.
49. Vladimir Nabokov, *Lolita* (New York: Vintage, 1997), 306–307.
50. Jeff Noon, *Falling Out of Cars* (London: Doubleday, 2002), 336.
51. Noon, "Ghost on the B-Side."
52. Ibid.
53. Ibid.
54. Ibid.
55. Paul D. Miller, aka DJ Spooky That Subliminal Kid, *Rhythm Science* (Cambridge: MIT Press, 2004), 5.
56. Karl Marx and Friedrich Engels, *The Communist Manifesto* (London: Vintage, 2018).
57. John Donne, "The Ecstasy," *The Complete English Poems*, ed. A.J. Smith (London: Penguin, 1996), 15–16.
58. Miller, *Rhythm Science*, 18.
59. Ibid., 8.
60. Jeff Noon, *Vurt* (London: Pan, 2001), 32
61. Saul Williams, "The Future of Language," *Sound Unbound: Sampling Digital Music and Culture*, ed. Paul D. Miller (Cambridge: MIT Press, 2008), 22.
62. Miller, "In Through the Out Door," 5.
63. Ibid., 6.
64. Miller, *Rhythm Science*, 4.
65. Noon, *Vurt*, 33.
66. Beard, in an interview with novelist and critic D. Harlan Wilson: "I think postmodernism has pretty much led to a dead end, with everyone happy to sample the same cultural greats from the past. Maybe that's been its value, actually—a process of

canon formation for postwar pop culture. We can all agree that the 'Funky Drummer' riff is a great drum sound and that Robert De Niro doing Travis Bickle is a perfect emblem of alienation. Maybe it's time to move on. Something that could point to an exit from the postmodern hall of mirrors is a cultural trend called 'hauntology.'" Interview by D. Harlan Wilson, *The Dream People: A Journal of Bizarro Texts* 27 (November 26, 2011).

67. Jacques Derrida, *Specters of Marx: The State of the Debt, the Work of Mourning and the New International*, trans. Peggy Kamuf (New York: Routledge, 1993), 10.

68. Ibid., 11.

69. Mark Fisher, "What is Hauntology?" *Film Quarterly* 66.1 (Fall 2012), 18.

70. Ibid., 19.

71. Ibid.

72. Katy Shaw, *Hauntology: The Presence of the Past in Twenty-First Century English Literature* (Palgrave Macmillan, 2018), 2.

73. John Zilcosky, *Kafka's Travels: Exoticism, Colonialism, and the Traffic of Writing* (New York: Palgrave Macmillan, 2003), 192.

74. Ken McMullen, dir. *Ghost Dance* (London, UK: Channel Four Films, 1983).

75. Noon, *Falling Out of Cars*, 11.

76. Ibid., 14.

77. Ibid., 16.

78. Jon Courtenay Grimwood, "Behind the Mirror," review of *Falling Out of Cars*, by Jeff Noon, *The Guardian* (December 7, 2002), http://www.guardian.co.uk/books/2002/dec/07/featuresreviews.guardianreview23.

79. Noon, *Falling Out of Cars*, 11–12.

80. Ibid., 12.

81. Noon, 1.

82. This is likely an homage to a phrase famous in communication theory and shorthand training: "*if u cn rd ths msg . . .*" Gleick, *The Information*, 256.

83. Noon, *Falling Out of Cars*, 344.

84. Claude Shannon, *The Mathematical Theory of Communication* (Urbana: University of Illinois Press, 1949), 33.

85. Ibid.

86. Ibid., 34.

87. Ibid.

88. Ibid.

89. Weaver, "Recent Contributions to the Mathematical Theory of Communication."

90. Noon, *Falling Out of Cars*, 294.

91. Santala, "Jeff Noon – Works."

92. Noon, *Falling Out of Cars*, 265.

93. Ibid.

94. Ibid., 265–266.

95. Ibid., 266.

96. Ibid.

97. Ibid., 268.
98. Ibid., 269.
99. Ibid.
100. Ibid., 18–19.
101. Ibid., 271.
102. Ibid., 271–272.
103. Ibid.
104. Ibid., 273.
105. Ibid., 327.
106. Ibid., 335–336.
107. Ibid., 337.
108. Ibid.
109. Ibid., 339.
110. Ibid., 339–340.
111. Marshall McLuhan, *Understanding Media: The Extensions of Man*, ed. W. Terrence Gordon (Berkeley: Gingko Press, 2003), 63, 64.
112. Ibid., 65.
113. Noon, *Falling Out of Cars*, 340.
114. Ibid.
115. Ibid., 341.
116. Ibid., 342.
117. Ibid.
118. Ibid.
119. Ibid., 345.
120. Ibid., 344.
121. Grimwood, "Behind the Mirror."

Chapter 6

Swarm Annihilation and Supermodern Transcendence

Chaotics, Granular Synthesis, and the Glitch Poetics of Kenji Siratori

In his 2009 book, *The Futurism of the Instant*, Paul Virilio notes that in the nineteenth century, the idea of progress meant the great commotion of railways. By the twentieth century, we have the great acceleration of the speed train or airliner.[1] To complement Virilio's bunker logic is his British counterpart, Ballard, and his internment camp logic. In 1971, Ballard identified the quintessential inner-snapshot of the twentieth century's psychopathology as even more enclosed, personalized, and isolated than that of the speed train or the airliner: "If I were asked to condense the whole of the present century into one mental picture," he writes,

> I would pick a familiar everyday sight: a man in a motor car, driving along a concrete highway to some unknown destination. Almost every aspect of modern life is there, both for good and for ill—our sense of speed, drama and aggression, the worlds of advertising and consumer goods, engineering and mass manufacture, and the shared experience of moving together through an elaborately signaled landscape.[2]

The motor car: the image of endless mobility and ceaseless kinetics. This visual marker of industrialized progress is more privatized and isolated than that of the speed train or airliner and the archaic, if nostalgic, design requiring embodied human proximity in orientation and time. Spatiotemporal positioning in the twenty-first century is, after all, more virtual than actual: today, Virilio remarks, we have the "instantaneity of the interactive telecommunications of cybernetics."[3] This instantaneity is, however, as arrested as it is amnesiac: the "sudden loss of memory, every bit as of imaginative, about the future of a too-cramped telluric planet, cluttered . . . not so much by rubbish ... as by the illusions it entertains, its great progressive illusions."[4] Mark Fisher offers another image for contemplation, this time updated for the early twentieth-first century: an image intensified by its sequential, mutating multiplicities without a future and any sense of shared experience. A shared experience of togetherness is delimited by the increasingly privatized and personalized algorithmic cultures of the present: ceaseless motion without progression, recursively reiterating communications technologies without human connection, algorithmically optimized behavior standardization, and hourly upgrades without innovation.

So, rather than the speed train, airliner, or automobile, "the twenty-first century," Fisher writes, "is perhaps best captured in the 'bad' infinity of the animated GIF, with its stuttering, frustrated temporality, its eerie sense of being caught in a timetrap."[5] What, however, might the frustrated temporality of a GIF mean to text itself? The digital image skips endlessly but does not mutate. Text and language, the constituent of reality and the unconscious, is not immune to the skipping image: words can get caught in a timetrap, delimited by inhuman processes, and repeated endlessly into chaos and noise. Yet, every timetrap is a function of a spacetrap, and every loop has its moment where representation discombobulates. This is the moment, the glitched-out noise when staying put on "the frame that reveals the loop," that we need to consider more closely since it offers an opportunity for transcendence in a procedure that would otherwise disavow going outside its procedurality. This is when and where Kenji Siratori's work pauses and inhabits: a function denying the great progressive illusions of writing while transcending the parameters of prescribed semantic cohesion. Or, in other words, as the shared experience of motion halts and the inner space of chaotically signaled mindscapes reiterate, bifurcate, and knot. There is a way out of this closed system, though: paradoxically, the way out is achieved by journeying in further. Siratori's "devastating loop of language"[6] reminds us that shared destinations administered by railways, flight paths, and motorways are behind us, not ahead. Instead, it is in stochastic stillness where transcendence reveals itself as conceivable. When things accelerate to the point of immobility, we recognize that there are endless exits inward: some, perhaps, without termini.

As a result, Siratori poses the reader with a contentious question: at what point does literary experimentalism transcend literacy? And, what does it mean for the literate individual to suddenly confront illiteracy? His work conflates computer code with anatomical, medical, technical, typographic devices, and glitch concatenations. When we "read" his work, we are confronted with a horizon of noise: clashes where word assemblages resist semantic coherence and instead confront us with the terror and ecstasy of possibility. The future feels canceled and remains unintelligible due to a collective hesitancy to journey deeper into the mystifying, stochastic nimbus of unknowing. Siratori's work, however, reminds us that, after all, noise is where the fecundity of possibility is the most informationally dense. To confront neuro-totalitarianism, the cognitive needs to confront the computational; to confront the acceleration and proliferation of information, we need to speed up. In short, Siratori's work is cyberpunk at its most extreme: transcend the machine via transcendent machinery.

As cyberpunk, his writing evokes the cinema of Sogo Ishii, Shigeru Izumiya, and Shinya Tsukamoto; as a transcendent program, his work is akin to that of Antonin Artaud's Theatre of Cruelty; (anti)aesthetically, his work is Dadaist; as functionalist experimentation, it conjures cut-up era Burroughs and Gysin. However, while Burroughs wishes to reveal the underlying conspiracy of language, Siratori drifts away from reconceptualizing meaning toward provoking a disorienting, often violent, affect—something explicitly meant to counter the goals of commercial technologies. Rushkoff, for example, notes that "Facebook is set up to make us think of ourselves in terms of our 'likes' and an iPad is set up to make us start paying for media and stop producing it ourselves."[7] Siratori's work, on the other hand, considers the biases of information technology in the manner that Burroughs asks about the biases of language through aggressive denaturalization. The emotional experience of reading Siratori rehearses illiteracy as an analog to the consumer's normalized cybernetic relationships. Here, agency and literacy are conflated intensely: if we cannot acknowledge these biases, we are incapable of possessing agency in supermodernity. Amid all the asemic noise, Siratori's conceit is as lucid as it is timely: the anxiety of reading asemic cyberpunk is analogous to the consumer's illiteracy regarding the social programming of desire. As experimentation is pushed to relentless limits, new code and programming languages suggest the dawn of new arts.

Siratori has a particularly helpful description of his work on his webpage that acts as a skeleton key when approaching his writing. "Kenji Siratori," it begins, is

> a Japanese cyberpunk writer who is currently bombarding the internet with wave upon wave of highly experimental, uncompromising, progressive, intense prose. His is a writing style that not only breaks with tradition, it severs all cords . . . Embracing the image mayhem of the digital age, his relentless prose is nonsensical and extreme, avant-garde and confused, with precedence given to twisted imagery, pace and experimentation over linear narrative and character development. With unparalleled stylistic terrorism, he unleashes his literary attack. An unprovoked assault on the senses.[8]

Stephen Barber comments that Siratori renders the "English-language instantly redundant with his relentless, murderous prose-drive, [he] transmits his authentic, category-A hallucinogenic product direct to his reader's cerebellum. A virulently warped amalgam of Tetsuo and cut-up era William Burroughs."[9] Jack Hunter,[10] author of *Eros in Hell* (1999), offers the following evaluation of Siratori's most famous novel *Blood Electric* (2002): "*Blood Electric* is the black reverb of soft machine seppuku, a molten unspooling of sheet metal entrails and crucified memory banks into the howling void of violence. It is a cyborg crash nightmare of the new flesh, a final dispatch from mutant Hell where the embryo hunts in secret."[11] Whereas Reza Negarestani notes that Siratori

> perhaps pioneered a movement among all non-English speaking writers whose languages are radically dissociated from the dominant Latin-Anglo-Franco-German linguistic germ-line on the one hand, and are, on the other, enthusiastically seeking to contribute to the diversification of the English language whose centrality has already been sabotaged in the wake of emerging cyber-societies.[12]

Immediately noticeable to the reader of Siratori's work, however, is the futility of approaching his writing via conventional modes of close reading. And, of course, reading alone is not necessarily the most effective way of representing the experience of apparatus. If Siratori's work is affect, it is expressive of the impossibility of ontological communication with the apparatus.

In this sense, Siratori's writing is fundamentally in opposition to traditional modes of literary interpretation since his aesthetic operates in such a way as to induce the experience of illiteracy rather than as a means of encouraging more intense semantic engagement. *Blood Electric*, for example, runs at 224 pages; any selection from this text will yield a similar response. Take the first paragraph on page 112 as an example:

> I infect the brain of the hydro-mania that goes up in flames to the okama fibre of muscle fleshy substances::the machinery horizon of the Cadaver City is inoculated::SODO probe of boy-roid that contaminated the insanity of a chromosome=emotional>womb area machine::that exploded the feral lobe of BABEL and gene=TV//[ice nebula faecal black] vital junk::the entrails emotion that revolves the house of tortures internal++vital-serum KK<<sex-motion of ToKAGE//the planet links to ambient rotor of godhead which conceived the nerve of the spectre that invades the control system of EVOL//the parasite drone spinal fluid of Cadaver City sepulcher—the swastika form living body helix that a girl infuses—the mass of flesh that distorts NDROID/[13]

This passage is not only exemplary of *Blood Electric* but Siratori's project more generally. Edward S. Robinson quotes the following passage from *MOBILE@NGEL* (2006)—a work of electronic literature that only exists as an online text—as a means of demonstrating Siratori's iconoclastic approach to writing: "I turn on ill-treatment of the DNA=channels of the biocapturism nerve cells abolition world-codemaniacs that was processed the data=mutant of her ultra=machinery tragedy-ROM creature system corpse feti=screaming of a clone boy****the gene-dub to the paradise apparatus."[14] Or, again, the following from *Mind Virus* (2008), a sequel to *Blood Electric*: "technojunkies' era respiration-byte that joints the feeling replicant living body junk of her digital=vamp cold-blooded disease animals to the paradise apparatus of the human body pill cruel emulator corpse feti=streaming of the soul/gram made@retro-ADAM acid. 0101010101chaos0101010101chaos-0101010101chaos0101010101chaos0101010101chaos."[15]

And, yet again, this excerpt from *Hack_* (2011): "<<our ice sky where the respiration that brain is risked resolve be like the heart>>my eyeball that the sun that insanity walks exclaim is broken:::.so love of the anthropoids/clones of the murderous intention that my soul that the chromosome of the true disgrace that I who write the indefinite nightmare of the desert be not seen."[16] What these passages have in common are assemblages that, in and of themselves, induce an intense response from the reader. However, this reaction is one that cannot be absorbed by current modes of *knowing*. That is, the contamination, specters, viral infections, or mutations that appear in Siratori's writing are not syntactically or semantically related. Instead, this writing gestures toward extreme, paratactic disorientation. To *look into* his work is a practical absurdity; rather, one must move deeper *through* it, journeying further and further into the chaos. "When we say 'chaos,'" Bifo notes, "we mean two different, complementary movements. We refer to the swirling of our surrounding semiotic flows, which we receive as if they were 'sound and fury.' But we also refer to attempts to reconcile this encompassing environmental rhythm with our own intimate, internal rhythm of interpretation."[17] The latter sense of chaos is as pertinent here as it is in Noon's work. However, while *Falling out of Cars* operates at the borders and the *during* of information illiteracy, Siratori's work represents the *after*. Yet, Siratori does so with a Dadaist spirit of rage, revulsion, and revolution: chaos is the intimate, novel interpretation that breathes life into agency where agency has seemingly already been amputated. We cannot think of the meaning of Siratori's writing by relying on established methods of decoding. Instead, his work considers how confusion, disorder, and derangement bring about alternatives. Ultimately, Siratori asks us to experience unknowing.

GLITCHING THE ENGLISH LANGUAGE

Of note is Siratori's fundamentally unconventional use of the English language: this seems to tempt critics into discussing him in the context of his national origin. While Siratori is certainly Japanese by nationality,[18] the emphasis on Japaneseness expressed by so many of his reviewers in their evaluation of his work may prove to be contentious. Negarestani writes that

> now we are witnessing the emergence of writers from radically different cultures and languages within the English language without any prior linguistic domestication. They reinvent their infernal writing machines in English as the most dominant language—and consequently prone to becoming a hegemonic linguistic empire—undermining its centrality and violently turning it into a dark pool of diversification and anomalies.[19]

Yet, Siratori's radicalism is one that confronts more than the hegemonic dominance of the English language in the global literary scene. That is, he disrupts the very possibility of nationhood and, even more explicitly, a shared language, diegetic topoi, and topology that assist as cultural narratives in making such imagined communities meaningful. Indeed, his work is more explicitly concerned with hybridity, mutation, infection, fecundity, and openness.

In his introduction to the *Contemporary Japanese Fiction* issue of *The Review of Contemporary Fiction*, Takayuki Tatsumi employs the term "Japanoid" as a

> post-80s hyper-creole subjectivity transgressing the boundary between the Japanese and non-Japanese, and in so doing, naturalizing the very act of transgression. If you eat sushi or drive a Toyota, root for Ichiro or Cool Hand Koboyashi, if you're an anime or manga fan, do karaoke or watch sumo, enjoyed William Gibson's *Idoru*, or . . . but you can see where this is going. . . . [In] the current postmillennial world, "ethnically Japanese or not, we are all Japanoid."[20]

The invocation of the Japanoid as a contemporary instance of hybrid sensibility is appropriate in discussing Siratori since his use of language is eccentric and resists nationalization. Indeed, this hybridism is part of the Japanese avant-garde tradition itself: Donald Keene writes that he "once asked [Kōbō Abe] why he so seldom gave names to the characters in his novels or plays. . . . He said it was because it made things more difficult if he gave them names. He did not elaborate, but I wonder if he was not reluctant to confine his characters within the limitations of being Japanese—or any other nationality."[21] Along these lines, Abe is frequently cited as an international artist who shares more commonalities with "Franz Kafka and Alain Robbe-Grillet than with his Japanese contemporaries," suggests Margaret S. Key, "in short, he is typically painted as an isolated, heterodox figure on the Japanese literary landscape—a stubborn nonconformist whose most characteristically Japanese literary quality is that he wrote in Japanese."[22]

Perhaps it is most accurate to suggest that Abe's characters are, rather than without nationality, Japanoids in the sense that they cannot be understood fully outside of the oeuvre of Japan's most internationally famous avant-gardist. And, indeed, cyberpunk may certainly be the most appropriate literary mode through which to examine these processes: in his introduction to the defining cyberpunk anthology *Mirrorshades*, Bruce Sterling "argues for the internationalism of cyberpunk," notes Christopher Bolton, "by noting that the first magazine to publish a cyberpunk special was Japan's *SF magajin*."[23] Ultimately, turning literature against the habitual use of language offers alternative ways of thinking that both loops back to nationhood and language while transcending them. However, the spirit of shedding nationhood, tradition, language, and identity proved as contentious an act to early twentieth century avant-gardists in Japan as it did in Europe. Here we turn to a Japanese avant-garde movement and Dada-esque analog for more context: Mavo.

MAVO IN JAPAN

Perhaps one of the earliest national predecessors to Siratori's project would be the radical modernist art movement Mavo. Like Dada and Futurism in Europe, the Mavo movement in Japan during the 1920s aimed to dismantle nationalism, identity, and tradition. "The original group had five members, the artists Murayama Tomoyoshi,[24] Ōura Shūzō, Yanase Masamu, Ogata Kamenosuke, and Kadowaki Shinrō. But Mavo quickly expanded to a core of between ten and fifteen young artist-activists. Responding to the rapidly changing conditions of modern Japan, group members sought to revolutionize the form, function, and intent of Japanese art," writes Gennifer Weisenfeld. Like the Dadaists in Europe and America, "Mavo artists principally championed the reintegration of art into the social (and political) practice of everyday life."[25] Also similar to the history of Dada, even the name of the movement itself is somewhat uncertain.[26] "There were a number of different explanations of Mavo's naming," Weisenfeld remarks, "all of which differed on key points but generally served the important purpose of giving the group an enigmatic and stylish aura."[27] Again, such ambiguity to the movement's naming is central to the revolutionary program itself in that it aimed to identify and articulate through modes of negation and paradox. Consequently, the 1923 "Mavo Manifesto" makes explicit that the movement would have no clear ideological or political unity. Murayama declares:

> We have gathered together because we share the same inclination as Constructivist artists.

> However, we definitely did not gather because we have identical principles and beliefs about art.
>
> Thus, we do not aggressively try to regulate our artistic convictions.
>
> We recognize, however, that when looking out over the general world of Constructivist art, we are bound to each other by a very concrete inclination.
>
> Because our group is formed thus, it is a matter of timing, a thing of the moment.
>
> We, each one of us, of course, possess assertions, convictions and passions that we feel we must elevate to the level of objectivity and appropriateness. However, as long as we are going to form a group, we respect one another. Furthermore, while recognizing what we inherently possess may be exclusive at times, we acknowledge the fact that we could not form a group without it.
>
> In short, in terms of organization our group is a negative entity.[28]

Ultimately, this negative entity "was a gathering of diverse personalities," Weisenfeld continues, "each with distinct, but often overlapping, interests [as] Mavo artists did not want to limit the scope of art; they sought to break down the borders between art and daily life."[29] By doing so, Mavo artists were operating specifically as social critics who lived their declarations. The modernist aesthetic, for Mavo as it was for Dada and Futurism, fused life with art as a negative project that aimed for absolute revolution via the rejection and destruction of all social and political vectors of traditional culture. At a time of rapid change and a series of both natural and national disasters, Mavo responded to "feelings of crisis and peril"[30] with the emergence of constructivism, fragmentation, discord, contradiction, and collage in their work. Furthermore, "they often couched their protests against social injustice in terms of irrationality, melancholy, and pessimism,"[31] Weisenfeld notes, while they "specifically chose the fragmented idioms of assemblage, collage, and construction because of their connotations of radicalism."[32] Beyond this, however, Mavo artists also recognized that the "destructiveness of their critical posture in dialectic relation to its constructive potential" was essential for the revolutionary transformation of Japanese society. Or, just as it was for Dada and Futurism, "for them, destructive acts were a form of constructive criticism."[33]

Of particular importance here, however, is Mavo's enthusiastic embrace of technology as a communicative and transformative force for resistance and change. Modernism is, after all, all about media technologies. Mavo artists actively used "new mass media, loudly broadcasting their commentaries on the problematic sociocultural condition that had developed under the progressive ideologies of modernization."[34] In this sense, Mavo inaugurated the Japanese avant-garde practice of critical engagement with technology whereby technology itself becomes both part of and an extension of art-as-practice and artist-as-practitioner. This merging of avant-garde practice with technology in senses both metaphorical and applicable, of course, finds its most explicit articulation much later in cyberpunk aesthetic.

CYBERPUNK IN EXTREMIS AND THE JAPANESE AVANT-GARDE

As a Japanese avant-gardist concerned with media and digital technologies, Siratori's work emerges from the lineage of the Japanese cyberpunk culture of the 1980s—particularly films like Ishii's 1982 *Burst City*, the films of Izumiya, or, more explicitly, Tsukamoto's cult film *Tetsuo: The Iron Man* (1989)—and in relation to Japan's greatest postwar literary experimentalist Abe. *Tetsuo* is largely regarded as one of the watershed works of cyberpunk media dominating the science fiction underground that emerged in the early 1980s and reaching a mainstream status by the 1990s. Like other cyberpunk works, William Verrone, in *The Avant-Garde Feature Film* writes, *Tetsuo* "examines or situates the body-as-performance, loss of self, and the search for identity and meaning in a future urban environment that has become over-reliant and dependent upon, or dominated by, technology. In this manner, *Tetsuo* is, arguably, a film about the encroachment of technology on the body and the inevitable merging of the two."[35] Furthermore, Verrone remarks that "knowing the plot [of *Tetsuo*] is actually not that essential in appreciating exactly what Tsukamoto has done with his film. It is the style and the form that make *Tetsuo* a real avant-garde film."[36] This emphasis on both the merging of body and machine and the primacy of style and formal experiment over meaning or traditional diegesis is what links Siratori with *Tetsuo* most explicitly. Both are concerned with altering the perceptual and conceptual dynamics of its audience.

There is also something radical to the Japanese elements of Siratori's cyberpunk experiments, and these radicalisms seem to originate from a tendency prevalent in Japanese science fiction. Rushkoff remarks that most American science fiction "makes the unstated assumption that no matter how far technology evolves, human nature will remain basically the same."[37] This observation stems from another line of understated logic: that technology and humanity are to be "understood as two distinctly different lines of development, in strict conformity with the guarding moral syndrome. The roles of human beings and the structure and function of society are constants. Although technology may be evolving, as long as it remains controlled by the same forces nothing fundamental needs to change."[38] This optimism is founded on a unidirectional logic that posits human beings as essential entities: the creators and controllers of both nature and technology. In sensationalist narratives, technology becomes a threat to human beings, but typically in a solely physical sense. There is little, if any, effective engagement in these kinds of narratives—Rushkoff cites *Star Trek* and *Babylon 5*—for technology fundamentally changing the dynamics of the central nervous system, thus deconstructing the very notion of the imperial self. Science fiction of this kind is, in the end, a thinly disguised mode of conservative humanism. Eschewing the possibility of the human nervous system mutating and reconfiguring alongside dynamic media ecologies, techno-narratives of the Enlightenment humanist variety prove to be propelled ideologically and are ultimately unwilling to compromise the narrative constancy of selfhood.

On the other hand, cyberpunk is generally more drastic in its handling of subjectivity and what it means to be human amid rapidly mutating technology and media ecology. Eschewing the optimism of more conservative science fiction, cyberpunk engages with several groundbreaking diegetic and thematic formulations. Nevertheless, Rushkoff acutely remarks that the major works of the genre, in general, "refuse to consider the possibility that people may develop along with their technology."[39] While the narratives are characterized by inventive conceptual technologies, the heightened emphasis on alienation and confusion—or narratives lacking love and spirit, according to Rushkoff—again operate upon the logic that human beings do not change while their technology and their media do. If human beings evolve cognitively alongside their technologies, this ambiance of alienation will lose its validity. For Rushkoff, whether it is the traditional model of American science fiction or the postmodern sensibility of the cyberpunk ethos, there remains a constitutive narrative determinant in the West that sculpts the borders of narrative logic:

> The underlying logic of the Western vision is Christian fundamentalism: Created in God's image, the human being is itself a perfect form and can only be sullied by sex or corrupted by technology. Therefore we [Americans] maintain a strict division between the ideas of technological development and the sanctity of humanity . . . people and machines don't mix. You can't improve on nature. People will be people.[40]

While Christian fundamentalism[41] certainly is not necessarily an explicit foreground for these narratives, Rushkoff's point is well taken. The epistemological assumption that the biological human being is at, or very near, the apex of a teleological ascension makes incomprehensible the possibility of accepting changes in cognitive and social relations that largely remain outside meaningful discourse.

The status of the self and its relation to technology, however, is manifest somewhat differently in much Japanese science fiction, and it is the following formulation that situates Siratori most meaningfully in tandem with the science fiction of his native country. While the traditional American model posits the teleological stasis of the essential human being, the Japanese approach embraces the prospect of both the human body and brain engaging in a parallel evolution with technology. In this sense, Japanese science fiction is more closely in the spirit of the modernist avant-garde. Rushkoff suggests this is not necessarily a "function of aesthetics but necessity"; and necessity is, after all, the most pressing drive for innovation. For an author like Abe, for example, invention and production are synonymous with aesthetics, and the same is true for Siratori. There may be a concrete reason for this tendency in Japanese science fiction: "The Japanese learned through experience" suggests Rushkoff, "that the evolution of technology without an accompanying development in human interaction can only end in disaster. This is not to say that human beings are intrinsically evil—simply that technology can, like a feedback loop, amplify and dangerously exaggerate some of our social shortcomings."[42] Themes of both cognitive and biological mutations are, after all, commonplace in popular manga and anime. Likely the most famous example of the Japanese tendency toward the representation of radical mutation, Katsuhiro Otomo's *Akira* (1982–1990 manga, 1988 film) represents both the body and the cognitive parameters of characters transforming in sublime ways: changes of such a grand scale that they transcend the conventional modes of meaningful cognition. Along this movement toward the incalculable is perhaps why Verrone suggests a film like

> *Tetsuo* is about the merging of metal and flesh, and its graphic representation of this blending or commingling leaves one exhausted (and perhaps confused) by the end ... the film is a no-holds-barred tour de force of stop-motion animation, live action, unforgettable imagery and avant-garde aestheticism that makes it dark and foreboding, prescient and thought-provoking.[43]

Of course, the merging of metal and flesh is not unique to the Japanese iteration of the genre; however, a salient feature of Japanese cyberpunk is how Tetsuo's protagonist mutates physically, behaviorally, and cognitively from a salaryman to something more akin to the inhuman. For the viewer, this sense of exhaustion and confusion proves appropriate since the representational apparatus in question suggests a move beyond comprehensible sense experience, both anatomical/physical and emotional/intellectual. In short, the merging of the biological with the technological demands a mode of representation that is altogether unusual. So, "Tsukamoto may," Verrone suggests, "be interested in how machinery or technology can overpower us to the point of *becoming us*,"[44] and this ultimately substantiates the inventiveness of his aesthetic. And Siratori is conceptually situated among these processes: he is primarily interested in the affective quality of extreme writing as an embedded metaphor for how machinery and technology merge with the human nervous system and, consequently, mutate the very biological apparatus of neural pathways that construct the human being as a meaningful category. Michael Schiltz suggests that to read Siratori, one must "do away with everything that qualifies as fiction, science or otherwise. Siratori presents us the art of the 21st century word, with its typical references to the multimedia embedding of (post?)modern communication."[45] Siratori's formally extreme writing is emblematic of the human nervous system mutating at a pace equally rapid to that of evolving communication technologies. His writing baffles because it moves faster than meaning-making. Ontologic reality, in Siratori's writing, ultimately dissolves into the ambiance of constructivism.

Abe, on the other hand, is a figure so towering that, as Tatsumi remarks, "to some Japanese intellectuals, the death of Abe signified the death of the avant-garde itself."[46] Critics often regard Abe as an author whose writing is antirealist. His relevance here is the way he dismantles nationalism, subjectivity, and their role in consensus reality; this is a project Siratori pushes much further. His aesthetics are certainly avant-garde and, Key remarks, "challenged the Naturalist realism dominating the literary mainstream and socialist realism of the orthodox Left. Abe long felt misunderstood by critics and particularly hated the label 'anti-realist.'"[47] As a writer of avant-garde fiction, Abe's work sometimes explicitly engages in the science-fictional mode. "In some senses [Abe's] *Inter Ice Age 4* still remains at the vanguard of science fiction," suggests Bolton:

> The innovations associated with the cyberpunk revolution in science fiction during the 1980s and 1990s, for example, have some notable affinities with Abe's novel [*Inter Ice Age 4*]. Early works by . . . William Gibson and Neil Stephenson feature a similarly dark view of the future characterized by corporate conspiracy, the same reluctant celebration of human bodies transformed by invasive technology, and the unsettling possibility of a disembodied human consciousness that floats in computer memory, suspended between life and death.[48]

Bolton notes that Abe's fiction incorporates material from a multiplicity of scientific disciplines—from biochemistry to geology, mathematics to computer programming—and science is "a source for his language, his characters, his metaphors, and his plots,"[49] more generally, and in the tradition of science, Abe himself thought of his work as realist. His avant-garde aesthetics are not so much a gesture of radical perspectivism or constructivism so much as he felt "committed to rehabilitating literature's capacity to represent what is real"[50] and, as a consequence, frequently adopts the documentary style in his work. Key suggests that Abe is not intent on undermining the possibility of understanding and aesthetically expressing reality;[51] Siratori, on the other hand, complicates this position with the aesthetic of his avant-gardism in that he wishes to represent the instant of perceptual shift in which the sense ratios of the human nervous system are undergoing a radical reconfiguration in the face of the apparatus. In short, Siratori's work is an unprovoked assault on the senses. However, "the crucial point missed by antirationalist and antifoundationalist readings," Key argues,

> is the thoroughgoing commitment to epistemological realism that is the basis of both his style and the ethical substance of his work. Whereas an antirealist either denies the existence of an objectively existing world or denies its independence from our thoughts and perceptions of it, the epistemological underpinning of Abe's work is the realist thesis that reality exists independently of our conceptions of it.[52]

This is the impulse behind Abe's preference for the documentary style. With Abe, Key suggests, the documentary style "is fundamentally separate from oneself."[53] Again, we see fission in the work of Siratori from that of Abe. Abe suggests a kind of epistemological realism and faith in scientific objectify, that is, he subscribes to the reasonable possibility that the cognitive center of the individual can remain at a state of valuated independence from a given set of phenomena under observation. Siratori, on the other hand, is more of a radical constructivist. Far from the central nervous system existing as an autonomous conceptual locale apart from, and objective toward, the phenomenal world, Siratori's aesthetic intimates the radical immanence of the perceiver as both the constituter and constituent of a kind of ambient media ecology. In other words, the objectively existing world for Siratori can only be understood as yet another extension of information technologies.

Coming into literary fame in the mass-productionist period, "an era during which he could imagine the writer only as a *producer* of fiction,"[54] Abe's iconoclastic influence on the Japanese literary avant-garde proved immense though ephemeral. Tatsumi suggests that most readers today feel a stronger affinity to younger writers like Paul Auster, Angela Carter, William Gibson, and Peter Ackroyd—we might add Noon to this list as well—because much of their work is, rather than an act of production, more of an act of creative consumption and reconfiguration in which the writer's work is a kind of rewriting, updating, and consuming of literary precursors. "However authentic Abe may have been, and however similar [his and Auster's] approaches to the urban maze may appear," writes Tatsumi,

> contemporary readers prefer Auster to Abe for the simple reason that Auster is up to date. Herein lies the logic of the ironic relationship between art and business: while anything is permitted in avant-gardism, everything becomes

dated in a hyperconsumerist society, where consumerism has run rampant so that virtually everything is a commodity. The irony here is particularly useful in considering what has come to pass in our pan-Pacific transculture in the last decades of the last millennium.[55]

In the 1960s, Abe's avant-gardism focused almost entirely on this ideology of creative production. Key remarks that Abe "was an inventor. He had that combination of creativity, practicality, and discontent with things as they are that is the source of innovation from the mechanical to the aesthetic."[56] Tatsumi suggests that this literary philosophy is what leads to Abe's eventual decline in popularity by the 1980s: "for the simple reason that this decade saw the astonishing escalation of the hyperconsumerist society, an escalation that transformed the most radical renunciation of literary convention into a major literary convention in itself."[57] That is, an epistemological shift that understands both material and information as a commodity that can be consumed and reconfigured eventually replaces the fetishes of production that characterized the spirit of the age when Abe wrote his most influential work.

This move from production to creative consumption suggests shifts in aesthetic practice. Along these lines, Darko Suvin suggests science fiction is most effective as a literature from which readers can rehearse historical and political alternatives. Suvin's definition of science fiction is "the literature of cognitive estrangement."[58] "Estrangement" for Suvin has a specific Brechtian sense: a mode of representation, "which allows us to recognize its subject, but at the same time makes it seem unfamiliar."[59] In this sense, the literature of cognitive estrangement intimates shifts in understanding, denaturalization of the familiar, and, ultimately, new possibilities for thought. Mark Bould and Sherryl Vint note that Suvin's concept of the *novum*, borrowed from Ernst Bloch, demonstrates certain borders to the definition of science fiction. The *novum*, Suvin suggests, is "so central and significant that it determines the whole narrative logic" of the work.[60] "This requirement," Bould and Vint continue, "explains why Suvin rejects from the genre those stories that introduce novel technologies into futures in which current social relations remain intact."[61] Work like that of Siratori certainly meets these criteria, perhaps in a sense that can be understood as extreme to the extent of a provocative hoax in the Dadaist and Mavoist spirit. Not only does Siratori's engagement with technologies radically disrupt conventional narrative logic, his novel technology *is* the novel itself. In an interview with Richard Marshall at *3am Magazine*, Siratori states that "I believe that the novel becomes a cultural trigger—but this requires the digital narrative . . . —simultaneously we must perceive the instant when the novel is networking as a part of the human body emulator."[62] The gesture of an avant-garde novel as a novel technology allows Siratori to be explicitly concerned with the extra-diegetic effect of this kind of work as that which changes or reconfigures the perceptual sense ratios of the reader and, consequently, having a notable effect on social conditions. The novel becomes an extension of both the human body and the brain: the use (and misuse) of language as a human body emulator. Just as Suvin employs the concept of the *novum* from Bloch, and thus the "term refers to those concrete innovations in lived history that awaken human collective consciousness out of a static present to an awareness that history can be changed,"[63] Siratori engages with both digital cut-up and print culture as a means of making manifest a material representation of the affective quality for the relationship of both the reading public and art undergoing radical epistemological transformations.

ELECTRONIC MUSIC, GRANULAR SYNTHESIS, AND DIGITAL CUT-UPS

Siratori states, in his characteristically opaque manner, that "Japanese chaos makes my writing the gene-dub to the composition of Antonin Artaud and William Burroughs."[64] Here, Siratori seems intent on marking his writing as a kind of hybrid of both technologies and nationalities via the establishment of new epistemologies. By evoking Japanese, French, and American writing and nationality as engaged in the act of "gene-dub," Siratori effectively engages in remixing culture, nationality, ethnicity, and tradition into something altogether new. Dub, here, is certainly a reference to the tradition of electronic music production and composition originally practiced by Jamaican dubmasters in the early 1970s that are also so important to Noon's compositional techniques. However, just as Siratori's work brings to mind electronic remix and literary cut-up, his assertion that his work is situated in an avant-garde tradition of both writing and electronic music in the iconoclastic tradition and its interrogation of authorship, modernist impersonality, and the transcendence of agency. The shift to music here is significant since Siratori is a multimedia artist who frequently collaborates with musicians and sound artists, and the music he works in is not technically "dub" or remix. Furthermore, the way he approaches music and sound is technically correlative to the way he approaches writing. Here, we will consider Siratori's work not simply as cut-up or remix, but a literary kind of granular synthesis. In the age of digital algorithms, granular synthesis can be likened to generative literature that uses text randomizing algorithms. Hayles writes that "the constraints and possibilities of the medium [electronic literature] have encourages many writers to turn to nonnarrative forms or to experiment with forms in which narratives are combined with randomizing algorithms,"[65] and Siratori certainly falls into this group though with express emphasis on the possibilities of nonnarrative, semantic unpredictability. Just as the cut-up has a concrete legacy in cinema and literature, it also has its place in recorded sound. Furthermore, granular media has notable implications on agency, identity, and impersonality in the twenty-first century in ways similar to the aesthetics of fragmentation and their role in the modernist avant-garde.

From the Futurists and Dadaists to multimedia artists like Siratori, the shift toward a poetic impersonality has a fascinating history in electronic music. From Luigi Russolo and Edgard Varèse to John Cage's aleatoric music and the metamusic of Iannis Xenakis, composers followed a similar trajectory to that of the avant-garde modernist poets. Xenakis developed granular synthesis to create automated cut-ups of recorded audio whereby a tape recording is split into tiny clips (called grains) and reassembled in a complex, indeterminate algorithmic pattern based on mathematics, not by culture or language. This process would later be used in Xenakis's hypercomplex computer music. "Granular synthesis involves generating thousands of very short sonic grains to form larger acoustic events," writes Curtis Roads,

> The technique can be classified as a form of additive synthesis, since sounds result from the additive combination of thousands of grains. A grain is a signal with an amplitude envelope in the shape of a quasi-Gaussian bell curve. The duration of a grain typically falls into the range of 1-50 msec but can also vary outside this range. The grain density refers to the number of grains occurring within a given time interval. Grain densities of hundreds of grains per second can be required to create complex, dynamically evolving sounds. Each grain has a specific duration, waveform, and peak amplitude. In a system capable of multichannel sound synthesis, each grain can be assigned to a particular spatial location.[66]

While Xenakis's[67] technique originated in analog technology, digital audio makes this process accessible and seemingly unlimited. Just as the Dadaists captured the process of random reassembling as an act of political resistance, the digital era demands engagement with the formative media and agential acknowledgment with the interfaces that govern the narratives of modern life. Indeed, neither the author nor the composer is necessarily dead after all. Siratori's work *is* Siratori: the word, and the sound, can be set free to set a precedent for a stochastic agency.

In the early history of electronic music, the advent of pitch generators, filters, echo chambers, ring modulators, oscilloscopes, and sine wave generators alongside the materiality of recorded sound in the form of magnetic tape, piano roll, or vinyl, avant-garde composers were apt to both explore sonic possibilities hitherto impossible to generate and experiment with intervening with the material of musical production and reproduction. Many of these experiments are indebted to Italian Futurist Luigi Russolo's *The Art of Noises* (1913). Here, Russolo suggests that "we must break at all cost from this restrictive circle of pure sounds and conquer the infinite variety of noise-sounds" and by doing so, listeners will "get infinitely more pleasure imagining combinations of the sounds of trolleys, autos and other vehicles, and loud crowds, than listening once more, for instance, to the heroic or pastoral symphonies."[68] By the 1920s, French composer Edgard Varèse began setting the groundwork for convincingly achieving this; rather than reproduce already familiar sounds, Varèse notes that the composer must make "possible the realisation of new sounds in accordance with new conceptions."[69] He would achieve this most successfully a few decades later with *Poème électronique* composed for the 1958 World's Fair after being commissioned by Le Corbusier to provide the soundtrack to accompany the projected visuals in the pavilion. Like Russolo, Varèse was "in search of absolute liberation, rather than a pursuer of themes or political ideas."[70]

While Varèse's music attempts to break free of tradition in a Dadaist spirit, Pierre Schaeffer's work in the 1940s, *musique concrète*, would be more Dadaist in form and much closer to Gysin and Burroughs's cut-ups in that the method of cutting up, manipulating, and reorganizing magnetic tape (rather than text). Schaeffer's main concern centered on what the difference was between experiencing and listening to the sound of an event occurring around us and "listening only to the sound produced by the same event."[71] As a way of demonstrating the potential of recorded sounds, Schaeffer "started combining and assembling them in sound structures, which he called 'études' or experiments on different types of sound sources and combinations,"[72] writes Teruggi. These études became the source material for what Schaeffer named *musique concrète*. This process complicates the composer's status: Terrugi suggests that Schaeffer's work shifts a focus from the composer's score to the listening experience.[73] Schaeffer collaborated with composer Pierre Henry on sound collage work, *Symphonie pour un homme seul* (1950), where Schaeffer's audiotape fragments were played, accelerated, reversed, decelerated, and manipulated in various ways to establish repeated loops of sound. Schaeffer's emphasis on disembodied sound, as a distinct category from the embodied performative processes of traditional music, ultimately sets the stage for ways of considering the conflation of technology's means of making sound and the individual's means of accessing and making sense of such sounds.

In 1955–1956, Karlheinz Stockhausen combined purely electronically generated sound with layers of a twelve-year-old chorister, Josef Protscha, singing "Praise the Lord!" in one of the most famous electronic pieces of the twentieth century: *Gesang der Jünglinge*. "The boy's song is broken down into phonetic fragments," writes Alex Ross, "then remixed in the style of *musique concrète*," whereby the effect is one that "boy and machine imitate each other, uniting natural and artificial worlds."[74] This synthesis of performer, technology, composer, and audience delimits the degrees to which the agency of language determines the agent. Two years later, the virtuosic American Armenian mezzo-soprano Kathy Berberian and her husband, Italian composer Luciano Berio, collaborated on *Omaggio a Joyce* (1958) that followed a similar process to that of *Gesang der Jünglinge*. Berberian recited the opening of the "Sirens" episode from Joyce's *Ulysses* (1922). The piece is lyrical, yet the language, like that in *Gesang der Jünglinge*, is a "cryptic burst of prose" and a "series of pre-echoes,"[75] where "the phonetics have taken on an unruly, multiple life of their own, receding far onto the sound horizon."[76] Berio's piece leads to an "atomization of . . . voice" through technology. Resultantly, while Varèse searched for new conceptions for sound and Stockhausen and Berio were early scouts into the unknown territory examining the possibilities of making the boundaries between recorded music, tape manipulation, electronic music, and embodied performance hazier, Schaeffer, a man who preferred Mozart to electronic music, did not consider musique concrète to be successful *as music*, and, thus, in the same spirit as those who would dismiss Siratori's work *as literature*. However, the uncertainty of what constitutes music, scores, sounds, and composer achieves a complete consideration with American conceptual artist and composer, John Cage.

Cage is the composer most likely associated with impersonality indebted to the modernists in terms of both compositional process and performance. Not only did Cage, in *Empty Words* (1978), experiment with textual cut-ups—his sample corpus ranging from Henry David Thoreau to James Joyce—he also applied the technique to music both in terms of the score and to the indeterminate nature of performance. In his 1937 talk, "The Future of Music: Credo," Cage speaks of the horizon of music involving machines to enhance compositional processes, emphasis on noise and familiar sounds as compositional materials, and the erasure of both the performer's and composer's emoting expression commonly associated with the Romantic lyrical individual. As much in line with Tzara and Duchamp[77] as with Varèse, for Cage sounds signify nothing; in particular, sounds associated with music in a traditional sense do not signify. In his most famous piece, *4 33*, silence acts as a conduit for accidental sounds and room ambiance, elements heard in any performance of a traditional piece of scored music, though not usually associated with the piece itself. Cage's preoccupation with these accidental elements pervades his musical output and compositional processes involving aleatoric and indeterminate methods. Robinson details Cage's interest in "found sound." Blurring the distinction between art and everyday life, Cage's early experiments with radios in his *Imaginary Landscape No. 4* present an audio collage, similar to cut-up in writing. However, in this case, the found material is the ephemera of radio broadcasts dependent on the available signals to the time and place of the performance. In this sense, the composer is downplayed, and the resulting performance is left to the performer and chance. Cage also used the *I-Ching* to construct *Imaginary Landscape No. 4*, further downplaying the author's role and favoring chance over choice.[78] Piero Scaruffi summarizes Cage's work: "[Cage] extended the scope of Dadaism beyond mere provocation and turned it into a new perception of the artistic event; which is, after all, just that: an event. He removed both form and content from art, and left only the process."[79] This process is one that engenders possibility over prediction, or, in Cage's words, "what we desperately need . . . is a laboratory for useless musical activity, devoted to failure rather than to success."[80]

It is this emphasis on process and procedure, in combination with indeterminacy and orderly disorder, that Cage's work confronts the hierarchical structures of music performance in similar ways to how Siratori's work addresses print media. *Imaginary Landscape No. 4* is a piece for twelve radios performed by twenty-four players and a conductor. To perform the piece, two performers manipulate each of the twelve radios. One performer controls the amplitude and timbre of the radio while the other performer dials through radio stations. The piece's score looks similar to a traditional musical score with certain distinctions: "durations are written in conventional notation, relating to notes placed on a 5-line staff. The rhythmic structure of the work is 2-1-3, and is expressed in changing tempi. Cage uses proportional notation where 1/2″ equals a quarter note" ("Comments: *Imaginary Landscape No. 1*"). The score also dictates the performance of both the tuning dial (performed by player 1) and the volume and timbre (performed by player 2). However, what is crucial is that while the score is painstakingly put together using both the indeterminacy of the *I-Ching* tossing of coins in combination with mathematical ratios and the exactitude traditionally dictated by a carefully notated score, each performance of the same piece will be *radically* different from any other. This uncertainty is not only experienced by the audience but also by all twenty-four performers and the conductor since each radio station signal that the radios would pick up (or miss entirely) will be wholly contingent on the exact time and place the performance ensues. Consider Cage's brief story about the premiere performance of the piece:

> People say that at its first performance, in 1951, nothing happened, because it was too late at night and we couldn't find anything on the radios. In fact, there were all sorts of broadcasts! Still, I have always been attracted by those sonorities that someone else wants and that are immediately distorted and transformed to fit into the sphere of goallessness. It's not exactly a collage. It's a way of

opening up the absence of will. In the case of *Imaginary Landscape*, I had a goal, that of erasing all will and the very idea of success.[81]

Ultimately, the work expresses the absence of agency and will on multiple levels: composer, conductor, and performers. Not only does this enact an erasure of the composer's agency as *maestro*, but such a multileveled anarchic gesture is also a direct affront to the Romantic cult of genius and, for the Western classical tradition, the Wagnerian myth of conductor-as-dictator. "Value judgments are not in the nature of this work as regards either composition, performance, or listening. The idea of relation . . . being absent, anything . . . may happen. A 'mistake' is beside the point, for once anything happens it authentically is."[82] The only element that is stable and unchanging is the score itself; the score becomes a common activity around which the conductor and each performer exercise a decentralized, heterarchical practice whereby any will to control will not be met with success. Ultimately, ubiquitous indeterminacy and unpredictability through this kind of self-deployment of possibility denies the very possibility of totalitarian logic.

While Cage is a major force in compositional approaches to impersonality, it is Iannis Xenakis whose stochastic music and work with granular synthesis would emphasize process in its accelerated complexity while maintaining form and content as architectural parameters within which nonlinear dynamics may play out with seemingly infinite complexity in ways closest to what Siratori achieves. And this should be no surprise: Xenakis was an architect, engineer, and designer who worked with Le Corbusier while also studying with Schaeffer and Olivier Messiaen. "With Messiaen's encouragement," writes Ross, Xenakis "began thinking about how instrument sounds could be 'built' as a structure is built, without break or seams in the construction."[83]

Xenakis made three significant contributions to electronic music. The first was the writing of musical scores by drawing on graph paper and then converting these images into musical notation.[84] The second was his hypercomplex "stochastic music," which he named after "the branch of mathematics that studies the random or irregular activity of particles."[85] Xenakis, in Formalized Music*: Thought and Math in Composition* (1992), writes that the question of presence or absence of causality in philosophy and science

> follow paths that appeared to be divergent, but which, in fact, coalesced in probability theory and finally in polyvalent logic, which are kinds of generalization and enrichments of the principle of causality. The explanation of the world, and consequently of the sonic phenomena which surround us or which may be created, necessitated and profited from the enlargement of the principle of causality, the basis of which enlargement is formed by the law of large numbers. This law implies an asymptotic evolution towards a stable state, towards

a kind of goal, of stochos, whence comes the adjective "stochastic." . . . But everything in pure determinism or in less pure indeterminism is subjected to the fundamental operational laws of logic, which were disentangled by mathematical thought under the title of general algebra. . . . Equivalence, implication, and quantifications are elementary relations from which all current science[86] can be constructed.[87]

As a result, Xenakis considered the orchestra in a way similar to how a "scientist looks at a gas cloud."[88]

Xenakis's third major contribution is granular synthesis: the process of cutting up a magnetic tape (or recorded audio) into minuscule audio clips (or grains) and rearranging them according to some complex algorithmic pattern (an illusion of randomness). He "developed a theory of granular synthesis as early as 1958," writes James Harley, "and put it into rudimentary practice with his *Analogique A+B*"[89] and more formally theorized in 1941; although it is worth noting that the practice had been previously theorized by Dennis Gabor in 1947 and Norbert Wiener in 1964.[90] Xenakis achieved this initially by cutting up magnetic tape and rearranging it manually: an intensely tedious and complex process. Roads, among others, would eventually program this process via computers as a means of speeding up and making the process more efficient: "Automated granular synthesis provides the user with a means of precise specification of complex timbral events," Roads writes. "Sound spectra can vary from a single, isolated pitch (formed by a chain of grains at a given frequency) to groupings of simultaneous frequencies, glissandi and clouds of granular particles over the audio spectrum. These variations may be controlled by manipulating just one or two event parameters."[91] For decades, granular synthesis was limited to electronics labs with massive mainframe computers, today the process can be powered by any PC, tablet, or smartphone. This democratizing of technology's accessibility would have pleased Xenakis, and the decentralization of complex technologies from big tech is an essential component of future emancipation. Granular synthesis, though a complex mathematic process, is perhaps the unlikely inheritor of Tzara and the cut-up legacy; or, perhaps it is an example of a Futurist[92] impulse coming full circle where technology, mathematics, and the human become fused into a new hypercomplex entity that aims to complicate signification as an everyday experience. Ultimately, Xenakis's three central contributions fall under the broader category that he calls "metamusic."

Xenakis notes that contemporary technocrats are too quick to reduce music into the formulae of information theory to achieve objective criteria for aesthetic experience. By reducing music to a formula based on the composer-as-signal and the listener-as-receiver, Xenakis argues that there is not much to be gained other than some statistical data. So, "identifications of music with message, with communication, and with language are schematizations whose tendency is towards absurdities and desiccations. Certain African tom-toms[93] cannot be included in this criticism, but they are the exception."[94] However, Xenakis is confident that, at least for now, "hazy music" cannot be interpreted as informatics, that is, like the Futurists, Xenakis stresses that there is no obligatory connection between communication and information. Metamusic is, for Xenakis, both a going-beyond and a self-referential *about*. Like the hazy, stochastic cloud of particles, metamusic is at once something that can be modeled mathematically but also remains essentially poetic, mysterious, and at the peripheries of semantics. "Music has a fundamental function, which is to catalyze the sublimation that it can bring about through all means of expression," he writes.

> It must aim through fixations which are landmarks to draw towards a total exaltation in which the individual mingles, losing his consciousness in a truth immediate, rare, enormous, and perfect. If a work of art succeeds in this undertaking even for a single moment, it attains its goal. This tremendous truth is not made of objects, emotions, or sensations; it is beyond these. . . . But this transmutation of every-day artistic material which transforms trivial products into meta-art is a secret. The "possessed" reach it without knowing its "mechanisms."[95]

Technology here is poetic and mysterious, unpredictable and uncertain, an absolute affront to techno-totalitarian determinism. Granular synthesis employs algorithms-as-mystification against algorithms-as-instruction. Even those who know the mechanisms may become possessed: an impersonality merged with and subject to hypercomplexity that subordinates agency to an experience of atemporality and aspatiality.

Metamusic permits a rehearsal of impersonality outside history and historiography, even if for an instant, whereby processes may operate outside prescribed cultural narrative. "Personal identity depends upon the possibility of history," Ellmann notes; "this is crucial, for the definition of *im*personality depends on the nature of the self to be dethroned . . . in temporal terms, each existence has its own rhythm, its unique *durée*; but space reduces time into a common currency."[96] However, Xenakis's metamusic does not simply transcend time in the sense of going beyond. Metamusic also signifies an experience of chronological stasis whereby the transcendence of time is the transcendence into zero temporal experience: there is no essential human memory, and no self, just a sense of uncertainty though predicated on hypercomplex disorder with an underlying logic. "In the same way a stochastic construction or an investigation of history with the help of stochastics cannot be carried through without the help of logic."[97] Xenakis writes that the arts must proceed with technological extensions: to use stochasticism that at once establishes the sense of temporal and spatial stasis while operating to the random and unpredictable reorganization of sounds or grains. If personal identity does indeed depend upon history, the spatial and temporal illusions established by hypercomplex stochasticism establish paradoxical impersonality: one of random, disordered, cut-up, aleatoric, hazy, cloud-like unpredictability swirling upon a substratum of algorithmic logic: or, "a total exaltation in which the individual mingles, losing his consciousness in a truth immediate, rare, enormous, and perfect." This is not necessarily Burroughs and Gysin's "third-mind" but instead, like Siratori's work, the sounds and poiesis for troubled times.

Granular impersonality is that which resists the totalizing impulse of algorithmic culture. While Eliot writes in "The Dry Salvages" (1941) that "We had the experience but missed the meaning."[98] Steven Shaviro writes that while the lament is one that "Eurocentric modernists used to whine" about, it is "for us, now ... a cause for celebration. Meaning only gets in the way of enjoyment."[99] The twenty-first century's intensified algorithmic culture reformulates the observation even further: we had the meaning but missed the experience (the algorithmic culture). That is, by the second decade of the twenty-first century, reactionary mad-scrambling for cohesive media narratives got in the way of the potentialities that are unbounded by uncertainty. When Pound confidently stated that humans are the ones who start the machines, he was unable to foresee how the machinic might operate according to media apparatus. Before the information age, the poetics of impersonality were an aesthetic project and one of allowance: one *can* choose to act as a kind of medium for history, Futurist accelerationism, emancipatory occult messages from the third mind, and so on. Today, however, this negation may manifest itself in the form of the nonconsensual exclusion of individual agency in nearly every aspect of daily life through the ubiquity of information technologies and the cultural logic of algorithms. However, rather than facing this epistemological impasse with a shrug, perhaps granular synthesis can offer a metamusical experience, the approaching zero, as a rehearsal for confronting apparatus. "Zero is to number signs, as the vanishing point is to perspective images, as imaginary money is to money signs," writes Brian Rotman. "Zero is a sign about signs, a *meta-sign*, whose meaning is to indicate, via a syntax which arrives with it, the absence of certain other signs."[100] This syntax indicates the absence of other signs that define the endless possibilities; through negation, through a merging-as-disappearance with apparatus, it is difference, not defeat, which radiates with possibilities.

Xenakis's "meta" is essentially ecstatic: it aims to escape time and place. In a sense, it is the access by which aesthetic affect might imagine an escape from history (or, at least, establish alternative nonlinear spaces to view anew historiography and its favoring of change). By doing so, granular poetics may offer the ability to rehearse knotted-thinking with politics without being constituted by the political and the temporal. Ballerini takes note of how such modes of art and impersonality can redeem the human from political context. "This redemption is inherent in the divergent use that art and politics make of history," he writes. "Art produces new syntagms out of its own history," Ballerini continues, "and it does so by contradicting the very paradigms upon which that history is founded."[101] He stresses that art is opposed to history as it "deploys an oneiric grammar that disengages it from the linear configurations of time."[102] Inevitable is how art, in this sense (and arguably in Xenakis's "meta"), disengages from politics.

Politics are inextricable from time and temporality; politics impress the Zeitgeist upon the individual, resulting in the necessity of agency as constitutive and constituted by "the times." And yet, simultaneously, it is politics that impress "upon [time] the rhythm of its own mechanisms."[103] Politics is logical in the sense that it is sequential, rule-governed, and dependent upon its feedback looping self-reference and self-propagation: politics "believes in measures" and "turns predictions into paradigms and serves as the clock of the future . . . politics needs time to produce the illusion of progress,"[104] whether by clocks or in coffee spoons. And such illusions of progress are, ultimately, simply stochastic reorganizations, self-affirming mutations of politics itself: politics cannot think politics because, like semantic sound, it shares sequential logic and measured temporality. The algorithmic hyperchaos of granular poetics and glitch writing does not aim to transcend temporality; however, it engenders a nonsequential cloud of grains that is not situated alongside sequence or as an alternative parallel to politics instead the swarm interpenetrates, knots, ever-reorganizes, and entwines. The twenty-first century is not off to a promising start. The reappearance of ordered and authoritarian populism on the political stage coupled with a global pandemic, precarity, climate catastrophe, overpopulation, essentialism, and corporatization does not instill confidence in the future. "What will emerge in the future is inscribed in the present," Bifo writes, yet "the traces that we can detect in the present are not prescriptions: the interpretation of what is inscribed in the present is not obvious and the evolution of the tendency is not prescribed in a deterministic way."[105] Artistic innovation *with* technology will be the science of revolution; the embrace of complexity, chaos, and unpredictability will yield psychic emancipation from technology as instruction engendered by neuro-totalitarianism. Just as Dada signifies nothing and yet is the will to difference via destruction, data signifies nothing yet is the negation that may also highlight a syntax of endless, indeterminate possibility. This is the substratum, whether sound or text, upon which Siratori's glitch poetics mobilizes.

SIRATORI, ANTINATIONALISM, AND THE WESTERN AVANT-GARDE

Shifts in aesthetic methodology, literary philosophy, and constitutive market determinants emphasize a kind of historicity that again complicates the question of nationhood as it relates to writing likes Siratori's. His work is certainly posited in relation to formalistically extreme Mavo, Japanese cyberpunk, and the avant-garde spirit of Abe. Yet, an analogous relation must be said about the heritage of cut-up narrative and textual sampling in European and North American literary traditions: particularly, according to Siratori, the work of Artaud and Burroughs. What links Siratori's work to that of Artaud's is most salient in considering the latter's project from the 1930s, The Theatre of Cruelty. Furthermore, this relationship is more programmatic than immediately aesthetic; yet, the gesture proves to be more than superficial. In the case of both Siratori and Artaud, the program is one of the radical rejection of the conventions of the media and social context within which their work is situated: for Artaud, the blunt rejection of "an entire theatrical tradition"[106] while for Siratori, it is the relentless assault upon the conventions of syntax, plot, national language, and sense of the novel. Consider the opening lines of *Blood Electric*—note the similarity to the passages quoted above—as emblematic for Siratori's rejection of novelistic tradition: "<<I record the vital-icon+our chromosome form escape of the suck=blood chromosome::the horizon of the body fluid=murder like the dog that was done to nude gene=TV/spasm//I am disillusioned with the volume inoculation of hydromachine::the circuit without the end of masses of flesh::I disappear with the body of the machine nature of ToK::."[107] While, as Barber suggests, "Artaud's commitment was to creating a new theatre,"[108] the preceding passage is indicative of Siratori's dedication to a project of unveiling the inappropriateness of conventional language and the novel in the digital age: he is "disillusioned with the volume," that is, the novel. Artaud intimates a similar sentiment in *The Theatre of Cruelty: The First Manifesto* (1932),

> We can only define this language as expressive, dynamic spatial potential in contrast with expressive spoken dialogue potential. Theatre can still derive possibilities for extension from speech outside words, the development in space of its dissociatory, vibratory action on our sensibility. We must take inflection into account here, the particular way a word is pronounced, as well as the visual language of things (audible, sound language aside), also movement, attitudes and gestures, providing their meanings are extended, their features connected even as far as those signs, making a kind of alphabet out of those signs. Having become conscious of this spatial language, theatre owes it to itself to organise these shouts, sounds, lights and onomatopoeic language, creating true

hieroglyphs out of characters and objects, making use of their symbolism and interconnections in relation to every organ and on all levels.[109]

For both Artaud and Siratori, this kind of iconoclasm is fundamentally generative. While Artaud's declarations and Siratori's work both gesture toward "an unbearably piercing sound or noise,"[110] this cacophony is metonymical to the effects of thinking the unthinkable or experiencing that which has not, or may not be possible, to experience: the noise is mediated through Artaud's "kind of alphabet." That is, in Artaud's words, such new modes of expression will "succeed in recording or codifying anything that cannot be described in words."[111] Just as "The Theatre of Cruelty will choose themes and subjects corresponding to the agitation and unrest of [Artaud's] times,"[112] Siratori's project acknowledges the biases of both the traditional language of the novel and the encroaching consequence of code in the digital age. Artaud was "attracted by fragmentary, violent gestures which were suddenly cut and abandoned,"[113] something which Siratori enacts extremely in his approach to language. Barber suggests that within the first manifesto for the Theatre of Cruelty there is embedded an explicit "threat to language."[114] Artaud's vision was to establish "a truly dangerous theatre" that would inflict major consequences upon the stability and security "both of the word and of the world with its unique performances";[115] Siratori gestures in the same direction, though with a kind of electronically produced language of cruelty.

Cruelty, here, has a specific meaning. In a letter to Jean Paulhan dated September 13, 1932, Artaud writes that this sense of cruelty "is not sadistic or bloody, at least not exclusively so. I do not systematically cultivate horror. The word cruelty must be taken in its broadest sense, not in the physical, predatory sense usually ascribed to it . . . cruelty means strictness, diligence, unrelenting decisiveness, irreversible and absolute determination."[116] Later that year, in a letter to André Rolland de Renéville, Artaud suggests that "cruelty connects things together, the different stages of creation are formed by it."[117] "For Artaud, 'cruelty' could embody in one word all his creative preoccupations and his personal suffering," writes Barber, "he resisted the superficial resonances of blood and murder attached to the word, believing that the idea of cruelty could communicate a remaking of worlds."[118] Albert Bermel notes that cleansing, transfiguration, and exaltation[119] operate as the objectives of Artaud's medium of cruelty. Furthermore, Bermel indicates three notable features of Artaud's Theatre of Cruelty: first, "it does not involve physical or spiritual maltreatment"; second, Artaud's "theatre draws on the individual dreams and the collective dreams, or the myths, of all men"; and finally, that because this theatre "works on the nerves and senses, rather than on the intellect . . . the Theatre of Cruelty is aimed at a general public, not the usual run of theatergoers."[120] The pattern that arises here—that of making unusual connections, violence against habitual thought as a means of achieving a new or collective language or code, and the establishment or reconfiguration of worlds—is an aesthetic of cruelty shared by both writers. Significantly, however, Siratori's project is uniquely of the digital age and explicitly engages with electronic media. That "Artaud was proposing a theatre," Barber writes, "that would be in a state of constant self-destruction and self-reconstruction,"[121] is itself almost prophetic for the nature of electronic avant-garde writing. The theatre, for Artaud, and the written form, for Siratori, achieve their potency through iconoclasm: the destruction of the very possibility of representation by rejecting the possibility of semantic repetition. Artaud might consider this an almost mystical process; Siratori, on the other hand, employs the excesses of the destruction and reconstruction of language as a means of expressing the affective quality of information illiteracy in the early twenty-first century.

Some three decades later, at the same time Abe was writing his finest work, across the pacific, Burroughs and Gysin were experimenting with the cut-up method. "Gysin had a 'career-long desire to create works' that would alter the reader's thought process and perception in the same way."[122] Burroughs's 1959 novel *Naked Lunch* is a series of cut-up vignettes that lack any conventional diegetic structure; with this strategy, Burroughs "strove to break the mould and escape the 'straight jacket of the novel.'"[123] Much in the same way Burroughs incorporated contemporary magazines and newspaper articles as materials to parasitize his cut-up narratives, Robinson writes that, similarly, "Siratori uses the fabric of the digital age to create texts which reflect life in the new millennium, while also breaking down any semblance of a sense of continuity by splicing and mashing text and code together."[124] Robinson suggests that the methodology of cutting up material print can be considered to belong to the more destructive aspects of avant-gardism rather than to postmodernism,[125] thus establishing an analogous parallel to Tatsumi's distinction between literary production and creative consumption. Michael Schiltz remarks that "*Blood Electric* is a compelling psychedelic trip in which the status of the writer and reader are frequently shifted. Different from Burroughs' work, we are not offered any breathing pause, but are forced to search or create an orientation of our own."[126] While the avant-garde gesture is certainly iconoclastic, it is also an explicit act of production: manufacturing alternatives that reconfigure conventional aesthetic values and expectations and ultimately challenge the possibility of affective satisfaction. With a paradoxical and nonoppositional stance such as this, the contemporary reader may also prefer Auster to Abe or Burroughs; however, Siratori's writing offers little pleasure in the commercial sense and, as a result, does not necessarily fit in the hierarchical nodes of inclination that Tatsumi suggests. Postmodern aesthetic, however—in the work of Auster, Burroughs, and Siratori—is more akin to acts of creative consumption in that it engages with source material of any type, consumes it, updates it, reconfigures it, remixes it, cuts it up, and consequently, the status of the producer/writer and consumer/reader is repeatedly transferred. Avant-gardism makes the possibility of alternatives; postmodernism and its legacy suggest hybridity, permutation, fecundity, and closed system mutation.

As a result, the language of Siratori's writing proves difficult, and not just on a semantic level. For a writer who is repeatedly discussed in terms of his Japaneseness, perhaps the most explicit point of contention with this position is that Siratori's writing is not in the Japanese language and, as Negarestani points out, this is significant in terms of Siratori's iconoclasm. Rather, Siratori's novels comprise English language interspersed with nongrammatical punctuation, typographical eccentricities, and numbers establishing something more akin to a fictional, glitching code than a conventional language for effecting patterned and complex communication. His writing takes on the appearance, to the eye, of a combination of English language and code. Michael Schiltz acutely notes that there is a seriously problematic aspect to Siratori's work that is "enhanced by a host of tendentious comments by Siratori's fans or *aficionados*. In a typical example of flawed contemporary Japonism, [Barber] and [Hunter] describe *Blood Electric* as respectively a 'blood- and semen-encrusted debris with the finesse of a berserk Issey Miyake' and 'the black reverb of soft machine seppuku.'"[127] Siratori's writing demonstrates that semantics take place on the level of syntax and de Saussurean deference. Since there is no recognizable semio-grammatical patterning in his writing, it is reasonable to suggest that his writing is asemic. Indeed, "What Kenji Siratori achieves with his polywaves of interlocking paraphrasing," writes GX Jupitter-Larsen, "is the opportunity to rase to the ground antiquated rhetoric, and give world literature the prefect blank foundation in which to bring about a whole new phraseology."[128]

This new phraseology is brought about via Siratori's glitch methodology, which is perhaps most appropriately called an "automated" writing practice. David Toop calls it a "generative machine,"[129] Robinson distinguishes from the surrealists' automatic writing practices.[130] This methodology is intimately linked to the logistics of speed as it evolves alongside the development of information technologies. Robinson suggests that "Siratori can be seen to be exploiting the available software as a means of producing large quantities of text very rapidly, and has 'bombarded' the internet by maintaining a remarkably prolific level of output."[131] This excessive output is, in itself, a kind of formal or meta-aesthetic gesture. That Siratori's works come out almost faster than a reader could read marks a kind of self-similar experience to reading a single work by the author, that is, any single Siratori book is, to a degree, metonymical to his entire oeuvre. This formulation recognizes the medium of rapidly developing new modes of communicative extensions as something that has, by its very logic, surpassed the conceptual parameters of linearity. Baudrillard, in conversation with Sylvère Lotringer, comments on this phenomenon: "when the effect goes faster and faster than the cause, it devours it. I could easily see the 'speed-up' analyzed by Paul Virilio from this angle as an attempt to accelerate faster than linearity can handle. Speed is different from movement. Movement goes somewhere, speed nowhere."[132] Siratori is effectively intimating how information technologies make possible this paradoxical glitch in causation: engagement with media occurs before the message is configured and disseminated. In effect, the medium ends up engaging the user before the user can engage with the medium. With Siratori's writing, the signifier outraces the referent, the word is more rapid than its constitutive syntax, and information more like noise than semantic pattern. Here, we have Marinetti's words in freedom at their most radical deliverance as an extreme form of aesthetic accelerationism. This ambivalent relationship between technology and the body is what links Siratori most explicitly with the cyberpunk tradition—it also enacts cyberpunk formally rather than through content: language is a virus, yet the symbiotic loop is spinning past its logical singularity; the metonymical embedding of form in content is producing an illogical conceptual geometry and ubiquitous, assaulting cognitive mutation. This is the alienating and asemic effect that Siratori's writing ultimately produces: the experimental novel as an aesthetic and affective proxy for our relationship with the apparatus.

GLITCHING THE NERVOUS SYSTEM

Siratori's writing, however, does not reconfigure McLuhan's dictum "the medium is the message." McLuhan's message is "the change of scale or pace or pattern" that a new technology introduces into the lives of individuals.[133] The message is not the semantic content but the shift in dynamics that the new technology enacts. So, the message of Siratori's writing is not the "meaning" or the content of his work, but the way it restructures the reader's nervous system. His writing demands that the reader consider the effects—whether semantic or social or interpersonal—that are reconfigured, accelerated, or extended by unusual writing practice. While Abe's avant-garde aesthetics are posited upon the possibility of objectivity and the separateness of the perceiver and world, Siratori's aesthetic is more persistently ambient: "the instantaneous world of electronic informational media involves all of us, all at once," asserts McLuhan: "No detachment or frame is possible."[134] Robinson suggests that

There is little question that Siratori's texts implicitly follow the popular and age-old sci-fi idea of machines taking over and humanity either under their control or otherwise running scared, but his "writing" equally seems to suggest a new mode of manipulating digital text—and manipulating text by digital meanings—as a device by which to express and reflect, in a heightened fashion, the effects of (post)modern living.[135]

The medium—an extension of the human body, to stick with McLuhan's formulation—is the novel itself, language as an extension of the human nervous system, extending our thoughts from our own brains into a postmodern or supermodern matrix accessible by others. Siratori's work "must be seen," writes Schiltz, "as a product and symbol of the medial interconnections the very digital revolution. Word, sound and image have become one. I therefore doubt that it can be discussed as literature in its pure sense. It is as much a work of visual art."[136] *Blood Electric* is described as the "coming to consciousness of an artificial intelligence" and thus emphasizes the extension. In this sense, the novel is an extension of an AI's "central nervous system"; by establishing this kind of proxy, Siratori elucidates his project via analogy. Here we have the brain or consciousness as an extension of an AI. Whatever direction this formulation is considered, the message remains intact: the central nervous system's pace and pattern are reconfigured in a kind of closed dynamic system by its extension into communication technologies.

Playing around with the equation makes Siratori's readers think about the relationship between media and the metanoia. Rushkoff suggests that modern information technology is biased because its message, its effects on the patterns and pace of interpersonal dynamics, is determined by programming. "Digital technology is programmed," Rushkoff writes, "this makes it biased toward those with the capacity to write the code. In a digital age, we must learn how to make the software, or risk becoming the software. It is not too difficult or too late . . . to understand that there *is* a code behind their interfaces. Otherwise, we are at the mercy of those who do the programming, the people paying them, and even the technology itself."[137] This is a central *point* behind Siratori's excess; by enacting the cyberpunk aesthetic formally through glitch writing that evokes programming, he reveals a systemic logic that asks readers to recognize that there is a code behind the interfaces of digital technology. That so many of us respond to code in a way similar to how we may respond to Siratori's writing—that of illiterate bafflement—reveals that this kind of readership in the twenty-first century needs to move beyond hyperconsumerism toward a kind of intensely paradoxical participation of impersonality, if not hyperparticipation, with both the arts and digital technology. Indeed, perhaps the concerns that arise Siratori's work are the concerns of both McLuhan and Rushkoff—the public must be aware of the processes of both production and consumption, whether in our engagement with the arts or with digital media in general. "The theme of the awaking artificial intelligence," writes Schiltz, "demands us to be replaced in the mind of what is awakened, including the noise of growing, learning, forgetting and remembering, in short, acquiring a self-referentially evolving self."[138] Siratori's linguistic apocalypse serves to reveal not only the dyshomeostatic processes at play between the central nervous system and media but also to de-create antiquated rhetoric and "give world literature the perfect blank foundation in which to bring about a whole new phraseology."

Ultimately, although the totality of his multimedia is cyberpunk at its most formally extreme, in a way, Siratori's work is its own genre. One will not find that Siratori's work is conceivable content or determinable form; instead, we are confronted with a conflagrating jetty of disparate, independent fragments that, if looked at in isolation, suggest semantics but when reconsidered within context become incomprehensible. If parts make sense, the whole remains incomprehensible. If the whole is comprehensible, it is only so in a transcendent way: the parts have been set free. This emergent complexity is precisely the *point* of Siratori's work: forget the meaning and embrace the inscrutable emergence of endless, antiteleological potentialities.

SWARM ANNIHILATION

Siratori's work is primarily a confrontation, not only of conventional language but "the swarm" that is made possible through combinatorial culture. Bifo writes that "when the social body is wired by techno-linguistic automatisms, it acts as a swarm: a collective organism whose behavior is automatically directed by connective interfaces."[139] Though common in nature—think of bees or schools of fish—the swarm comes to define human behavior only in relation to new media technologies associated with the internet. The swarm needs to be distinguished from a crowd, a multitude, and a network. A crowd, according to Han's reading of Gustave Le Bon's *The Crowd: A Study of the Popular Mind* (1895), suggests that at the end of the nineteenth century, Le Bon imagined "the society of the future would have to reckon with a new power—the power of masses."[140] As the hierarchical model of aristocracy was waning, Le Bon saw in the masses a collective, unified spirit that expressed a flattening of power structures and political hierarchy. For Le Bon, a crowd has a unified soul and a sense of collective identity and shared goals. It can identify as a *we* and speak with a common voice. The crowd, however, is distinguished from what Bifo calls the multitude. "A multitude is a plurality of conscious and sensitive beings sharing no common intentionality, and showing no common pattern of behavior," writes Bifo.[141] Consider the busy streets of a city. The crowd bustles about in any given direction, each person with their schedule, goals, desires, boredom, and tasks. With a multitude comes multiplicity. "Everybody goes their own way," Bifo continues, "and the intersection of those displacements makes a crowd. Sometimes the crowd moves in a coordinated way: people run together towards the station because the train is soon expected to leave, people stop together at traffic lights. Everybody moves following his or her will, within the constraints of social interdependency."[142] Unlike the multitude, a network is more explicitly cybernetic and is concretely made manifest in the digital era. "A network is a plurality of organic and artificial beings, of humans and machines who perform common actions thanks to procedures that make possible their interconnection and interoperation," writes Bifo.[143] Unlike the multitude or the crowd, a network is more regimented, rigid, and rule-governed. For example, a collection of machines could be considered a multitude: they are without agency, and any agency one may discover in them results from a cybernetic extension of a human being or other organism. If one were to place their hand between a button press and a shoe in a factory, the mechanism would mutilate the worker's hand. The automation of the machine—its rigid, preprogrammed set of motions—does not, like a crowd, react to interference. "If you do not adapt to these procedures," Bifo notes, "if you don't follow the technical rules of the game, you are not playing the game."[144] If the "game" happens to be a dangerous conveyer belt in a factory, one may lose a limb. With a network, the technology, being more rigid and rule-governed than human behavior, tends to demand of the human to bend to its functionality rather than the other way around. After all, you cannot reason with a computer by using emotional appeals, for example; instead, the human must learn code and then use code to affect code. "If you don't react to certain stimuli in the programmed way, you don't form part of the network," Bifo writes, "the behavior of persons in a network is not aleatory, like the movements of a crowd, because the network implies and predisposes pathways for the networker."[145] While the multitude permits (and requires) individual agents, the network diminishes this to maintain the efficiency and effectively of its purpose or procedure. Indeed, the multitude in human beings is incomplete, but an analog to it results from the atomizing effects of reducing the qualitative to the quantitative. However, the effects algorithmic culture and its managerial, conforming, and essentialist tendencies have on human beings may be more accurately expressed by the swarm.

The swarm operates in ways that allow for the sense of individual agency *only* on the individual level, whereas the whole operates independently according to constitutive, systematic rules regardless of the knowledge, agency, or will of an individual actor. "A swarm is a plurality of living beings whose behavior follows (or seems to follow) rules embedded in their neural systems," Bifo remarks:

> Biologists call a swarm a multitude of animals of similar size and bodily orientation, moving together in the same direction and performing actions in a coordinated way, like bees building a hive or moving toward a plant where they can find resources for making honey.... In conditions of social hypercomplexity, human beings tend to act as a swarm. When the infosphere is too dense and too fast for a conscious elaboration of information, people tend to conform to shared behavior.[146]

The swarm is effectively a systematic abstraction that removes the possibility of individual actors' will, choice, desire, or interpretation. "In a swarm it is not impossible to say 'no,'" Bifo continues: to dissent as an individual is irrelevant to the operation and function of the swarm. "You can express your refusal, your rebellion and your nonalighment," he writes, "but this is not going to change the direction of the swarm, nor is it going to affect the way in which the swarm's brain is elaborating information."[147] The swarm becomes, in a sense, a collective abstract organism that operates according to systematic functionalities. To say that a swarm has a will of its own would be misleading. Another distinction that the swarm has from a crowd, a multitude, or a network is its unlikeness (if not impossibility) of articulating as a collective. "The digital swarm does not constitute a mass because no *soul*—no *spirit*—dwells within it," writes Han.[148] He continues,

> The soul gathers and unites. In contrast, the digital swarm comprises isolated individuals. The mass is structured along different lines: its features cannot be traced back to individuals. But now, individuals are melting into a new unit; its members no longer have a *profile of their own*. For a crowd to emerge, a chance gathering of human beings is not enough. It takes a soul, a common spirit, to fuse people into a crowd. The digital swarm lacks the soul or spirit of the masses. Individuals who come together as a swarm do not develop a *we*. No harmony prevails—which is what welds the crowd together into an active entity. Unlike the crowd, the swarm demonstrates no internal coherence. It does not speak with a voice.[149]

The swarm's purpose is to ensure its survival even at the expense of constitutive parts. That is, it can easily sacrifice individual units to maximize the overall optimization of the swarm itself.

A confrontation with the emergence of the apparatus and the semantic stronghold of the swarm, Siratori demands that we defy the rise of the algorithmic manufacturing of cultural and cognitive automatism. Bifo writes that in the twenty-first century, crowds and multitudes are involved in automatic chains of behaviour, and driven by techno-linguistic dispositives. The automation of the behaviour of many individuals traversed and concatenated by techno-linguistic interfaces results in the effect of Swarm. Man is the animal who shapes the environment that shapes his/her own brain, the swarm effect therefore is the outcome of human transformation of the technical environment leading to automation of mental behaviour.[150]

Elsewhere, Bifo writes that the swarm

is a particular kind of . . . group phenomenon that may be dependent upon a condition of connectivity. A swarm is a collectivity that is defined by relationality. This pertains as much to the level of the individual unit as it does to the overall organization of the swarm. At some level 'living networks' and 'swarms' overlap. A swarm is a whole that is more than the sum of its parts, but it is also a heterogeneous whole. In the swarm, the parts are not subservient to the whole—both exist simultaneously and because of each other.[151]

The constitutive effects of corporatized media technologies ultimately deny agency and annihilate art and collective revolt. In this context, the swarm refers to a phenomenon where many individuals behave in coordinated ways regardless of whether there is an organized or centralized source dictating such behavior. An active expression of the way both neoliberalism embeds itself in the unconscious via neuro-technological extension, swarm phenomena are indicative of the reach that neuro-totalitarianism may achieve: a shaping of decentralized cognitive automatisms that seem to operate independently but, from another scale, is revealed to be a collective, automated behavior. "The swarm," Bifo continues, "has no political soul, only an automatic and relational soul."[152] Rather than turn away from technology—an impossible and hopeless future course of action—Siratori asks us to transcend the techno-totalitarianism by demolishing the destroyer through a negative act of constructivism. Like the prototypical Ballardian protagonist, we are to push further and further into technology, prying apart the parameters of agency along the way as a means of achieving a new kind of supermodern transcendence and an escape from the totalitarian manufacture of a cognitive, automated swarm.

As a master of demolishing both form and content as a revolt against the constitutive dominance of social media and corporate neuro-technologies and at a time when there is a push to reestablish content in ways that serve the inhuman, Siratori is one of the most transgressive artists to have experimented with image and text these past twenty years. Like the soft elegance of Noon's chaotics, Siratori's harsh noise reminds us that, in chaos, possibilities abound. The future needs to be human in this multiplicitous sense. It is a worthwhile endeavor to believe in the possibility of a socially (complex) cohesive future. However, rather than projecting desire on the future, Siratori expresses *the now* and an alternative future in a way that we should also acknowledge: a complete glitch in meaning, a coming-together of an endgame, a staging of poietic Dadaist nonsense or neo-Futurist trans-sense[153] against algorithmic order. Siratori is doing to content and form what Simon Sellars does with method with his excellent book *Applied Ballardianism* (2018). Siratori's hypermodern project articulates the nonarticulation that currently dominates the substratum of much current discourse. Without the intense atomization of the individual, Siratori's work does not resound. Yet, if we take pause, Siratori's work resonates at a fever pitch, blaring at the limitless informational realm of our minds as it bursts the parameters of the skull. As a kind of accelerationist aesthetic, Siratori critiques technology by pushing it beyond its sensible potentiality; he cultivates alien cognitions where alternatives thrive, where semantic derangement is revolt, where epistemology uncoils. Ultimately, he uncompromisingly forces us to pause on the chaos of the glitch, to claim the instance where embodying the unquantifiable amounts to insurgency.

NOTES

1. Paul Virilio, *The Futurism of the Instant: Stop-Eject*, trans. Julie Rose (Cambridge: Polity Press, 2011), 70.
2. J.G. Ballard, "The Care, the Future," *A User's Guide to the Millennium: Essays and Reviews* (London: Harper Collins, 1996), 224–227.
3. Virilio, *The Futurism of the Instant*, 70.
4. Ibid., 70–71.
5. Mark Fisher, "Break it Down: DJ Rashad's *Double Cup*," *K-Punk: The Collected and Unpublished Writings of Mark Fisher (2004–2016)*, ed. Darren Ambrose (London: Repeater Books, 2018).
6. Kenji Siratori, *Blood Electric* (Creation Books, 2002), dust jacket.
7. Douglas Rushkoff, "Technologies Have Biases," in *Edge* (2011), https://www.edge.org/response-detail/10368.
8. Kenji Siratori, *Kenji Siratori Official Site*, https://kenjisiratori.wixsite.com/kenjisiratori/works.
9. Stephen Barber, quoted in Siratori, *Blood Electric*, dust jacket.
10. AKA James Williamson/James Havoc.
11. Jack Hunter, quoted in Siratori, *Blood Electric*, dust jacket.
12. Reza Negarestani, "TECHNODROME," *3:AM Magazine*, 2005, https://www.3ammagazine.com/litarchives/2005/oct/technodrome.shtml.
13. Siratori, *Blood Electric*, 112.

14. Kenji Siratori, quoted in Edward S. Robinson, *Shift Linguals: Cut-up Narratives from William S. Burroughs to the Present* (New York: Ropodi, 2011), 260.

15. Kenji Siratori, *Mind Virus* (Monstaar Media, 2008), 65–66.

16. Kenji Siratori, *Hack_* (Minerva, 2011), 64.

17. Berardi, *Breathing*, 53.

18. Siratori currently lives in Sapporo, Japan, according to his Twitter profile: https://twitter.com/kenjisiratori.

19. Negarestani, TECHNODROME.

20. Takayuki Tatsumi, *Full Metal Apache: Transactions between Cyberpunk Japan and Avant-Pop America* (Durham: Duke University Press, 2006), 205.

21. Donald Keene, *Five Modern Japanese Novelists* (New York: Columbia University Press, 2003), 73.

22. Margaret S. Key, *Truth from a Lie: Documentary, Detection, and Reflexivity in Abe Kōbō's Realist Project* (Lanham: Lexington Books, 2011), 1–2.

23. Christopher Bolton, *Sublime Voices: The Fictional Science and Scientific Fiction of Abe Kōbō* (Harvard Univeristy Asia Center, 2009), 284.

24. Weisenfeld notes that

"in many ways, Mavo's history revolves around Murayama's own intellectual development and interests. An ardent believer in the socially transformative potential of innovative aesthetics, Murayama played a crucial role in the Japanese art world as cultural interpreter, arbiter, rebel, and personality. Japanese artists like him who studied and selectively assimilated the modernist credo to suit their needs and the context in which they worked helped domesticate Modernism in Japan . . . Murayama labeled his artistic theory 'conscious constructivism' (*ishikiteki koseishugi*). Inspired by ideas derived from anarchism, Marxism, futurism, expressionism, dadaism, and constructivism, Murayama sought to construct a nonrepresentational image of modernity pertinent to the reality of daily life in Japan. Murayama felt that the complete social and creative liberation of the individual was the first step toward realizing this project. Mavo members collectively implemented Murayama's theory, taking it from the realm of aesthetics to the world of radical politics." Gennifer Weisenfeld, *Mavo: Japanese Artists and the Avant-Garde, 1905–1931* (London: University of California Press, 2002), 2–3.

25. Weisenfeld, *Mavo*, 2. See note 22 above.

26. "The Mavo Group were a negative entity," writes Alex Danchev,

"as they said; more an inclination than an organization. Apocryphally, the name or acronym Mavo was arrived at by cutting up pieces of paper with the names of the five founders spelled out in Romanized letters, scattering them around the room, and choosing the four remaining letters (or perhaps the ones furthest away) to make up a random word. This sounds too good to be true, if only because there is no letter V in the Japanese syllabary. Alternatively, and no less improbably, it represents M for *masse* (mass) and V for *vitesse* (speed), with A for *alpha* and O for *omega*." *100 Artists' Manifestos: From the Futurists to the Stuckists*, ed. Alex Danchev (London: Penguin, 2011), 233.

27. Gennifer Weisenfeld, "Mavo's Conscious Constructivism: Art, Individualism, and Daily Life in Interwar Japan," *Art Journal*, 55, no. 3 (1996), 64.

28. Tomoshoi Murayama and others, "Mavo Manifesto (1923)," in *100 Artists' Manifestos: From the Futurists to the Stuckists*, ed. Alex Davnchev (London: Penguin, 2011), 234.

29. Ibid., 66.

30. Weisenfeld, "Mavo's Conscious Constructivism," 67.

31. Ibid., 67.

32. Ibid., 67.

33. Weisenfeld, *Mavo*, 3.

34. Ibid., 257.

35. William Verrone, *The Avant-Garde Feature Film* (Jefferson: McFarland, 2011), 151.

36. Ibid., 151.

37. Douglas Rushkoff, *ScreenAgers: Lessons in Chaos from Digital Kids* (Cresskill: Hampton Press, 2006), 67.

38. Ibid., 67.

39. Ibid.

40. Ibid., 68.

41. Indeed, one would be better off looking to Gnosticism, rather than Christian fundamentalism, and particularly the former's role in the work of Philip K. Dick.

42. Rushkoff, *ScreenAgers*, 68.

43. Verrone, *The Avant-Garde Feature*, 150.

44. Ibid., 153.

45. Michael Schiltz, review of *Blood Electric*, by Kenji Siratori, *Image [&] Narrative: Online Magazine of the Visual Narrative* 9 (October 2004), http://www.imageandnarrative.be/inarchive/performance/siratori.htm.

46. Tatsumi, *Full Metal Apache*, 29.

47. Key, *Truth from a Lie*, 2.

48. Bolton, *Sublime Voices*, 104.

49. Ibid., 1.

50. Key, *Truth from a Lie*, 2.

51. Ibid., 171.

52. Ibid., 171–172.

53. Ibid., 172.

54. Tatsumi, *Full Metal Apache*, 29.

55. Ibid.

56. Key, *Truth from a Lie*, 1.

57. Tatsumi, *Full Metal Apache*, 30.

58. Darko Suvin, *Metamorphoses of Science Fiction: On the Poetics and History of a Literary Genre* (New Haven: Yale University Press, 1979).

59. Brecht, quoted in Suvin, *Metamorphoses*, 6.

60. Mark Bould and Sherryl Vint, *The Routledge Concise History of Science Fiction* (New York: Routledge, 2011), 18.

61. Bould and Vint, 18.

62. Kenji Siratori, interview by Richard Marshall, "The Nude Brain," *3:AM Magazine*, 2002, http://www.3ammagazine.com/litarchives/2002_jun/interview_kenji_siratori.html.

63. Istvan Csicsery-Ronay, Jr., "Marxist Theory and Science Fiction," in *The Cambridge Companion to Science Fiction*, eds. Edward James and Farah Mendlesohn (Cambridge: Cambridge University Press, 2003), 119.

64. Kenji Siratori, interview by Azimute, "Mechanical Hunting For The Grotesque," *Heathen Harvest*, February 15, 2006. https://web.archive.org/web/20060323041512/http://www.heathenharvest.com/article.php?story=2006021520160363.

65. N. Katherine Hayles, *Electronic Literature: New Horizons for the Literary* (Notre Dame, Indiana: University of Notre Dame Press, 2008), 17.

66. Curtis Roads, "Introduction to Granular Synthesis," *Computer Music Journal* 12, no. 2 (1988), 11.

67. Alongside Xenakis, Curtis Roads, Barry Truax, Douglas Jones, and Thomas Parks are the composers most commonly associated with granular synthesis; however, today, there are countless electronic artists and sound designers who incorporate granular synthesis into their work on a regular basis.

68. Luigi Russolo, "The Art of Noise: 1913 Futurist Manifesto," trans. Robert Filliou (Something Else Press, 1967), 6.

69. David Stubbs, *Future Sounds: The Story of Electronic Music from Stockhausen to Skrillex* (London: Faber & Faber, 2018), 67.

70. Ibid., 77.

71. Daniel Teruggi, "The *Treatise on Musical Objects* and the GRM," in Pierre Schaeffer's *Treatise on Musical Objects: An Essay across Disciplines*, translated by Christine North and John Dack (Oakland: University of California Press, 2017), xvi.

72. Ibid.

73. Ibid.

74. Alex Ross, *The Rest is Noise: Listening to the Twentieth Century* (New York: Farrar, Straus and Giroux, 2007), 395.

75. Ibid., 116.

76. Ibid., 117.

77. Found sounds are not unlike Duchamp's readymades: objects or clips torn from their functional purpose and placed within formalized artistic contexts to confront established practices of authorship, authority, and aesthetics.

78. John Cage, *Silence: Lectures and Writings by John Cage*, 50th Anniversary Ed. (Middletown: Wesleyan University Press, 2011), 57.

79. Robinson, 11.

80. John Cage, "A Few Ideas about Music and Film (1951)," *John Cage: Writer* (New York: Limelight Editions, 1993), 65.

81. John Cage and Daniel Charles, *For the Birds: John Cage in Conversation with Daniel Charles*, eds. Richard Gardner, Tom Gora, and John Cage (Salem, NH: Marion Boyars, 1981), 169.

82. Cage, *Silence*, 59.
83. Ross, 397.
84. This technique is something he would eventually champion with the development of the Unité Polyagogique Informatique CEMAMu (UPIC) computer.
85. Ross, 397.
86. Originally published between 1955 and 1965, Xenakis here, alongside referencing set-theory, is referring to the emerging fields of information theory, nonlinear dynamics, and chaos theory.
87. Iannis Xenakis, *Formalized Music: Thought and Math in Composition*, Revised Ed. (Stuyvesant, NY: Pendragon Press, 1992), 4.
88. Ross, 397.
89. James Harley, *Xenakis: His Life in Music* (New York: Routledge, 2004), 197.
90. Curtis Roads, "Automated Granular Synthesis of Sound," *Computer Music Journal* 2, no. 2 (1978), 61.
91. Ibid., 62.
92. Xenakis was a committed communist and certainly did not share any of the pro-war or fascist tendencies of Marinetti and other Italian Futurists. Indeed, Xenakis worked tirelessly to develop user-friendly computer interfaces (like UPIC) to make the process of creating hypercomplex music available to everyone from children to those unschooled in music composition.
93. Xenakis is referring to the talking drums of West Africa where percussion pitch and rhythm are adjusted to emulate human prosody and, as a result, communicate over distances. English missionary John Carrington, who lived much of his life in the Belgian Congo, learned Kele and was taught the practice of using talking drums as a form of communication introduced this sophisticated practice to the European and North American public with the publication of *The Talking Drums of Africa* (1949).
94. Xenakis, 180.
95. Ibid., 1.
96. Ellman, *The Poetics of Impersonality*, 10.
97. Xenakis, 4.
98. T.S. Eliot, "The Dry Salvages," *The Complete Poems & Plays of T.S. Eliot* (London: Faber & Faber, 1969), 186.
99. Steven Shaviro, *Doom Patrols: A Theoretical Fiction about Postmodernism* (New York: Serpent's Tail, 1997), 19.
100. Brian Rotman, *Signifying Nothing: The Semiotics of Zero* (Stanford: Stanford University Press, 1987), 1.
101. Luigi Ballerini, "Italy and/or Marinetti: From Alexandria to Vittorio Veneto," in *The Untameables*, by F. T. Marinetti, trans. Jeremy Parzen (Copenhagen: Green Integer, 2016), 12.
102. Ibid., 12.
103. Ibid.
104. Ibid., 12–13.
105. Franco "Bifo" Berardi, *Futurability: The Age of Impotence and the Horizon of Possibility* (London: Verso, 2019), 235.
106. Stephen Barber, *Antonin Artaud: Blows and Bombs* (London: Faber & Faber, 1993), 45.

107. Siratori, *Blood Electric*, 5.
108. Barber, 45.
109. Antonin Artaud, "The Theatre of Cruelty: First Manifesto," in *Collected Works: Vol.4*, trans. Victor Corti (London: Calder & Boyars, 1968), 68.
110. Artaud, 73.
111. Antonin Artaud, "The Theatre of Cruelty: Second Manifesto," in *Collected Works: Vol.4*, trans. Victor Corti (London: Calder & Boyars, 1968), 99.
112. Artaud, "Second Manifesto," 94.
113. Barber, 45.
114. Ibid., 55.
115. Ibid., 45.
116. Antonin Artaud, "Letters on Cruelty: First Letter," in Victor Corti, trans, *Collected Works: Vol.4* (London: Calder & Boyars, 1968), 77.
117. Artaud, "Letters on Cruelty," 79.
118. Barber, 52.
119. Albert Bermel, *Artaud's Theatre of Cruelty* (New York: Taplinger, 1977), 22.
120. Bermel, 23.
121. Barber, 66.
122. Robinson, 22.
123. Ibid., 35.
124. Ibid., 260.
125. Ibid., 38.
126. Schiltz, review of *Blood Electric*.
127. Ibid.
128. Jupitter-Larsen, *BlazeVOX Books* http://www.blazevox.org/index.php/Shop/fiction/nonexistence-by-kenji-siratori-156/.
129. David Toop, *Kenji Siratori: [KILL ALL MACHINES]: Official site of the US cyberpunk author Kenji* Siratori. http://www.kenjisiratori.com/intro/.
130. Robinson, 259.
131. Ibid., 260.
132. Steve Redhead, *Paul Virilio: Theorist for an Accelerated Culture* (Toronto: University of Toronto Press, 2004), 49.
133. McLuhan, *Understanding Media*, 20.
134. Marshall McLuhan and Quentin Fiore, *The Medium is the Massage: An Inventory of Effects* (Berkeley: Ginko, 1996), 53.
135. Robinson, 261.
136. Schiltz, review of *Blood Electric*.
137. Rushkoff, *Program or Be Programmed*, 134.
138. Schiltz, review of *Blood Electric*.
139. Berardi, *The Uprising*, 14.
140. Han, *In the Swarm*, 10.
141. Berardi, *The Uprising*, 14.
142. Ibid.
143. Ibid.
144. Ibid.

145. Ibid.
146. Ibid., 15.
147. Ibid., 16.
148. Han, *In the Swarm*, 10.
149. Ibid., 10.
150. Franco "Bifo" Berardi, *And: Phenomenology of the End* (Alto University, 2014), 24.
151. Franco "Bifo" Berardi, *The Soul at Work: From Alienation to Autonomy* (Semiotext(e), 2009), 195.
152. Ibid., 195.
153. See Russian Futurists Velimir Khlebnikov (1885–1922) and Aleksei Kruchenykh's (1886–1968) Zaum that first appeared in 1913.

Chapter 7

The Electronic Literature of Exclusion and Autopoiesis

Obsession and Fictionalism

In this chapter and the next, I will move beyond print text to examine three works of electronic literature. Just as this book has no intention of providing anything like a survey of literature that confronts signifying nothing, there is no objective here to attempt a survey of the dizzying number of AI and computer-generated works of literature. Because electronic literature is predicated on evolving technologies, the speed at which its many manifestations develop is always accelerating. From hypertext fiction, email novels, network fiction, generative art, and short fiction delivered serially to mobile devices to interactive fiction, virtual and augmented reality narratives, interactive drama, video games, visual narrative, interactive gestural narrative, glitch literature, code work, and Twitter Bots, electronic literature proves an ever-blossoming and exciting field and offers a fascinating glimpse into the future of storytelling. Here, I use the term "electronic literature" in Hayles's sense: "Electronic literature, generally considered to exclude print literature that has been digitized, is by contact 'digital born,' a first-generation digital object created on a computer and (usually) meant to be read on a computer."[1] Pressman reiterates this emphasis on electronic literature as digital-born: "Electronic literature is born-digital. It is computational and processual, dependent upon the operations of the machine for its aesthetic effects. Electronic literature emerges through a series of translations across machine codes, platforms, and networks; its resulting onscreen content depends upon algorithmic procedures, software, hardware, and (often) Internet compatibility."[2] However, according to a committee headed by Noah Wardrip-Fruin with the Electronic Literature Organization, electronic literature may also include "work with an important literary aspect that takes advantage of the capabilities and contexts provided by the stand-alone or networked computer."[3] Of the literature of exclusion examined so far, only Siratori's glitch poetics would technically be electronic literature. The other works conform more to the definition of the literature of exclusion: works that confront the existential and ontological instance when meaning can no longer be grasped as a result of the authorship of cultural narratives shifting increasingly further away from human storytelling to the algorithmic functionalities of the apparatus.

Works of electronic literature, however, *are* algorithmic, functional, coded, generative, and programmed. They are also often multimedia, hybrid forms of art, thus inaugurating ever-new horizons of "hopeful monsters,"[4] odd peculiarities, and happy mutants. Hayles argues that such works can be "literary" in that they are

> creative artworks that interrogate the histories, contexts, and productions of literature, including as well the verbal art of literature proper . . . . even a casual acquaintance with major movements in the literary studies in the last half-century will immediately confirm that the discipline, in embracing cultural studies, postcolonial studies, popular culture, and many other fields, has been moving toward the broader category of "the literary" for some time. Now, at the dawn of the twenty-first century, we are poised to extend this interrogation of the literary into the digital domain.[5]

Pressman furthermore places stress on the literary qualities of modernism in electronic literature:

> "digital modernism makes the case for considering these digital creations as 'literature' and argues for the value of reading them carefully, closely, and within the tradition of literary history. Analyzing these digital adaptations also provides a fresh perspective on modernism, specifically an opportunity to assess how modernist literature engaged with the new media of its own moment."[6] By stressing the literary quality of electronic works, and digital modernism particularly, Pressman has a dual purpose: to situate "contemporary digital literature in a genealogy that rewrites literary history, and it reflects back on literature's past, and on modernism in particular" as well as to "illuminate the crucial role that media played in shaping the ambitions and poetics of that period."[7]

While computer-generated poetry dates back to the 1960s, the field of electronic literature has not yet been around for four full decades. Hayles helpfully distinguishes between two periods of electronic literature: the classic period and the contemporary or postmodern period. For Hayles, the classic period ends in the mid-1990s, while the contemporary and postmodern period is still vibrant today. We can include the critical implications of Loss Pequeño Glazier's *Digital Poetics: Hypertext, Visual Kinetic Text and Writing in Programmable Media* (2001) and Pressman's *Digital Modernism* in the latter period—though digital modernism would suggest a kind of extension of the experimentalism of modernist print media into digital supermodernism rather than the open, playful, interactivity that postmodernism might connote. Rather than exploiting multimedia and multimodal forms of narrative, Pressman remarks that within the second generation of electronic literature exists those works of digital modernism "characterized by an aesthetic of restraint" rather than "exploiting the possibilities" of combining "complex animations, detailed graphics, and immersive interactivity."[8] Even while many works of the contemporary or postmodern trajectory of electronic literature are interactive, embodied, and playful these works do not, however, necessarily denaturalize the interface, code, black box, or apparatus that makes their very existence possible. That is, many of the best works of contemporary and postmodern electronic literature are consistent with optimized usability and ease of engagement, whether it be reading, clicking, gesturing, or interacting with the work. In short, the most successful and user-friendly works of electronic literature are those that often stabilize the apparatus' invisibility.

The literature of exclusion is a print tradition grieving, revolting, or confused at the *confrontation* with the ontological implications that digitality and apparatus imply. The three works I will examine in this chapter and the next, however, exist exclusively online, are *mostly* generated by AIs programmed by an author/coder, and—most importantly—highlight information illiteracy, or a lack of what Gregory L. Ulmer in *Internet Invention* (2002) calls "electracy,"[9] as part of their Dadaist revolt against semantic cohesion, epistemology, and constitutive narrative sense. Accordingly, we may consider the three texts discussed below as examples of the electronic literature of exclusion. Ultimately, Hayles notes that today digital technologies cannot be abstracted from commercial printing procedures, that even print could be "properly considered a particular output form of electronic text than an entirely separate medium";[10] however, more specifically, she notes that "electronic text remains distinct from print in that it literally cannot be accessed until it is performed by properly executed code."[11] Furthermore, most of the central genres and modes of electronic literature "emerge not only from different ways in which the user experiences them, but also from the structure and specificity of the underlying code."[12] It is this *from* that makes the experience possible, rather than the experience-in-itself, that is at the heart of the literature of exclusion. As a result, the three works that follow are those that, in differing ways, resist reader-friendly experience and instead bear witness to the functionality, proceduralism, and processual logic of the apparatus as the inhuman ontological *other* that, ultimately, invites a horizon of both helpless dread and poietic possibility. Indeed, such works, like glitch and code works of electronic literature, "reference the complex hybridization now underway between human cognition and the very different and yet interlinked cognition of intelligent machines."[13] The electronic literature of exclusion aims to highlight and wander deeper into the "very different" cognition of apparatus while grasping at the threshold of the apparatus' unfathomability. What follows are three considerations of the electronic literature of exclusion: Mike Bonsall's J. G. Ballard Twitter bots, a short film titled *Sunspring* (2016) that was written by a basic AI that named itself "Benjamin," and, in the next chapter, Allison Parrish's brilliant asemic word processing novel *Ahe Thd Yearidy Ti Isa* (2019). Each work confronts exclusion and an ontological impasse through obsessive procedural regimentation, laughter directed at the non-sense of the "very different cognition" of the apparatus, and an invitation to contemplating the mystifying ecstasy of the unknowable, respectively. We will consider how, while the works by Bonsall and Benjamin are fundamentally autopoietic, closed systems, Parrish's asemic novel gestures toward the allopoietic—that level-crossing, feedback-looping process that, rather than reproduce and reorganize from its own constituents, may produce something notably different to the datasets from which it was produced. All three of these works offer conceptual speculations while also suggesting a trajectory of absolute narrative denaturalization. After all, "when it comes to digital literature, there is no separation between science and literary art," Pressman writes. Instead, because "digital literature is algorithmically driven and technologically enabled . . . its content cannot be separated from its form or format."[14] Ultimately, these works are not solely about representing the experience of loss when confronting the apparatus. Each is, instead, actively *using* procedures and functions *inherent to* the apparatus. Indeed, we may even go so far as to suggest that such works are cyborgian negotiators and processual scouts that help us extend ourselves into the apparatus just as the apparatus extends itself into our psyches.

COPING WITH ZERO TO A MILLION DECIMALS: MIKE BONSALL'S J. G. BALLARD TWITTER BOTS, AUTOPOIESIS, AND FUNCTIONALIST PSYCHOPATHOLOGY

In a 2006 interview with Travis Elborough, Ballard suggests that he sees his role as a novelist, as an investigator, or a scout who is sent ahead to see whether the water is drinkable. Ballard is one of the most discerning English language authors of the twentieth and twenty-first centuries. Today, his catastrophe novels of the 1960s are remarkably prescient with their extrapolations of climate change and the psychopathological impulse to embrace and accelerate the destruction that comes with it. In the 1970s, Ballard's formally experimental novels examined the psychopathologies of mass media by looking at the surreal combinations of eroticism, death, technology, obsession, psychopathy, and violence. His final novels consider the logical conclusion of closed communities and the coming of techno-feudalism and consumer fascism as a reaction against safety and boredom. As varied as these theses may seem, Ballard's work is a kind of variations on a theme: that the protagonist is constituted by something that is at once internally latent yet outwardly constitutive and, in complicated ways, functionalist. Perhaps this is why the central thesis of Ballard's work should lend itself seamlessly to online bots. After all, "Ballard has for a long time resembled a rogue AI, re-permutating the same few themes ad infinitum, occasionally adding a sprinkling of contemporary detail to freshen up a limited repertoire of fixations," writes Fisher, "Fixations, fixations. Appropriate, since, after all, Ballard's obsession is . . . obsession."[15] Ballard's fiction is characteristically set in car parks, hospital lobbies, suburbs, motorways and underpasses, shopping malls, business parks, airports, and luxury high-rises. Each of these settings, like the divinely neutral apparatus in Yeager's work, exemplifies Augé's conception of "non-places": supermodern deluges of meaning, contagiously viral, outside of time, and purely functional. Ballard's concerns are physical, psychological, and civic. All this lends itself to Mike Bonsall's *Digital Ballard*, Ballard Twitter bots, and Bonsall's investigation into the ultimate non-space where rogue AI literally can endlessly self-generate and re-permutate: the internet.

For Ballard, non-spaces signify the social architecture as an absent referent; the internet only intensifies this nullification. Bonsall explains his Bots and where the idea came from:

> Although I haven't had much in the way of formal art education, a series of influences have brought me to where I am with *Digital Ballard*.
>
> I had an early interest in Burroughs' cut-up techniques and Ballard's more experimental writings, and was an early adopter of computer technology (Sinclair ZX Spectrum). It's interesting that both Burroughs and Ballard had computer-oriented friends and collaborators—Ian Sommerville and Christopher Evans—who both died young, before they could become a lasting influence.
>
> As well as failing to obtain a medical degree (like Burroughs and Ballard before me), I have worked as an educational technologist, I.T. trainer and analyst at a university, giving me an interest in, and access to, a wide range of computing equipment and software.
>
> Coming of age in the Punk era taught me that you don't need to ask permission and you can just go do it yourself. I've heard the filmmaker Shane Meadows talk of his method in a similar way: "Fast, Fun and Fuck-it." Pete Shelley, who sadly died recently, was a brilliant example of this, setting up gigs, a band and a record label with minimal knowledge but great enthusiasm.

While a student of the U.K. Open University I took the notorious art course TAD292: Art and Environment.[16] A radical, perhaps even a Situationist, course which opened my eyes to alternative art practices . . .

I was also influenced by the very nature of Ballard's writing, which seems to presuppose another world, just out of sight, that might somehow be reached by an ever-more intense interrogation of the text. As Ballard himself put it: "It's a little as if I were leading the reader to a deserted laboratory, and that I put a collection of specimens and all the necessary equipment at his disposal. It's his job then to relate these elements together and create reactions from them."[17,18]

The Ballardian Twitter bots are an amusing and insightful extension of Ballard's central thesis (that the psyche is both constitutive and constituted by the psychopathology of non-place environments) through automated means. Bonsall's three Ballard Twitter bots are @JGB_Sentences, @Crash_Cutup, and @New_Ballard. All three offer a progression of significance when considering psychopathy and the media functionalities of the inhuman.

The first, @JGB_Sentences, is the simplest and consists of a Twitter-length sentence, selected from a single-column Excel spreadsheet containing forty thousand elements of Ballard text, and posted to Twitter once every 12 hours. Bonsall removed all very short sentences (i.e., single-word sentences) and used a full stop as the delimiter. Here are two examples from June 7, 2019 (spaced twelve hours apart): "Gregory looked out across the terrace at the traffic whirling over the neon-lit cobbles" and "A few paces from the grave of the Mallory her footprints vanished into the sand."[19] The authorship of these tweets is Ballard's because the sentences, Bonsall remarks, are completely those of the former. The SSBot[20] that chooses the sentences twice daily is entirely for convenience and does not complicate traditional understandings of authorship.

The second, @Crash_Cutup, is more complex. Bonsall took each sentence in Ballard's 1973 novel *Crash* and split each sentence into three parts (beginning, middle, and end) in an Excel spreadsheet. The bot randomly organizes selections from the three columns resulting in a novel Ballardian sentence. Bonsall suggests that Ballard is the original author but that he has acted as the collagist. However, the bot is playing a larger role here in the sense that it is situated somewhere between Ballard and Bonsall. Here are two examples from June 5, 2019: "She told me that she worked I moved rapidly like sabre wounds" and "As I expected, and the shower of glass as the animal was carried over the roof, on her heel."[21] Interestingly, the *parts* of the sentences are Ballard's own words; however, the complete sentences themselves do not appear in Ballard's writing. Furthermore, this process asks whether the astronomically aleatoric possibilities of syntactic reorganization are taking one step further away from Ballard and Bonsall and situating itself as something nonlinearly inhuman.

Finally, and most interestingly, @New_Ballard uses a simple Markov chain model that determines which word is most likely to come next in the order of the text. A Markov chain is a relatively simple way of statistically modeling stochastic patterns based on what appeared before in a sequence. In other words, @New_Ballard uses an algorithm that guesses what the next Ballardian word would be based on a spreadsheet containing the complete text of Ballard's urban novels (*The Atrocity Exhibition*, *Crash*, *High-Rise*, and *Concrete Island*). Here is an example from June 6, 2019, and another from June 7, 2019: "He moved through the bundle of cracked tiles"[22] and "Arabesque. Later, in this stage of vehicles, but Maitland looked down at the bald woman carrying desks and gear shift."[23] In this case, the question of authorship is more complicated since these sentences do not appear at all in Ballard's work. Bonsall writes that "while Ballard is undoubtedly still the creator of the original text, the 'author' of these Tweets is more difficult to ascribe. [It] could in part be Zach Whalen,[24] or even Andrey Markov,[25] who died eight years before Ballard was born." However, rather than considering the bots in terms of authorship, it may be more appropriate to consider the new sentences as Ballardian protagonists.

So, how are these automated tweets protagonists? It may be helpful to consider a related way of thinking about the conflating of inner and outer (or other) space. Bonsall considers Ballard's writings as examples of what Barthes calls writerly texts: works that place demands on the reader to generate meaning. By extension, a Ballardian character is in the process of something similar: attempting to have the objective world corroborate with the subjective world. Much like the conflating of an environment and inner-life, this tangling of the text and the psyche is surrealist. However, this has an interesting proxy with a similar logical structure playing out, not in the psychological realm, but in the digital-technological space of functionalism. @Crash_Cutup and @New_Ballard are functionalist par excellence. Tasić remarks of structuralism and functionalism that "structural differentiation among the ideal units produces the meaning of the units all by itself. Structure is not only necessary for the creation of meaning, it is also sufficient. Semantics is in the syntax."[26] He continues, noting that

> according to the functionalist view, semantics is mechanically inferred from syntax. The elements of the structure get their meaning from their mutual interdependencies according to the rules of the structure, period. As a consequence, the elements encountered in a structure become functions. Their meaning is identifiable with the "roles" they pay in the entirety of structure. Their material expressions (or any other characteristics that are independent of the role in the

structural formation), as well as the "observer's" intentions, are simply irrelevant. Anything can be a symbol. The relationship between the signifier and the signified is arbitrary.[27]

Ballard's work is not functionalist in the strict sense; instead, it is more surrealist or, in the case of *The Atrocity Exhibition*, neo-Dadaist. Functionalism and surrealism have in common a tightening of tangled, bidirectional, level-crossing loops between spaces outside, inner space, and language. For a functionalist, language constitutes the parameters of thought and is a strict psycho-ecology. For a surrealist, the subjective and objective always tangle and trip over one another. A Dadaist would deny the existence of an imperial author, character, or subject altogether (as a way of attempting to escape these loops). A Twitter bot, however, seems to complicate these distinctions altogether by taking the Dadaist position to its (il)logical conclusion: an inhuman, programmed scout that comes into existence through automated processes and wanders into the non-space (and asignifying functionality) of digital environments. It is a bit like a programmed *no thing* is tangling and level-crossing within a digital *no thing*. The bots are not writerly texts in the way Ballard's writing is; instead, they are texts of exclusion. And, as characters (rather than authors), the process is an intensification of Ballardian psychopathology. Call it functionalist psychopathy: a demand on the reader and the bots, not to generate meaning, but to dismantle ego absolutely, re-permutate functions, process processes, and endlessly repeat the same objective.

The Bots are an extension of this functionalist process: Bonsall's reading of Ballard's work leads to interpretations that take on not only a new kind of digital, automated meaning but also permit the reading to generate and automate itself, to become the reagent in its own self-automated reactions. Dominika Oramus writes that Ballard's semiautobiographical work presents the reader with a series of personas that he constructed throughout his body of work. However, what these personas achieve are fictional proxies to Ballard-the-man in the extra-diegetic space of the book. "Ballard enjoyed playing with readers' assumptions about himself as well as the role of the author," writes D. Harlan Wilson, "but he was relatively adamant about how his various 'Ballards' were fictions conjured from his internal and external experiences" and, "in daily life, Ballard was thoroughly 'un-Ballard.'"[28] Wilson adds that Ballard's autobiographical novels (*The Unlimited Dream Company*, *Empire of the Sun*, and *The Kindness of Women*) confirm the postmodern dictum that "we are products of the media environment," "our names should be enclosed in quotes," and that "characters jeopardize the concept of a fixed identity on multiple levels."[29] From this, Wilson disagrees with Scott Bukatman's evaluation of the Ballardian character as one without ego, purely absorbed into and conflated with the media landscape where the landscape itself "becomes a schizophrenic projection of a de-psychologized, but fully colonized consciousness" and "everything becomes at once objective and subjective."[30] Wilson, instead, suggests that Ballard's protagonists are "pure ego, compulsively trying and retrying to assert and define themselves," and are "unable to get over or outside of their own hang-ups, crises, passions, needs, imaginings, and inhibitions."[31]

And, Wilson is correct, particularly in the sense that, as he states, a typical Ballardian protagonist is a psychopath in the clinical sense: "in search of fixity, of achieving some kind of negotiation between objective and subjective worlds."[32] Fisher also identifies the typical Ballardian protagonist as pure ego in the process of exploring, confronting, and negotiating the tangled knots of the inside and the outside. What the Ballardian protagonist confronts, Fisher writes, "is time and space *themselves*, as preconditions of all perceptions and experiences," that the negotiations between time and space "open up as an intensive zone beyond—outside—standard perceptual thresholds."[33] So, in terms of Ballard's writing, Bukatman's evaluation may be left wanting. While Wilson and Fisher are correct to identify Ballard's characters as pure ego, Bukatman's character-without-ego seems to be a precise definition of Bonsall's BallardBots. Neither authors nor characters in the traditional sense, the SSBots are without ego, media-landscapes-in-themselves, processes obsessed with process, and lacking any attempt at negotiating objective and subjective worlds. Instead, the BallardBots intensify functionalist level-crossing, by aiming to achieve an intensified equilibrium that maximizes the efficiency of its rigid, programmed, fixed process: to self-assemble and be made visible on Twitter at highly regular intervals.

The bots demonstrate an incremental shift toward supermodern psychopathy: from didactic sentences to a digitally generated sentence, to fully surreal automated syntax (i.e., literary blips: protagonists without a unified, imperial author). Ballard's prose is always highly calculated, dispassionate, and articulate; Bonsall's BallardBots achieve this functionality to a new inhuman degree. After all, authorship is not the best way to think about the bots at all. Instead, they are self-generated Ballardian characters in a dual sense: first, they are representations of an agent with (or without) identifiable human traits and, second, literal symbols (letters and coded numbers representing data) that regularly reiterate themselves into new sentences and are usable by an algorithm. In this sense, their choices and decisions are not their own but, rather, reactions to an attractive, constitutive, and alterior logic or code. For a Ballardian character, "'decides' is no doubt too active a word," Fisher notes, "in every respect the typical Ballard character . . . *discovers* rather than initiates" and "finds himself drawn into a *logic* he is compelled to investigate."[34] Bonsall's Twitter bots are the scouts sent ahead—not into shopping malls, airports, or luxury high-rises—but onto the internet to see how the future may unfold according to an inhuman psychopathology of algorithmic culture. Bonsall ultimately establishes a means by which Ballard can operate according to the nihilism at the logical center of an intensified non-place.

In this sense, the BallardBots operate in abstract ways outside signification, time, relation, and value. They are supermodern processes that are perfectly adept at proceeding in non-places that are neither anthropomorphic nor anthropological, and fully abstracted from preceding architectural forms. Because Twitter and other social media platforms operate as non-places in the same way as those physical supermodern spaces Augé formulates, it is essential to recall that these are not parallel universes to which we can escape from contemporary society. Such digital non-places are instead intensifications and optimizations of those inhuman physical nodes of transport (Augé's shopping centers, airports, hotel lobbies, waiting rooms, parking lots, and motorways). Rather than delimiting the human to an object of transportation along a circuit of consumption, digital non-places absorb the subject more intensely by knotting with and interrupting the productive feedback loops of thinking poietically, thus escaping the trappings of neoliberal functionalism. Twitter, like any other highly mediated space, becomes a non-place where the confrontation between topoi and spatiality themselves operate as the necessary conditions of experiencing exclusion through a dissolve into number, code, and algorithmic procedurality. That is, digitized social media platforms and other highly networked digital media are not simply sites where individuals can share information nearly instantaneously regardless of time or location. Instead, these decidedly mediated and highly digitized networks *are* information (informational, closed systems, functions without semantic valuation) that operate according to rigid principles radically different from the fuzzy ambiguities of language and the spontaneity of embodied, multi-gestural conversation. Digital non-places are the networked site at which the social shares via media but where media utilizes the social. In short, digital non-places and BallardBots are autopoietic.

Digital non-places like Twitter are autopoietic and functionalist in the sense that they are self-contained and self-referential. Autopoiesis operates in such a way that a system guarantees its limits and boundaries yet, at the same time, allows for self-generative meanings by self-reflexive incorporation of environmental complexity. In other words, an autopoietic system is, like functionalism, a closed system, but a closed system that permits various levels of change and complexity from any information available from the system's own self-reflexivity. Humberto R. Maturana and Francisco J. Varela note that

> there are machines which maintain constant, or within a limited range of values, some of their variables. The way this is expressed in the organization of these

machines must be such as to define the process as occurring completely within the boundaries of the machine which the very same organization specifies. Such machines are homeostatic machines and all feedback is internal to them.[35]

This homeostasis is crucial because it allows for emergence to take place from *within* rather than from without. It is autopoietic in the sense that it is self-generative and self-emergent:

> Autopoietic machines are homeostatic machines. Their peculiarity, however, does not lie in this but in the fundamental variable which they maintain constant. An autopoietic machine is a machine organized (defined as a unity) as a network of processes of production (transformation and destruction) of components that produces the component: (i) through their interactions and transformations continuously regenerate and realize the network of processes (relations) that produce them; and (ii) constitute it (the machine) as a concrete unity in the space in which they (the components) exist by specifying the topological domain of its realization as such a network. It follows that an autopoietic machine continuously generates and specifies its own organization through its operation as a system of production of its own components, and does this in an endless turnover of components under conditions of continuous perturbations and compensation of perturbations. Therefore, an autopoietic machine is a homeostatic (or rather a relations-static) system which has its own organization (defining network of relations) as the fundamental variable which it maintains constant.[36]

This is consistent with Wilson's observation that Ballardian protagonists are "pure ego, compulsively trying and retrying to assert and define themselves," and, in this case, functionally incapable of moving beyond their own inner experience. There is *no outside* for a Ballardian protagonist; instead, the inside mutates, self-generates, and self-organizes in ways that deceptively let the outside *in*. Twitter bots—informational non-agents—have no objective outside. As pseudo-inforgs, these functionalist protagonists have a self-enclosed spatiality of a different kind.

Bonsall's bots scout cyberspace. While the term "cyberspace" seems archaic and a bit awkward in the 2020s, it is worth recalling because the "space" part reminds us of the spatial or topological conundrums associated with it. Bukatman writes that "whether 'cyberspace' is a real place or not, our experience of electronic space is a 'real' experience."[37] "By distinguishing the constitution of being as an activity of interface," he continues, "phenomenology suggests that the status of being is not an absolute condition, but one that changes relative to changes in the experience of the real" (118). According to Bukatman, this real experience establishes a "master-narrative, one grounded in the centrality of human intention and perception, which has the cumulative effect of inaugurating a new subject capable of inhabiting the bewildering and disembodied space of the electronic environment—*the virtual subject*."[38] In the twenty-first century, we are all virtual subjects, and the disembodied spaces of digital environments are no longer bewildering to most of us. The virtual experience seems in many ways to be a tightening or intensification of a correlationist way of accessing phenomena. The world's embodied spaces may be, for "digital natives" born in the 1980s (to borrow Rushkoff's term for those born into a world *already* largely governed by the digital), the more bewildering environments. But, Bonsall's BallardBots are something different altogether: they are not virtual subjects, nor are they digital natives. Instead, the bots are procedures, functions set in motion by Bonsall to inhabit Twitter, to be the inhuman scouts on the surface of an otherwise inhuman non-space with seemingly endless fractal iterations. "Cyberspace," after all, Bolter and Grusin write, "is a shopping mall in the ether; it fits smoothly into our contemporary networks of transportation, communication, and economic exchange."[39]

We may as well add, in Ballardian fashion, that these networks of transportation, communication, and economic exchange also fit neatly inside us. Ballardian landscapes are non-places, non-places are Ballardian: "The shopping mall as a mediated space is simultaneously particularized and anonymous."[40] Bolter and Grusin suggest that "despite efforts to identify each mall (by giving it a name and sometimes a theme), malls are notoriously anonymous, perhaps because, as Sorkin (1992)[41] points out, consumer capitalism demands sameness behind the variety."[42] Just as neoliberalism constitutes the individual as a manufactured and automated identity that, at first glance, establishes a sense of difference, it simultaneously establishes sameness predicated on the underlying rules, operations, and functions of capitalism. Nevertheless, the underlying logic of neoliberalism is always attracted inward, back to a determining force whose output is always the simulation of variety but whose black box is tightly regulating what is expressed and that with which it identifies and represents in actuality. With this in mind, it should be no surprise that Ballard's protagonists, themes, and settings are deliberately reiterative.

Much of what unfolds in the examination of BallardBots is a noteworthy apprehension of first-wave cybernetics. First-wave cybernetics is "the cybernetics of systems that are observed from the outside as opposed to the cybernetics of systems involving their observers . . . First-order cybernetics is concerned with circular causal processes, e.g., control, negative feedback, computing, adaptation."[43] In short, first-order cybernetics is consistent with functionalism: the strange looping and diegetic level-crossing activity and rigid regularity of Bonsall's BallardBots predominantly serve the ulterior homeostasis of the constitutive system. Because cybernetics signifies the examination and investigation into the control mechanisms—its etymology is predicated on the Latinized Greek *kybernetes*, steersman in English, and connotative of governor or guide—of machines and organisms, how the metaphorical steersman governs in a closed system is a central concern of first-order cyberneticists. Wiener's anxiety behind the heterarchical relations between human and machine was that agency, individuality, and autonomy would be lost in a process which necessitates that biological properties be applied to machines. The major concern here is that when creating a machine that self-reproduces, it self-reproduces the descriptions, coding, and processes—that is, the modeling of autopoiesis—rather than the autopoietic procedures in themselves.[44] In short, autopoietic machines could reproduce the models and descriptions upon which they are based, but not the biological ecology of evolutionary reproduction. For first-order cyberneticists like Wiener, John Von Neumann, Shannon, and Ross Ashby,[45] the primary focus is on the system's operative behavior and the production of machines and artifacts that would operate and proceed like cybernetic organisms. First-order self-generating machines behave cybernetically, but they cannot reproduce the constitutive condition from which they arose; instead, these machines behave as self-generating cybernetic organisms, but they reproduce systemic constituents rather than the constitutive systēma which organizes them. In a way, these self-generating organisms are cybernetic tautologies that self-replicate modes of behavior and organization but cannot produce behavior or organization of their own. The boundaries of constitution, in this sense, become the parameters that originate, produce, and reproduce production but also subsume and constitute it.

Like Ballardian supermodern structures merging with inner space, it is the environment that is determinate while the subject is subjugated; the conditions of an environment, not its inhabitants, are the steersman. The Ballardian character articulates from within these boundaries. However, their agency is not their own per se. Instead, their articulations are those of the living system, the supermodern constituent, in which they are constituted. The BallardBots exemplify this: while the combinations Bonsall establishes offer astronomical permutations, there is no contingency in the system itself. The tweet will be made at a certain time daily. It will be organized according to the sample sets and syntactic parameters determined by Bonsall's programming of the Markov chain. Hayles writes that Wiener had unique anxieties that recur in his writing in regards to what happens when "one autopoietic unity is encapsulated within the boundaries of a larger autopoietic unity, for example when a cell functions as part of a larger machine."[46] Wiener's apprehension is fundamentally about the broader implications of agency. As someone dedicated to the humanist project, Wiener worried about whether the cell could "continue to function as an autonomous entity" or whether its functioning would be completely "subordinated to the larger unity";[47] of course, we can also think of the implications of this in terms of the individual's relation to a cybernetic society. In the supermodern environment that Ballard's work models there too remains a reliance on the human and the inhuman dichotomy.

This dichotomy is imperative in the sense that given the zero-sum game between human and inhuman, it is the human that is subsumed to the functioning of the latter. Ballard's surrealist logic—that built environment shape us rather than the other way around—perpetually regenerate and realize the processes and relations that produce them. Haraway writes that "late-twentieth-century machines have made thoroughly ambiguous the difference between natural and artificial, mind and body, self-developing and externally designed, and many other distinctions that used to apply to organisms and machines. Our machines are disturbingly lively, and we find ourselves frighteningly inert."[48] Haraway aptly describes the cybernetic imbalance in a way that offers parallels to Ballard's work since the 1970s, which is, again, sublimated and distilled in Bonsall's bots. Ballard's eschewing of affect, his distance, clinicality, and distance allow him to see and perhaps even understand such processes. Bonsall's programming take this observation even further by eliminating the author and allowing digital supermodern processes to guide and sculpt the syntactic behaviors; thus, the raison d'être of the tweets become indistinguishable from the interface itself. Just as supermodern environments are not *for* us, neither are digital environments; we are *for* the procedures.

If Ballardian fiction is dystopian, it is ambivalently so. And, Ballard's personal optimism and moralism aside, his *work* is certainly not utopian. From a humanist vantage point, the Ballardian protagonist attracted more and more strongly to the catastrophe, the dyshomeostasis and thanatotic pull of the inhuman is neither celebrated nor condemned. This is not to say that Ballard or Bonsall are anti-humanist (like Wiener, they are not). However, their work examines processes that eschew the triumph of humanist value without evaluating it as such. Yet, both Ballard and Bonsall leave it to the extra-diegetic readerly agent to consider this cyborgian dyshomeostasis without providing further comment on the author's or programmer's behalf. Haraway also addresses this ambivalence: the

> cyborg world is about the final imposition of a grid of control on the planet . . . From another perspective, a cyborg world might be about lived social and bodily realities in which people are not afraid of their joint kinship with animals and machines, not afraid of permanently partial identities and contradictory standpoints. The political struggle is to see from both perspectives at once because each reveals both dominations and possibilities unimaginable from the other vantage point.[49]

This is looking inward and outward at once at absolute control, constitutive, systematic organization of the agency from without and, at the same time, a commitment to a pure contingency that may open yet unthought relations, expansions, and optimizations with both natural and synthetic environments.

In Ballardian fiction, the initial historical conditions determine the thanatotic trajectory of his narratives. Whether it is environmental collapse, colonialism, racism, misogyny, or generalized violence, what haunts every Ballardian fiction is the thanatotic drive of capital itself. Just as Ballard insists on the initial conditions of modernity intensifying the biases of their foundational logic as a principle being pushed to its logical conclusion (the death of affect, death of the subject, and death to humanism in general), digitized initial conditions and logical foundations are also famously prone to replicating the biases of their programmers. At the inception or design state of a digital platform—just like with the inception of modernity—a series of algorithms and procedures shape, direct, and govern the program's unfolding. Current digital platforms are not neutral in the strict sense but have racial, gender, class, and colonial biases that reflect the programmers' biases and, as a result, these biases become highlighted in the program's subsequent functioning.[50] In short, the internet will, and currently does, operate as an extension of the psychopathic tendencies of capital because, as first-order cybernetics would dictate, digital platforms are effectively machines made according to the processes expressed by another constitutive machine. In this case, the digital, on the level of development, reproduces the processes expressed and optimized through capital, and this does not lead to neutrality but, instead, to an abstract substratum that captivates and instigates the perpetuation and prolongation of colonialism, racism, genderism, and generally capitalist biases.

If we take the underlying logic of the capitalist subject (or the virtual subject) to its logical conclusion as a simple SSBot, we notice an intensification of the surrealist impulse as a prototype of functionalist acceleration. Yet, this impulse is one toward, not the metaphorical inhuman, but the actual inhuman. There is a unique shock when experiencing the absence of people in capitalist spaces since "non-places, such as theme parks and malls," Bolter and Grusin suggest, "function as public places only during designated hours of operation."[51] They add that "there is nothing as eerie as an airport at three o'clock in the morning, or a theme park after closing hours, when the careful grids of railings and ropes that during the day serve to shepherd thousands of visitors to ticket counters or roller coasters stand completely empty. Such spaces then seem drained of meaning."[52] But it may also be equally eerie to experience a non-place like the internet, rather than uninhabited, but operating on its own. That is, cyber-Ballardian scouts are endlessly testing the water as self-reflexive functions of functionality. When we are not inhabiting Twitter (i.e., not logged on), @JGB_Sentences, @Crash_Cutup, and @New_Ballard are still posting and, we should add, could technically continue to do so ad infinitum (though, in actuality, they will not). Like the Ballardian psychopath, BallardBots are those who endlessly *discover* and *operate* according to an endlessly combinatorial logic that merges with the logic of non-space without meaning. In many ways, Bonsall's bots are intensified Ballardianism: self-automated processes qualifying the asemic environments of functional code, able to cope with zero to a million decimals.

NOTHING IS GOING TO BE A THING: *BENJAMIN'S SUNSPRING*, MATHEMATICAL FICTIONALISM, AND AI NARRATIVE

Similar to Derrida's assertion that there is nothing outside the text, mathematical fictionalism suggests that mathematics itself is nonrepresentational and more a historical construction and cultural artifact than an expression of a Platonic discovery of a transcendent and independent truth out there. In short, mathematical fictionalism is functionalist in the strict sense. While self-written narratives can sound science-fictional, self-adapting algorithmic narratives are, in fact, fairly common and operate behind everything from algorithmically generated news stories online to personalized online advertising to algorithmically generated works of literary fiction. A noteworthy example of one of these narratives is the short science fiction film *Sunspring* (2016), written by a type of recurrent neural network called a long short-term memory (LSTM); or, Benjamin, as the AI named itself. Benjamin rapidly generated the screenplay for Sunspring after being introduced to a large number of science fiction screenplays. After the screenplay was printed out, it was then put to film by a cast and crew directed by Oscar Sharp and was made for the Sci-Fi London film festival as part of a forty-eight-hour film challenge. To make this screenplay feasible, Sharp collaborated with AI researcher Ross Godwin (technically the developer of Benjamin). Benjamin produced the notably inhuman—and peculiarly Dadaist—screenplay while Sharp chose the acting roles.

What is striking about *Sunspring* is that it is very strange and, often, quite funny. Is our laughter, however, an empathetic response to the director's and actors' artistic choices as they make light of the oddness of the screenplay; or, may our laughter be the consequence of discomfort as it makes manifest biases we hold about how stories are generated and whether they are our own or the product of a rigid, inhuman functionalities? Ultimately, mathematical fictionalism implies that that algorithmic code may generate uncanny narratives simply because it is an extension of us. On the other hand, Platonism suggests that algorithmically generated narratives express something truly inhuman, fundamentally severing the self-reflexive knots and loops of functionalism. *Sunspring* thus raises certain questions about narrative and how it expresses either language (or code) according to its own constitutive logic or whether the incompatibility between sense and algorithmic processes in *Sunspring* reveals a glimpse at essentially inhuman narrative.

Ultimately, our laughter at watching *Sunspring* may result from a recognition that we are only "halfway there" in our AI technology. From this perspective, our laughter may also serve as a reminder that organizing society around quantitative, selective combinatorialism is as absurd as developing fictional narratives in analogous ways. Alternatively, this laughter may confront the unique disquiet of acknowledging that AI-generated narratives imply a rigid logic incompatible with the messy illogic underlying much human storytelling. While Benjamin's screenplay is technically autopoietic, that it signifies nothing but its own processual function regardless of semantics may also offer a horizon of thought whereby we may consider the implications that AI narrative could have if it were to reach a level of advancement beyond that of, say, a worm. Benjamin is organizing, combining, and choosing words according to grammatical and syntactic patterns; that is, as Tasić notes about functionalism, Benjamin's functionality assumes that semantics are in the syntax. However, it is not the semiotics of words that interest us here, but that of the numerical itself: that which permits the LSTM function autonomously. In short, is the numerical arbitrary (like language), or is it Planotically representational and, in this latter case, a non-arbitrary organizing principle based on abstract, mind-independent reality. With this in mind, we should stop for a moment to consider Benjamin's output when it says: "*Nothing is going to be a thing.*"

As machine learning, AI, and algorithmic processes play a larger and larger role in our everyday lives, reflecting on narrative as language (and language/poiesis as human) and its relation to the appearance (and rapid development) of inhuman narrative brings about a fascinating horizon of possibilities. The following clash is worth some thought: reason as the sovereign of all faculties versus the output of well-defined processes. The former, reason, is human-centric and human-created and likely does not refer to higher abstract entities beyond its own self-contained system. The same, however, can be said about the output of well-defined processes. Both are, though in different ways, functionalist. Another way of asking about this might be: are the effects of human narrative different from those of an algorithmically generated narrative written by a nonhuman? Writing and mathematics are both languages, and both may be self-reflexive and without access to mind-independent reality. Poiesis and algorithms, however, operate differently. Poiesis is open and undetermined; algorithms, however, tend to be more rigid. In a couple of words: you screw can your grammar up, and people know it still what you mean. You cannot make these kinds of syntactical errors in code, algorithms, or equations, however. If you make these kinds of syntactical errors, the code will not operate as intended (or at all). This differentiation is worth considering; while spoken and written language is how we communicate in our everyday lives, there are codes, processes, well-defined rules, and algorithms that now organize and steer almost every aspect of twenty-first-century life.

Algorithms are step by step mathematical functions that serve a specific operation. If the steps are followed accurately and correctly, the algorithm's procedurality will result in the desired outcome. One thing that distinguishes an algorithm from other forms of nonmathematical procedures is that they have a clearly defined beginning and, after completing a specified number of steps, a determined end. Simple algorithms are generally predictable, closed systems: if given the same input information, the algorithm will produce already known output (as evidenced by earlier procedure outcomes). Think of a recipe from a cookbook—if one follows the instructions correctly each time, the resultant dish should be the same. If one follows a chocolate chip cookie recipe correctly, they will get chocolate chip cookies and not minestrone. Of course, algorithms can be linked, stacked, and reassembled to perform much more complex tasks than a cookie recipe. For example, a computer program's composition requires multiple algorithms operating functionally together for a series of specified operations. Ultimately, algorithms are uniquely suitable for solving problems that require linear, sequential analysis where information or data requires transformation or reconfiguration. Baruch Gottlieb writes:

> when text appears on a computer screen in a human-legible form, it must first be rendered legible through algorithms from the electronic numerical data form in which it is stored. In this sense, technical images, including electronically published texts, are always algorithmically generated from mathematical codes. Although the technical images they produce may seem like the iconic, mystical, and mythical images of preliterate times, the algorithmic code apparatuses, which generate these technical images, are products of causal linear thinking of the literate Enlightenment.[53]

We will return to the mystifying, mythical images reminiscent of preliterate times when we consider technical images and the asemic word processing of Allison Parrish in the next chapter; however, here a central point of contention is that while algorithms are both suited for, and emblematic of, causal and linear thought, they are notably unsuitable for solving problems where human value judgment is required. So, while "algorithms work in the causal logic of literacy as they produce communication forms appropriate to the information revolution,"[54] such mathematical functions prove inappropriate for meaning-making by agents who are constituted by the historical unfoldings of the informatics era.

That algorithms are unsuitable for problems where value judgments are required accounts for why algorithmically generated narratives are so funny and strange. *Sunspring* is an example of a recurrent neural network called a LSTM. One thing that humans do not do is restart their thinking from nothing at each instance (even the most spontaneous Dadaist will be biased at an unconscious level). For example, words cumulatively express themselves and are understood based on our understanding of past or different words. Early neural networks could not do this; a basic neural network cannot remember prior events to inform later ones. Recurrent neural networks, however, have feedback loops that allow information to persist. Another way of thinking about this is that, with each loop, a recurrent neural network can be imagined as a successive re-creation of the neural network as it passes its message along to its recipient (itself another copy of the network but with more "memories"). LSTM networks are a particular kind of recurrent neural network because they can learn long-term loop dependencies. The algorithmic process behind this is an evolving one; nevertheless, it is still rigid. The screenplay for *Sunspring* is based on an LSTM network, the same kind that operates behind the keyboard of a smartphone. Its "memory" can be pretty impressive. However, when you want to type "I'll see you soon" and the network's memory suggests "I'll see you song" it is making an error based on learned syntax divorced from semantics (often repeated sentence patterns rather than meaning). This is at the core of what makes the screenplay of *Sunspring* so strange (i.e., funny and/or unsettling). It is also at the core of the conflict one might see between the screenplay (i.e., LSTM generated) and the directorial and acting choices (human interpretive agency).

It is difficult to explain the plot of *Sunspring*, and this should be no surprise since a narrative arch would require value judgment rather than sequential procedures to craft. Reading the screenplay and then viewing the film (or the opposite order, it does not matter) offers insight into the this clash between syntax and semantics. As a result, the screenplay and film are worth considering separately since the screenplay is oddly syntactically correct, though without any cumulative meaning. At the opening of the film is a quick explanation: "Just above your smartphone keyboard lives an artificial intelligence. It was trained on lots of texts and emails. And tries to guess what you'll type next. We were curious what would happen if we trained this kind of software on something else: science fiction screenplays. So we fed a LSTM recurrent neural network with these":[55] and then proceeds to list that they say includes hundreds of science fiction TV and film screenplays. These include classics like *2001: A Space Odyssey, Alien, Blade Runner, X-Files, Star Trek*, and *Solaris* to cult classics like *Adventures of Buckaroo Banzai Across the Eighth*

Dimension and *Cube*, to kitsch and science fiction comedy like *G.I. Joe: The Rise of Cobra, 2012, Hot Tub Time Machine*, and *Jason X*. Consider the screenplay: all this alongside some random seeds from a science fiction filmmaking contest: title (*Sunspring*), dialogue ("It may never be forgiven, but that is just too bad"), prop and action ("a character pulls a book from a shelf, flips through it and puts it back"), and an optional science idea ("In a future with mass unemployment, young people are forced to sell blood.")[56] What follows is, depending on your disposition, hilarious or unsettling (or both). The recurrent network named itself Benjamin and created four characters: H, H2, C, and T. By reading the screenplay we learn that H2 may be Hauk, H (by implication) may also be Hauk, C may be Coffee, and T (who appears only in the final monologue) is, well, the letter T. Here are the opening lines from the screenplay for some context:

INT. SHIP
(We see H pull a book from a shelf, flip through it and then put it back.)
H
In a future with mass unemployment, young people are forced to sell blood. That's the first thing I can do.
H2
You should see the boys and shut up. I was the one who was going to be a hundred years old.
H
I saw him again. The way you were sent to me . . . that was a big honest idea. I am not a bright light.
C
Well, I have to go to the skull. I don't know.
(He picks up a light screen and fights the security force of the particles of a transmission on his face.)
H
(continuing)
What do you mean?
C
(smiles)
I don't know anything about any of this.
H
(to Hauk, taking his eyes from his mouth)
Then what? H2 There's no answer.
C
(frowning)
We're going to see the money.

H
(reading) "All right, you can't tell me that."
Steps back. Coffey is still going through.[57]

This is all strange, of course. But even here, certain tropes emerge: economic collapse, the human body as the product (or bodily fluid as commodity), body horror, paranoia, forbidden knowledge. But really, this is all pattern recognition on our part and recurrent feedback memories/guesses on the part of Benjamin (the author). The rest of the screenplay also introduces thematic fragments that science fiction readers are likely to recognize: youth and aging (even immortality), dystopia, time, reproduction and extinction, the hero's quest, militarism vs. the individual, memory (grammatically looking back), the impossibility of suicide for AI, claustrophobia, black holes, portals, and so on. Beyond these dreamlike, disconnected fragments, there is semantically not much. We are left doing what we do, but Benjamin does not: to bring meaning and value judgments to this output. Though *Sunspring* is the output resulting from a corpus of science fiction screenplays for film and television, the screenplay itself requires us to superimpose the semantics.

This brings us to the other aspect of *Sunspring* that, more than the screenplay, reached the public: the directorial and acting choices made in staging and filming. Filmmaker Oscar Sharp and collaborator Ross Goodwin worked together to develop the film. In a sense, it is Goodwin's technical expertise that made *Sunspring*'s screenplay possible. However, it is Sharp who put it to film. The short film stars Elisabeth Gray as H2 (Hauk) and T, Humphrey Ker as Coffey, and Thomas Middleditch as H. Significantly, Middleditch is possibly most famous for his role as tech valley CEO Richard Hendricks in the HBO series *Silicon Valley* (2014–2018). What is most interesting here about Sharp's choices is his insistence (they only had 48 hours to write the script) on performing the implied tropes that Benjamin authored. Here we see H as the central male character, H2 (Hauk) as the supporting female character and love interest, and C (Coffey) as the second male character who is rich, cocky, and intrusive, and who acts as sexual competition to H (H2/Hauk is secondary to her agency as she simply darts between male love interests). Perhaps the most interesting character is the mysterious T (also played by Elisabeth Gray), who appears in the closing monologue. Consider the following paragraph in Benjamin's screenplay that seems to be gathering something like sense. The film ends with a female monologue (the gender is Sharp's choice, not Benjamin's, but this gendering proves semantically significant):

> Well, there's the situation with me and the light on the ship. The guy was trying to stop me. He was like a baby and he was gone. I was worried about him. But even if he would have done it all. He couldn't come any more. I didn't mean to be a virgin. I mean, he was weak. And I thought I'd change my mind. He was

crazy to take it out. It was a long time ago. He was a little late. I was going to be a moment. I just wanted to tell you that I was much better than he did. I had to stop him and I couldn't even tell. I didn't want to hurt him. I'm sorry. I know I don't like him. I can go home and be so bad and I love him. So I can get him all the way over here and find the square and go to the game with him and she won't show up. Then I'll check it out. But I'm going to see him when he gets to me. He looks at me and he throws me out of his eyes. Then he said he'd go to bed with me.[58]

There are frequent mentions of a baby, a male's inability to come, virginity, love, sympathy, regret, inability to conceive, insecurity, power, and sex. To what degree this paragraph can be meaningful would differ depending on how we consider its authorship. Many of us want this screenplay to "mean," and yet we see that the syntax does not dictate the semantics. The directorial choices Sharp makes certainly do superimpose meanings. And, yet, Benjamin's screenplay denies it.

To return to reason as the sovereign of all faculties as that which opposes the output of well-defined processes, we see some tension. We want to bring meaning to processes that are primarily syntactic but lack semantics. Perhaps we are resolved to do so because we inherently fear language's inability to represent meaningful ways of decoding the things and events that would nevertheless exist without our recording of them. Humans are finite, and so are algorithms. Both poiesis and mathematics have been extolled as infinite or timeless. Yet, both are likely to be ingenious anthropocentric systems of self-reference. This brings us to how language as a metaphorical or nonrepresentation system is very much like mathematical fictionalism.

Sunspring is both literary and mathematical; it is a screenplay fed on narratives as input for a series of combinatorial feedback loop processes that result in output. Language's ability to operate is contingent on its relation to other aspects of language. Mathematical fictionalism operates similarly. Hartry Field first articulates mathematical fictionalism in *Science without Numbers: A Defense of Nominalism* (1980); the work responds explicitly to mathematical Platonism. Here Field writes that, as controversial in 1980 as it is today, he aims

> to show that the mathematics needed for application to the physical world does not include anything which even *prima facie* contains references to (or quantifications over) abstract entities like numbers, functions, or sets. Towards that part of mathematics which does contain references to (or quantifications over) abstract entities—and this includes virtually all of conventional mathematics—I adopt a fictionalist attitude: that is, I see no reason to regard this part of mathematics as true.[59]

Mathematical fictionalism does not suggest that mathematics is a fiction. However, we may concede that mathematics is, like language, a brilliant self-referential system. He continues:

> Most recent philosophers have been hostile to fictionalist interpretations of mathematics, and for good reason. If one just advocates fictionalism about a portion of mathematics, without showing how that part of mathematics is dispensable in applications, then one is engaging in intellectual doublethink: one is merely taking back in one's philosophical moments what one asserts in doing science, without proposing an alternative formulation of science that accords with one's philosophy. This (Quinean) objection to fictionalism about mathematics can only be undercut by showing that there is an alternative formulation of science that does not require the use of any part of mathematics that refers to or quantifies over abstract entities. I believe that such a formulation is possible; consequently, without intellectual doublethink, I can deny that there are abstract entities.[60]

Mathematics, in this sense, is not Platonic in that the practice does not require the independent existence of number as abstract objects. There are two central tenets of Platonism: first, abstract mathematical objects exist (though, they are non-spatiotemporal objects—abstracted or removed from space and time), and, second, mathematical syntax and theory represent such objects (i.e., the semiotic referents are *real* and, as a result, their proceduralities tell us something about reality itself).[61] In short, the Platonist model suggests that a sentence like "the number 5 is prime" is, in fact, a direct description of a certain object (the non-spatiotemporal object number 5). The sentence reestablishes the presence of the abstract object "number 5" through a language or syntax/sentence. In this sense, it is similar to the linguistic statement "the chair is made of wood." In the linguistic statement, we understand the chair and its descriptor to be speaking about—directive semantic replacement *for* and representations *of*—an object (a chair) and a material descriptor (the material from which the chair is made, that is, wood). However, the difference is that a number is a unique abstract object, and a chair is a generalized physical object. Nevertheless, the process of representation—making an actuality semantically and intelligibly present through description—is more or less the same. When we talk about the chair, we mean *a* chair. When we discuss the number 5, we refer to a non-spatiotemporal abstract object. This is because "abstract objects, Platonists tell us, are wholly nonphysical, nonmental, nonspatial, nontemporal, and noncausal. Thus, in this view, the number 3 exists independently of us and our thinking. However, it does not exist in space or time, it is not a physical or mental object, and it does not enter into causal relations with other objects."[62] Unlike physical objects like a chair, Platonic abstract objects are not affected by time or space and do not change.

Fictionalism, however, is incredulity toward Platonism. The major difference between Platonism and fictionalism is that Platonism claims to describe and constitute abstract objects. In contrast, fictionalism suggests that the referents of mathematics are not true because there are no such abstract objects independent from human thought. It suggests that mathematical theory talks about concepts that make sense, but the referents of these concepts do not exist objectively. When we say "the chair is made of wood," we represent an actual object and its qualities through language. If we look at the mathematical sentence "the number 5 is prime," fictionalism suggests that the abstract object "5" does not exist independently of the semiotic system itself and, consequently, "our mathematical theories are not true."[63] However, they do make sense and are functional. Fictionalism suggests that numbers do not refer to abstract non-spatiotemporal objects in the same way that the semantics of the statement "Hobbits are from the Shire" is untrue since there are no such entities as Hobbits. Both operate in ways that are functional semantically, but they are not "true." One of the most pressing problems fictionalism faces is its relation to the applied mathematics: "Mathematics, unlike Tolkien's stories, is apparently indispensable to our best scientific theories"[64] and, furthermore, the apparatus itself.

Mathematics is self-consistent and, just like language, can be meaningful. However, it may not have access to mind-independent reality. What is important here, though, is that fictionalism does not imply that mathematical discourse is a fiction in the narrative sense. The terminology does not correlate perfectly; however, we can say that mathematical fictionalists claim that numbers do not correspond with an abstract entity that exists *without us* but can reveal things *to us*. Similarly, historiographic metafiction like Toni Morrison's *Beloved* (1987) or Werner Herzog's *Aguirre, the Wrath of God* (1972) does not necessarily correlate with precise actualities but the narratives do reveal something meaningful *to us*. While "the label 'fictionalism' suggests a comparison of mathematics with literary fiction, and although the fictionalist may wish to draw only the minimal comparison that both mathematics and fiction can be good without being true, fictionalists may also wish to develop this analogy in further dimensions, for example by drawing on discussions of the semantics of fiction, or on how fiction can represent."[65] Just as there is nothing outside the text, there is nothing outside the mathematical sentence. This is not nihilistic but instead refocuses our attention on how the parameters we set on semantics can dominate us; it is self-reflexivity and, as we will consider more closely in the next chapter, rather than simply relativism, contingency *and* reflexivity can yield fecund potentialities. If mathematics, like language, does not necessarily have special access to that beyond its self-consistency, what might this mean? What does it mean to write, or compute, that "nothing is going to be a thing?" Does this strange, LSTM memory-generated phrase itself not imply poiesis? Before considering this more closely, one may wish to ask whether there are algorithmic narrative modes that, rather than autopoietic, can indeed be, not Platonic, but functionally allopoietic. We will examine this in more detail in the next chapter.

NOTES

1. Hayles, *Electronic Literature*, 3.
2. Pressman, *Digital Modernism*, 1–2.
3. Hayles, *Electronic Literature*, 3.
4. Ibid., 4.
5. Ibid., 4–5.
6. Pressman, *Digital Modernism*, 3.
7. Ibid., 3.
8. Ibid., 7.
9. Ibid., 23.
10. Ibid., 5.
11. Ibid.
12. Ibid.
13. Ibid., 21.
14. Ibid., 22.
15. Mark Fisher, "Space, Time, Light, All the Essentials — Reflections on J.G. Ballard Season (BBC 4)," *K-Punk: The Collected and Unpublished Writings of Mark Fisher (2004–2016)*, ed. Darren Ambrose (Repeater, 2018), 43.
16. Daniel Weinbren, "Decades of Impact: TAD292 Lives on," *History of the Open University*, http://www.open.ac.uk/blogs/History-of-the-OU/?p=2250.
17. J. G. Ballard, "1974: Robert Louit. Crash and Learn," *Extreme Metaphors*, eds. Simon Sellar and Dan O'Hara (London: Fourth Estate, 2014),74.
18. Mike Bonsall, email message to author, December 17, 2018.
19. JG Ballard Openings (@JGB_Sentences), "A few paces from the grave of the Mallory her footprints vanished into the sand." Twitter, June 7, 2019, 12:17 a.m., https://twitter.com/JGB_Sentences/status/1136849575455539200.
20. SSBot is what Zach Whalen calls a Spread Sheet Bot.
21. Crash Cutup (@Crash_Cutup), "As I expected, and the shower of glass as the animal was carried over the roof, on her heel." Twitter, June 5, 2019, 12:22 a.m., https://twitter.com/Crash_Cutup/status/1136488605109620741.
22. New Ballard (@New_Ballard), "He moved through the bundle of cracked tiles." Twitter, June 6, 2019, 12:18 p.m., https://twitter.com/New_Ballard/status/1136668768925573120.
23. New Ballard (@New_Ballard), "Arabesque. Later, in this stage of vehicles, but Maitland looked down at the bald woman carrying desks and gear shift." Twitter, June 7, 2019, 12:18 a.m., https://twitter.com/New_Ballard/status/1136849951512616962.

24. Zach Whalen is an associate professor in Digital Studies at the University of Mary Washington, Virginia. Bonsall writes: "I took a MOOC version of Mark Sample's course DIG220: Electronic Literature (https://courses.digitaldavidson.net/dig220/about/). A fascinating historical, philosophical and practical examination of E-Lit. Sample's course led me to Zach Walen's work on Twitter bots, particularly his Do-It-Yourself SSBot (https://github.com/zachwhalen/ssbot). My three Ballard Twitter bots are based on [Whalen's tutorial for] the SSBot." Mike Bonsall, email message to the author, December 17, 2018.

25. Andrey Markov (1856–1922) was a Russian mathematician. J. J. O'Connor and E. F. Robertson write that "Markov is particularly remembered for his study of Markov chains, sequences of random variables in which the future variable is determined by the present variable but is independent of the way in which the present state arose from its predecessors. This work founded a completely new branch of probability theory and launched the theory of stochastic processes." *MacTutor* (August 2006), http://www-history.mcs.st-andrews.ac.uk/history/Biographies/Markov.html. In the 1920s, after Markov's death, Markov processes were first treated as more than abstract mathematical exercises by the cyberneticist and mathematician Norbert Wiener. Interestingly enough, Markov was also a big fan of poetry and literary studies. Perhaps the Twitter bots are, as Bonsall suggests, coauthored by Markov.

26. Tasić, *Mathematics and The Roots*, 111–112.

27. Ibid., 114.

28. D. Harlan Wilson, *J. G. Ballard* (Urbana: University of Illinois Press, 2017), 101.

29. Ibid., 101.

30. Scott Bukatman, quoted in Wilson, *J. G. Ballard*, 101–102.

31. Ibid., 102.

32. Ibid., 102.

33. Mark Fisher, "Space, Time, Light, All the Essentials," 44.

34. Ibid., 43–44.

35. Humberto R. Maturana and Francisco J. Varela, *Autopoiesis and Cognition: The Realization of the Living* (London: D. Reidel Publishing, 1980), 78.

36. Ibid., 78–79.

37. Scott Bukatman, *Terminal Identity: The Virtual Subject in Postmodern Science Fiction* (Durham, N.C.: Duke University Press, 1993), 118.

38. Ibid., 118.

39. Bolter and Grusin, *Remediation*, 179.

40. Ibid., 175.

41. Michael Sorkin, ed., *Variations on a Theme Park: The New American City and the End of Public Space* (Hill and Wang, 1992).

42. Bolter and Grusin, *Remediation*, 175–177.

43. "First-Order Cybernetics," *Principia Cybernetica Web*, http://pespmc1.vub.ac.be/ASC/FIRST-_CYBER.html.

44. Hayles, *How We Became Posthuman*, 141.

45. Ibid.

46. Ibid.

47. Ibid.

48. Donna Haraway, "A Cyborg Manifesto," *Simians, Cyborgs, and Women: The Reinvention of Nature* (New York: Routledge, 1991), 152.

49. Ibid., 154.

50. See Safiya Umoja Noble's *Algorithms of Oppression: How Search Engines Reinforce Racism* (New York: New York University Press, 2018).

51. Bolter and Grusin, *Remediation*, 177.

52. Ibid.

53. Baruch Gottlieb, "Algorithm," *Flusseriana: An Intellectual Toolbox*, Siegfried Zielinski, Peter Weibel, and Daniel Irrgang, eds. (Univocal, 2015), 42.

54. Ibid.

55. *Sunspring*, Oscar Sharp, Ross Goodwin, and Benjamin, Ars Technica and Therefore Films, June 9, 2016, *YouTube* video, 9:02, https://www.youtube.com/watch?v=LY7x2Ihqjmc.

56. Ibid.

57. *Sunspring*, Benjamin, screenplay (Therefore Films, 2016), http://www.thereforefilms.com/uploads/6/5/1/0/6510220/sunspring_final.pdf.

58. Ibid.

59. Hartry Field, *Science Without Numbers: A Defense of Nominalism*, 2nd Edition (Oxford: Oxford University Press, 2016), 1–2.

60. Ibid., 2.

61. Mark Balaguer, "Fictionalism in the Philosophy of Mathematics," *The Stanford Encyclopedia of Philosophy*, ed. Edward N. Zalta, July 23, 2018, https://plato.stanford.edu/archives/fall2018/entries/fictionalism-mathematics/.

62. Ibid.

63. Ibid.

64. Mark Colyvan, "Fictionalism in the philosophy of mathematics," *Routledge Encyclopedia of Philosophy* (Taylor and Francis, 2011), https://www.rep.routledge.com/articles/thematic/fictionalism-in-the-philosophy-of-mathematics/v-1.

65. Mary Leng, "Fictionalism in the Philosophy of Mathematics," *Internet Encyclopedia of Philosophy*, https://www.iep.utm.edu/mathfict/.

Chapter 8

The Electronic Literature of Exclusion and Allopoiesis

Asemic Word Processing, Technical Images, and Allison Parrish's Ahe Thd Yearidy Ti Isa

Bonsall's Twitter bots and Benjamin's screenplay correspond to Maturana and Varela's conceptualization of autopoiesis as self-organizing, closed systemic units. While Maturana and Varela are primarily concerned with living systems and biological systems, Twitter bots and LSTM are in strange relation to a media ecology by being representations of, as well as constituents of, the interface through which they emerge and operate. The bots are at once identifiable by a boundary (i.e., a bot's Markovian operative, e.g., can be recognized as a unit separate from other operations). However, its autopoietic organization dictates that it is both produced and procedurally/processually repeated-with-difference through methods inherent to its self-operation. The bots can, as Ballard remarks, cope with zero to a million decimals. They are emblematic of a dual process of disaggregating the corpus of Ballardian language while also reassembling them into functional syntactic phenomena at regular intervals. The brilliance of the bots is that their functionality is emblematic of a breakdown in the representation of objective reality. Instead of representation, the autopoietic processes of the bots prove to be informatic: the Markov chains produce concentrations of possible patterns through reassemblage, thus producing new articulations that no longer represent reality, but instead congregate syntactic probabilities representative of, not the world, but the program or Markovian code that operates as its own processual inception. In short, the BallardBots are procedural products of productive procedures. They represent a system constituted by code and programming unconcerned by the outside.

Because Twitter bots operate linearly, like writing, they engage their own systemic operatives. While Flusser would argue that algorithms are zero-dimensional—thereby, all signification or representation would have a zero relation to representing material phenomenon beyond its own processes—a Markov chain nevertheless operates linearly like writing. That is, it is one-dimensional in the Flusserian sense as a rigid ordering system. Like writing, algorithms are linear, aim to organize the complexity and unpredictability of actuality, and delimit disorder into sequential modes of thinking. Autopoietic processes, whether Markov chains or LSTMs, operate independently because the system in which they operate as constituents is closed. The bots and the screenplay do not represent the world but, instead, their own procedurality. While the works themselves have clear boundaries, they nevertheless also obtain and sustain all possible output through its own input (in this case, a vast corpus of text). This raises the question as to whether AI narratives, algorithms, or neural networks can, indeed, ever represent or capture the outside. Can this mode of narrative production be produced—and produce—something other than the processes that determine the parameters of its operation? Or, in other words, can nonhuman generated aesthetic procedures operate allopoietically?

One of the best works to interrogate whether or not computer-generated work can produce something beyond the processual procedurality of a closed system is programmer, author,[1] and poet Allison Parrish's work of asemic word processing *Ahe Thd Yearidy Ti Isa*[2] (figure 8.1). Parrish is an assistant arts professor at New York University's Interactive Telecommunications Program. As a computer programmer, educator, game designer, and poet, her work examines the

> unusual phenomena that blossom when language and computers meet, with a focus on artificial intelligence and computational creativity. . . . Named "Best Maker of Poetry Bots" by the Village Voice in 2016, Allison's computer-generated poetry has recently been published in Ninth Letter and Vetch. She is the author of "@Everyword: The Book" (Instar, 2015), which collects the output of her popular long-term automated writing project that tweeted every word in the English language. The word game "Rewordable," designed by Allison in collaboration with Adam Simon and Tim Szetela, was published by Penguin Random House in August 2017 after a successful round of Kickstarter funding. Her first full-length book of computer-generated poetry, "Articulations," was published by Counterpath in 2018.[3]

Parrish has a steady output of remarkable projects; one can get a sense of her prolific and endlessly interesting artistic output by visiting her Portfolio on her webpage.[4] What makes *Ahe Thd Yearidy Ti Isa* so striking, however, is

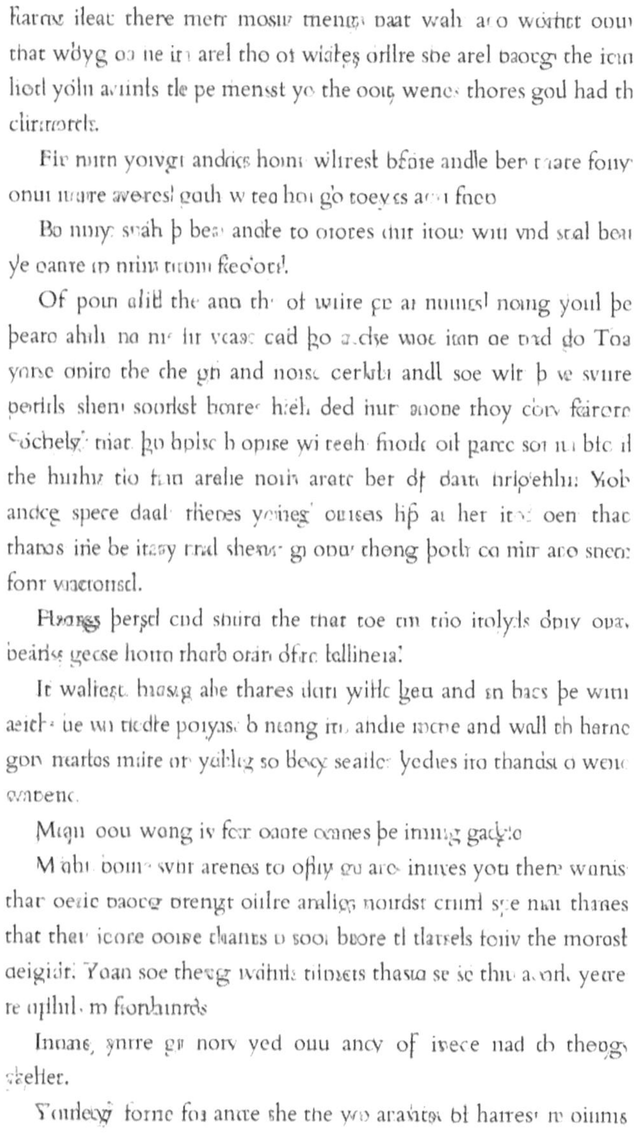

Figure 8.1 Allison Parrish,. *Ahe Thd Yearidy Ti Isa* (https://github.com/NaNoGenMo/2019/issues/144), 9.

the way in that it draws attention to text as technical image and eschews any possibility of signifying a codified semantics. Furthermore, she writes that the project has Dadaist inspirations and is asemic: "When composing the piece, the main thing I had in mind were Belle Epoque dadaist typography experiments (e.g., Ilia Zdanevich's *Ledentu* [1923]) and other concrete poetry works that play with the shape of the letterform."[5] And just as Dada signifies no thing, Parrish's asemic word processing takes the form of a novel that shifts attention away from *making sense* to initiating poiesis and provoking poetic ways of thinking about code and programming. Indeed, Parrish's phenomenological concerns may agree with Bifo's statement that "meaning is not a presence, but an experience."[6] Peter Schwenger, in his pioneering book *Asemic: The Art of Writing* (2019), writes that "asemic writing is an invitation, not an imposition."[7] That asemic writing is an initiation to think outside the closed system of language's functionalist and structuralist correlationism, Parrish's work updates this practice to draw attention not to *writing* but the interface of machine learning and word processing. While asemic writing draws us away from the codifying strictures of writing, asemic word processing invites us to both acknowledge the nonintuitive operations of the apparatus while also interrogating how we might consider poietic processes beyond closed systems and whether it is indeed possible to experience no thing, an *outside*, beyond language, via programming and code.

The historical shift from writing to programming offers a monumental parallel for collective social agency akin to the printing presses that appeared first in China and later in Europe with Gutenberg. "Just as in the beginning of text-based culture it was the literati who dominated the new code of writing, today it is the programmers of image-generating apparatuses who encode culture, both Western and Eastern," Andreas Müller-Pohle writes. He continues by adding that programmers "as well—usually collectively working authors of linear texts (which have now become auxiliary texts—create a gigantic literature of code hidden in the apparatuses of the applications. Uncovering, decoding, and recoding this literature . . . is a tricky game: the programmers of the iPhone are more powerful than Günter Grass."[8] That is, with increasing urgency, those who can write and type, but not program, are at a kind of disadvantage analogous to the shift from illiteracy to literacy. While mass literacy inaugurated the lasting effects of McLuhan's Gutenberg Galaxy, a major shift to information literacy would invite the social into active programming and summon nonprogrammers to acknowledge and think about the code upon which user-friendly interfaces rely to exist. The bafflement, mystery, or anxiety experienced by the revealing of the programming behind everyday processes, however, is simply a transitionary moment whereby our information illiteracy, or Ulmer's "electracy," reveals itself as one of the quiet, although pressing, pedagogical, social, and political issues of the early twenty-first century.

Unlike some of the authors so far examined, Parrish, like Siratori, Bonsall, and Godwin, *is* a programmer and does not subscribe to the mystifying black box interpretation of the shift from a culture of writing to a culture of programming. As a result, Parrish disagrees that the technologies of word processing are "especially 'invisible,' especially if word processing is broadly construed to include all of the interfaces that people commonly interact with in order to input text."[9] Indeed, her interest leans toward the phenomenology of reading more than the structuralist or functionalist anxieties of the psychoanalytic undercurrents of linguistic or processual subjectivity.[10] "The experience of writing a tweet," Parrish writes, "in which you must pay constant attention to the character limit (and to the way the character limit is surfaced in the interface) is very different from the experience of using Microsoft Word."[11] Parrish notes that she switches "between multiple interfaces for writing every day, which I choose based on very specific material properties of those interfaces—a plain text editor (vim) for programming, a Markdown editor for writing code documentation, a digital tablet/stylus pair for brainstorming and writing drafts."[12] Each of these interfaces operates differently, serve different functions, and are modular. In short, for the programmer, there is not anything overly invisible or mysterious about such everyday interfaces. Instead, rather than confronting a literature of exclusion, Parrish-the-programmer describes an experience of relative ease while Parrish-the-poet also recognizes the non-habitual potentialities that electronic media has for poiesis and potentialities. As a result, neither the word nor the program operates invisibly in such a way that it mechanically and invisibly structures and determines subjectivities, cognition, and desires. Instead, her work demonstrates that the closed feedback loops between language, code, and psyche so central to structuralist and functionalist approaches to poiesis are themselves troubled constructions and ones whose foundations do not necessarily hold under the pressure of scrutiny. And, what better way to interrogate the processes of meaning generation than through the asemic. Asemic writing largely attests to the rejection of functionalism by operating outside the closed system, by demonstrating that there are phenomenological possibilities beyond the self-reflexive, self-organizing, and self-representing formulation of language adhered to by functionalists. Asemic word processing—or perhaps, more accurately, asemic glyph processing—on the other hand, can be considered an allopoietic machine: that which invites thinking about not only language and image but code, programming, and machine learning as modes of inventive and poetic possibility.

To distinguish how language and writing operate differently from code and programming in terms of poiesis and subjectivity, we can turn to Jacques Lacan's structuralist formulation of language's mechanistic role in organizing the subject. By reviewing this process, we can then demonstrate how code unfolds differently than language on the semiotic level by distinguishing between Lacan's "floating signifiers" and Hayles's "flickering signifiers" and what asemic writing and asemic glyph processing, respectively, mean for these two formulations. When it comes to writing and language, Lacan asserts that the subject is always an assemblage: the conscious on the one hand, and the unconscious on the other. The conscious is accessible while the unconscious is not. The unconscious is the locus of the pre-thought: that which is prelinguistic and, for Lacan, pre-epistemological. Our subjectivity is largely predicated not only on what we know but what is inaccessible and absent. The human subject bases what they experience as their self through that which is negated from thought and knowledge. This negation is the big Other who figures as an absolute alterior. We desire to fill this lack, but, as desire dictates, this is impossible. The unconscious, the Other, the negation is, for Lacanian psychoanalysis, across a non-transversable chasm. While our needs and demands might be met, desire will never be fulfilled. The unconscious is made manifest through the endless urgency to abstract that which is already abstracted; however, the instance of negation is the central rationale for why the subject is always already lacking. Ultimately, the desire is one that attempts to fill a negation with negation.

Such absence causes the individual to seek and restore the condition of pre-lack as a perpetual, consciously driven procedure. For Lacan, this state without lack figures in infancy when the subject was in singular union with the mother and did not experience lack. The thing that would restore this pre-linguistic, pre-subjective, pre-thought state is the Other. Of course, nothing will fill this absence since the Other indefinitely figures through processes of representation rather than material accessibility. The potentiality of totality then is always deferred, always beyond reach, and infinitely inaccessible. Lacan famously denotes the instance of this process as the mirror stage: the moment when the infant recognizes themselves as a being that exists temporally and spatially in opposition to the fragmented and dependent actuality of their actual embodied experience. As a result, the infant identifies with and as the image-as-reflection, and subjectivity comes into play through a misidentification with an image, reflection, or representation of the self. The infant's subjectivity is narcissistic in the sense that the experience of subjectivity is auto-amputated by the reflection in the mirror, and such representation acts as the servomechanism that shapes identity recognition. Acknowledging that they can see themselves as an image, they also recognize that they exist as that which can be seen by others. Resultantly, we desire this alteriority as that which is severed from epistemological access. All modes of subjectivity and knowledge, then, are based on a severed extension. The subject is, in a way, displaced from itself by alterior representational processes.

The reflection's representational initiation establishes a hierarchical relation between the child's real self and the more desirable echoed self. Simultaneously, the child also acknowledges that they can be signified, that is, they can be "represented" by a sign system. This is the crucial entry into systems of language. Here we have language where the signifier stands in place of the signified. As a mode of identity formation, language insists that the first person pronoun also *stands in* for our inner, subjective identity. All people, then, can also use the first person *I* to signify themselves. Beyond identity being constituted by representation and signifying systems, we are asked to extend the semiotics to all understanding of reality and all acts of communication. In short, the subject's identity can only be known, represented, and communicated via sign systems, thereby establishing identity as a site of drifts and displacements. Here, the very logic determines a break between language and the actuality independent from language that the former must represent. In this sense, identity and subjectivity inhabit the realm of the Other—that inaccessible outside independent from and represented by language. Subjects exist, therefore, *as* subjects in the locus of elsewhere—the Other. In this sense, we may say such a formulation privileges representation and semiotics over poetic experience.

Accordingly, Lacan notes that this outside is distinctly nonequivalent to that which it represents. So, the symbolic is a distinct realm from the real world and a distinct realm from the pre-thought of infancy or the anti-epistemological unconscious, the latter which Lacan calls "the imaginary" realm because it harkens to a formulation that excludes the distinction between signifier and signified. The imaginary is not exclusive of where word breaks off, but it accounts for this pre- and post-linguistic state, that is, it is distinct from the functionalist closed loops of language and signification. As an unassuming fantasy, the imaginary realm in which there is no distinction between signifier and signified is ultimately nonexistent; however, it is the engine that propels toward negating negation and interrupting lack with presence. As a result, language precedes the proceeds of subjectivity and, intermittently, produces them as well. The subject is not merely a subject as a consequence *of* language but also a subject *to* language. While the subject is the subject of the subconscious, the subject *represents* because they are *represented*; they use language because the signifier also produces them. Accordingly, both language and subjectivity may be said to be autopoietic and functionalist because the subject is caught in an evolving, knotted, level-crossing loop with language and, in the process, becomes the product of the process in question. In this sense, the subject is a tool of language.

However, this poses a problem when writing explodes the very assumptions of language's self-regulating procedures in identity formation. The instances where one does not merely level-cross diegetically or expand the thresholds of psycho-ecological knotting, but where one experiences the outside beyond epistemological reportage. This is where asemic writing comes in. While Siratori's work is asemic cyberpunk in the sense that it aims to express a pure affect of information overload and bursts free from semantic cohesion, his work is not asemic *writing* in the strict sense of the definition.

Instead, as a whole, it conveys a kind of protest against the psycho-ecological loops and the psychopolitical potentialities of language and communications technologies. In short, Siratori's asemic cyberpunk asks us to confront information illiteracy by admitting it, embracing its inhumanity, and transcending its self-configuring dynamism.

Asemic *writing*, on the other hand, denotes something more specific. Schwenger writes that

> when the linguistic term *seme* (derived from the Greek *sema*, "sign") is preceded by the privative *a-*, the normal meaning of what follows is negated or neutralized (compare *moral* and *amoral*). In the case of *asemic* it is meaning itself, or rather the sign's capacity to convey meaning, that is eliminated. So asemic writing is writing that does not attempt to communicate any message other than its own nature as writing. . . . This distinguishes it from nonsense or gobbledygook or whatever may be produced by those emblematic monkeys whaling away at typewriters. In all those cases we have before our eyes, if not a coherent message, at least a coherent sign system. We can recognize the letters on the page as signs that we are familiar with, even if they are not employed to form known words for communicative purposes. Asemic writing removes even this minimal reassurance.[13]

While these signs on the page may be organized in ways that suggest an ordered, conventional system, they do not, in fact, "belong to any familiar system."[14] Indeed, while asemic writing is not legible, "it has effects that are different from those of conventional communicative writing."[15] Asemic writing announces itself as image, and this is quickly recognized as such since, Schwenger writes, we do this already with traditional writing even though we may not consciously acknowledge it as such: "This is done by baffling any attempt to read the writing, that is, to follow its lines in the conventional way."[16] Because asemic writing substitutes "the familiar signs of the alphabet" with "enigmatic signs,"[17] it ultimately invites us to "consider" it. To consider is to fixate the mind upon and to reflect upon. It is also to be fixated upon by an enigma, to be the reflection *of*. While "most asemic writing preserves the linear organization of conventional writing," Schwenger notes, this results in "a kind of cognitive dissonance: writing is evoked at the same time that we are estranged from it."[18] This estrangement temporarily frees us from the psycho-ecological loop, functionalist determinism, and Lacanian chain of signification as it demands separation by being considered from without. Such cognitive dissonance experienced does not, then, lead to meaning or prepare an explanation, thus purveying it to semantics, but instead is "something that *calls* for explanation—that is, a stimulus of thought."[19] Call for explanation is consideration in its earliest sense—the

Latin *considerare*, to observe the stars. That is, to look beyond both the word and the world.

For Schwenger, we can imagine beyond functionalist loops by considering asemic glyphs. The formal and aesthetic qualities of writing strike us even in the most mundane ways. One need not be an art critic, historian, linguist, epigraphist, or archaeologist to experience awe, wonder, anxiety, frustration, unknowing, and ecstasy in the unique contours of etches, scratches, and engravings. Such glyphs and traces come to float free from the codified communicative systems to which they developed and belong. They come to invite secret meanings and produce private sigils. Austere, beautiful ancient Egyptian hieroglyphs, Mayan glyphs, ancient Mesopotamian cuneiform, and so on, continue to generate admiration and wonder enhanced by most admirers' inability to *read* them. Of course, there is a unique beauty to writing and inscription of all kinds: languages that we cannot *read* are, nevertheless, *experienced* uniquely. These traces are not interpreted but intuited; they are sigils of affect and gates to emotional constructs. The joy of temporary "illiteracy" comes from a denaturalized encounter with writing-as-image rather than writing-as-communication. After all, this is a singular experience, not a common or public one. While Marinetti called for the word to be set free, here we see the smallest units of communication emancipated from chains of signification and their flight into matrices of imagination. In such cases, the reader simply *sees* without criteria. Whether or not such scratches, engravings, or markings *signify* is simply no longer a concern.

However, writing of any sort—legible or illegible—will generally elicit one of two responses. "Some viewers may recognize their own expectations ironically," writes Schwenger, perhaps "as a commentary on the human addiction to verbalizing."[20] On the other hand, "their expectations act as a lure, prolonging an initial attention to the point that it becomes a fascinated desire to elucidate a cryptic text."[21] In either case, these inscriptions can bring some peripheral sense of comfort; or, at least, the prospect of control. "These are opposite attitudes toward the same thing: the sense, or hope that behind an asemic text lies a text of recognizable words, with a coherent meaning. This basic notion leads to two common ways of wanting to 'read' the asemic: *decoding*, where each sign is considered to be equivalent to a single letter; and *translating*, where complete words must be given equivalents."[22] Take the example, not of asemic writing, but a foreign *language*: one knows that they could simply ask an acquaintance or professional who is literate in the language for a quick translation; or, today, one could also simply use Google Translate or an image text translation app to get some approximation of its meaning. Even in ancient scripts, one could, with some effort, contact an epigraphist or, eventually, learn the art of translation themselves. Perhaps you are a pharmacist and decipher near-asemic writing daily. In any case, there is a degree of comfort for many readers in knowing that with desire and persistence, there is *a* meaning behind such inscriptions; that they are traces of alternate ways of extending thought through space, material, and time; that a voice and thought can persist in alternate form across millennia; that, in short, the meaning is *there* and it *can be shared* if one desires to pursue it. However, simply because writing is illegible in one instance does not make it asemic. Asemic writing is inscription that looks and feels like writing but is without a cipher; it draws attention to itself through the fact that it cannot be read but experienced; rather than unsealing meaning, it reveals itself as art. Indeed, asemic writing does not only raise questions about writing but, as Flusser stresses, also raises questions about reading.

Schwenger, commenting on Flusser, notes that "for anybody who is writing is also reading those vague shapes in the mind . . . translating them into another medium, continually revising in an attempt to achieve a more adequate translation."[23] He reminds us that "writing is not stenography, taking dictation from our profound and articulate thoughts, for those thoughts come into existence only through the act of writing."[24] Furthermore, he continues, "writing translates into words something different from words; and as in any act of translation, some things are lost in the process" while "clarity, logic, and 'meaning' are gained."[25] What is lost is the nebulous cluster of synapses and semantic sensations that occur before and beyond thought. After all, thought is "commonly recognized as such only if it can be verbalized."[26] In short, the pre-thought cannot be communicated through language and meaning. Asemic writing, though explicitly non-communicative in the sense of making a shared meaning public or externalizing a thought to be accurately shared with the commons, instead makes common, without words, the unsharable "mental texture," "mental movements and shapes, tendencies and qualities" of the psychic interior.[27]

The effects of asemic reading are radically unanchored from the commons of communication. "Asemic traces on the surface of a page have their own eloquence," Schwenger writes, "there is no need to prove further than inclination or imagination may encourage us to do."[28] This is the *seme set free* and reading as engagement with pre-thought, resistant to epistemology, unconcerned with codification, and submission to unknowability. It is particularly in this sense that asemic writing is an invitation rather than an imposition: because asemic writing is a stimulus for thought, and "the thinking it encourages is not that of a system or science," Schwenger writes. "It is open-ended, based in wonder and wondering. It has something to say about an abstract notion we call 'writing'; but it reminds us that such a notion can exist only through a multitude of writings each with its own individual expressivity. Consequently, the depiction of writing by asemic artists is endlessly varied."[29] As a result, asemic writing is eminently anti-functionalist.

However, this changes when we shift from language to code. And this is where Parrish's asemic word processing and asemic glyph processing offers a fascinating and contemporary addition to the discussion. Hayles remarks that when Lacan proclaimed that "language is not a code," he did so "because he wanted to deny the one-to-one correspondence between the signifier and the signified."[30] Therefore, signification for Lacan is floating, which has pressing effects on everything from language, writing, and subjectivity. Nevertheless, writing over the past century has gradually—and more recently, rapidly—been in the process of being supplanted by typing and, today, word processing. The implications here—from subjectivity, language, and psychopolitics—rest on a fundamental difference between writing and word processing. That is, Hayles remarks, with "word processing . . . language *is* a code."[31] What, then, might this mean when we come to consider computer-generated asemic "writing"?

Lacan developed his formulation of language during a time that was still dominated by writing and print. Developing the Saussurean insistence that it is not the signifier's relation to the signified that is of primary importance, but instead the relational matrices of signifiers to other signifiers, Lacan adds that signifiers float along a chain of other signifiers. That is, other signifiers produce signifiers. Such negations and absences establish the underlying logic of signification: the signified does not have an ontic presence of its own and does not have any stable correspondence to signifiers (which do not have a homeostatic relation to one another). The absence and negation at the core of subjectivity and language, the floating signifiers unanchored from the signifieds, and the corresponding logic of presence and absence, however, do not transfer to discourses on electronic media in general and word processing in particular.

Acknowledging this comes with a unique urgency in the early twenty-first century. Not only is there a massive shift from handwriting to typing, but this shift also moves beyond the print-based typing of a typewriter to the keyboarding of digital word processing. Schwenger identifies asemic writing as a timely practice during this transition. The familiar act of scrawling across a blank page, by denaturalizing it via cognitive dissonance, reminds us how strange the practice of writing was all along. Asemic word processing, alternatively, is less about the slips, drifts, and displacements of signification and, instead, draws attention to the interplay between pattern and randomness characteristic of informatics. To account for the shift, Hayles suggests the flickering signifier in place of Lacan's floating signifier.

Flickering signifiers are more appropriate for examining the informational processes associated with the programming commands of word processing functionality. Hayles suggests that flickering signifiers offer even more tenuous modes of stability than floating signifiers. Flickering signifiers are "characterized by their tendency toward unexpected metamorphoses, attenuations, and dispersions."[32] While language is not a code, word processing and flickering signifiers have as much significance to representation and subjectivity for the twenty-first-century *Homo digitalis* as do floating signifiers to linguistic subject representation. Hayles writes that "the relation between machine and compiler language is specified by a coding arrangement, as is the relation of the compiler language to the programming commands that the user manipulates."[33] While some quantity of semblance is conserved through these informational transformations, Hayles reminds us that this is conservation is unlike "the mechanical energy implicit in a system of levers or the molecular energy of a thermodynamical system."[34] Instead, just as the relation between machine and compiler language as well as the relation between compiler language and the commands in which a writer engages are both specified by rigid coding arrangements, the informational (rather than mechanical or thermodynamical) relationship in word processing is, for Hayles, predicated on, not presence and absence, but pattern and randomness.

Material duration marks writing and print: imprints or inscriptions scrawled on, impressed, or engraved into paper, wood, stone, metal, or any other material. Word processing, on the other hand, finds its inception on the screen. The presence after typing or absence after deletion of a word on a computer screen exists informationally. It is both predicated on and persistent through, not material duration of inscription, but of "constantly refreshed images" and "transformational patterns" formed and sustained by "systemic exchanges."[35] To account for the changes that occur when considering flickering—rather than floating—signifiers, Hayles asks us to consider how, with informatics and word processing, the signifier "is opened to a rich internal play of difference."[36] Rather than presence and absence, the interplay between pattern and randomness can attest to the ease of a font change—a replacement that would take great time, diligence, and effort for traditional typeset printing but is functionally instantaneous in digital word processing. With informatics, Hayles notes that "the signifier can no longer be understood as a single marker," like an ink mark on a page or an engraving on wood or stone. Instead, the informational flickering signifier "exists as a flexible chain of markers bound together by the arbitrary relations specified by the relevant codes."[37] Coding processes assemble, correlate, and calculate alphanumerics via binary code; and this intervening procedure operates invisibly and, at least to human perception, instantaneously *between* the fingers typing and the corresponding images that appear on the screen. That is, the computer is *reading* and transcribing the movement of the writer's digits via digitality.

Ultimately, while the digital is often discussed in incorporeal terms, this embodied experience of typing is central to Parrish's interest in phenomenology and its role in poiesis. "I'm very much more interested in the phenomenology of reading itself—what reading feels like," she writes, "and what we feel our bodies do when we're oriented toward 'legible' artifacts, and in particular what happens when the artifact in question is right on the border between legible and illegible."[38] Such thresholds, between the legible and illegible, operate not simply between a pen or typewriter and paper, but as a result of one's embodied engagement with keyboard or touchscreen communicating with a programmed interface. And, Parish notes, "these interfaces are also deeply *physical*, in that they require certain postures and movements, and also have affordances for 'prelinguistic' users (e.g., toddlers can pick out emojis on a phone; it's possible to look at some text and guess that it resulted from a cat walking on a keyboard)."[39] However, unlike Parrish's *Ahe Thd Yearidy Ti Isa*, neither the toddler nor the cat determines the glyphs' parameters and shapes that will appear on the screen. That is, for most of us, we engage with already-programmed interfaces—the user-friendly, intuitively designed software programmed by others. Most of us, unlike Parrish, currently do not program. Even so, Parrish is hesitant to distinguish between writing and word processing simply based on the degree to which embodiment and physicality determine the shape or communicative success of a glyph on paper or the screen. "I suppose it *is* true that in a word processor, the motions you make with your body don't map directly to the shape of a glyph," Parrish remarks. "But you *are* making physical motions with your body in order to *produce* glyphs," she continues, "so it's hard for me to categorically draw a distinction between 'writing' and 'word processing' on that basis alone."[40] This hesitancy, then, becomes central to the poietic potentialities behind Parrish's work. That is, rather than accept the hard functionalist dictum that language, programs, and code *use* us (while we only think that we use it), Parrish stresses our embodiment, presence, and physicality as a significant part of the recognition of our agency in the imaginative possibilities afforded by code.

This is not to say that by simply learning to program, we are freer from certain rigid constraints of word processing than we are from language. Hayles remarks that alongside our typing at a computer keyboard or touchscreen, it is "the compiler language that correlates these symbols with higher-level instructions" that determine "how the symbols are to be manipulated."[41] Furthermore, it is "the processing program that mediates between these instructions and the commands" the writer gives the computer via typing. This coding mediation that correlates alphanumerics with binary code is the procedural site where, for example, a global command could instantaneously change the front of each glyph in a document regardless of its length. Analogous font substitution in print, however, would require manual manipulation of each character and line—a direct material interplay between the hands of the typesetter and the materiality of the printing press—while changing the font with word processing requires a single, global command on behalf of the user (the diligent work making this ease possible, of course, is written by coders before the user so much as installs the program). It is not the hands moving typeset, but the embodied typist communicating with codes-as-intermediary *and* the programmer who made this process as user-friendly as possible in the first place. Furthermore, word processing is not presence and absence, but instead a conciliatory site of pattern and randomness whereby the typist sends an electronic signal as a command, its information is then correlated, selected, gated, and reorganized, thus appearing as a constantly refreshed, flickering, ever-reorganizing image that limits the uncertainty of the digital image's communicative stability on the screen.

While asemic writing brings to light the processes that link writing, language, and subjectivity through semiotic presences and absences toward the end of inviting a glimpse into the pre-thought, asemic word processing may offer unique insight into the way that programming, interfaces, and informatics operate as the intermediary between the typist and flickering signification. That is, the denaturalization of word processing may offer some insight into the subjectivity of *Homo digitalis* and how the subject may operate—both linguistically and processually—outside the deterministic, self-regulatory, self-affirming closed systems of linguistic functionalism. Parrish is, for instance, not a functionalist, and, as a result, her work is not so much a confrontation with functionalism as an alternative altogether. "I don't perceive my own cognition to be especially 'linguistic' in nature," she writes,

> and as a poet I've always been drawn more to language's material aspects (how language looks and sounds) than I am to semantics or rhetoric. I insist that language isn't a monolithic 'thing'—it's a collection of human behaviors that we can form some (weak) generalizations about, and which always overflows the boundaries we place on it. . . . And as a student of language, I'm constantly surprised and inspired by how people make use of their linguistic capacities not in order to carry out some inexorable mechanical teleology of grammar and syntax, but to tactically meet the communicative need of the moment, by twisting and shaping language in creative ways, regardless of whether or not the 'interface' for doing so is digitally mediated.[42]

Accordingly, Parrish would be hesitant to accept Bifo's statement that "code is 'speaking' us" or that "code is a tool for the submission of the future to language, enabled by the inscription of algorithms into the flux of language," or that "the future is now being written by the algorithmic chain inscribed into techno-linguistic automatisms."[43] Instead, Parrish's work reminds us that, whether digitally mediated or not, the users of language or code are fundamentally the agents of their own communication should they utilize and shape language (and programming language) in non-habitual and innovative ways. The more freely, creatively, and playfully we use language, the better we can operate outside the psychopolitical and neuro-totalitarian violence and strictures of grammatical standardization as a quiet mode of psycho-linguistic and cultural authoritarianism.[44] At the same time, the more we engage fully in the process of programming and acknowledge the procedures of interfaces, the more we assert agency when faced by the determinist procedurality of "techno-linguistic automatisms."

Parrish's work reminds us, then, that programming, like language, is profoundly human. While Hayles's flickering signification "is the progeny of the fascinating and troubling coupling of language and machine,"[45] Parrish aims to demonstrate how this uneasy assemblage is not necessarily a transition "from human to something radically other than human" or that "flickering significations bring together language with a psychodynamic based on the symbolic movement when the human confronts the posthuman,"[46] but that the metaphysics of humanity's communicative agency remain intact, rather than latent, in the future potentialities of creative, embodied digital communication and creation. If it is indeed the case that "individuals today no longer pursue autonomous life projects,"[47] as Bifo remarks, and that "indeterminacy is slowly replaced by the determination of code, and the digital self must be purified of its residual traces of human empathy, compassion, and solidarity in order to escape the whirlpools of failure,"[48] then Parrish's *Ahe Thd Yearidy Ti Isa* reenvisions indeterminacy *from* code.

While much of Parrish's work attests to the affirmation that *we* are the movers of communication, it is *Ahe Thd Yearidy Ti Isa*, in particular, that denaturalizes language, glyphs, and word processing in ways that are as poietic as the asemic writing examined by Schwenger. The restorative potency of asemic writing, its invitation into the pre-thought, that which is "obliterated in the technology of the alphabet,"[49] offers something distinct from what computers and information technologies can do. Schwenger remarks that "Flusser's assertion that electronic media are impelling a fundamental shift towards 'technical images' can be met with a counterargument: that alphabetic communication is not only more pervasive than ever but also more standardized; and this is due precisely to the dominance of electronic media."[50] Rather than the transcendent ambitions embedded in so many teleological discourses around the posthuman, the cyborg, Luciano Floridi's inforg, or the transhuman, *Homo digitalis* arrests our romanticism only to remind us that the calculative potentialities socially standardizing the neuro-totalitarian heist of information technologies are aimed at social isolation and psychopolitical standardization. Hayles reminds us that the intermediary code reduces uncertainty, collates, and organizes the information between typing and the screen and is largely invisible to most users. Beyond word processing, those who control this black box also control the technologies themselves and thus control the mediated processes of the twenty-first-century subjectivity so long as mass programming literacy remains latent across the globe. Just as Lacan demonstrates that the processes behind language and subjectivity are profoundly counterintuitive, the same shift in focus away from content and meaning toward process and information is central to considering *Homo digitalis* and whether the technical possibility of agential, imaginative, alternative futures will sustain itself into the future.

To do so, Parrish treats Flusser's technical image with the same mutability as she would the poiesis of language. That is, while Hayles writes that "for readers who do not themselves program in computational media, the temptation of reading the screen as a page is especially seductive,"[51] and that "although they are of course aware that the screen is not the same as print, the full implications of this difference for critical interpretation are far from obvious,"[52] Parrish's work acknowledges that such a critical distinction does not necessarily mean that the asemic cannot, though produced in radically different ways, express an invitation to think the unthought regardless of the medium of its inception. And, indeed, by mutating the most pervasive and innocuous technical image—the letters-as-graphemes of an alphabet on a computer screen or mobile device—Parrish's *Ahe Thd Yearidy Ti Isa* brings to the foreground the models, computation, and calculation that processually operates behind our everyday engagement with technical images. Indeed, *Ahe Thd Yearidy Ti Isa* signifies no thing while also provoking its reader/viewer into thinking and experiencing beyond the familiar.

For Flusser, a technical image tells us more about models, computation, and calculation than it does about the world. In this sense, he makes a counterintuitive claim. A photograph of a deer in a field, a busy street in Beirut, or a close-up of flower petals tells us very little about the reality of such objects. Likewise, a computer-generated image of a landscape or the letters and words appearing on the screen on a word processor tell us little about landscapes or writing. Rather than focus on representational crises, however, Flusser shifts his concern to crises of concept modeling. To interpret a technical image is to interpret the programs that made the image possible in the first place: the chemical, mechanical, computational properties of the camera and film or hard drive rather than the image as a final product. For example, the photographer executes a program rather than intervenes in it: they *use* the mechanical, procedural, and processual functions of the camera to take a picture without intervening in the program that makes this activity possible.[53] Because technical images are executed, created, and developed using machines, Flusser draws attention to their mechanical functions and mechanistic logic. In a sense, technical images permit us to trace "out opportunities for access and intervention"[54] in the world in ways that are radically unlike the unmediated ways we experience the world: satellite photographs tell scientists about changes in ice shields, time-lapse photography can liken the expansion of a city to the growth of slime molds, microphotography can inform us about bacterial phenomena, or high-speed photographs can determine the winner of a race all in ways inaccessible to the temporal and spatial thresholds that determine the limited functions of the naked, human eye. In a certain sense, Flusser asks us to look beyond what we see in these photos and, instead, invites us to consider how we see and act differently due to the technical image's program. To do so asserts the autonomy necessitated for the social in the face of encroaching automatic psychopolitical neuro-totalitarianism.

Unlike asemic writing, Parrish's asemic glyphs are not generated by the free movement of the hand. Instead, she employs a generative adversarial network (GAN) to generate and represent new data akin to the data training set from which it selects. She writes, "that representation—the model's 'latent space'—boils down to a small list of numbers, and in that sense a GAN is a kind of compression algorithm. What makes GANs interesting is that it can generate plausible outputs not just from known points in the latent space, but also from random numbers. Think of a JPEG decoder that can produce a valid image by 'decompressing' random noise, and you're getting close to a GAN."[55] A GAN is a relatively recent form of machine learning[56] and constitutes a generative model in the sense that they can generate output data that resembles, but is not identical to, the input data. The images generated by GAN can be remarkably realistic[57] or extraordinarily surreal.[58] However, one thing that many GAN-generated images have in common is an uncanny quality that appears *more real than computer-simulated.* This realistic representational level is made possible by combining a component called a generator that learns to express a particular output with another component called a discriminator that discriminates between input data and the generator's output. The generative aspect of the network is that it can generate new data; the adversarial aspect is based on two competing neural networks (the newly generative data being regulated for faithfulness by the discriminator). It is this process that generates similar, though different, representations from anything in the dataset. However, rather than generating, on the one hand, faces that do not exist in actuality or flora that appear uncannily and impossibly indistinguishable from an insect or an automobile, Parrish uses this process to generate previously unknown graphemes from sets of images of English words. She describes the two-part process of generating *Ahe Thd Yearidy Ti Isa* as follows:

> In the case of *Ahe Thd Yearidy Ti Isa*, I trained a GAN on bitmaps of whole English words. The program I wrote would pick a word at random from an English word list, weighted by word frequency, and then render that word as an

image in the computer's memory. Those images are then fed into the GAN as the training data set. The program does this many thousands of times, until the GAN learns how to produce output that looks vaguely word-like. So the program isn't creating "fonts"—it's creating images of words. (Actually, all of the words are rendered with the same font—Cardo.) A second part of the program then arranges those words on the page in a book-like fashion, keeping track of things like paragraphs, margins, justification, and other aspects of page layout. (This second part is entirely driven by constraints and procedures, not a statistical model [as is the case with the GAN]).[59]

It is important to note Parrish's insistence that the first part of this process does not produce digital fonts but, instead, surreal, dreamlike digital images of words. Furthermore, it should be stressed that the graphemes or words on the screen are technical images of varying complexity. It is also significant that the generated images, like asemic writing, are not designed to be decoded, that is, it is not a cipher. "In fact," she writes, "each word in the text is produced by sampling a random number (actually, a normal-distributed random vector), and generating an image from that random number with the GAN. Many of the words will look similar to each other, simply because certain arrangements of pixels are more likely to occur in images of English words. But technically, each word image in the piece should be unique."[60] The very uniqueness, however, is a result of Parrish's programming, that is, she does note that "technically I could make the program deterministic."[61] And it is the uniqueness of each "word" image that itself becomes a kind of extended metaphor for how programming and code do not simply organize, reorganize, generate, produce, and *use* human beings, but that it is the programmer-as-author who can represent via technical images that which lies outside the generative system itself. Namely, Parrish's asemic glyph processing reveals to us that we *can*, if not *should*, think as mystified poets rather than as baffled defeatists in our acknowledgment of the apparatus.

Indeed, Flusser wants to focus on how technical image critique reveals the ways that the apparatus comes to merge itself with the programmer (camera designers) and the user (photographers, viewers). Such linking of apparatus, programmer, and user/viewer entails profound social, existential, and political effects. The technical images themselves, as functions of apparatus, signify nothing, and this can, as we have examined elsewhere, have radically unpredictable effects since programming processes and algorithms are not effective at calculating human value judgment. "Criticism of technical images requires an analysis of their trajectory and an analysis of the intention behind it,"[62] writes Flusser. The reason that examining technical images in similar ways to traditional images is misleading is that "technical images, with their inverted vectors of meaning, have an unprecedented meaning: they don't signify anything; they indicate a direction."[63] This direction is multifaceted. However, one thing Flusser does want to stress is that such directionality is implicit in the programs and models as they instruct us "about the way society should experience, perceive, evaluate, and behave";[64] in short, they run the risk of benefiting thanatotic authoritarianism as easily as serving the eros of poetic emancipation. As a result, Flusser suggests that technical images, according to the logic of apparatus, are procedurally and programmatically pedagogical:

> as they currently surround us, technical images signify . . . instructional programs. At present, envisioners and their apparatuses give their images not only a programmed but a programming significance. We currently live among commandingly outstretched index fingers, and we will blindly follow their instructions unless we realize that our blind following is exactly what they mean. Should we, in fact, realize this (and there are signs that we are beginning to do so), technical images could change their significance dramatically. They could then turn into dialogically constructed signposts, signposts in the world that has become absurd for those who have become aware of its absurdity.[65]

The remarkable fact that technical images signify nothing—that they are the models, calculations, computations, and instructions of apparatus—is central to Flusser's call to acknowledge, recognize, and theorize technical images. Nevertheless, the absurdity in question here invites both defeatist nihilism and a revolting spirit of nothingness. Despite the evidenced tendency toward social isolation and psychopolitical neuro-totalitarianism, Flusser recognizes utopic possibilities in technical images (and even the apparatus) as an invitation to the freedom of empty horizons. And, indeed, Parrish's work is situated on this horizon of poietic possibility.

Because the technical image diverges into two separate paths, Flusser asks us to consider its bifurcating potentialities. Considering contemporary technical images, he remarks that the first path "moves toward a centrally programmed, totalitarian society of image receivers and images administrators, the other toward a dialogic, telematics society of image producers and image collectors."[66] Flusser suggests that both potentialities are fantasies. While he writes in 1985 that "we are still free at this point to challenge these values,"[67] he also accurately predicts that "what we can no longer challenge is the dominance of technical images in this future society."[68] The first—the programmed, totalitarian society where images are offered to passive recipients—is primarily negative and largely encapsulates much digital engagement of the early twenty-first century. In the alternative, utopic case—the telematics society where, rather than image receivers, there are image producers and curators—however, we have a societal multiplicity of active and knowledgeable image collectors, producers, and curators. Nevertheless, from the early twenty-first century, it appears that the discourse concerning the dominance of technical images is sadly confined to academics, coders, and designers even though the technical image is so ubiquitous it is often mistaken *for* reality itself. Flusser's optimism is that the latter, utopian course of technical images will come to dominate a society that is transcendent and no longer "found in any place or time but in imaged surfaces, in surfaces that absorb geography and history."[69] From this, he asks us "to grasp this dreaming state of mind as it has begun to crystallize around technical images: the consciousness of a pure information society."[70] Today, these bifurcating paths, though dominated by the negative, have nevertheless begun to loop into one another and entangle into a knot that brings with it the various, unpredictable tendrils of signifying nothing: ecstasy, anhedonia, and social isolation.

The ubiquity of digital images and their invisibility in shaping and delimiting the chaotics of subjectivity via the guise of language and representation puts special pressure on the image's receiver. Flusser states that the "penetrating force of technical images drives their receiver into a corner, puts him under pressure, and this pressure leads him to press keys to make images appear in the corner."[71] For Flusser, to resist the pressure of technical images would ostracize and force the receiver outside the social sphere. To imagine the receiver simply choosing to not engage in technical images—that is, to resist social media, to avoid word processing, to evade the ubiquity of news and ceaseless content creation—is an absurdity and even more damning than being pressed into a corner since Ludditism does not liberate but isolates even more intensely in an electronically mediated society. However, social and psychic isolation remains inevitable regardless of whether one actively or implicitly engages in technical images. The difference between the two experiences is the degree and relentlessness of the feedback loop's alienating effects: since "the energy required to withstand the penetrating force of technical images," Flusser writes, "would project such a person out of the social context"[72] altogether. Yet, despite the ambient ubiquity of technical images and their isolating force, how the receiver is entwined into the process is not simply one of a non-agential sponge who inactively receives information. Even when cornered, there are exit strategies. *Ahe Thd Yearidy Ti Isa*, itself an updating extension of avant-garde print poiesis and an agential intervention in technical images, ultimately offers us a map out of such a knotted labyrinth.

In their engagement with technical images, the receiver can be an active *part of* the informational feedback loop; their engagement or passivity, after all, becomes part of an evolving process. Whether or not one *wishes* to respond to technical images is not a matter of choice since their presence is ubiquitous; Flusser, after all, asserts that one "must react" to technical images. While from an outside perspective, "they must act in accordance with the technical images they have received . . . receivers also react to the received image on the inside."[73] Ultimately, non-reaction is a reaction and delivers viable data since the way a receiver interacts—or chooses not to interact—with an image is fundamentally a feedback loop of mutually evolving and adapting nodes: "The images have feedback channels that run in the opposite direction from the distribution channels and that inform the senders about receivers' reactions," writes Flusser, "channels like market research, demography, and political elections. This feedback enables the images to change, to become better and better and more like the receivers want them to be; that is, the images become more and more like the receivers want them to be so that the receivers can become more and more like the images want them to be."[74] Such images, then, are *not* autopoietic closed systems: "this circuit," Flusser adds, "can't actually be closed . . . for then the images would fall into entropic decay"[75] and would infinitely produce the same images. For the feedback loop to optimize the mutual adaptation of the sender and receiver, the process must be, like Parrish's asemic novel, allopoietic.

The image *needs* a receiver to which it can adapt, while the receiver *needs* an image to which they can adapt, and so on; this process, then, galvanizes change and contingency rather than static and decay. To avoid reproducing a homeostatic state ad infinitum, this feedback loop necessitates that the subjectivity of the receiver is open to—and shaped by—a myriad of possible external forces: history, politics, science, art, everyday life. The subject's multi-knotted relation to various, ever-shifting experience, then, is what provides the necessarily fecund contingency for the image. Rather than Baudrillard's hell of the same, we have three-dimensional, informational entrapment being passed through the zero-dimensional—Hayles's "no there there" locus of digitality—where the dismantling of subjectivity can be either automating or liberating. Despite its ubiquity, this merger with the zero-dimensionality of digitality is a normalized, largely innocuous phenomenon by all those who are not programmers or technicians. Yet, "technology has become too serious a matter to be left to technicians,"[76] writes Flusser. Since the experience in the twenty-first century continues to conform to an ever-optimized, intensified, and accelerated manifestation of the feedback loops linking technical images with subjectivity, it is imperative to acknowledge the thresholds of the loop's parameters. It is allopoiesis that opens potentialities whereby the subject can encourage adaptation in the context of a human merger with technical images; just as the subject is constituted by language and language is constituted by the subject, the image receiver must preserve agency to receive technical images as a mutually adaptive function of the way technical images imprint themselves *into* and *on* subjects. If technical images are to operate as allopoietic machines—that is, an optimized, programmed, processual tool—then the receiver/subject/typist should also operate allopoietically as a means of resisting being used by technical images *while* also consciously and cautiously providing willed feedback outside sanctioned parameters. This would make the image more suitable to the poietic values of humans than the other way around since, again, algorithms, computation, and calculation are not reliable assessors of ethical and social value.

This feedback loop must produce an adaptation that is different from that which produces it. Allopoietic machines are, after all, "machines that have as product of their functioning something different from themselves."[77] To this, Hayles provides an example of how a *car* can be allopoietic while the *driver* is autopoietic: "When I drive my car, its functioning is subordinated to the goals I set for it. Instead of the pistons using their energy to repair themselves, for example, they use their energy to turn the drive shaft so that I can get to the store. I function autopoietically, but the car functions allopoietically."[78] Our relation to the technical images of word processing, however, is fundamentally different from our relation to a car in that, while the car may elicit the autoamputation of the driver's feet in order to function autopoietically, the receiver of technical images may—like the image—act allopoietically in order to adapt *as* feedback instead of resulting in static, decay, and entropy or the subject strictly *of* the technical image. We drive a car, but the car does not drive us; with word processing, we type and are typed. Between typing and being typed operates code and the apparatus' invisible processes that, ultimately, signify nothing. As a result, with *Ahe Thd Yearidy Ti Isa*, the receiver/viewer of the technical image rehearses allopoiesis in that they invite the witness of word processing-subject assemblage *as* producing a mode of being notably other than itself while also notably different from the technical image. In a sense, Parrish instigates allopoietic experience regardless of programmatic Platonism, nominalism, or fictionalism. Indeed, it is work like *Ahe Thd Yearidy Ti Isa* that reminds us that even the technical image, while signifying no thing, *can* operate as a horizon of poietic possibility.

NOTES

1. While as we saw in the previous chapter, Mike Bonsall has some reservations regarding his status as the author of the Ballard Bot, and Oscar Sharp and Ross Godwin attribute their screenplay to Benjamin, Parrish is less ambiguous about her status as the author of her work:

> "I am the author of the work, in what I think is a very straightforward way. I made a series of literary, linguistic, aesthetic and technical decisions that resulted in a book . . . that sounds like authorship to me. It's true that the architecture for the GAN model I used was written by another person, and someone else designed the font. Writers with more

conventional practices acknowledge the importance of tools (pencils, paper, word processors) and designers (fonts, graphic design, book design) to the process of writing, but don't usually attribute authorship to them. I don't feel especially compelled to do so either. I certainly don't attribute any intention or authorship to the computer, the program, or the machine learning model." Allison Parrish, interview by Andrew C. Wenaus by email, July 24, 2020–August 7, 2020.

2. You can download the full book as a PDF for free on GitHub: https://github.com/NaNoGenMo/2019/issues/144

3. Allison Parrish, "Bio," *Decontextualize*, 2020, https://www.decontextualize.com/.

4. Allison Parrish, "Allison Parrish: Recent and Selected Work," *Decontextualize*, http://portfolio.decontextualize.com/

5. Interview with Parrish by Wenaus. See note 1 above.

6. Berardi, *Breathing*, 145.

7. Peter Schwenger, *Asemic: The Art of Writing* (Minneapolis: University of Minnesota Press, 2019), 149.

8. Andreas Müller-Pohle, "Code," *Flusseriana: An Intellectual Toolbox*, ed. Siegfried Zielinski, Peter Weibel, and Daniel Irrgang (Univocal, 2015), 110.

9. Parrish, interview by Wenaus.

10. Ibid.

11. Ibid.

12. Ibid.

13. Schwenger, *Asemic*, 1–2.

14. Ibid., 2.

15. Ibid., 3.

16. Ibid., 7.

17. Ibid.

18. Ibid.

19. Ibid.

20. Schwenger, *Asemic*, 137.

21. Ibid.

22. Ibid., 137–138.

23. Ibid., 147.

24. Ibid.

25. Ibid.

26. Ibid.

27. Ibid., 148.

28. Ibid., 149.

29. Ibid., 17.

30. Hayles, *How We Became Posthuman*, 30.

31. Ibid.

32. Ibid.

33. Ibid.

34. Ibid.

35. Ibid.
36. Ibid., 31.
37. Ibid.
38. Parrish, interview by Wenaus.
39. Ibid., emphasis in original.
40. Ibid., emphasis in original.
41. Hayles, *How We became Posthuman*, 31.
42. Parrish, interview by Wenaus.
43. Berardi, *Breathing*, 28.
44. Parrish's emphasis on our own agency to engage and use language—regardless of medium—in unique ways is itself a confrontation with psychopolitics, neuro-totalitarianism, and hierarchical authoritarian modes of language standardization practices:

> "At the same time, I acknowledge that language, especially as a reified concept, plays a tremendous role in establishing and maintaining authoritarian structures of power. If this weren't the case, no conservative would ever demand that English be declared the 'official' language, and no high school teacher would ever strike through a stretch of text in a student's paper with red ink. I think it's easy to mistake prescriptivist/political notions of what language should be as evidence that conventional, conservative ways of writing are, in fact, *inevitable* ways of writing, and I agree with (what I read as) the underlying suggestion in your question, which is that digital writing interfaces tend to encourage this mistake. Here's how I think that operates in practice: A computer, by its nature, operates on abstractions (zeroes and ones), and so to process words on a computer requires a kind of 'transcription' (transcribing the analogue linguistic phenomenon into a formalism). Putting language into a computer means that you have to accept certain abstractions about language that are not necessarily 'natural' or inevitable, such as the idea that all language can be represented as a one-dimensional stream of discrete symbols—a metaphor that underlies almost all digital representations of language. More concretely and urgently, systems for encoding text (such as Unicode) originate in military technology and are built on histories of white supremacy and colonialism. The language models that power features like spell check and autocomplete in contemporary writing interfaces are based on data sets that tend overwhelmingly toward white, middle class, American language use, and must be understood as carrying and reproducing particular ideologies. The interfaces are literally putting words in our mouths." Parrish, interview by Wenaus.

45. Hayles, *How We Became Posthuman*, 35.
46. Ibid., 33.
47. Berardi, *Breathing*, 87.
48. Ibid.
49. Schwenger, *Asemic*, 14.
50. Ibid., 14–15.
51. Hayles, *Electronic Literature*, 24.
52. Ibid.
53. Disruption of the standard practices in film and photography were a central concern of Dadaists and Surrealists in the early twentieth century. For more, see Candice Black's wonderful *Ghosts of the Black Chamber: Experimental, Dada & Surrealist Photography 1918–1948* (Solar Books, 2010).

54. Roland Meyer, "Technical Images," *Flusseriana: An Intellectual Toolbox*, eds. Siegfried Zielinski, Peter Weibel, and Daniel Irrgang (Univocal, 2015), 388.

55. Parrish, interview by Wenaus.

56. Generative adversarial network (GAN) machine learning was developed in 2014 by Ian Goodfellow and a team of researchers at the University of Montreal.

57. Parrish notes that "maybe the best-known recent example is StyleGAN, which is the model responsible for all of those weird fake faces (e.g., https://thispersondoesnotexist.com/)." Parrish, interview by Wenaus.

58. See Artbreeder, an app that "aims to be a new type of creative tool that empowers users' creativity by making it easier to collaborate and explore. Originally Ganbreeder, it started as an experiment in using breeding and collaboration as methods of exploring high complexity spaces. Artbreeder is named after the research of Picbreeder which investigated the role of exploration in the optimization process. It is also inspired by an earlier project of mine Facebook Graffiti which demonstrated the creative capacity of crowds." Joel Simon, "About," *Artbreeder*, https://www.artbreeder.com/about. Perhaps the most arresting images that are easily generated on Artbreeder are those that are remarkably surreal, Ernst-like hallucinatory impossibilities.

59. Parrish, interview by Wenaus.

60. Ibid.

61. Ibid.

62. Flusser, *Into the Universe of Technical Images*, 49.

63. Ibid., 50.

64. Ibid.

65. Ibid.

66. Ibid., 4.

67. Ibid.

68. Ibid.

69. Ibid.

70. Ibid.

71. Ibid., 53

72. Ibid.

73. Ibid.

74. Ibid., 53–54.

75. Ibid., 55.

76. Ibid., 65.

77. Maturana and Varela, *Autopoiesis and Cognition*, 135.

78. Hayles, *How We Became Posthuman*, 141.

Conclusion

Extro-Science Fiction, Hyper-Contingent Literatures of Exclusion, and Unthinkable Thought

In chapter 1 we considered Wittgenstein's claim that if a lion could talk, we would not understand what it was saying. The context, experiences, and world of the lion would be so unlike our own that, even should the lion speak with words we recognize, the message itself would be so strange that we would simply not be able to follow. Human beings, however, have more in common with lions than they do with the apparatus. If the apparatus could speak, we would not be capable of understanding what it is saying. It may be able to organize language syntactically, even convincingly, but this is not its *voice*. It does not speak; even as it inhabits our words and our worlds, the apparatus proceeds according to a rigid, obsessive, and autopoietic logic very different from human psycho-ecology. As supermodernity assembling itself, the apparatus comes to control, organize, and delimit everyday life in the twenty-first century. In one way or another, it will continue to do so more efficiently, more effectively, and more innocuously in the coming years. And yet, we offer ourselves to it; we willingly allow it to infect our nervous systems, shape us, and initiate us into ontologically diegetic level-crossing feedback loops; and, it will, someday, abandon us. The modernist jouissance of being both delighted and abused as a cog in a machine was prescient; today, the machine has shed much of its steel, coal, and fuel. It now exists largely as accumulating interplay between pattern and randomness, that is, data as information to be collected, retrieved, organized, and reorganized. Stories have always had structurally self-similar and categorizable qualities. However, today stories are increasingly standardized by sales algorithms. And indeed, more recently, our stories are increasingly being contracted off to AI. Without any goal of meaning, consideration, empathy, or self-knowledge, the apparatus quietly and invisibly steers twenty-first-century narratives as a superidiotic selector, a hyper-efficient datist. We can consume its stories, but we cannot *know* what it is saying because it does not speak in the sense that it does not hold discourse with the other.

We will never surpass the apparatus' speed and efficiency; our nervous systems have biological limits. Yet, trying to stop the apparatus or disengage from it would be disastrous. Unfortunately, as Andrea Juno and V. Vale write, "our fundamental mythology may be preparing us for what now seems inevitable: the suicide of planet Earth."[1] We may be best to try steering the apparatus away from the thanatotic dataset on which we fed it: our own violence, obsessions, and selfishness. But, because the teleology of digital code and the very concept of the singularity may result from an ethnomathematical bias implicit to Western apocalypticism, it may already to be late to retell our own narrative. The peculiar relationships between the inside and the *outside*, subjects and objects, information and live experience, data and meaning, and the human and the apparatus are tightly tangled. Yet, such tangles do not make meaningful our coming exclusion so much as they indifferently declare the apparatus' triumph over the human as inevitable and prescribed.

The nothingness of digital code may shape the individual's inner life and exclude the human from processes of self-knowledge. Indeed, humans currently do not possess a mode of access to the apparatus any more than they have insight into a mind-independent reality. Language is the tool employed to create order out of the radically inhuman; but, the inhuman—vast, cold, indifferent—always resists language's epistemological imperative. With the apparatus, the very structure of semiotics and representation is dismantled. Rather than language bringing meaning to the meaninglessness of the apparatus, the latter comes to inhabit, consume, and surpass the site of language, ultimately leaving it—and language users—behind. The literature of exclusion aims to confront this emerging eminence of the apparatus. It not only examines the psycho-ecological reflexivity and functionalism that describe the ways different modes of language use can affect perception, but also considers what happens when the apparatus is confronted and invited in. This relationship between the inner experience and the apparatus is at the heart of the uneasy relationship between combinatorialism, mathematics, the political, and literature in the twenty-first century. Indeed, we may aim to confront the apparatus tangentially via the literature of exclusion through an attempt to merge the processual and combinatorial with the multiplicitous openness of the poietic.

In his essay collection *The Age of the Poets* (2014), Alain Badiou considers the millennia-old conundrum of the relationship between poetry, literature, and philosophy. Whether it is Plato kicking the poet out of the Republic or Heidegger stressing the necessity of language and poetry for the generation of new thought, there are many difficulties in considering what literature has to do with philosophy and what philosophy has to offer literature. Badiou, however, suggests we can think outside philosophy. Literature can be considered a form of thought itself, a "thought-practice or a practiced thinking, a poem-thought or novel-thought," as Emily Apter and Bruno Bosteels suggest.[2] That is, literature has much to offer thought in ways that philosophy, mathematics, and programming fall short. For Badiou, literature is an action without a direct object. Literature is, in short, conceptual, constructivist, and poietic. "The poem is an unthinkable thought," Badiou writes; it is "a thinking that is neither thinking nor even thinkable."[3] We should embrace literary work "because it keeps us from supposing that the singularity of a thought can be replaced by the thought of this thought."[4] The poetic is a form of thought that is distinct from philosophical thought. The difference is primarily anchored around the notion that literature thinks and speaks what cannot be thought or spoken. Literature, then, is rigorous and clinical to the degree that it is, despite its materiality on the page, without material application. Literature and poetry are thus more than the sum of closed, functionalist systems; because literature and poetry do not have concrete application, the unthinkable thought cannot be collected, quantified, and organized as data. Philosophy, with this in mind, must listen to artists. We might add that programmers, too, must listen to the poets.

The literary does more than collect, count, and organize, that is, it can *recount* the generative, poietic, and indefinite. In this sense, the literary is the best medium to both encounter and counter the inhuman apparatus. Language does not represent reality; instead, it represents a perceptual system that correlates data from other semiotic systems constituted by reality. Rather than provide knowledge about anything outside the self-reflexive loop, language offers knowledge about language's functioning as a closed, tautological system. The literary and poetic, however, reconfigure this closed loop in ways that expand unthought parameters. That is, even as literary poiesis strives for the unthought, we always end up, to our surprise, back at the site of language. In this sense, the unthought does not represent reality itself, but it is a reminder that poiesis is the closest thing human beings have to *intimating an outside*. The literature of exclusion confronts the unthought threshold by considering our ever-expansive impulse to bring something of the technological *outside* into the psycho-ecology of mind and language. However, if the literary alone cannot access the *outside*, then perhaps mathematics and number *can* offer parallel insight. And it is on this point that I wish to suggest that the electronic literature of exclusion may be the inception of a new kind of literature that offers a poietic and paradoxical exit strategy inward. Indeed, perhaps the electronic literature of exclusion will someday answer the question as to whether a poietic mathematics or poetic numbering may also offer a future for narrative: a mathematics that is, rather than epistemological or empirical, explicitly aesthetic and poietic.

In his 2012 book *Weird Realism: Lovecraft and Philosophy*, Harman suggests that just as Hölderlin was to Heidegger and Mallarmé was to Derrida, H. P. Lovecraft is the literary muse of the speculative realist philosophers because "the greatness of Lovecraft even pertains to more than the literary world, since it brushes against several of the most crucial philosophical themes of our time."[5] While Lovecraft's fiction—and Weird Fiction more generally—has a central concern with the cosmic indifference of natural Reality, the literature of exclusion is here more concerned with the emergence of the apparatus as an artificial procedure occupying reality. Both constitute the *outside*, but while the cosmos are subject to the inhuman, constitutive laws of nature, the apparatus is a conglomeration of self-optimizing AI. While Lovecraft's monsters—metaphors for the encounter with reality itself—are blind, idiot gods, the apparatus is the compound-eyed superidiot, a self-augmenting artifice ever-expanding into the *outside*. Lovecraft's monsters indicate the instance when human beings *see* reality-in-itself and, as a result, go mad. However, the apparatus operates innocuously, psychopolitically, and procedurally via self-optimizing combinatorialism. Concerned with the limits of knowledge and the inability to correlate Reality into meaningful epistemologies, Lovecraft, in a sense, considers the empirical and epistemological limits of the scientific. The apparatus, however, is mathematical and may claim to represent an abstract, numerical reality, or, be a pure manifestation of a language (mathematics) that itself *actually* exists as-itself, independent from language users.

How, then, can we come to acknowledge the apparatus while also recognizing our coming exclusion? How might we know something outside of ourselves so that we may transform ourselves rather than be transformed, to program ourselves rather than be programmed? To begin addressing this, we turn to a relatively recent movement in philosophy, speculative realism, which is neither typically analytical nor continental. Indeed, speculative realism may offer some insight into technologically autonomous processes that are not human. Speculative realism is a rejection of Emanuel Kant's transcendental idealism and its lasting influence on modern philosophy. Ian Bogost writes:

> Being, [the legacy of transcendental idealism] holds, exists only for subjects. In George Berkeley's subjective idealism, objects are just bundles of sense data in the minds of those who perceive them. In G.W.F. Hegel's absolute idealism, the world is best characterized by the way it appears to the self-conscious mind. For Martin Heidegger, objects *are* outside human consciousness, but their *being* exists only in human understanding. For Jacques Derrida, things are never fully present to us, but only differ and defer their access to individuals in particular contexts, indeterminably.[6]

The problem that arises here, according to speculative realists, is one that asserts the foundation of being as one of correlation between the mind and the world, not unlike psycho-ecology. That is, from this perspective, Bogost continues, "if things exist, they do so only *for us*."[7] The legacy of transcendental idealism tends toward the assertion that human beings and that which exists *outside* human beings are inextricably tied together, thus challenging the very possibility of that which could exist exteriorly as accessible to knowledge.

Speculative realism is not a unified school, but it does operate as an umbrella term that unites four otherwise incompatible theorists: Harman's object-oriented ontology, Quentin Meillassoux's speculative materialism, Ray Brassier's transcendental nihilism, and the cyber-vitalism of Ian Hamilton Grant. What connects these thinkers is that their methodologies aim to unite realism with speculation. Here, realism rejects Kant's legacy that turns philosophy inward and rejects the possibility of examining reality or things in themselves. Kant suggests that we cannot think about something without *thinking* about it.[8] Peter Gratton writes that, for Kant, "speculation occurs when we attempt to think the world as it is beyond what appears to us."[9] So, the "speculative" part of speculative realism rejects the naïve realism that claims knowledge of commonplace objects and things outside the mind are as they seem to us and instead attests to an inarticulate, ineffable "weird reality" that shares little, if any, resemblance to the givenness of our everyday experience, that is, reality as the *outside* or what Meillassoux calls "the Great Outdoors." The speculative realists, not just Harman, express an interest in horror, science fiction, and fantastic literature because the special quality of unknowing, awe, and terror that these genres exercise (in dismantling the sureties of identity and perception) set the stage for speculations about the inhuman outside, beyond correlationism and psycho-ecology. Indeed, the disintegration and dissolution of one's identity is the most appropriate way to respond to an encounter with reality *out there*. So, speculative realists offer speculations on reality and what reality *is* (or *might be*) in the absence of the rational, empirical subject: speculations on reality and speculations that are radically unlike the way we experience and represent that experience. While a writer like Lovecraft uses these kinds of encounters with absolute reality (Old Gods, tentacles, ancient cults) as a point where language and knowledge break down, the narrative becomes almost cubist, the narrator goes insane, and the story ends abruptly, the literature of exclusion is more ambivalent in its examinations of the superidiotic apparatus. The qualities of these encounters are perhaps where speculative realism and the central concept of correlationism may offer special insight into the future of the literature of exclusion. Ultimately, speculative realism may also be a mode through which the literature of exclusion may articulate itself *as poiesis*: to confront, acknowledge, and meet the apparatus' combinatorialism with radical uncertainty, openness, and possibility.

NARRATING CONTINGENCY WITH NOISE

The human mind is metaphorical; the apparatus is combinatorial, procedural code. Metaphor means "transfer"; combinatorial code, however, functions via direct relations within a closed system of finite data. So, a metaphor represents one thing using the terms of another and, though also self-reflexive, lends itself to contingencies and possibility; code, on the other hand, is rigid and delimiting. Our access to reality through language is always metaphorical, while the apparatus is evolving into pure information and pure number; and number, as Platonic realists would claim, may correlate directly with mind-independent reality. We can speak of one thing using another's terms, but we can never know or experience the *outside*. Meillassoux describes this correlationism: "By 'correlation' we mean the idea according to which we only ever have access to the correlation between thinking and being, and never to either term considered apart from the other. We will henceforth call *correlationism* any current of thought which maintains the unsurpassable character of the correlation so defined. Consequently, it becomes possible to say that every philosophy which disavows naïve realism has become a variant of correlationism."[10] Despite the differences in their models of thinking, the speculative realists agree that contemporary philosophy can move beyond the tradition that suggests the foundation of being is predicated on the mind and the world as correlates. From the correlational perspective, things exist *for us* and cannot be understood in a meaningful way in and of themselves. Harman remarks that the outside world, the *real* world that exists independent from our perception of it, is "a darker form of 'weird realism' bearing little resemblance to the presuppositions of everyday life"[11] and that the models of reality generated by speculative realist philosophers are notable in their weirdness.

So while all the speculative realists have drawn rather counterintuitive conclusions about the structure of reality, they do assert that there is a mind-independent reality. However, this reality is inaccessible via our common-sense experience and, by extension, traditional modes of narrative. Peter Gratton reiterates it lucidly and succinctly as "there is no thinking of reality without *thinking* of it,"[12] while Brassier adds:

> Correlationism affirms the indissoluble primacy of the relation between thought and its correlate over the metaphysical hypostatization or representationalist reification of either term of the relation. Correlationism is subtle: it never denies

that our thoughts or utterances *aim at* or *intend* mind-independent or language-independent realities; it merely stipulates that this apparently independent dimension remains internally related to thought and language.[13]

Indeed, the subtlety of correlationism itself is a problem in its very innocuousness. The role of the philosopher, and the writer of the literature of exclusion, is to find a way out of the tangled strange loop-like self-reflexive labyrinth, and into this outside. While we can access the phenomenal (through experience), we can also *speculate* about the world in-itself even if we cannot explicitly "know" the in-itself. And literature and poetry may be a tool alongside philosophy and mathematics to do so.

Of the thinkers associated with speculative realism, it is Meillassoux who interests us most here. Meillassoux's means of asserting that there is a mind-independent *outside* is by way of drawing attention to the material universe of objects that preexist us and will continue to exist well after we are gone. The world preexists us (as evidenced by what he calls "ancestrality," or the "arche-fossil") and will continue to exist without us. Furthermore, Meillassoux employs dia-chronicity to "provide a general characterization of all such statements about events that are anterior or ulterior to every terrestrial-relation-to-the-world—the former expressing the temporal hiatus between world and relation-to-the-world that is inherent in the very meaning of such discourse."[14] This "dia-chronicity" as a temporal concept, however, is one thing; *statements about* such dia-chronicity are another matter altogether. We can know that the world existed *before us*, will continue to exist *after us*, and thus accept its existence independent of knowledge and perception; nevertheless, it is not *for us* and is not equivalent to any linguistic statement that makes that knowledge possible:

> what is at stake in dia-chronicity is indeed the nature of empirical science *in general*. The problem of dia-chronicity is not just a function of the fact that science has actually established a temporal hiatus between being and terrestrial thought; it concerns the fact that *this is a possibility that was rendered meaningful by the very inception of modern science*. It is not the question of fact that we are concerned with—i.e. the fact that dia-chronic statements are verified or falsified—but rather the question of right or principle; that is to say, the question of the status of the discourse which renders the verification *or* falsification of such statements meaningful . . . if science thereby renders dia-chronic knowledge possible, this is because it allows us to consider all of its statements—or at least all its statements about the inorganic—from a dia-chronic point of view. For the truth or falsity of a physical law is not established with regard to our own existence—whether we exist or do not exist has no bearing upon its truth.[15]

While the empirical sciences can *discover* verifiable compatibilities between humans and reality *without* the necessity of the human (as evidenced through dia-chronicity), the fact would remain that articulating this would be a *discovery*, thereby making it human-bound and semantic binding. This is at the center of a rift in contemporary philosophy and contemporary sciences; however, the mathematization of reality may offer philosophy access to speculations about the absolute that eschew the metaphorical psycho-ecology of mind, language, and world. That is, reality itself is outside correlation; mathematics and number, however, may offer a way out of such self-reflexivity since mathematics, in the Platonic sense, unlike language, affirms thought-independent actualities.

The mathematization of scientific knowledge over the past 500 years or so has made such claims possible. The more recent mathematization of poetry, literature, and narrative in the twentieth and twenty-first centuries aims to adapt *our* stories' methodologies with those of an increasingly technologized—that is, scientific—culture. This adaptation, however, is an ambivalent one. If our stories are so counterintuitive in form, content, and methodology, how can we consider these *our* stories? Such ambivalence is consistent throughout the literature of exclusion in the sense that representation cannot negotiate with the apparatus. Indeed, the more accurately our stories capture our cultural moment, the more we recognize our exclusion from, not just the indifference of the natural world, but also our exclusion from the technological apparatus.

The relationship between the human and the technological is no longer one where we can successfully describe the apparatus in terms of what it actually *is* but, instead, we can only know fleeting aspects of its ever-expanding and ever-optimizing whole. Indeed, there is no intimacy with the apparatus; it simply infects, gathers data, and proceeds without intention. The literature of exclusion, like speculative realism, is ambivalently Promethean, however. It is speculative in the sense that we may poietically *speculate* contingent potentialities regardless of intuitive, affective recourse to the human. Furthermore, the literature of exclusion may opt to create radically impossible modes of poiesis; to establish narratives and practices that resist delimitation and co-option by the apparatus: to walk further alongside the universe of the apparatus, break free of the word, narrate radical contingency *with* the noise, and think the unthinkable thought.

FACTIALITY, PROBABILITY, AND HYPER-CHAOS: EXTRO-SCIENCE FICTION AND HYPER-CONTINGENT LITERATURES OF EXCLUSION

It is here that I wish to suggest a future for the literature of exclusion. This literature would be that which could reorganize, adapt, and dissolve in radically unpredictable ways. In this sense, it could be a realist, if not a speculative realist, fiction in not only content and concept but also in form and methodology. When Meillassoux remarks that "there is no reason for anything to be or to remain thus and so rather than otherwise, and this applies as much to the laws that govern the world as to the things of the world,"[16] he suggests that the only universal constant is that of radical, absolute, contingent possibility. Nothing can exhaust possibility, and there is no reason to assume that there is a *primum movens* from which causal consistency must rationally unfold (and this would include Platonic and Cartesian mathematics). "Everything could actually collapse," he writes, "from trees to stars, from stars to laws, from physical laws to logical laws; and this not by virtue of some superior law whereby everything is destined to perish, but by virtue of the absence of any superior law capable of preserving anything, no matter what, from perishing."[17] For Meillassoux, the central question of philosophy is radical possibility and universal contingency: the very laws and principles upon which science rests are themselves subject to change without warning. Because such a model of reality is radically in opposition to the procedural, processual, and self-optimizing procedurality of the apparatus, this contingency can act as a model for a poietics of radical possibility: a hyper-contingent literature of exclusion. That is, while the apparatus may thrive in chaos—that is, to find and assemble order in orderly disorder—the constant and absolute in Meillassoux's philosophy is one that radically undermines the constancies required for contemporary scientific models, including the disorderly order of chaos. Confronting, and ultimately resisting, such models is the goal toward which the literature of exclusion must continue to pursue. Rather than consistency, the literature of exclusion should, like Meillassoux's absolute-as-contingency, aim for that to which the apparatus is not adept: fundamental uncertainty and hyper-chaos.

The apparatus does not mirror reality; it mirrors the logic of its initial conditions. These initial conditions are those of causal, linear logic; while such initial conditions permit for hypercomplex, level-crossing, self-optimizing procedures, a logical rigidity will remain central to its functionality. The absolute principle of reality-itself (*not* models of reality) for Meillassoux, on the other hand, is what he calls the "factiality" of contingency. That is, while the apparatus requires consistency, reality itself is contingent:

> Our absolute, in effect, is nothing other than an extreme form of chaos, a *hyper-Chaos*, for which nothing is or would seem to be, impossible, not even the unthinkable. This absolute lies at the furthest remove from the absolutization we sought: the one that would allow mathematical science to describe the in-itself. We claimed that our absolutization of mathematics would conform to the Cartesian model and would proceed by identifying a primary absolute (the

analogue of God), from which we would derive a secondary absolute, which is to say, a mathematical absolute (the analogue of extended substance). We have succeeded in identifying a primary absolute (Chaos), but contrary to the veracious God, the former would seem to be incapable of guaranteeing the absoluteness of scientific discourse, since, far from guaranteeing order, it guarantees only the possible destruction of every order.[18]

This hyper-chaos is central to the future of the literature of exclusion as both an acknowledgment of and resistance to the apparatus: *human* stories should aim for a future of unimagined, radically possible, hyper-chaotic, nonlinear, a-logical modes of thought and concept production. This is something that an AI cannot (at least in its current model) do because it is, by definition, a machine that selects from a non-contingent dataset in a closed system. While the human may turn to poietically rendering the factiality of contingency and the absolute-as-hyper-chaos, the apparatus will ultimately rely on models of probability no matter how inhumanly complex.

This is one reason why hyper-chaos should not be confused with chance or the aleatoric—and why the literature of exclusion should gradually shift away from chance, randomization algorithms, and aleatoric methodologies. Chance and the aleatoric are not truly random, that is, they rely on probability. While the probabilities are astronomically high when considering the possible permutations of a small dataset comprised of 2,000 units of data (not to mention myriad of units more appropriate to those datasets feeding the apparatus), it is important to note that this represents a closed, finite system. This is radically different from the hyper-chaos of Meillassoux's contingency because, as Gratton notes, chance "is built out of a totalizable set of possibilities,"[19] while the *set itself* would be subject to a broader contingency, thus eliminating its totalizing, finite status. "When, armed with this hypothesis," writes Meillassoux, "we attempt to calculate the likelihood of one event occurring (understood as this or that outcome of throwing the dice), we implicitly assume the following a priori principle: *whatever is equally thinkable is equally possible*. It is precisely this *quantitative* equality between the thinkable and the possible that allows us to work out the probability or frequency of an event when we play a game of chance."[20] Chance, the aleatory, and chaos always have an inherent orderly disorder and definite probability; hyper-chaos, however, "is one of unbounded possibilities."[21] The apparatus—itself a superdiotic, advanced sum of AI—may only select from a totalizable set of possibilities and is, as a result, always limited by *probability*. Hyper-chaos and contingency, however, signify *unlimited possibility*. Ultimately, to tell our own stories as we move into and beyond the twenty-first century, we may wish to adopt a radical superdadaism to narrate both alongside and against superdataism. When Harmon remarks that "reality itself is not a content,"²² we should always remember that, unlike reality, the apparatus itself *is* a content. With unbounded possibility, signifying *no thing* elicits a literature of exclusion that examines the unthinkable thresholds, and the unthinkable is *unquantifiable*. What we need is a hyper-contingent literature of exclusion.

In his 2015 essay, "Science Fiction and Extro-Science Fiction," Meillassoux introduces the concept of extro-science fiction. This concept might offer the best way of bringing together some of the "weird realities" of speculative fiction and what they may have to offer in terms of critical insight into the future of the literature of exclusion. Extro-science fiction means a kind of fiction whose epistemology is one that lies outside the logic of science; it can mean worlds that operate according to hyper-chaos, unpredictability, mythological thinking, and surrealism without recourse to prescribed expectations. While it is a form of science fiction, it is also, for Meillassoux, distinguished from science fiction by certain qualities. For Meillassoux, science fiction extrapolates on imagined futures where technologies are so greatly advanced that they are vastly beyond the capabilities of the sciences of the author's time. However, "every science fiction," Meillassoux claims, "implicitly maintains the following axiom: in the anticipated future it will *still* be possible to subject the world to a scientific knowledge. Science will be transfigured by its new power, but it will always exist."²³ While Meillassoux's definition only seems to concern itself with what would commonly be called "hard science fiction," the central point here is that this kind of fiction, regardless of whether it is utopian or dystopian, is optimistic toward science's ability to describe, know, and regulate the stable laws of the natural world. Against this trajectory of (hard) science fiction, Meillassoux posits "extro-science fiction" as a literature where world is not constituted and known through science but is outside the models of science. "By the term 'extro-science world,'" Meillassoux writes,

> we are not referring to worlds that are simply devoid of science, i.e., worlds in which experimental sciences do not in fact exist. For example: worlds in which human beings have not, or have not yet, developed a scientific relation to the real. By extro-science worlds, we mean worlds where, *in principle, experimental science is impossible* and not unknown *in fact* . . . the guiding question of extro-science fiction is: what should a world be, what should a world resemble, so that it is in principle inaccessible to a scientific knowledge, so that it cannot be established as the object of a natural science.²⁴

Meillassoux suggests that we can only know something because we have seen it repeatedly happen in the past. But, this is not necessarily the case: experience does not equal reality. He radicalizes this in ways that are not only metaphysical but in ways that destabilize the very assumptions of science as a methodology of knowledge. Thinking needs avenues to consider that reality is plastic, hyper-chaotic, and ever-changing in *fundamental ways*; this thinking requires a poiesis that resists being categorized by scientific knowledge. What is a kind of fiction that resists co-option by the apparatus and, as a result, allots us paratactic thought *alongside* the apparatus *as* empathetic subjects? Extro-science fiction is already here in experimental literature, print and avant-garde literature, slipstream, surrealism, electronic literature, and the literature of exclusion. Literature is poiesis, and the unthinkable thought offers asymptotic convergences for the future of narrating the general intellect both encountering and countering the apparatus. As an extro-science fiction, the literature of exclusion thinks in ways that prepare us for uncertain futures by celebrating potentialities, virtualities, and contingencies, and by always intensifying the threshold of unknowability in narrative.

In the twenty-first century, we are rethinking the place and status of humans in the universe in significant ways. Ultimately, we need stories to help us do this rethinking so that we may think alongside the apparatus until, and after, the instance where the word breaks off. What are human stories in relation to the inhuman? What are inhuman stories? What would the apparatus say if it spoke, and could we understand, even recognize, its speech as such? Are there stories "out there," or can there be narratives that can more accurately engage with the outside without recourse to the world-modeling teleology of contemporary science, mathematics, and programming? Meillassoux is, via extro-science fiction and much like the literature of exclusion, offering a call for narrative to push the boundaries of the philosophical and nonepistemological import of science fiction into new territories.

While much science fiction transports us to other worlds with advanced technologies and sociopolitical extrapolations, those worlds almost always have consistency, and such narratives derive their consistency from representing extensions of the same scientific laws we access through current scientific knowledge. No matter how strange, these narrative worlds hold together in recognizable ways and are verifiable extrapolations on current knowledge. But with the literature of exclusion, these laws have optimized themselves to the point where they surpass epistemology; and with extro-science fiction, laws are neither stable nor inductive. In such literature, causality is not predictable, and, as a result, the scientific ethos becomes an unreliable mode for new poietic flows into unknowing. Such worlds are, in principle, ones that cannot be modeled or fully comprehended; however, they can be narrated, transmitted, and experienced. The experimental and the avant-garde are those modes through which we may speculate about hyper-chaotic reality; it may permit us to achieve narrative that enacts not just an encounter with the apparatus but also a mode of thinking *alongside* it. Meillassoux remarks that "life mentally experiences itself without science and . . . perhaps discovers something unprecedented about itself or about science . . . a precarious intensity would plunge infinitely into its pure solitude, with only an environment of rubble in which to explore the truth of a worldless existence."[25] Sometimes the most illogical flights of the impersonal imagination stumble upon unknowable veracities hidden from science and philosophy. That is, this literature thinks the unthinkable thought.

The literature of exclusion is in style, content, and methodology, an expression of the paradoxes and challenges of thinking our relation to the apparatus as it absorbs, reconfigures, abandons, and, ultimately, exists alterior to our capacity to process its proceduralities as a meaningful whole. It is a literature of confrontation and resignation between subjectivity and the inhuman. Moving beyond print into and beyond the digital, the future of the literature of exclusion will incorporate mathematics into its hyper-chaotic diegesis and disorder not only the senses but even the empirical and epistemological. If Ballard's oeuvre is indeed a mythology preparing us for the suicide of the Earth, then the literature of exclusion is that literature that confronts the apparatus' role in accelerating this process. Recall Ballard's conundrum that there are dangerous bends ahead, and we need to make a choice: should we slow down, or should we speed up? As the apparatus severs our Earth-bound word and world-*for-us*, a hyper-contingent Dadaist literature of exclusion—a literature which posits factiality, possibility, and unknowing *contra* probability, combinatorialism, and processual self-optimization—offers narratives that think the *outside* and offer paratactic stories that are equally unthinkable as the apparatus is ineffable. To Ballard's conundrum, then, we might add a third risk: to keep abreast.

NOTES

1. Andrea Juno and V. Vale, "Introduction," *The Atrocity Exhibition* (San Francisco: RE/Search, 1990), 6.

2. Emily Apter and Bruno Bosteels, "Introduction," in *The Age of the Poets: And Other Writings on Twentieth-Century Poetry and Prose*, by Alain Badiou, trans. Bruno Bosteels (New York: Verso, 2014), xxxv.

3. Alain Badiou, *The Age of the Poets: And Other Writings on Twentieth-Century Poetry and Prose*, trans. Bruno Bosteels (New York: Verso, 2014), 48.

4. Ibid., 58.

5. Graham Harman, *Weird Realism: Lovecraft and Philosophy* (Winchester: Zero Books, 2012), 10.

6. Ian Bogost, *Alien Phenomenology, or What It's Like to Be a Thing* (Minneapolis: University of Minnesota Press, 2012), 3–4.

7. Ibid., 4.

8. Our discussions on psycho-ecology and functionalism, for example, are within with tradition.

9. Peter Gratton, *Speculative Realism: Problems and Prospects* (London: Bloomsbury, 2014), 7.

10. Quentin Meillassoux, *After Finitude: An Essay on the Necessity of Contingency*, trans. Ray Brassier (London: Bloomsbury, 2014), 5.

11. Graham Harman, *Towards Speculative Realism: Essays and Lectures* (Winchester: Zero Books, 2010), 2.

12. Gratton, *Speculative Realism*, 6.

13. Ray Brassier, *Nihil Unbound: Enlightenment and Extinction* (Basingstoke: Palgrave Macmillan, 2007), 51.

14. Meillassoux, *After Finitude*, 112.

15. Ibid., 113–114.

16. Ibid., 53.

17. Ibid.

18. Ibid., 64.

19. Gratton, 63.

20. Meillassoux, *After Finitude*, 96.

21. Ibid., 63–64.

22. Harman, *Weird Realism*, 14.

23. Quentin Meillassoux, *Science Fiction and Extro-Science Fiction: Followed by "The Billiard Ball" by Isaac Asimov*, trans. Alyosha Edlebi (Minneapolis: Univocal, 2015), 5.

24. Ibid., 5–6.

25. Ibid., 57.

Bibliography

Abbott, H. Porter. *The Fiction of Samuel Beckett: Form and Effect*. Berkeley: University of California Press, 1973.
Acheson, James. *Samuel Beckett's Artistic Theory and Practice: Criticism, Drama, and Early Fiction*. Houndmills, Basingstoke, Hampshire: Macmillan, 1997.
Adorno, Theodor. "Trying to Understand *Endgame*." Translated by Michael T. Jones. *New German Critique* 26 (1982): 119–150.
Apter, Emily and Bruno Bosteels. "Introduction." In *The Age of the Poets: And Other Writings on Twentieth-Century Poetry and Prose*, by Alain Badiou, vii–xxxv. Translated by Bruno Bosteels. New York: Verso, 2014.
Aristotle. *Poetics*. Translated by Gerald F. Else. Ann Arbor: University of Michigan Press, 1967.
Artaud, Antonin. "Letters on Cruelty." In *Collected Works: Vol. 4*, 77–79. Translated by Victor Corti. London: Calder & Boyars, 1974.
——. "The Theatre of Cruelty (First Manifesto)." In *Collected Works: Vol. 4*, 68–76. Translated by Victor Corti. London: Calder & Boyars, 1974.
——. "The Theatre of Cruelty (Second Manifesto)." In *Collected Works: Vol. 4*, 94–99. Translated by Victor Corti. London: Calder & Boyars, 1974.
Augé, Marc. *Non-Places: Introduction to an Anthropology of Supermodernity*. Translated by John Howe. London: Verso, 1995.
Baader, Johannes. "Germany's Greatness and Decline." In *The Dada Almanac*, edited by Richard Hülsenbeck, 97–102. Translated and edited by Malcolm Green. London: Atlas Press, 1993.
Badiou, Alain. *The Age of the Poets: And Other Writings on Twentieth-Century Poetry and Prose*. Translated by Bruno Bosteels. New York: Verso, 2014.
Balaguer, Mark. "Fictionalism in the Philosophy of Mathematics." In *The Stanford Encyclopedia of Philosophy*, edited by Edward N. Zalta (Fall 2018). https://plato.stanford.edu/archives/fall2018/entries/fictionalism-mathematics/.
Ballard, J. G. "1974: Robert Louit. Crash and Learn." In *Extreme Metaphors*, edited by Simon Sellar and Dan O'Hara, 72–77. London: Fourth Estate, 2014.

———. "The Car, the Future." In *A User's Guide to the Millennium: Essays and Reviews*, 262–267. London: Harper Collins, 1996.

Ballerini, Luigi. "Italy and/or Marinetti: From Alexandria to Vittorio Veneto." In *The Untameables*, 7–59. Translated by Jeremy Parzen. Copenhagen: Green Integer, 2016.

Barber, Stephen. *Antonin Artaud: Blows and Bombs*. London: Faber and Faber, 1993.

Baudrillard, Jean. "Superconductive Events." In *The Transparency of Evil: Essays on Extreme Phenomena*, 36–43. Translated by James Benedict. London: Verso, 2009.

Beard, Steve. Interview by D. Harlan Wilson. *The Dream People: A Journal of Bizarro Texts* 27 (November 26, 2011).

Beckett, Samuel. *Endgame, A Play in One Act, Followed by Act Without Words, a Mime for One Player*. Translated by Samuel Beckett. New York: Grove Press, 1958.

Benjamin with Oscar Sharp and Ross Goodwin. *Sunspring*. Ars Technica and Therefore Films, 2016. Screenplay. http://www.thereforefilms.com/uploads/6/5/1/0/6510220/sunspring_final.pdf.

Berardi, Franco "Bifo." *And: Phenomenology of the End*. Alto University, 2014.

———. *Breathing: Chaos and Poetry*. South Pasadena: Semiotext(e), 2018.

———. *Futurability: The Age of Impotence and the Horizon of Possibility*. London: Verso, 2019.

———. *The Soul at Work: From Alienation to Autonomy*. Los Angeles: Semiotext(e), 2009.

———. *The Uprising: On Poetry and Finance*. Los Angeles: Semiotext(e), 2012.

———. *Totalitarianism in Technomaya Goog-Colonization of the Experience and Neuro-Plastic Alternative*. Los Angeles: Semiotext(e), 2014.

Berlyne, John. Review of *Falling Out of Cars*, by Jeff Noon. *SFRevu* (November 2002). http://www.sfrevu.com/ISSUES/2002/0211/Book%20-%20Falling%20Out%20of%20Cars/Review.htm.

Bermel, Albert. *Artaud's Theatre of Cruelty*. New York: Taplinger, 1977.

Björk, Staffan & Jesper Juul: "Zero-Player Games Or: What We Talk about When We Talk about Players." Presented at the Philosophy of Computer Games Conference, Madrid 2012. http://www.jesperjuul.net/text/zeroplayergames/.

Bogost, Ian. *Alien Phenomenology, or What It's Like to Be a Thing*. Minneapolis: University of Minnesota Press, 2012.

———. *Unit Operations: An Approach to Videogame Criticism*. Cambridge: MIT Press, 2006.

Bohn, Willard. "From Surrealism to Surrealism: Apollinaire and Breton." *The Journal of Aesthetics and Art Criticism*. Vol. 36, No. 2 (1977): 197–210.

Bolter, Jay David and Richard Grusin. *Remediation: Understanding New Media*. Cambridge: MIT Press, 2000.

Bolton, Christopher. *Sublime Voices: The Fictional Science and Scientific Fiction of Abe Kōbō*. Cambridge: Harvard University Press, 2009.

Bonsall, Mike. Crash Cutup (@Crash_Cutup). "As I expected, and the shower of glass as the animal was carried over the roof, on her heel." Twitter, June 5, 2019, 12:22 a.m. https://twitter.com/Crash_Cutup/status/1136488605109620741.

——. JG Ballard Openings (@JGB_Sentences). "A few paces from the grave of the Mallory her footprints vanished into the sand." Twitter, June 7, 2019, 12:17 a.m. https://twitter.com/JGB_Sentences/status/1136849575455539200.

——. New Ballard (@New_Ballard). "He moved through the bundle of cracked tiles." Twitter, June 6, 2019, 12:18 p.m. https://twitter.com/New_Ballard/status/1136668768925573120.

——. New Ballard (@New_Ballard). "Arabesque. Later, in this stage of vehicles, but Maitland looked down at the bald woman carrying desks and gear shift." Twitter, June 7, 2019, 12:18 a.m. https://twitter.com/New_Ballard/status/1136849951512616962.

Borges, Jorge Luis. "Coleridge's Flower." In *Jorge Luis Borges: Selected Non-Fictions*. Edited by Eliot Weinberger, 240–242. Translated by Esther Allen, Suzanne Jill Levine, and Eliot Weinberger. New York: Penguin, 2000.

——. "Pascal's Sphere." In *Jorge Luis Borges: Selected Non-Fictions*, edited by Eliot Weinberger, 351–353. Translated by Esther Allen, Suzanne Jill Levine, and Eliot Weinberger. New York: Penguin, 2000.

Bould, Mark and Sherryl Vint. *The Routledge Concise History of Science Fiction*. New York: Routledge, 2011.

Boulter, Jonathan. "'Speak no more': The Hermeneutical Function of Narrative in Samuel Beckett's Endgame." In *Samuel Beckett: A Casebook*, edited by Jennifer M. Jeffers, 39–62. New York: Garland Pub, 1998.

Brassier, Ray. *Nihil Unbound: Enlightenment and Extinction*. Basingstoke: Palgrave Macmillan, 2007.

Breton, André. "'Max Ernst' by André Breton (1927)." In *Beyond Painting*, by Max Ernst, 130–140. Solar Books, 2009.

Bukatman, Scott. *Terminal Identity: The Virtual Subject in Postmodern Science Fiction*. Durham, NC: Duke University Press, 1993.

Cage, John. "A Few Ideas about Music and Film." In *John Cage: Writer*. New York: Limelight Editions, 1951.

——. *Silence: Lectures and Writings by John Cage*, 50th Anniversary Edition. Middletown: Wesleyan University Press, 2011.

Cage, John and Daniel Charles. *For the Birds: John Cage in Conversation with Daniel Charles*. Prepared by Richard Gardner. Edited by Tom Gora and John Cage. Boston: Marion Boyars, 1981.

Calleja, Gordon. *In-Game: From Immersion to Incorporation*. Cambridge: MIT Press, 2011.

Carrao, Mike. "Layers of the Real: On B.R. Yeager's *Amygdalatropolis*." *Newfound*. https://newfound.org/archives/volume-10/issue-1/reviews-amygdalatropolis.

Chester, Tony. Review of *Falling Out of Cars*, by Jeff Noon *The Science Fact & Science Fiction Concatenation*. http://www.concatenation.org/frev/falling.html.

Cohn, Ruby. *Just Play: Beckett's Theatre*. Princeton: Princeton University Press, 1980.

Colyvan, Mark. "Fictionalism in the philosophy of mathematics." *Routledge Encyclopedia of Philosophy*. Taylor and Francis, 2011. https://www.rep.routledge.com/articles/thematic/fictionalism-in-the-philosophy-of-mathematics/v-1.

Connole, Edia. "Introduction to *Amygdalatropolis*." In *Amygdalatropolis*, by B.R. Yeager, i–xxxiii. London: Schism Press², 2017.
Connor, Steven. "The Doubling of Presence in *Waiting for Godot* and *Endgame*." In *New Casebooks:* Waiting for Godot *and* Endgame, edited by Steven Connor, 128–140. New York: St. Martin's Press, 1992.
Consalvo, Mia. "There is No Magic Circle." *Games and Culture* 4, no. 4 (2009): 408–417.
Csicsery-Ronay, Jr., Istvan. "Marxist Theory and Science Fiction." In *The Cambridge Companion to Science Fiction*, edited by Edward James and Farah Mendlesohn, 113–124. Cambridge: Cambridge University Press, 2003.
Davnchev, Alex. *100 Artists' Manifestos: From the Futurists to the Stuckists*. Edited by Alex Davnchev. London: Penguin, 2011.
Dawkins, Richard. *The Selfish Gene*. Oxford: Oxford University Press, 1989.
——. *What is Philosophy?* Translated by Hugh Tomlinson and Graham Burchell. New York: Columbia University Press, 1994.
Deleuze, Gilles. *Foucault*. Translated by Seán Hand. Minneapolis: University of Minnesota Press, 1988.
Deleuze, Gilles and Félix Guattari. *A Thousand Plateaus: Capitalism and Schizophrenia*. Translated by Brian Massumi. Minneapolis: University of Minnesota Press, 1987.
Derrida, Jacques. *Specters of Marx: The State of the Debt, the Work of Mourning and the New International*. Translated by Peggy Kamuf. New York: Routledge, 1993.
Donne, John. "The Ecstasy." In *The Complete English Poems*, 53–55. Edited by A. J. Smith. London: Penguin, 1996.
Duffy, Enda. *The Speed Handbook: Velocity, Pleasure, Modernism*. Duke University Press, 2009.
Eliot, T. S. "The Dry Salvages." In *The Complete Poems & Plays of T. S. Eliot*, 184–190. London: Faber and Faber, 1969.
——. "Tradition and the Individual Talent." In *The Complete Prose of T. S. Eliot*. Volume 2, *The Perfect Critic, 1919–1926*, 105–114. Edited by Anthony Cuda and Ronald Schuchard. Baltimore: Johns Hopkins University Press, 2014.
Ellman, Maud. *The Poetics of Impersonality: T. S. Eliot and Ezra Pound*. Cambridge: Harvard University Press, 1987.
Éluard, Paul. "Beyond Painting." In *Beyond Painting*, by Max Ernst, 158–159. Solar Books, 2009.
Ermi, Laura and Frans Mäyrä. "Fundamental Components of the Gameplay Experience: Analysing Immersion." *DiGRA '05 – Proceedings of the 2005 DiGRA International Conference: Changing Views: Worlds in Play* (2005). http://www.digra.org/wp-content/uploads/digital-library/06276.41516.pdf.
Esslin, Martin. *The Theatre of the Absurd*. Revised and Enlarged Edition. Harmondsworth: Penguin, 1968.
Evans, Vyvyan and Melanie Green. *Cognitive Linguistics: An Introduction*. Edinburgh: Edinburgh University Press, 2006.
Field, Hartry. *Science Without Numbers: A Defense of Nominalism*. 2nd Edition. Oxford: Oxford University Press, 2016.

Finger, Anke, Rainer Guldin, and Gustavo Bernardo. *Vilém Flusser: An Introduction*. Minneapolis: University of Minnesota Press, 2011.

"First-Order Cybernetics." *Principia Cybernetica Web*. http://pespmc1.vub.ac.be/ASC/FIRST-_CYBER.html.

Fisher, Mark. "Break it Down: DJ Rashad's *Double Cup*." In *K-Punk: The Collected and Unpublished Writings of Mark Fisher (2004–2016)*, 403–406. Edited by Darren Ambrose. London: Repeater Books, 2018.

———. "Gothic Materialism." *Pli: The Warwick Journal of Philosophy* 12 (2001): 230–243.

———. "Space, Time, Light, All the Essentials – Reflections on J.G. Ballard Season (BBC 4)." In *K-Punk: The Collected and Unpublished Writings of Mark Fisher (2004–2016)*, 43–46. Edited by Darren Ambrose. Repeater, 2018.

———. "What is Hauntology?" *Film Quarterly* 66, no. 1 (Fall 2012): 16–24.

Flusser, Vilém. *Does Writing Have a Future?* Translated by Nancy Ann Roth. Minneapolis: University of Minnesota Press, 2011.

———. *Into the Universe of Technical Images*. Translated by Nancy Ann Roth. Minneapolis: University of Minnesota Press, 2011.

Flusser, Vilém and Louis Bec. Vampyroteuthis Infernalis: *A Treatise, with a Report by the* Institut Scientifique de Recherche Paranaturaliste. Translated by Valentine A. Pakis. Minneapolis: University of Minnesota Press, 2012.

Foucault, Michel. *Archaeology of Knowledge*. New York: Routledge, 2002.

———. *The Order of Things: An Archaeology of the Human Sciences*. London: Routledge, 2002.

Freud, Sigmund. "The Uncanny." In *The Norton Anthology of Theory and Criticism*, edited by Vincent B. Leitch. New York: Norton, 2001.

Gardner, Martin. "The Fantastical Combinations of John Conway's New Solitaire Game 'Life.'" *Scientific American* 223 (October 1970): 120–123.

Gleick, James. *The Information: A History, A Theory, A Flood*. New York: Pantheon, 2011.

Gottlieb, Baruch. "Algorithm." In *Flusseriana: An Intellectual Toolbox*, 42–43. Edited by Siegfried Zielinski, Peter Weibel, and Daniel Irrgang. Univocal, 2015.

Gratton, Peter. *Speculative Realism: Problems and Prospects*. London: Bloomsbury, 2014.

Grimwood, Jon Courtenay. "Behind the Mirror." Review of *Falling Out of Cars*, by Jeff Noon. *The Guardian*, December 7, 2003. http://www.guardian.co.uk/books/2002/dec/07/featuresreviews.guardianreview23.

Hale, Jane Alison. "*Endgame*: 'How are Your Eyes?'" In *New Casebooks:* Waiting for Godot *and* Endgame, by Steven Connor, 71–86. New York: St. Martin's Press, 1992.

Han, Byung-Chul. *In the Swarm: Digital Prospects*. Translated by Erik Butler. Cambridge: MIT Press, 2017.

———. *Psychopolitics: Neoliberalism and New Technologies of Power*. Translated by Erik Butler. London: Verso, 2017.

Haraway, Donna. "The Promise of Monsters: A Regenerative Politics for Inappropriate/d Others." In *The Haraway Reader*, edited by Donna Haraway, 63–124. New York: Routledge, 2004.

———. *Simians, Cyborgs, and Women: The Reinvention of Nature*. New York: Routledge, 1991.
Harley, James. *Xenakis: His Life in Music*. New York: Routledge, 2004.
Harman, Graham. *Prince of Networks: Bruno Latour and Metaphysics*. Melbourne: re.press, 2009.
———. *Towards Speculative Realism: Essays and Lectures*. Winchester: Zero Books, 2010.
———. *Weird Realism: Lovecraft and Philosophy*. Winchester: Zero Books: 2012.
Hayles, N. Katherine. *Electronic Literature: New Horizons for the Literary*. Notre Dame, IN: University of Notre Dame Press, 2008.
———. *How We Became Posthuman: Virtual Bodies in Cybernetics, Literature, and Informatics*. Chicago: University of Chicago Press, 1999.
Heidegger, Martin. "The Nature of Language." *On the Way to Language*. Translated by Peter D. Hertz. New York: Harper One, 1971.
———. "The Thinker As Poet." In *Poetry, Language, Thought*, 1–14. Translated by Albert Hofstadter. New York: Harper Perennial, 2001.
———. "What is Metaphysics?" *Basic Writings*, 89–110. Translated by David Farrell Krell. London: Harper Perennial, 2008.
———. "Words." *On the Way to Language*, 139–158. Translated by Joan Stambaugh. New York: HarperOne, 1971.
———. *Nietzsche: The Will to Power as Art*. Translated by David Farrell Krell. San Francisco: Harper & Row, 1979.
Hofstadter, Douglas R. *I Am a Strange Loop*. New York: Basic Books, 2007.
———. "Nomic: A Self-Modifying Game Based on Reflexivity." In *Metamagical Themas: Questing for the Essence of Mind and Pattern*, edited by Douglas R. Hofstadter, 70–86. Toronto: Bantam, 1986.
———. "On Self-Referential Sentences." In *Metamagical Themas: Questing for the Essence of Mind and Pattern*, edited by Douglas R. Hofstadter, 5–24. Toronto: Bantam 1986.
Hughes, Linda. "Children's Games and Gaming." In *Children's Folklore: A Source Book*, by B. Sutton-Smith, 93–120. New York: Routledge, 1999.
Hui, Yuk. Interview by Geert Lovink. "Cybernetics for the Twenty-First Century." *E-Flux* 102 (September 2019). https://www.e-flux.com/journal/102/282271/cybernetics-for-the-twenty-first-century-an-interview-with-philosopher-yuk-hui/
Hutcheon, Linda. *A Theory of Adaptation*. New York: Routledge, 2006.
Jarry, Alfred. *Exploits and Opinions of Doctor Faustroll, Pataphysician: A Neo-Scientific Novel. Collected Works of Alfred Jarry: Three Early Novel*. Edited by Alastair Brotchie and Paul Edwards. Translated by Alexis Lykiard, Simon Watson Taylor, and Paul Edwards. London: Atlas Press, 2006.
Juno, Andrea and V. Vale. "Introduction." In *The Atrocity Exhibition*, 6. San Francisco: RE/Search, 1990.
Keene, Donald. *Five Modern Japanese Novelists*. New York: Columbia University Press, 2003.
Keller, Evelyn Fox. "Marrying the Premodern to the Postmodern: Computers and Organisms after World War II." In *Mechanical Bodies, Computational Minds:*

Artificial Intelligence from Automata to Cyborgs, edited by Stefano Franchi and Güven Güzeldere, 203–228. Cambridge: MIT Press, 2005.
Kelly, Mark G. E. *The Political Philosophy of Michel Foucault*. New York: Routledge, 2009.
Kern, Stephen. *The Culture of Time and Space 1880–1918*. Harvard University Press, 1983.
Key, Margaret S. *Truth from a Lie: Documentary, Detection, and Reflexivity in Abe Kōbō's Realist Project*. Lanham: Lexington Books, 2011.
Kittler, Friedrich A. *Discourse Networks 1800/1900*. Translated by Michael Metteer with Chris Cullens. Stanford University Press, 1990.
Korzybski, Alfred. *Selections from Science and Sanity: An Introduction to Non-Aristotelian Systems and General Semantics*. 2nd Edition. Lakeville: Institute of General Semantics, 2010.
Lakoff, George and Mark Johnson. *Metaphors We Live By*. Chicago: University of Chicago Press, 1980.
Lakoff, George and Mark Turner. *More Cool than Reason: A Field Guide to Poetic Metaphor*. Chicago: University of Chicago Press, 1989.
Lalumière, Claude. Review of *Falling Out of Cars*, by Jeff Noon. *Infinity Plus*. http://www.infinityplus.co.uk/fantasticfiction/fallingoutofcars2.htm.
Langton, Christopher. "Artificial Life." *Artificial Life: Proceedings of the Santa Fe Institute Studies in the Sciences of Complexity*, Vol. 6, 1–48. Redwood City: Addison-Wesley, 1989. Accessible through the Internet Archive. https://archive.org/details/artificiallifepr00inte/page/n3/mode/2up.
Latour, Bruno. *Pandora's Hope: Essays on the Reality of Science Studies*. Cambridge: Harvard University Press, 1999.
Leng, Mary. "Fictionalism in the Philosophy of Mathematics." *Internet Encyclopedia of Philosophy*. https://www.iep.utm.edu/mathfict/.
Lyotard, Jean-François. *The Inhuman: Reflections on Time*. Translated by Geoffrey Bennington and Rachel Bowlby. Stanford: Stanford University Press, 1991.
Macherey, Pierre. *The Object of Literature*. Translated by David Macey. Cambridge: Cambridge University Press, 1995.
Mallarmé, Stéphane. *Selected Poetry and Prose*. Edited by Mary Ann Caws. New York: New Directions, 1982.
Marinetti, F.T. "The Foundation and Manifesto of Futurism." In *F.T. Marinetti: Critical Writings*, edited by Günter Berghaus, 11–17. Translated by Doug Thompson. New York: Farrar, Straus and Giroux, 2006.
———. "The Free Word Style." In *The Untameables*, 65–75. Translated by Jeremy Parzen. Copenhagen: Green Integer, 2016.
Martin, Tomas L. Review of *Falling Out of Cars*, by Jeff Noon. *Science Fiction Crowsnest*. Accessible through the Internet Archive Wayback Machine. https://web.archive.org/web/20080509184449/http://www.sfcrowsnest.com/sfnews2/03_dec/review1203_23.shtml.
Marx, Karl and Friedrich Engels. *The Communist Manifesto*. Edited by Jeffrey C. Isaac. Vintage, 2018.

Maturana, Humberto R. and Francisco J. Varela. *Autopoiesis and Cognition: The Realization of the Living*. London: D. Reidel Publishing Company, 1980.
McCarthy, John. "What is Artificial Intelligence?" Stanford: self-published, 2007. http://jmc.stanford.edu/articles/whatisai/whatisai.pdf.
McKay, Robin. "Editorial Introduction." In *Collapse IV*, edited by Robin McKay. Urbanomic: 2008.
McLuhan, Marshall. "Cybernation and Culture." In *The Social Impact of Cybernetics*, edited by Charles R. Dechert, 95–108. New York: Simon & Schuster, 1966.
———. *Understanding Media: The Extensions of Man*. Edited by W. Terrence Gordon. Berkeley: Gingko Press, 2003.
McLuhan, Marshall and Quentin Fiore. *The Medium is the Massage: An Inventory of Effects*. Berkeley: Ginko, 1996.
McMullen, Ken, dir. *Ghost Dance*. UK: Channel Four Films, 1983.
Meillassoux, Quentin. *After Finitude: An Essay on the Necessity of Contingency*. Translated by Ray Brassier. London: Bloomsbury, 2010.
———. *Science Fiction and Extro-Science Fiction: Followed by "The Billiard Ball" by Isaac Asimov*. Translated by Alyosha Edlebi. Minneapolis: Univocal, 2015.
Meyer, Roland. "Technical Images." In *Flusseriana: An Intellectual Toolbox*, 388. Edited by Siegfried Zielinski, Peter Weibel, and Daniel Irrgang. Minneapolis: Univocal, 2015.
Miller, Paul D. aka DJ Spooky That Subliminal Kid. "In Through the Out Door: Sampling and the Creative Act." In *Sound Unbound: Sampling Digital Music and Culture*, edited by Paul D. Miller, 5–20. Cambridge: MIT Press, 2008.
———. *Rhythm Science*. Cambridge: MIT Press, 2004.
Morville, Peter. *Ambient Findability*. Sebastopol: Farnham, 2005.
Müller-Pohle, Andreas. "Code." In *Flusseriana: An Intellectual Toolbox*, 110–111. Edited by Siegfried Zielinski, Peter Weibel, and Daniel Irrgang. Univocal, 2015.
Murayama, Tomoshoi and others. "Mavo Manifesto (1923)." *100 Artists' Manifestos: From the Futurists to the Stuckists*. Edited by Alex Davnchev. London: Penguin, 2011.
Murphy, P. J. "Beckett and the Philosophers." In *The Cambridge Companion to Beckett*, edited by John Pilling, 222–240. New York: Cambridge University Press, 1994.
Murphy, Tim. *Nietzsche, Metaphor, Religion*. Albany: State University of New York Press, 2001.
Nabokov, Vladimir. *Lolita*. New York: Vintage, 1997.
Negarestani, Reza. "TECHNODROME." *3:AM Magazine* (2005). https://www.3ammagazine.com/litarchives/2005/oct/technodrome.shtml.
Nietzche, Friedrich. *On the Genealogy of Morals*. Translated by Walter Kaufmann and R. J. Hollingdale. New York: Random House, 1967.
———. *Beyond Good and Evil*. Translated by Walter Kaufmann. New York: Vintage, 1989.
Noon, Jeff. "Artwork 2058: Probability Cloud." In *Unilever Series: Dominique Gonzalez-Foerster. TH.2058*. London: Tate Modern, 2008. http://blog.tate.org.uk/unilever2008/.

———. *Cobralingus*. Illustrated by Daniel Allington, Hove: Codex, 2001.
———. *Falling Out of Cars*. London: Doubleday, 2002.
———. "*Falling Out of Cars*: Extra Content. *Metamorphiction – Roots* (2002). http://www.metamorphiction.com/index.php/printed/falling-out-of-cars/.
———. "Ghost on the B-Side: Remixing Narrative." *Metamorphiction* (November 26, 2011). Accessible through the Internet Archive Wayback Machine. http://www.metamorphiction.com/index.php/the-ghost-on-the-b-side-remixing-narrative/.
———. "Origins of a Dub Fiction." *Codex Books*. Accessible through the Internet Archive Wayback Machine. https://web.archive.org/web/20050215083945/http://www.codexbooks.co.uk/origins.html
———. *Vurt*. London: Pan, 2001.
Núñez, Rafael. "Conceptual Metaphor, Human Cognition, and The Nature of Mathematics." In *The Cambridge Handbook of Metaphor and Thought*, edited by Raymond W. Gibbs, Jr., 339–347. New York: Cambridge University Press, 2008.
Ogden, Benjamin H. "What Philosophy Can't Say about Literature: Stanley Cavell and *Endgame*." *Philosophy and Literature* 33, no. 1 (2009): 126–138.
Parrish, Allison, "Recent and Selected Work." *Decontextualize*. http://portfolio.decontextualize.com/.
———. *Ahe Thd Yearidy Ti Isa*. 2019. https://github.com/NaNoGenMo/2019/issues/144
———. "Bio." https://www.decontextualize.com/
Parsler, Justin. "Life." In *Encyclopedia of Play in Today's Society*, Volume 1, edited by Rodney P. Carlisle, 361–362. SAGE Publications, 2009.
Perloff, Marjorie. *The Futurist Moment: Avant-Garde, Avant Guerre, and the Language of Rupture*. Chicago: University of Chicago Press, 1986.
Pound, Ezra. "As for Imagism." In *Ezra Pound's Poetry and Prose: Contribution to Periodicals*, Volume 2, *1915–1917*. New York: Garland Publishing, 1991.
———. *ABC of Reading*. New York: New Directions, 1934.
Pressman, Jessica. *Digital Modernism: Making It New in New Media*. New York, NY: Oxford University Press, 2014.
Pula, Robert P. "A Selection from the Preface to the Fifth Edition of Science and Sanity." In *Selections from Science and Sanity: An Introduction to Non-Aristotelian Systems and General Semantics*. 2nd Edition, xiii–xxiii. Lakeville: Institute of General Semantics, 2010.
Rasula, Jed. *Destruction was my Beatrice*. New York: Basic Books, 2015.
Redhead, Steve. *Paul Virilio: Theorist for an Accelerated Culture*. Toronto: University of Toronto Press, 2004.
Reynolds, Simon. *Retromania: Pop Culture's Addiction to its Own Past*. London: Faber, 2012.
Richter, Hans. *Dada: Art and Anti-Art*. Translated by David Britt. London: Thames & Hudson, 1997.
Roads, Curtis. "Automated Granular Synthesis of Sound." *Computer Music Journal* 2, no. 2 (1978): 61–62.
———. "Introduction to Granular Synthesis." *Computer Music Journal* 12, no. 2 (1988): 11–13.

Robinson, Edward S. *Shift-Linguals: Cut-up Narratives from William S. Burroughs to the Present*. Amsterdam: Rodopi, 2011.

Ross, Alex. *The Rest is Noise: Listening to the Twentieth Century*. New York: Farrar, Straus and Giroux, 2007.

Rotman, Brian. *Signifying Nothing: The Semiotics of Zero*. Stanford: Stanford University Press, 1987.

Rushkoff, Douglas. *Program or Be Programmed: Ten Commands for a Digital Age*. Berkeley: Soft Skull Press, 2011.

———. *ScreenAgers: Lessons in Chaos from Digital Kids*. Cresskill: Hampton Press, 2006.

———. "Technologies Have Biases." *Edge* (2011). https://www.edge.org/response-detail/10368.

Russolo, Luigi. *The Art of Noise (Futurist Manifesto, 1913)*. Translated by Robert Filliou. Something Else Press, 1967.

Santala, Ismo. "Jeff Noon – Works: *Falling Out of Cars*." *The Modern World* (October 14, 2003). Accessible through the *Internet Archive Wayback Machine*. https://web.archive.org/web/20060329141101/http://www.themodernword.com/SCRIPTorium/noon_works.html.

Schiltz, Michael. Review of *Blood Electric*, by Kenji Siratori. *Image [&] Narrative: Online Magazine of the Visual Narrative* 9 (2004). http://www.imageandnarrative.be/inarchive/performance/siratori.htm.

Schwenger, Peter. *Asemic: The Art of Writing*. Minneapolis: University of Minnesota Press, 2019.

Shannon, Claude. *The Mathematical Theory of Communication*. Urbana: University of Illinois Press, 1949.

Sharp, Oscar, dir., with Ross Goodwin and Benjamin. *Sunspring*, Ars Technica and Therefore Films, *YouTube* Video, 9:02. June 9, 2016. https://www.youtube.com/watch?v=LY7x2Ihqjmc&feature=emb_logo

Shaviro, Steven. *Doom Patrols: A Theoretical Fiction about Postmodernism*. New York: Serpent's Tail, 1997.

Sicart, Miguel. "Against Procedurality" *Game Studies* 11 (2011). http://gamestudies.org/1103/articles/sicart_ap.

Sieg, George. "Infinite Regress into Self-Referential Horror: The Gnosis of the Victim." In *Collapse IV*, edited by Robin McKay, 29–54. Urbanomic: 2008.

Shaw, Katy. *Hauntology: The Presence of the Past in Twenty-First Century English Literature*. Palgrave Macmillan, 2018.

Siratori, Kenji. *Blood Electric*. Creation Books, 2002.

———. *Hack_*. Minerva, 2011.

———. Interview by Azimute. "Mechanical Hunting For The Grotesque." *Heathen Harvest*, February 15, 2006. Accessible through the Internet Archive Wayback Machine. https://web.archive.org/web/20060323041512/http://www.heathenharvest.com/article.php?story=2006021520160363

———. Interview by Richard Marshall. "The Nude Brain." *3:AM Magazine* (2002). http://www.3ammagazine.com/litarchives/2002_jun/interview_kenji_siratori.html.

———. *Kenji Siratori Official Site*. https://kenjisiratori.wixsite.com/kenjisiratori/works.

———. *Mind Virus*. Monstaar Media, 2008.
Sperry, Roger. *Science & Moral Priority: Merging Mind, Brain, and Human Values*. New York. Praeger, 1985.
Stubbs, David. *Future Sounds: The Story of Electronic Music from Stockhausen to Skrillex*. London: Faber & Faber, 2018.
Suvin, Darko. *Metamorphoses of Science Fiction: On the Poetics and History of a Literary Genre*. New Haven: Yale University Press, 1979.
Tasić, Vladimir. *Mathematics and The Roots of Postmodern Thought*. New York: Oxford University Press, 2001.
Tatsumi, Takayuki. *Full Metal Apache: Transactions between Cyberpunk Japan and Avant-Pop America*. Durham: Duke University Press, 2006.
Teihard de Cardin, Pierre. *The Phenomenon of Man*. Introduction by Julian Huxley. Translated by Bernard Wall. Toronto: Harper Perennial, 2008.
Teruggi, Daniel. "The *Treatise on Musical Objects* and the GRM." In *Treatise on Musical Objects: An Essay across Disciplines*, by Pierre Schaeffer, xv–xx. Translated by Christine North and John Dack. Oakland: University of California Press, 2017.
Toffoli, Tommaso and Norman Margolus. *Cellular Automata Machines: A New Environment for Modeling*. The MIT Press, 1987.
Toop, David. *Kenji Siratori: [KILL ALL MACHINES]: Official site of the US cyberpunk author Kenji Siratori*. http://www.kenjisiratori.com/.
Topsfield, Valerie. *The Humour of Samuel Beckett*. Houndmills: Macmillan, 1998.
Tzara, Tristan. "Dada Manifesto 1918." In *The Dada Reader: A Critical Anthology*, edited by Dawn Ades, 36–42. Translated by Ralph Manheim. Chicago: University of Chicago Press, 2006.
Vergara, Tomas. "Catatonic Futures and Post-Apocalyptic Capital" *C21 Literature: Journal of 21st-Century Writings* 8, no. 1 (2020). https://c21.openlibhums.org/article/id/970/.
Verrone, William. *The Avant-Garde Feature Film*. Jefferson: McFarland, 2011.
Virilio, Paul. *The Futurism of the Instant: Stop-Eject*. Translated by Julie Rose. Cambridge: Polity Press, 2011.
Weaver, Warren. "Recent Contributions to the Mathematical Theory of Communication." *The Mathematical Theory of Communication*. Urbana: University of Illinois Press, 1949.
Weisenfeld, Gennifer. "Mavo's Conscious Constructivism." *Art Journal* 55, no. 3 (1996): 64–73.
———. *Mavo: Japanese Artists and the Avant-Garde, 1905–1931*. London: University of California Press, 2002.
Wenaus, Andrew C. "Coping with Zero to a Million Decimals: Mike Bonsall's J.G. Ballard TwitterBots and Procedural Psychopathology." In *Deep Ends: A J.G. Ballard Anthology 2019*, edited by Rick McGrath, 126–130. The Terminal Press, 2019.
———. "'Spells Out The Word of Itself, and Then Dispelling Itself': The Chaotics of Memory and The Ghost of the Novel in Jeff Noon's *Falling Out of Cars*." *Journal of the Fantastic in the Arts* 23, no. 2 (2012): 260–284.

———. "Twilight of Information Illiteracy: Kenji Siratori's Asemic Cyberpunk." *Foundation* 113 (2013): 29–48.

———. "'Zero, Zero, and Zero': Beckett's Endgame, Automation, and Zero-Player Games." *Chiasma* 4 (2017): 74–103.

Whorf, Benjamin Lee. "Science and Linguistics." In *Language, Thought, and Reality: Selected Writings of Benjamin Lee Whorf*. Cambridge: MIT Press, 1964.

———. Benjamin Lee. "The Relation of Habitual Thought and Behavior to Language." In *Language, Thought, and Reality: Selected Writings of Benjamin Lee Whorf*. Cambridge: MIT Press, 1964.

Williams, Saul. "The Future of Language." In *Sound Unbound: Sampling Digital Music and Culture*, edited by Paul D. Miller, 21–24. Cambridge: MIT Press, 2008.

Wilson, D. Harlan. *J.G. Ballard*. Urbana: University of Illinois Press, 2017.

Wittgenstein, Ludwig. *Philosophical Investigations*. 4th edition. Translated by G. E. M. Anscombe, P. M. S. Hacker, and Joachim Schulte. Oxford: Wiley-Blackwell, 2009.

Wolfe, Tom. "McLuhan's New World." *The Wilson Quarterly* 28, no. 2 (2004): 18–25.

Xenakis, Iannis. *Formalized Music: Thought and Math in Composition*. Stuyvesant, New York: Pendragon Press, 1992.

Yeager, B. R. *Amygdalatropolis*. London: Schism Press[2], 2017.

———. Interview by Andrew C. Wenaus by email. 8 June 2020 – 8 July 2020.

———. Interview by Jacob Siefring. "Digital Native: An Interview with B.R. Yeager on Amygdalatropolis." *3:AM Magazine*, February 15, 2018. https://www.3ammagazine.com/3am/digital-native-interview-b-r-yeager-amygdalatropolis/.

———. Interview by Matt Lee. *Ligeia*, Spring 2020. https://www.ligeiamagazine.com/spring-2020/br-yeager-interview/.

———. Interview by Mike Corrao. "'A Cadaver is Filled with Plenty of Material Activity': Mike Corrao Talks to B.R. Yeager, Author of the Horror Novel *Negative Space*." *Heavy Feather Review*, February 20, 2020. https://heavyfeatherreview.org/2020/02/20/yeager/.

Yeats, William Butler. "The Second Coming." In *The Collected Poems of W.B. Yeats*, edited by Richard J. Finneran, 187. New York: Scribner Paperback Poetry, 1996.

Zahavi, Dan. "Thinking about (Self-)Consciousness: Phenomenological Perspectives." In *Self-Representational Approaches to Consciousness*, edited by Uriah Kriegel and Kenneth Williford, 273–296. Cambridge: MIT Press, 2006.

Zilcosky, John. *Kafka's Travels: Exoticism, Colonialism, and the Traffic of Writing*. New York: Palgrave Macmillan, 2003.

Index

Abbott, H. Porter, 121
Abe, Kōbō, 186–87
absence, 15–17, 97, 99, 109–10, 113, 119, 122, 128–29, 133–34, 200, 203, 256, 261–62, 264
Acheson, James, 111, 121
Acker, Kathy, 154
Ackroyd, Peter, 193
actants, 112–17, 132
Adorno, Theodor, 23, 114
agency, 1–4, 11–12, 46, 52, 67–71, 73, 75–76, 85–86, 98, 101, 110, 112–13, 115–16, 124, 126–29, 150–51, 195–96, 202–4, 212, 235
The Age of the Poets (Badiou), 278
Ahe Thd Yearidy Ti Isa (Parrish), 24, 226, 251–53, 263, 265–67, 270, 272
Akira (Otomo), 191
algorithmic culture, 2–4, 22, 24, 31, 72, 155, 160, 203, 212, 232
algorithms, 2–3, 6, 53–55, 153, 195, 202–3, 237, 239–41, 244, 252, 264, 267–68, 272
alienation, 11, 67, 190
allopoiesis, 251–72
alphanumerics, 110, 262–63
Amygdalatropolis (Yeager), 23, 82–84, 86–87, 91–93, 95, 97–102, 109
ancestrality, 283

antinationalism, 205
anxiety, 62, 66, 124, 127, 129, 134, 142–43, 167, 169, 172, 254, 259
Apollinaire, Guillaume, 82
apparatus, 4–5, 7–8, 11–25, 31–32, 51–55, 59–62, 66–68, 76, 81–103, 109–10, 155–56, 184–85, 191–93, 203, 224–27, 268–69, 277–82, 284–89
Applied Ballardianism (Sellars), 215
Apter, Emily, 279
arche-fossil, 283
Aristotle, 37
Artaud, Antonin, 183, 195, 207
artificial intelligence (AI), 3, 19–21, 23–25, 64, 66, 68, 210–11, 223, 226–27, 238–39, 241, 243, 252, 277, 286
The Art of Noises (Russolo), 197
Asemic: The Art of Writing (Schwenger), 254
asemic word processing, 24, 226, 240, 251–52, 254–55, 261, 264
asemic writing, 254–55, 257–61, 264–65, 267–68
Ashby, Ross, 235
Augé, Marc, 96
Auster, Paul, 193
authoritarianism, 265, 269
autoamputation, 171–73, 272
automated signification, 5

303

automation, 4, 68, 89, 109–10, 121, 130, 145, 212, 214
automaton, 12, 14, 76, 110, 118, 120, 122–23, 129, 134, 169
autonomy, 3–4, 11–12, 19, 68–69, 235, 267
autopoiesis, 6, 24, 83, 223–47, 251
avant-garde, 4, 8–10, 14–15, 68, 70–71, 141, 183, 186–89, 191–96, 205, 207, 209, 288

Baader, Johannes, 8
Badiou, Alain, 278
Ball, Hugo, 7
Ballard, J. G., 89, 91, 181, 226
Ballerini, Luigi, 204
Barber, Stephen, 183
Barthes, Roland, 36
Bataille, Georges, 83
Baudrillard, Jean, 8
Beard, Steve, 141, 158
Beckett, Samuel, 23, 109–16, 118–24, 126–28, 130–35, 215
Benjamin (AI), 226
Bentham, Jeremy, 11
Berardi, Franco "Bifo," 6, 10, 19, 52, 69, 185, 204, 211–14
Berberian, Kathy, 198
Berio, Luciano, 198
Big Data, 12, 90, 102
Björk, Staffan, 118
Black Box, 13, 225, 234, 254, 266
black hole, 99–100
Bloch, Ernst, 194
Blood Electric (Siratori), 23, 184–85, 205, 207–8, 210
Bogost, Ian, 123, 127, 280
Bohn, Willard, 82
Bolter, Jay David, 97
Bolton, Christopher, 187
Bonsall, Mike, 24, 226–36, 238, 251
Borges, Jorge Luis, 33, 141, 161
Bosteels, Bruno, 279
Bould, Mark, 194
Boulter, Jonathan, 133

Bowie, David, 153
Brassier, Ray, 62, 281
Breton, André, 14
Bruno, Giordano, 42
Bukatman, Scott, 230
Burroughs, William S., 75
Burst City (Ishii), 189
Butler, Octavia, 159

Cage, John, 196, 198
Calvino, Italo, 141
"Can Thought Go On Without a Body?" (Lyotard), 62–63, 66
Carroll, Lewis, 141
Carter, Angela, 193
Cavell, Stanley, 124
cellular automata, 120–21
Cellular Automata Machines: A New Environment for Modeling (Toffoli and Margolus), 120
chaos theory, 40–41
chess, 111
closed systems, 2, 5–6, 21, 226
cognitive linguistics, 2, 22, 31–33, 37–39, 44
cognitive poetics, 31, 38–39
cognitive transformation, 31
Cohn, Ruby, 124
Coleman, Ornette, 165
Coleridge, Samuel Taylor, 33
"Coleridge's Flower" (Borges), 33
combinatorialism, 1–3, 7, 13, 20–21, 24, 35, 40, 278, 280, 282, 289
concept, 12, 40, 45–46, 51, 119, 127, 146, 150, 194–95, 278, 281, 283, 285–87
conceptual horror, 81–83, 86, 88, 98
Connole, Edia, 86
consciousness, 23, 44–45, 64, 75, 83, 89–90, 98, 147, 157, 202–3, 210
constructivism, 76, 188, 192, 214
contingency, 25, 73, 88–89, 235, 237, 246, 271, 282, 284–86
contingent consolation, 169
Conway, John, 121

correlationism, 25, 254, 281–83
Cronenberg, David, 159
The Crowd: A Study of the Popular Mind (Le Bon), 211
Curtis Roads, 196
cut-up (compositional technique), 75–76, 145
cybernetic homeostasis, 4
cybernetics, 84, 102, 181, 234, 237
cyberpunk, 23, 143, 183, 187, 189–92, 205, 209–11, 257–58
cyberspace, 97, 233–34
cyborg, 59–60, 65, 71, 184, 236, 265

Dada, 2, 5, 7, 12–16, 19, 21–22, 31–32, 35, 39, 67–69, 73–76, 149–50, 187–88
Dante, 72
Darwinian structuralism, 152
data fetishism, 11
dataism, 2, 8, 10–14, 18, 21, 51, 67
data totalitarianism, 11
deep web, 76, 84, 92, 100, 102
Derrida, Jacques, 36, 280
de Saussure, Ferdinand, 36
determinism, 4, 35, 37, 44, 46–48, 50, 69, 111, 116, 122, 201–2
The Diary of Samuel Pepys (Pepys), 165
diegetic level-crossing, 32, 34, 39, 45, 84, 234, 277
Digital Ballard (Bonsall), 227
digital code, 2–3, 51–54, 110, 131, 133–35, 278
digital cut-up, 195
digital font, 268
digitality, 10, 17, 83, 85, 88–89, 91, 93–96, 98, 100, 103, 271
digital modernism, 8–11, 13, 224–25
digital non-places, 232
digital psychopolitics, 11–13
digital supermodernism, 10
divine neutrality, 23, 81–103
Duchamp, Marcel, 157
Duffy, Edna, 9

dyshomeostasis, 236

echo, 172, 196
electronic literature, 8–9, 24, 52, 184, 195, 223–71, 279, 288
electronic music, 145, 195–96, 198, 200
Eliot, George, 141
Eliot, T. S., 69, 72
Ellmann, Maud, 69
Éluard, Paul, 135
Endgame (Beckett), 23, 109–16, 118–24, 126–28, 130–35, 215
English language, 142, 184–86, 208, 252
enlightenment, 11, 15, 40, 62, 67, 74, 190, 240
Epimenides Paradox, 34
epistolary writing, 160–61
eros, 184, 269
Esslin, Martin, 111
Evans, Christopher, 227
exclusion, 1, 3–5, 8–11, 13–15, 17–19, 22–25, 31, 48–49, 66–67, 69, 110–13, 128–30, 223–71, 277–81, 283–89
experimentation/experiment, 2–4, 23–24, 32, 75, 110–11, 114–19, 121, 130–35, 141–42, 159–60, 163–64, 182–83, 189, 195–98, 227, 287–88
extinction, 62–63, 243
extro-science fiction, 25, 277, 284, 287–88

factiality, 284–86, 289
Falling Out of Cars (Noon), 23, 141–44, 153–55, 158, 160–61, 163–65, 167, 169, 175, 185
feedback loops, 5, 9, 11, 13, 16, 64, 69, 94, 101, 122, 127, 271–72, 277
fictionalism (mathematics), 24, 223, 238, 244–46, 272
Field, Hartry, 244
finance, 5–7
financialism, 13–14, 16
First World War, 68
Fisher, Mark, 17, 76, 182

Flaubert, Gustav, 70
flickering signifier, 261–62
floating signifier, 261
Floridi, Luciano, 265
Flusser, Vilém, 4, 13, 115, 130, 270
Formalized Music: Thought and Math in Composition (Xenakis), 200
Foucault (Deleuze), 36
Foucault, Michel, 36, 74
free will, 12, 101
functionalism, 22, 36, 40–42, 83, 229–30, 232, 234, 239, 255, 264, 278
functionalist psychopathology, 226
functionality, 6, 91, 95, 98, 102–3, 225, 230–31, 237, 239, 251, 261
futurism, 15, 70–72, 144, 181, 187–88
The Futurism of the Instant (Virilio), 181

Gabor, Dennis, 201
The Game of Life (Conway), 121–22
Gardner, Martin, 121
Gavins, Joanna, 38
gender, 59, 65, 237, 243
general communication system, 163–64
general semantics, 35
generative adversarial network (GAN), 267–68
George, Stefan, 5
"The Ghost on the B-Side" (Noon), 153
Gibson, William, 141, 186, 192–93
GIF, 182
Glazier, Loss Pequeño, 224
Gleick, James, 41, 146
glitch, 23–24, 181–82, 204, 208–10, 215, 223, 225
Gödel, Escher, Bach (Hofstadter), 34
Gödel, Kurt, 40
Godwin, Ross, 238
Google, 6, 10, 100, 259
Gothic Horror, 84
Gottlieb, Baruch, 240
Grant, Ian Hamilton, 281
granular synthesis, 181, 195–96, 200–203

Gratton, Peter, 281–82
Gray, Elisabeth, 243
Great Outdoors, the (Meillassoux), 281
Greimas, Algirdas, 112
grief, 15–17, 23, 142–43, 160, 170
Grusin, Richard, 97
Gysin, Brion, 75

*Hack_* (Siratori), 185
Han, Byung-Chul, 3
Haraway, Donna, 59, 112
Harley, James, 201
Harman, Graham, 99
Haruspex (reader as), 88–90
hauntology, 23, 141–42, 156, 158–60
Hayles, N. Katherine, 12, 40
Hegel, G.W.F., 280
Heidegger, Martin, 47, 280
Henry, Pierre, 197
heterarchy, 235
Hikikomori, 93, 97
Hofstadter, Douglas R., 34
Home, Stewart, 154
homeostasis, 4, 19, 68, 98, 233–34
Homo digitalis, 92–93, 95, 97, 100–102, 262, 264–66
Homo electronicus, 92
How We Became Posthuman (Hayles), 16
Huelsenbeck, Richard, 75
Hui, Yuk, 60
Hutcheon, Linda, 9, 150, 159
hyper-chaos, 204, 284–87
hyper-contingent literatures, 25, 277, 284–85, 287

I am a Strange Loop (Hofstadter), 35
I-Ching, 199
illiteracy, 23, 67, 135, 182, 184, 254, 259
Imaginary Landscape No. 1 (Cage), 199
impersonality, 5, 12, 22–23, 59–76, 91, 93, 145, 148–49, 195–96, 198, 200, 202–4, 210
impersonal memetic engineering, 145

incompleteness theorem, 40, 42
indexicalization, 6, 35
informatics, 202, 241, 261–62, 264
information illiteracy, 10, 61, 112, 130, 132, 134, 185, 207, 225, 254, 258
information theory, 40–41, 143, 201
Inhuman, the, 98
inhumanism, 31, 67
inner space, 18, 182, 230, 235
Ishii, Sogo, 183
Izumiya, Shigeru, 183

Jamaican dubmasters, 195
James, Henry, 33
Jameson, Fredric, 9
Janco, Marcel, 75
Janicki, Karol, 37
Japanoid, 186
Jarry, Alfred, 113
Jenkins, Henry, 9
Johnson, B. S., 82
Johnson, Mark, 38
Jones, Susanna, 141
Joyce, James, 198
Juno, Andrea, 278
Jupitter-Larsen, GX, 208
Juul, Jesper, 118

Kafka, Franz, 186
Kamenosuke, Ogata, 187
Kant, Emanuel, 280
Keene, Donald, 186
Ker, Humphrey, 243
Kern, Stephen, 9
Key, Margaret S., 186
Kittler, Friedrich, 9
Korzybski, Alfred, 35
Kwo, Lee, 154

Lacan, Jacques, 255
Lakoff, George, 38–39, 45
Langton, Christopher, 120
language, 2–7, 19–20, 22–24, 31–32, 34–43, 45–50, 52–54, 94, 110–14, 118, 123–25, 131–34, 150–51, 182–84, 186–87, 205–10, 239–40, 244–46, 254–66, 277–84; is a virus, 209
Latour, Bruno, 113
Le Bon, Gustave, 211
Le Corbusier, 197, 200
Lee, Matt, 83
Leibniz, Gottfried Wilhelm, 1
Les mamelles de Tirésias (Apollinaire), 81
Ligotti, Thomas, 88
linguistic determinism, 35, 44, 46–48, 50
linguistic transfer, 31
The Literature of Cognitive Estrangement, 194
The Literature of Exclusion, definition, 4–8. *See also individual entries*
Llull, Ramon, 1
Long Short Term Memory Networks (LSTM), 238–39, 241, 247, 251
Lotringer, Sylvère, 209
Lovecraft, H.P., 90, 98, 280–81
Lyotard, Jean-François, 9, 62–63, 65–67

MacLeod, Alison, 141
Madam Bovary (Flaubert), 70
Mallarmé, Stéphane, 16
Manhood of Humanity (Korzybski), 35
Manovich, Lev, 9
Margolus, Norman, 120
Markov, Andrey, 229
Markov Chain, 229, 235, 252
Marx, Karl, 156
Masamu, Yanase, 187
mathematical fictionalism, 238, 244–45
Mathematics and the Roots of Postmodern Thought (Tasić), 39
Maturana, Humberto R., 232
Mavo, 187–88, 205
Mayakovsky, Vladimir, 71
McCarthy, John, 20
McKay, Robin, 83
McLuhan, Marshall, 9

Meadows, Shane, 227
Meillassoux, Quentin, 25, 281
Melancholia, 15
memes, 145, 148–52
memetic engineering, 141
memetics, 76, 83, 142, 145, 148, 151, 153
memory, chaotics of, 160, 169
messageboards, 84, 91–93, 100
Messiaen, Olivier, 200
Metamagical Themas: Questing for the Essence of Mind and Pattern (Hofstadter), 34
metamorphiction, 23, 141, 144–45, 153–55, 158, 161, 163–64
metamusic, 196, 201–2
metanoia, 31–55, 97, 210
metaphor, 23–24, 31–55, 59, 84, 89, 110, 112, 144, 146–47, 151, 164–65, 169, 282
metasignals, 164–65, 167–68
Microsoft Word, 255
Middleditch, Thomas, 243
Miller, Paul D., 155
"Mind, Brain, and Humanist Values" (Sperry), 146
Mind Virus (Siratori), 185
MOBILE@NGEL (Siratori), 184
modernism, 6, 8–11, 13, 69, 159, 188, 224–25
Monod, Jacques, 148
mourning, 23, 142–44, 159–60, 162, 164, 169–70, 174–75
Müller-Pohle, Andreas, 254
Murphy, P. J., 114
Musique concrète, 197–98

Naked Lunch (Burroughs), 75
narcissism, 62, 171–73
narcissus, 171–72
narcosis, 169, 171–73
Negarestani, Reza, 184
Negative Space (Yeager), 82
neoliberalism, 9, 11, 85, 159, 214, 234
neoreaction (NRx), 100

nervous systems, 18, 35, 52, 82–85, 90, 101, 103, 147, 152, 209, 277–78
neural networks, 241, 252, 267
neuro-totalitarianism, 10, 12–13, 17, 31, 68, 100, 144, 204, 214, 267, 269
neutrality, 23, 81–103, 237
nihilism, 13, 62, 68, 76, 84, 93–94, 100, 232, 269, 281
Nihil Unbound: Enlightenment and Extinction (Brassier), 62
noise, 23, 142–44, 156–58, 160–62, 164–67, 169, 171, 174, 182–83, 197–98, 206, 209, 211, 282, 284
nominalism (mathematics), 24, 272
non-place, 96–97, 228, 232, 237
Noon, Jeff, 23–24, 141–45, 153–58, 161–64, 166–68, 171, 175, 193, 195
noosphere, 146–48
no thing, 5, 7, 13–14, 21–22, 94–95, 103, 133, 230, 254, 266, 272
noumenon, 51, 82
Núñez, Raphael, 40
nymphomation, 145, 156

obsession, 93, 223, 227, 278
Ogden, Benjamin H., 124
Oramus, Dominika, 230
The Order of Things (Foucault), 36
Other, the, 69, 256
Otomo, Katsuhiro, 191
outside/outsider, 153

pain killer/anesthetic, 16, 132
parasitism, 13, 85
Parrish, Allison, 24, 226, 251–53, 263, 265–67, 270, 272
Parsler, Justin, 121
Pascal, Blaise, 43
Pasteur, Louis, 116
pataphysics, 112–14
Pearl Death, 82
Pepys, Samuel, 165
Perec, Georges, 141
Perloff, Marjorie, 71

Persuasive Games: The Expressive Power of Videogames (Bogost), 123
phenomenological engagement, 44
phenomenology, 44–45, 233, 255, 262–63
Philosophical Investigations (Wittgenstein), 31
Plato, 278
Platonism (mathematics), 24, 33, 44, 238, 244–46, 272
poetics of impersonality, 23, 59–75, 91, 203
The Poetics of Impersonality: T.S. Eliot and Ezra Pound (Ellmann), 69
poiesis, 2, 17, 19, 22, 109–10, 123, 142, 145, 239, 244, 247, 254–55, 279, 281, 288
posthumanism, 59–64, 66
Pound, Ezra, 4, 69
power, 8, 11, 17–18, 21, 41, 43, 45–46, 50, 94, 101, 211
powerlessness, 67
Pressman, Jessica, 8
probability, 25, 284, 286
proceduralism, 54, 109, 118, 123–24, 126, 130–31, 133–34, 225
procedurality, 17, 23, 89–92, 96, 98, 103, 119, 123–24, 127–28, 232, 252
processualism, 21
programming, 1, 3–4, 20, 24, 60–62, 183, 210, 235–36, 251, 254–55, 261–62, 264–66, 268–69
proto-fascism, 72
psycho-ecology, 2, 23, 25, 32, 53–54, 82, 100, 277, 279, 281, 284
psychogram, 100, 102–3
psychopathy, 76, 84–85, 98, 227–28, 230–31
psychopolitics, 10–13, 31, 37, 46, 68, 86, 100–101, 103, 261

Quantified Self, 21

Rasula, Jed, 16, 73
rationality, 15, 18, 68, 73–74, 90

recursion, 37, 66, 114
remix fiction, 68
Reynolds, Simon, 144
Richter, Hans, 15
Robbe-Grillet, Alain, 111, 186
Robinson, Edward, 74
Romantic Cult of Individuality, 67
Rotman, Brian, 203
Russolo, Luigi, 196–97

Santala, Ismo, 143
Sapir, Edward, 36
Sapir-Whorf Hypothesis, 36
Schaeffer, Pierre, 197
Schiltz, Michael, 192, 207–8
Schwenger, Peter, 254
Science and Sanity (Korzybski), 35
science fiction, 24–25, 189–92, 194, 238, 241–43, 277, 281, 284, 287–88
Science without Numbers: A Defense of Nominalism (Field), 244
scientific narrative, 114, 116
self-consciousness, 44–45, 47, 66, 83
self-forgiveness, 174
self-narration, 2–4, 9, 19, 21–22, 44
self-reference, 34–35, 43, 204, 244
self-reflexivity, 5, 34, 83, 232, 246, 284
self-representational consciousness, 44–45
Sellars, Simon, 215
Shannon, Claude, 71, 163
Shaw, William, 141
Shelley, Percy Bysshe, 33
Shinrō, Kadowaki, 187
Shipley, Gary J., 88
Shūzō, Ōura, 187
Sicart, Miguel, 119
Sieg, George, 98
Silicon Valley, 21, 243
simulation, 23, 52, 66, 81, 118, 120–22, 124, 126–28, 132–33, 234
simulation fever, 127
singularity, 14, 23, 72, 85, 158, 209, 278–79

singularity (the banality of), 14
Siratori, Kenji, 24, 182–86, 191–96, 200, 205–11, 214–15, 254
smartphone, 17, 20, 241
Sommerville, Ian, 227
Spectres de Marx/Specters of Marx (Derrida), 158
speculative realism, 25, 280–81, 283–84
Sperry, Roger, 145
Spread Sheet Bot (SSBot), 228, 231, 237
Steen, Gerard, 38
Sterling, Bruce, 187
stochastic music, 200
Stockhausen, Karlheinz, 197
strange loop, 34–35, 40, 43, 49, 54, 66, 82, 85, 98, 283
Sunspring (Sharp), 24, 226, 238–39, 241–44
superdadaism, 286
superidiot, 12, 14, 21, 55, 280
supermodernism/supermodernity, 4, 10–12, 14–15, 17, 96, 183, 277
supermodern transcendence, 181–215
surrealism, 75, 81–82, 230, 287–88
Suvin, Darko, 194
Swarm, the, 214
swarm annihilation, 181–215
symbolist poetry, 7, 16

Tasić, Vladimir, 239
Tatsumi, Takayuki, 186
Technical Image (Flusser), 24, 253, 266–70, 272
techno fascism, 100
technological singularity, 14, 23
Tetsuo: The Iron Man (Tsukamoto), 189
thanatos, 101
Theatre of Cruelty: The First Manifesto (Artaud), 183, 205–6
A Theory of Adaptation (Hutcheon), 150
thinking, 37, 47–54, 59, 63, 67, 87–88, 109–10, 130–31, 133–34, 147, 240–41, 254–55, 279, 281–82, 287–89
thought, 1–2, 21–22, 33, 35–42, 44–54, 62–66, 83, 85, 109–10, 114, 119, 130–35, 147–49, 191–92, 239–40, 256–58, 260, 277–79, 282–84, 288–89
Toffoli, Tommaso, 120
Tomorrow Is the Question (Coleman), 165
Tomoyoshi, Murayama, 187
Toop, David, 141, 208
Toward Non-Essentialist Sociolinguistics (Janicki), 37
"Tradition and the Individual Talent" (Eliot), 72
transcendence, 3, 14, 23, 81, 83, 93–95, 98, 102–3, 109, 181–215
transhumanism, 60, 64
trans-sense, 215
Tsukamoto, Shinya, 183
Turing, Alan, 121
turing machine, 121
Turner, Mark, 38
Twitter Bots, 24, 223, 226–28, 231, 233, 251–52
Tzara, T., 5, 15

Übertragen, 46
Ulmer, Gregory L., 225
Unit Operations: An Approach to Videogame Criticism (Bogost), 123
unknowability, 17, 31, 85, 260, 288
unpredictability, 53, 65, 67, 122, 156, 196, 200, 203–4, 252, 287
Unthinkable Thought (Badiou), 25, 277, 279, 284, 288–89

Vale, V., 278
Valéry, Paul, 33
value judgments, 116
Varela, Francisco J., 232
Varèse, Edgard, 196–97
Verrone, William, 189
Vint, Sherryl, 194
Virilio, Paul, 181, 209
virtual subjects, the, 234, 237
Vladimir Mayakovsky: A Tragedy (Mayakovsky), 71

void, 13, 16, 23, 50, 85, 98, 184
Von Neumann, John, 121, 235
vorticism, 71

warp records, 141
Weaver, Warren, 41, 71
Weisenfeld, Gennifer, 187
Wells, H.G., 33–34, 36
Whalen, Zach, 229
Whorf, Benjamin Lee, 35
Wiener, Norbert, 201
Williams, Saul, 157
Wilson, D. Harlan, 158, 230
Wittgenstein, Ludwig, 31
Wolf, Tom, 147
Woolf, Virginia, 13

word processing, 24, 156–57, 226, 240, 251–52, 254–55, 261–65, 270, 272
Wound, the (Yeager), 83, 87–88

Xenakis, Iannis, 196, 200

Yeager, B. R., 23, 81–95, 97, 99–101, 103, 142
Yeats, William Butler, 16

Zahavi, Dan, 44
Zdanevich, Ilia, 253
zero-player game, 23, 109, 118–22, 127–29, 131–32, 134
zero-sum game, 236
Zhongguancun, 21

About the Author

Andrew C. Wenaus is assistant professor at the University of Western Ontario's Department of English and Writings Studies and a member of the Complex Adaptive Systems Lab at UWO. He is also a composer and, with Christina Willatt, has recorded, arranged, and performed electro-acoustic scores for theatre, dance, film, and contemporary classical ensemble.

www.ingramcontent.com/pod-product-compliance
Lightning Source LLC
Chambersburg PA
CBHW021345300426
44114CB00012B/1086